Live Happy. Live Healthy. Live NOW.

BEATING THE ODDS
THE SUCCESS STORY OF NOW FOODS AND THE FAMILY BEHIND IT.

A WORM'S EYE VIEW

BY DAN RICHARD

Sixth Edition 2021

Every effort has been made to ensure that the historical and biographical information contained in this book is accurate. The opinions expressed in this book represent the personal views and historical research of the author.

Printed in the United States of America
ISBN: 1-890612-31-6

Author Info: C/O NOW Foods
               244 Knollwood Drive
               Bloomingdale, IL 60108
               dan.richard@nowfoods.com

Live Happy. Live Healthy. Live NOW.

BEATING THE ODDS

CONTENTS

PREFACE

The odds are stacked high against any new business. They are stacked even higher against small, family-owned businesses that start up without extensive trade or management experience. Every year nearly one million new businesses are launched in the U.S. and 30% of those will be closed by the end of the first year. Within five years, more than 60% of new businesses fail. Within ten years, 90% are gone. Of the surviving businesses, only a handful will grow to become national success stories while remaining privately owned.

Succession to the next generation is an entirely separate problem. While over 80% of America's corporations are family owned or controlled, only 30% of all family owned businesses survive to the second generation. At best, 10% will succeed to the third generation while remaining as a private enterprise. Combined together, the odds are very slim that new family businesses will survive to the third generation, while remaining privately owned.

Betty, Elwood, Sharon, David, Dan

Our family business has also overcome the social and business stigmas that used to be associated with health food companies. Most people simply aren't ready to change their lifestyles in order to feel better. Because of many factors, the FDA (Food and Drug Administration) and, to a lesser degree, the FTC (Federal Trade Commission) have made selling natural foods very difficult for over half a century. By standing the test of time, NOW Foods and the Richard family have shown that natural food products are legitimate and helpful.

NOW Foods has beaten the odds and is a living testament to the American success story. My grandfather, Paul Richard, started our family heritage in the natural foods field in 1949, and my father, Elwood Richard, expanded the business substantially, adding four related businesses to the fold. Today, all five businesses are alive and well with NOW Foods as the lead company. NOW has an interesting story to tell that should inform, surprise, enlighten and, hopefully, entertain readers with many interests. We have beaten the odds and they are now in our favor.

Dan Richard   May, 2002, Revised 2005, 2009, 2013, 2017, 2021

FOREWORD

"That's the craziest idea I've ever heard" I responded to Geraldine, our New York City representative, who suggested this very book. "I don't have the interest or the time, and even if I were to write a book, it would be about my Christian faith and not about business." Yet somehow it didn't take long for my firm negative reply to give way to possibilities about including my faith (very briefly) in a book about our family business. That little seed Geraldine planted in my mind soon took root and the results are presented in this small book.

For years NOW Foods has called itself a "Christian Principled" business, which is a reflection of some family members and senior managers. The phrase "do unto others as you would have them do unto you" became part of NOW's culture and continues as long as the spirit of our founder, my father Elwood, lives on. Though we're far from perfect, and always will be, our agreed-upon ethics are something for me to be proud of. It's good to work at a company where the people and products are part of the solution, rather than part of the problem.

Natural foods are part of the solution for people wanting to have physical health above a mediocre level. As a well-read manager within the natural foods industry, I've found research and personal use of natural products to be compelling for better health. My goal in writing this book is twofold: First, as one interested in history, to record historical events within NOW Foods and the natural foods movement as a testimony to my children and to others interested in the success of our family business. Second, to announce the inside workings at NOW, so that customers will have increased confidence in the people and products that appear in public as "NOW."

Normally a bird's eye view would be suitable for "taking pictures" of a success like NOW. However, I firmly believe that NOW Foods has been an outstanding success, growing from under $1 million in sales in 1985 to over $800 million in 2021, entirely due to the grace of God. Therefore, the inside story of our third-generation business will be told not from a bird's eye view, but a worm's-eye view. Having worked at nearly every job within our business over the past forty years, my hope is that you will walk in my shoes while you view our story. *I am that worm. (Psalm 22:6)*

ACKNOWLEDGEMENTS

I wish to acknowledge my entire family, whose business history has made this work possible. Many different family members have helped with proofreading and made suggestions that, I hope, have made this effort more readable, accurate and useful. Of note are Uncle Lou, David, and Dana who helped in other ways as well. This book is dedicated to my father, Elwood, who has been an inspiration to myself and to so many others I have worked with. The spirit of NOW Foods is Dad, and will remain that way as long as the business and family adhere to the core values he left us.

Finally, I wish to present this record to my wife, Beth, and three children: Nathan, Faith and Adam. May you each grow to appreciate the labors of your grandfather and great-grandfather.

RICHARD FAMILY TREE*

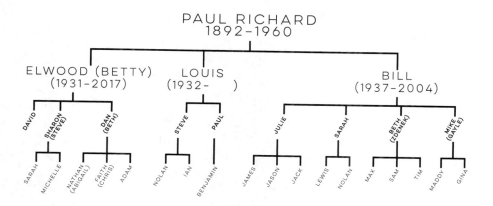

*Includes grown family members who have worked at NOW Foods or Fearn or who own stock in 2017.

> *"Generations come and generations go,*
> *but the earth remains forever.*
> *What has been will be again,*
> *what has been done will be done again;*
> *there is nothing new under the sun."*
> **Ecclesiastes 1: 4, 9**

1948–1960

1948 seems like a long time ago. The world was a very different place from what we see today. The entire industrial world was recovering from the horrors of World War II, Israel was reborn as a nation and the Cold War was just getting started. U.S. scientist A.E. Mirsky discovered ribonucleic acid (RNA) in human chromosomes and the junk food revolution formally began with a new hamburger café opened by Richard and Maurice McDonald.

In Chicago, a new industry called "health foods" was in its infancy and a company called Fearn was about to change hands. The new owner, Paul Richard, would help expand the potential of soybeans as a food and as a supplement in the United States. He would begin a family legacy of supplying health food stores with unique, quality foods that made a difference in people's lives. And he would do it in memory of his good friend, Dr. Charles Fearn, who started Fearn Soya Foods as a business to supply soy products to American hospitals and drug stores.

IN THE BEGINNING

Although soybeans were an important part of Asian diets for many centuries, they were almost unknown in the United States until World War I. When the war effort began to burden the nation's agricultural and shipping capacities, President Woodrow Wilson was informed that the soybean might be able to help the nation's problems by providing troops with high protein foods that could easily be transported. In 1917, the U.S. Government summoned Charles E. Fearn, M.D. to the United States to help develop a soybean industry as part of the war effort. Dr. Fearn was a surgeon major in the Royal Army Medical Corps and had been in charge of a hospital in England prior to his coming to the U.S. He was recognized as a leading soybean authority and, in addition, was the first to discover biochemical relationships between B vitamins.

As Dr. Fearn began consulting on growing soybeans and processing methods, the war ended and he turned his attention to promoting the soybean in various commercial ventures. In 1920, Dr. Fearn started the Soyex Company in New York, which was one of the first processing plants for soy in the U.S. However, the public did not seem ready for the new soy foods and the company failed soon after. In 1923, Dr. Fearn moved to Chicago where he started Fearn Laboratories, later to become Fearn International. Here he partnered with a friend and developed Viana, the first liquid diet formula; Solac, an all-soybean infant formula; and Full Fat Soya Powder. When that partnership fell through, Dr. Fearn started Fearn Soya Foods in 1925, in which he developed soy cereals, soy pancake mixes and soy milk powder.

Dr. Fearn was well known to every major company and researcher in the new soybean industry. He was granted U.S. citizenship by an Act of Congress and continued to work with the Department of Agriculture throughout his years. In 1937, Dr. Fearn exchanged letters with Dr. Charles H. Mayo, founder of the Mayo Clinic in Rochester, MN, about using SOY-O cereal in their dietetics clinic. Margaret Rudkin of Pepperidge Farms wrote Dr. Fearn on Dec. 22, 1938 requesting information about experimenting with soybean flour. And the original Kraft family spoke with Dr. Fearn about using his soy powders in their products. Interestingly, in 1937, a letter from A.V. Sadacca of Battle Creek Scientific Foods stated: "I do believe that it is a good move for you to go to California, inasmuch as most of the health addicts are located there." Yes, 1937!

Unfortunately, Dr. Fearn never earned a fortune from the soybean industry since his business ventures mostly failed and Fearn Soya Foods only had one other employee at the time of his death. He died July 31, 1949 in Elgin, IL without a will and no relatives in the U.S.

A NEW BEGINNING

Paul Richard had been one of Dr. Fearn's close friends, one of the few who had not taken advantage of him. In 1947, Paul was a printing salesman and flour broker who had sold products to Dr. Fearn for about 15 years. He had been trained as a pharmacist and had actually been the youngest registered pharmacist in the state of Indiana by the time he was nineteen. Paul also worked in various trades including as a Pinkerton detective, a forest ranger at Yellowstone, a cowpuncher for a railroad and as a porter on a Pacific ocean liner! As a close friend, Paul filled in for Dr. Fearn when health forced him to stop working in early 1947. Paul saw potential in Fearn Soya Foods and purchased the company at auction from the State of Illinois for $750 plus $400 debt, which was two months rent at 355 West Ontario Street in Chicago.

One of the first things Paul Richard did with the business was to fill orders that had been sitting in the office for some time. Dr. Fearn had grand visions of selling Soy products to hospitals and pharmacies and didn't care to even fill orders that were mailed to him from health food distributors. Fearn Soya Foods was still not Paul's full time job, but he had a good business sense and knew that an order was an order. An early challenge came when the lone employee, Renee Kozuchowski, refused to provide Paul with the formulas for the original Fearn products because she felt that the company should have been hers. Paul Richard had to experiment for awhile before rediscovering the right combinations and enabling the business to continue.

By early 1950, Fearn was still a side business with only one part-time employee, Paul, working Saturday's and some evenings. Paul Richard continued to work as a printing salesman for Kokomo Lithograph of Kokomo, IN throughout the entire time he owned Fearn Soya. He was very frugal in his business dealings and had made a practice of buying odd lots of paper and then selling them or using them himself. As a salesman, Paul knew actual print costs and was able to quote customers print jobs on the spot, leaving many buyers in disbelief. He also knew printing process costs and was able to get his own printing costs very low as he often would know the cost before the printers would. Fearn Soya was quite a small company for a number of years.

Listed below are records of Fearn distributor sales, plus the number of wholesalers (jobbers) the company utilized per year.

YEAR	$SALES	DISTRIBUTORS
1950	$6,200	5
1951	$7,600	8
1952	$20,300	12
1953	$16,900	8
1954	$19,900	13
1955	$27,300	11
1956	$38,500	17
1957	$56,300	20
1958	$58,500	19
1959	$72,200	21
1960	$103,700	22

Original Fearn Soya packages

DISTRIBUTOR RULES

For much of the 20th century, wholesale health food distributors dominated the business and controlled manufacturers as well as retailers. These jobbers hoarded territories so that suppliers were forced to sell to the key distributors or face a huge obstacle for selling in that area. In 1950, Fearn only sold four products and the distributors were: Specialty Foods in NY, Health Food Distributors in MI, Health Food Jobbers in IL, Pavo in MN and Morton's Health Foods. Prior to this, Dr. Fearn had made great efforts to sell his soy products to hospitals and pharmacies. Paul Richard also tried to sell to pharmacies at first, but this proved fruitless and the soy products found a welcome home in the budding health food industry. Paul Richard introduced Chocolate Soy Flour in 1950 as one of the first protein supplements available. Apparently this product contained 47% protein, which was a breakthrough in those days and more affordable than meat or milk sources of protein.

About 1950 a teacher named Eugene Feuchtinger discovered that voice muscles could be improved with dietary protein, resulting in improved voice tone. He experimented with many singers by recording voice lessons both before and after using protein. One student was Irwin Johnson, who became so convinced of this theory that he guessed that all body muscles would be improved by simply ingesting higher levels of protein. Johnson researched protein sources and discovered that soybeans contain the highest level of protein. He wrote to many suppliers and processors of soybeans and eventually found Paul Richard at Fearn.

Original Fearn Soya Protein label with picture of Bill Richard

Paul Richard made a deal with Irwin Johnson, a major body building promoter, to supply a custom protein powder for his business. Fearn mixed and packaged the protein for 25 cents per pound bag, though promotion expenses and profit by Johnson made the retail price $1.00 per bag. Interestingly, Johnson later moved to Hollywood, where he changed his name to Rheo Blair and became a nationally known personality with many enterprises. Shortly after this, Fearn also sold protein powders to Hoffman Products, which later became York Barbell in Pennsylvania. Bob Hoffman was to become the leading protein supplier in the 1970s and 1980s and Paul was always nostalgic about having helped Hoffman get started in that business.

Compared to Dr. Fearn, Paul Richard was a hands-on employer who preferred to pack flour, load trucks, pay bills and do many repetitive tasks himself. This was in contrast to Dr. Fearn who had been an English Gentleman and tended to avoid getting his hands dirty. By 1960, when Fearn had grown to have six employees, Paul would still be the one to unload truckloads of flour by hand. He also kept his desk in the production area in order to keep an eye on the basics of his business, all the while still selling flour and printing jobs as a broker.

About 1957, Paul and his wife Verna took a trip to Alaska for six weeks and Bill, the youngest son, was allowed to "run" the business in their absence. The family lived in Oak Park at the time and Bill was going into his senior year of high school. There was a big storm and a flood inundated the entire area. Power lines were down and standing water was about 18 inches deep. Authorities wouldn't allow Bill access to the plant due to the extreme danger. At the warehouse bags of flour and cartons were stored on the ground level and it became a horrible mess of smelly, soaked bags and boxes. Bill couldn't contact his parents, who were camping, but he worked hard to clean up the mess before they came back. The business basically stopped for almost two weeks while new supplies had to be ordered.

THE FAMILY GETS INVOLVED

Paul Richard had three sons named Elwood, Lou and Bill. These three worked at the small plant on Saturdays, packaging and mixing flour products mostly. They had great fun while learning the business from the bottom up. Elwood still recalls what they called "soy ball fights" – something that wasn't advertised to customers at the time!

In 1949, Elwood graduated from high school and was the first to go off to college. As early as 1948, Elwood, Lou and Bill had used Fearn's new high protein soy powder to help improve their running times in cross-country. It worked. Each of the brothers was able to reduce their distance running times enough to be noticeable. They each credited the Fearn protein powder for their improvement in running times and continued to supplement their diets with it throughout their school years.

During graduate school at Indiana University Elwood and his wife, Betty, had their first son named David. Elwood had majored in Physical Chemistry, with a minor in Biochemistry, and had been taking a course called Radiochemistry. At the time, the dangers of radioactivity were not well known and nuclear testing was in full swing. Elwood's radio chemistry class read the background counts each day during testing at Los Alamos and found that it tripled when the radioactive cloud came over from 1500 miles away. Although tests showed no significant exposure, it soon became clear that something wasn't very natural about that lab. David was born with a deformed thumb that required surgery as an infant and Elwood later realized that radioactivity, even in small doses, could strike and alter DNA with severe consequences. Elwood later worked at Nuclear Chicago from 1957-1960 where he was an associate physicist who worked with radiation detectors. These experiences and later discoveries led Elwood to be very cautious about today's careless use of food irradiation.

In 1958, Betty Richard worked at Fearn for her first and last day. She was called in to help package flours and felt the work was too physically demanding for her to work every day. Her fond memory is that she set a new production record that day, while trying to impress her boss and father-in-law. About that time, the company started using a "cuss jar", which meant that if anyone swore at work, they would have to put five cents per swear word into the jar. When enough money was collected, everybody went out to dinner for free with "cuss money." This volunteer plan worked surprisingly well, though I wonder how today's unions would view such a "tax" on employees.

In 1960, Elwood's mother, Verna, became ill with cancer and Elwood took time off to research and study cancer in search of a cure. Many hours were spent examining the literature for anything that could solve this immediate problem and Elwood still kept very large files about cancer research for decades. Unfortunately, Verna died in July, 1960 and Elwood joined the family business full time. Initially, Elwood's job was to fill mail orders which averaged about 6-8 orders per day. This was quite routine until one day when True Story Magazine wrote a "slim" article suggesting Fearn's low-fat soy powder was the best diet product. Within days, orders started coming in en masse, many with checks or cash. Soon, 100-150 orders per day were flowing in and Fearn's business was booming. The whole business only employed about 6 people in 1960, so everyone had to work especially hard just to keep up with the mail!

This great gift to the business ended up having a sad and unpredictable end. Paul Richard was in relatively good health despite two heart attacks and high cholesterol. The stress from the influx of business may have been what caused a final heart attack, which ended in his death on November 23, 1960. Three sons were left without both parents within six months and Fearn Soya lost its owner and business driver. The ancient proverb remains true, *"Many are the plans in a man's heart, but it is the Lord's purpose that prevails." (Proverbs 19:21)* Death is rarely according to our timetable and Paul's death was certainly a major hurdle for the growing business and family.

> *"So I saw that there is nothing better for a man*
> *than to enjoy his work, because that is his lot.*
> *For who can bring him to see what will happen after him?"*
> **Ecclesiastes 3:22**

1960-1968

1960 began a revolutionary decade within the United States and worldwide. From Cuba to Vietnam, Berlin to Jerusalem, American Civil Rights to South Africa's Apartheid, the world was changing. Assassinations were far too common while East and West both raced to be the first to put a man on the Moon. The Cold War was heating up and Fidel Castro sided with the Soviet Union because of American "economic aggression." As Kennedy debated Nixon on television for the first time, TV viewers liked the better looking Kennedy, while radio listeners thought Nixon was the man of the hour. America, meanwhile, braced for a decade of cultural revolution that changed our nation, for better or for worse.

The Richard sons, Elwood, Lou and Bill, inherited a health food business that none of them really wanted. Elwood had plans to return to graduate school and devote his life to the sciences as a science teacher. He had two young children, a sickly wife and the responsibility of being the eldest son in the family. Lou had spent eight years studying engineering, physics and mathematics and had just been hired by the Martin Company in Denver as a rocket scientist. In 1960, his research on liquid hydrogen helped lead to fuel for the first manned flight to the moon. Bill was earning his MBA from M.I.T., studying and planning for a successful career in the corporate world. He prepared for technical management and actually wrote his thesis on *"Consumer Knowledge of Health Food Products".* Their father, Paul, had left the business equally to them and there wasn't much to do except carry on their father's torch and make the business the best it could be. Elwood was left holding the bag as the eldest son and the one who was already working in the business. Lou and Bill were interested in Fearn, but were unable to be directly involved initially.

When Elwood started managing Fearn, he was only 29 years old and fairly inexperienced in the business world. He was quickly baptized by fire when the True Story craze ended and Fearn's business returned to its prior sales level. This would normally be okay, but Paul had hired about six extra workers to handle the windfall, not knowing that the dramatic influx of business would only be temporary. Elwood began managing a company that very soon had nearly twice as many employees as it needed and couldn't go on much longer with not enough work to do. He had the painful job of laying off about six good workers and later called it one of the worst days of his life. This really, really bothered Elwood. The experience was so painful that Elwood vowed that he would never be responsible for letting that happen again. It was just too difficult and unfair. Fifty years and thousands of employees later, Elwood can sleep peacefully at night knowing that he has never laid off anyone since that fateful day in 1960.

FEARN MOVES ALONG

From 1960 to 1967, sales at Fearn grew only about 6% per year, ending 1967 at about $180,000. Elwood, Lou and Bill became intimately involved in the business as each of them had to agree on each new distributor the company added. Whenever a new distributor approached Elwood to add the Fearn line, Elwood would write a letter to Lou and Bill, lay out the pros and cons and then they would decide together if the customer deserved distributor pricing. Surprisingly, about half of those discussed were not suitable as many retailers tried to act as distributors and weren't really in the business of servicing other stores.

During this time, Elwood took a few courses at Roosevelt University and was unsure how his role would continue. He had inherited the head job in a business that didn't captivate him. He also had a very young family and a wife, Betty, who had severe allergies, so life was extremely busy. In 1961, Elwood and Betty took a month off from work to explore other areas of the country that might be more helpful for her allergies. They spent time in Denver, Phoenix and San Diego, but ended with no noticeable improvement in Betty's health. She remained chronically ill for many years, but eventually felt well enough to continue life in the Chicago area.

Meanwhile, Lou married in 1961 and took an eight month trip around the world. He had taken a leave of absence and planned to return to his job in Denver, but his experiences in traveling the world led him back to his roots in the Chicago area where he wasn't quite sure what he would do next. In 1962, Lou decided to join Elwood at Fearn and see if their father's business was something that would satisfy his quest. Lou assumed this would be short term and he eventually left to explore the theological field from 1966 – 1969. During those years together, both brothers were responsible for all management/operation functions including selling, package design, new products, billing and new equipment at Fearn. In 1964, they started oil roasting soybeans and developed a nice business producing and selling Soy-O-Snacks.

In 1962, Elwood dealt with a problem that, unfortunately, was to repeat itself a number of times with different people. While totaling the numbers for mail order sales, Elwood found that they did not add up. Elwood checked and rechecked every possible option and came to the clear conclusion that one of his key employees had stolen the missing funds. He quickly confronted the surprised worker, who had been a close and well liked friend of the family and whose mother was the main supervisor. The young man wouldn't admit any fault initially, and even swore on his father's grave, but later in the day he confessed and had to be removed from his job. *"Truthful lips endure forever, but a lying tongue lasts only for a moment." (Proverbs 12:19)* Events like this are very sad to anyone who has had a similar experience, especially so when the thief is a close, trusted friend who was as much a part of the business as anyone.

While the health food industry was still getting established, Fearn was struggling with its primary customer – distributors – who practically owned the industry. Because Fearn sold food products like soy flour, soybeans, pancake mixes and other flours, the company couldn't ship direct to retailers and was forced to rely on an unstable group of middleman distributors. In 1960, Fearn sold products through 22 natural food distributors, of whom nearly half were out of business eight years later. Distributors were very financially unhealthy and this trend continued for several decades when weak distributors were long gone and new, mega distributors controlled vast portions of the health food trade. In 1961, Fearn's leading distributors were: Kahan & Lessin, Akin's - Tulsa, Health Food Jobbers, Sherman, Balanced Foods, Good Health, Health Food Distributors, Landstrom and NuVita. It was about this time that some of the leading distributors met together privately in an effort to collectively increase their margins from 20% to 25%. Elwood became aware of this and helped to publicize these illegal meetings to industry manufacturers and retailers. The Department of Justice looked into the matter and some manufacturers that sold through distributors tried to break free and sell direct to stores. The most visible and successful company was the William Thompson brand of vitamins, which became the #1 brand while mostly being sold direct to stores. Bill Thompson was a popular industry personality who was well liked and who was able to sell his brand direct to better stores, while using distributors for the smaller stores.

HEALTH HOUSE BEGINS

By 1962, Elwood decided to open his own health food store for three reasons: First, to learn more about the health food business from the retailer's point of view. He knew enough about overall health from Fearn and his own family, but he didn't have a connection with the public to see what they wanted and what would work. A retail store would be a convenient way to study the market, while building on Fearn's small mail order division. Second, an independent store would be able to keep an eye on distributors, who had just started duplicating Fearn's products in their own private brands. For several years Elwood kept his ownership of Health House a secret so that he could talk to representatives from distributors and manufacturers with their guard down. And third, Elwood felt that health food retailing would be a good business to make money, while at the same time helping people become healthier. Once again, Elwood, Lou and Bill were equal financial partners in the new retail venture, with Elwood leading the charge for day-to-day business.

Elwood lived in Elmhurst, IL and found a retail site in town that looked ideal. He quickly signed a lease for the store, but soon discovered that the building was one inch over the correct property line and a legal tangle ensued. Nine months later, an alternate site was chosen, on Second street in downtown Elmhurst. Elwood operated as an absentee owner, hiring a Cuban refugee as the first manager. Elwood was desperate for anybody to fill this job and the young woman was equally desperate for a job. At that time, very few people were willing to take on this position in a store that didn't show much promise, and even fewer were qualified with a nutrition education. The young woman was intelligent, personable and a ready worker, but she spoke broken English and knew nothing about health foods or retail management. Some days, sales were as low as $15 for the entire day! The health food movement was still very young, struggling financially and definitely not recognized as a bona fide industry. The term "health food nut" came to life and I recall my father being the subject of many "friendly" jokes.

Somehow Health House began selling over $2,000 per month in 1964 and a new customer named Florence Shibley began frequenting the store. She started working on Saturday's in late 1964 and became manager full time in 1965. Florence became such an important part of Elwood's success that words can only begin to express his appreciation for her. She had a very kind way of servicing customers and later had customers drive up to 100 miles to visit her and the store. She was a dedicated believer in natural foods and a born sales lady. Florence worked full time, and then some, while Elwood put in about 12 hours at the store per week in addition to 60 hours at Fearn. Florence single-handedly built Elwood's retail store into a success and annual retail sales are recorded below:

YEAR	$SALES
1964	$25,392
1965	$38,292
1966	$49,404
1967	$65,604
1968	$79,572

In 1968, Elwood had his only serious problem with Florence and it happened like this. After five years of losing money at the store, Health House finally made a profit and Elwood decided to give raises to the employees that made the store successful. He increased Florence's pay from $1.30 per hour to $1.55 per hour and gave a second lady a nickel raise to celebrate. Surprisingly, Florence became enraged at her co-worker's raise, because she felt that the other lady was not worth the increase! She was so upset that she walked out of the store during midday and didn't return. Elwood chased after her and, eventually, settled her down enough to reconsider her decision. In the end, Florence came back to the store only after Elwood promised her that he would open a second store that she would run basically on her own. In 1969, the Lombard Health House opened and quickly became a success. Within three years, Florence had that store humming, selling over $140,000 in Lombard alone in 1971. The other lady, Helen Howard, stayed in Elmhurst and became quite a health believer herself. She developed inoperable breast cancer and began reading Adelle Davis' words of wisdom in her books. Helen eventually put her cancer in remission and cured herself by consuming very high doses of antioxidant vitamins C and E.

Meanwhile, at Fearn, another big break came when Fearn's high protein powder was used by the U.S. team that climbed Mt. Everest in 1963. This was major publicity for Fearn and led to a whole campaign of window banners, store literature, industry news and a rush on the product. 'High Protein Food' was labeled "for athletes, body builders, and those wishing to develop strong muscles. A natural food supplement containing all needed amino acids, in convenient form for energy, vigor and vitality. High in biological value, pleasant tasting and economical." Somehow that old-time marketing verbiage looked partly extra honest and partly extra promotional. "You can set records too", ads claimed. In one sense this was quite true as Elwood, Lou and Bill all used soy protein powder in their high school years, and each noticed better times in distance running after using the product. Elwood later did research with Joe Newton, the Elmhurst high school cross-country coach, using soy protein for endurance. Joe Newton was such a running icon, winning many state and national cross-country championships, that he later became the only high school cross-country coach to serve on the Olympic Committee!

Fearn booth at the NNFA Trade Show

Another interesting side note to Fearn's soy protein efforts was that Bill Richard was photographed by a semi-professional for the front of the label. He was the strongest of the three brothers and looked in fine form throwing a shot put on the new label. As runners, Elwood and Lou were both too skinny to be seriously used for a muscle product. But Bill provided a 1960s, hulky look that was probably modern for the day, but today looks retro with old school shorts.

THE NEED FOR NOW

One day in 1968 Elwood was working at his Health House store in Elmhurst and a problem erupted that led to the creation of NOW. At the time, Elam Mills was the leading brand of flours, corn meals, grains, peanut butter and more, and had been recently sold to another company, which started selling those products in grocery stores. Elwood was unhappy about this, because his local Jewel grocery store was a very large store and could sell at lower prices. Elam Mills had been sold in every health food store, so dropping the line didn't seem like a practical idea. Because he was so busy, it never quite sank in that Jewel was offering the same Elam Mills products at his wholesale cost.

One day a customer walked in to Health House and was outraged that he had overpaid on Elam Mills products. He called Elwood "a dirty robber" and walked out. When a second customer repeated the same complaint loudly, it bothered Elwood to his core because he agreed that they were correct and had a right to be angry. The products did cost too much and the same item shouldn't be available at 2/3 the price just two blocks away. Elwood was really touched by these events and he immediately made plans to make sure that he would never be in such an embarrassing situation again. He quickly came up with a strategy that would allow his small hole-in-the-wall store to be able to compete with the "big boys." Never again would high prices drive his customers to shop elsewhere. It was time for his upstart health food store to provide good prices in addition to the healthy products, nutritional knowledge and excellent customer service. It was time for Elwood to beat the odds and change the game in his favor.

Because Elwood was still the president of Fearn, he knew raw material costs, blending costs, shipping costs, packaging costs and distributor costs. He also knew that the Fearn plant had excess packaging capacity particularly between jobs, when extra hands were available. He couldn't sell his own Fearn products directly to his store, because that might upset his local distributor, and since the health food business was so small, that could have created even bigger problems at Fearn. So Elwood decided to package his existing bulk flours at the Fearn plant with a different name and a different label. The new package would be sold direct to his store, eliminating the distributor markup, salesman commissions and normal freight costs. By leveraging the Fearn resources, Elwood had a plan that made sense and he had the willpower to make it happen.

Bill Richard (second from left) and Elwood Richard (right) with two customers

The name "N O W" was chosen because industry standards were a big concern and this acronym stood for Natural, Organic and Wholesome. Elwood and Lou defined these categories specifically so that there would not be confusion over what is natural and what is not. For instance, Natural meant that "agricultural chemicals were used to raise these products, but no preservatives or chemicals of any type were used in processing, preparing or preserving the product." Likewise, Organic meant "grown on composted soil, raised, processed and preserved without the use of chemical fertilizers, herbicides, pesticides, fumigants or chemicals of any type in any step." Finally, Wholesome meant "Synthetic, but identical to natural in molecular shape and structure." An example of wholesome might be Vitamin C, which is naturally sourced from corn, but is synthesized in several production processes. Another is the amino acid L-methionine, which is the naturally occurring form, compared to DL-methionine, which is not naturally produced from a food. Incidentally, the name NOW has no relation to the National Organization of Women, which also goes by the same name, NOW. To my knowledge, NOW Foods claimed the name first in 1968, though it was not officially incorporated until 1973. Every once in a while we still get questioned about our name and the other NOW. In general, I've found that women tend to like the association, which is in name only, while men don't give the matter a second thought!

The first NOW products packaged at Fearn for Health House were Non-Fat Dry Milk Powder, Soy Powder, Soy Protein, Whole Wheat Flour, Corn Meal and Vitamin E. This new venture was destined to reinvent distribution within natural foods stores as the low-cost strategy has proved to win the day. Even quality Fearn products could be made affordable, given the right circumstances, and Elwood ended up being ahead of his time with this idea. For about 25 years, no other major vitamin brand followed this strategy of focusing on value. All of the 'leading' brands either sold direct at high profit margins or through distributors who increased the end cost as well.

As 1968 ended, Fearn was growing nicely, Health House was finally profitable and NOW Foods had started as a minor private label in one small health food store. Who would have thought that from that humble beginning NOW would grow into the large corporation that it is today? Certainly not Elwood, who only wanted to supply his store with products that would compete on the basis of value. Even he couldn't start dreaming yet about supplying tens of millions of consumers every year with a brand of products like NOW does today. The revolution had begun and it was time to start another new business in the fledging natural foods industry. As the good book says, *"By wisdom a house is built, and by understanding it is established; by knowledge the rooms are filled with all precious and pleasant riches." (Proverbs 24:3-4)*

> *"So whatever you wish that men would do to you,*
> *do so to them; for this is the law and the prophets."*
> **Matthew 7:12**

1969–1977

1969 was a revolutionary year in many respects. The infamous Woodstock Music Festival awakened an entire nation to the vast numbers and pent up emotions behind the country's youth movement. The Middle-East welcomed two new leaders, Yassir Arafat of the PLO and Muammar Quaddafi of Libya, both world figures who dominated their respective peoples for decades. The U.S. finally won the race for putting the first man on the moon when Neil Armstrong uttered his famous quote, "that's one small step for man, one giant leap for mankind." And the legacy of Vietnam was lived in these years, a time when America was becoming much less known as 'the beautiful', and much more 'the polluted.'

In 1969, Elwood was fully engaged in running three separate businesses, which were each tailored to the fringe movement known as "health foods." Fearn – the natural food manufacturing division – reached its zenith during the 1970s, growing rapidly in sales while introducing many new products and becoming the first in the industry to package with stabilizing nitrogen flushing. Health House – the retail health food arm – grew dramatically from one to five stores in only four years, including the opening of the largest natural foods store in the Midwest. NOW Foods – the private label for Health House – grew because of the stores and soon began to reach out to other local health food stores willing to take on a generic line of natural foods and vitamins. Elwood was extremely busy at this time and the workload only increased as growth and unexpected problems took their toll.

FEARN MAKES ITS MOVE

Fearn grew about 30% in 1970, as Lou Richard returned to the family business in which he still had a major stake. 1971 was even better as Fearn took advantage of the booming health food market and actually jumped 77% in one year. It was during this time that the Richard brothers first considered selling Fearn outright or merging with other companies. In 1971, Elwood and Lou had formal discussions with Nutrition World, a Minnesota retail chain, about merging their businesses and going public. Several parties were interested in purchasing Fearn and a letter of intent was signed in 1972 to sell the company to one of them. Due to financing problems, the buyer was unable to come up with enough cash and the deal fell apart.

About this time, Fearn's finances were full of debt. In April of 1972, the company's bank put Fearn on an accounts receivable program, severely limiting working capital to complete expansion plans. Fearn had just tripled its warehouse space, added new machinery and introduced a number of new products. The sudden growth spurt and capital investments needed to continue almost ended up ruining the company! Fortunately, Chuck Fanaro, a friend of Elwood's, came to the rescue and loaned the company enough money to continue operations.

In November, 1971, Fearn purchased a very small company called D. Needham Sons & Co. for $405. This small firm was founded in 1878 and made red clover extract, which sold at $2.00 for 6 ounces of powder. In the 1950s, tests had been run at the University of Wisconsin for the treatment of cancer. The prior owner spent about $750 for the research, but the end results on mice were inconclusive. Fearn bought the company for next-to-nothing, and pretty much got next-to-nothing from it. Though the product showed promise, the lack of solid research hindered sales efforts and red clover extract soon faded out of the business.

1970's Fearns new packaging

Elwood and Lou shared a passion in running Fearn, and trying to influence the natural foods movement in a direction towards higher quality. In the early 1970s, Quaker Oats introduced a new "100% natural" Crunchy Granola that some felt was misleading. Lou felt that the term 'natural' should be restricted to foods that did not contain preservatives, synthetic ingredients, or artificial chemicals used in processing. Fearn developed comprehensive definitions for the terms 'natural', 'organic' and 'health food', and Lou actually went to Washington, D.C. to testify before the Federal Trade Commission on a proposed regulation to define these same terms. Due to the change in administrations in 1980, and a new anti-regulatory sentiment in Congress, the proposed rule was never adopted. But in some ways, it had been helpful to Elwood and Lou because it stimulated them to think through exactly what these terms meant for Fearn and NOW products. They asked questions of vendors that were unheard of at the time. Sometimes the answers weren't very forthcoming. As it became clear what their standard for 'natural' really meant, it became more difficult and more expensive to find clean ingredients that met their strict requirements.

Fearn exhibited at the 1970 NNFA (National Nutritional Foods Association) national trade convention and Elwood came home with a wide array of business ideas that he was determined to implement. He saw many changes taking place in the health food industry and anticipated even more. Elwood wrote an extensive report for his brothers, complete with the following predictions that have eventually proved true:

- General Nutrition Centers were growing quite rapidly and Elwood guessed that GNC could supply one third of all goods sold in the health food industry. Although GNC never met that lofty estimate in dollars, its 8000+ stores do dominate all U.S. health food stores in 2018.

- The FDA hearings to eliminate capsules or tablets sold without prescriptions for potencies over 150% of the RDA (recommended daily allowance) would fail. Still, as a hedge, Elwood proceeded to introduce over 75 powdered supplements just in case new regulations caused traditional supplements to be phased out. "Take a Powder" became a new slogan that helped NOW launch the only line of pure or complexed powdered vitamins, minerals, amino acids and digestive aids.

- That health food products would move into supermarkets within a couple of years, despite retailer furor over sales to discount operations. Elwood felt the #1 brand Thompson did cross the line and initiated sales to supermarkets. Unfortunately for Thompson, health food retailers boycotted the brand and supermarkets proved to be much less suitable or friendly compared to independents. Thompson's name was marred and it is still trying to recover decades after multiple owners ran the top brand into the ground.

- That the level of technical knowledge within the industry would increase substantially in years to come. In 1970, research was not as advanced as today and government resistance to alternative health products greatly hindered technical information and open communication to the public. This would change greatly with the passing of The Vitamin Bill in 1976, which provided Americans with basic freedoms to choose and use supplements based upon their own informed decisions.

- That wholesaler dominance would draw to a close as more and more stores started buying direct from manufacturers. As a result of wholesaler's sales to supermarkets, independent health food stores started their own private label lines that would only be available at their store. Both retailers and manufacturers began trying to find ways to bypass distributors as price competition drove businesses to seek new venues and alliances.

LOU AND ELWOOD CHANGE ROLES

In 1972 Lou became President of Fearn while Elwood spent the majority of his time at his retail stores and distribution center. Lou and Bill sometimes saw things differently than Elwood and the time seemed to come for the family to deal with the changing times. Elwood had different dreams than his two brothers, though they all wanted to supply independent health food stores with quality, real quality, natural food products. Accomplishing changes within family dynamics can sometimes leave bitter feelings, but these brothers managed to keep busy growing their related businesses and it all seems more appropriate years later. Lou's engineering skills helped Fearn introduce the first nitrogen flush packaging in the natural food industry. The 'Naturefresh' process was used in products like wheat germ to extend shelf life and avoid early spoilage. This unique process worked quite well and helped Fearn become the top-selling brand of wheat germ in health food stores.

In 1971, Elwood and Lou helped to start the National Nutritional Foods Association's (NNFA) Standards Committee. They reserved a large room at the convention hotel in Portland, Oregon and invited all of the exhibitors and suppliers to attend. The room was packed and there was a lively discussion of the need for industry standards. After considerable discussion and follow-up communication, the NNFA officially organized the Standards Committee and Danny Wells, a well known industry figure for decades, became the head. NNFA members were asked to complete information sheets on each of their products, and these sheets were assembled into the Standards Handbook. Unfortunately, some members did not comply and the Handbook was always incomplete. Lou was elected to the Standards Committee and served as the Chairman of the Food Division for eight years. Lou was also elected to serve as Chairman of the Manufacturing Division of NNFA. Out of these early committees has come NNFA's TruLabel and GMP programs, both of which NOW Foods has enthusiastically participated in and supported.

HEALTH HOUSE EXPANDS & CHANGES NAMES
In 1968, Elwood had promised Florence Shibley her own store and this started an amazing run of retail growth. The Lombard Health House opened in 1969 and took off far quicker than expected. In 1970, a third location was added in Skokie and the fourth opened the following year in Berwyn. Listed below are retail sales totals for the stores as they grew at a frenetic pace.

YEAR	$SALES	STORES
1968	$79,572	Elmhurst
1969	$229,596	Elmhurst, Lombard
1970	$558,936	Elmhurst, Lombard, Skokie
1971	$727,534	Elmhurst, Lombard, Skokie, Berwyn
1972	$987,264	Elmhurst, Lombard, Skokie, Berwyn, Downers Grove

In 1972, Health House was forced to change its name due to a bizarre series of unexpected events. The new Berwyn store opened in a former grocery store location and, at 6,000 sq. ft., was the largest natural foods store in the Midwest. It had a 1970s juice bar, an absentee owner and a host of employee problems that weren't known until the entire business almost went bankrupt!

The Berwyn store opened in late 1970 and sold a record amount from day one for a Health House store. On paper the store was profitable almost from the start, but somehow the store was consuming money in ways that weren't fully understood. The Elmhurst store manager had been promoted to run the superstore and he virtually ended our family business due to his extensive thievery of store products. The manager had opened his own personal store in a nearby town while he was still Elwood's trusted manager in Berwyn. Apparently he had set up a convenient situation for himself where he would steal large amounts of inventory from Health House on a regular basis and use it to supply his own start-up store. Even after the manager left Elwood's store, he continued to regularly steal inventory from the Berwyn store with the help of the new manager. That man was later known to be a professional thief who had a partner who was a real burglar alarm expert.

Eventually Elwood hired a private detective who caught the ex-employee red-handed and had Chicago police arrest him. His weak defense was that he was merely "transferring" goods that he intended to pay for later. The case went to trial and the ex-manager managed to escape punishment on a technicality as Chicago police did not have jurisdiction to make an arrest in Berwyn. Those who are familiar with Chicago and Berwyn's political and legal histories of corruption won't be surprised by such levels of injustice. Crime seems to pay in the short term, though *"riches do not profit in the day of wrath." (Proverbs 11:4)* In a short time, Elwood's natural food empire nearly went up in smoke and Elwood needed to put in 100-hour work weeks for nearly two years to stabilize the business and help the stores survive.

To add insult to injury, the same manager incorporated his own store with the same retail name – Health House – as Elwood's store because Elwood had never properly incorporated the retail store name. As a result, Elwood, Lou and Bill met November 17, 1971 and determined to change the name of the retail stores to avoid litigation. Names discussed included: The Fruitful Yield, NOW, To Your Health, Ounce of Prevention, The Hump-Backed Whale, Rich Earth, All in the Family and Fertile Plains. One month later the name "Fruitful Yield" was chosen and that name has been used in the Richards' retail stores ever since.

FDA VS. HEALTH FOOD MOVEMENT

By the mid-1960s, the FDA had begun a series of "big brother" initiatives that threatened the entire health food industry. The fringe health food movement somehow caught the government's attention in the wrong way and the FDA and FTC proceeded to wage war against an honest industry trying to help people's health. Hard to believe? Sure, but the facts are history and Frank Murray chronicled the battle in his detailed book, "More Than One Slingshot."

"Why would government agencies, which are partially funded by taxes from the health food industry, attack the health food industry? The motives become clear when you realize that critics of the health food industry often go to work as Washington bureaucrats after working in the food and chemical industries, and they later return to high-paying jobs in these same industries. Conflicts of interest, you say? Of course!"

In the late 1960s and early 1970s, Elwood and Lou found themselves pulled into political conflicts that threatened their retail business as well as their entire customer base for Fearn and NOW Foods. All of their eggs were in one big basket and the FDA pursued an illogical strategy of squashing the health food trade regardless of right or wrong. Listed below are some of FDA's worst public decisions as late as 1975:

1. That vitamin E and zinc were both considered non-essential nutrients.

2. That vitamin potencies in excess of 150% of the current RDA would only be available by prescription from a doctor. You could drink all the orange juice you wanted, but a mere 100 mg vitamin C tablet would only be available at a drug store under doctor's orders.

3. That health food stores should not be allowed to sell nutritional books or dispense nutritional information!

4. That the average American diet is so ideal that supplementation is not necessary, and likely more harmful than helpful anyway. Because the RDAs were designed for healthy 22-year-old males, the FDA assumed the same nutrient requirements would work for everyone else.

5. That FDA had a right to ban all safe supplements which failed to meet officially determined standards.

6. That non-essential nutrients (CoQ10, ginkgo biloba, L-carnitine, evening primrose oil, echinacea, etc.) would be prohibited from being listed on labels or in advertisements. At the time of this proposed regulation, even important minerals like potassium, chromium and selenium were considered non-essential and would have been virtually banned. A supplier could have added lecithin to a heart or brain formula as long as the labels and advertisements didn't say so.

7. That there is no nutritional difference between a natural source and a synthetic source vitamin. Indeed, the official "Findings of Fact" concluded that natural source vitamins may contain other ingredients which may <u>limit</u> their absorption.

If this sounds like the dark ages, it was - for the health food movement. Is it really possible for an unbiased, scientific group of bureaucrats to come up with worse rubbish?

The natural foods industry fought back and won a key appeal August 15, 1974 that reversed earlier FDA initiatives and proved to be a landmark decision. In 1973, Senator William Proxmire (D-WI) introduced the Food Supplement Amendment in support of individual rights to buy vitamins without excessive regulations.

A number of public hearings were held involving senators, congressmen, experts such as Dr. Linus Pauling, and lay people. The war of words ended April 22, 1976 when the Historic Heart and Lung Act was signed into law with the "Vitamin Bill" (Proxmire Act) attached. This sweeping victory provided the health food industry and the Richard businesses with legitimacy and security in a regulatory environment that had been threatening alternative health businesses for decades.

WELCOME ABOARD AL POWERS

On March 4, 1974 Al Powers joined NOW Foods as an accountant who could help Elwood with some big business expertise. Al had worked at Carson Pirie Scott department stores and became their youngest manager ever. He became the Assistant Comptroller and gained broad experience in Carson's management trainee program which involved all aspects of that business. Eventually Al tired of big business politics and he welcomed the change to a hands-on position where he could make a real difference.

What Al didn't know at the time was that NOW Foods and The Fruitful Yield were on the edge of bankruptcy and heading there fast. In 1973, the businesses lost about $100,000 as more retail theft continued and NOW Foods was paying start-up costs in the form of new products, new employees, new advertising and new customers. When Al first visited the Berwyn store, he saw a disorganized, loose, sloppy operation with no security in place and no formal goals set up for managers. Al jumped into the retail side

1. Al Powers (second from right) with Franko Columbo (right) in the 1970's

of the business only because he was skilled and available, and the situation looked so bleak from an organizational perspective. Initially, Al had to clean up some inefficient retail practices, get rid of dishonest employees, implement a security program and set up formal goals and expectations for each store manager. Al also had the job of meeting the weekly payroll requirements with virtually nothing in the bank.

Al still has distinct memories from 'the good old days' at the old Fearn building. As an educated accountant, Al was very surprised to see Elwood regularly using a slide rule to do all business calculations. Even in 1974 slide rules were obsolete to everyone – except maybe Elwood! (Believe it or not, in 2004 the president of NOW Foods still used a slide rule in preference over "slow" calculators for a variety of daily calculations.) Even though a slide rule is inexact at certain decimal points, it has served Elwood surprisingly well over the years. To anyone born after World War II it is a wonder that slide rules are even close to being correct and a bigger surprise that anyone knows how to use one!

The Berwyn store continued to suffer excessive inventory shrinkage throughout 1974, as up to six employees were fired for stealing. Al and a private detective sometimes stayed up all night outside the Berwyn store in order to catch the thieves in action. One time the private investigator actually had to pull a gun to arrest a bodybuilder who resisted the attempted arrest. Another employee opened his own store in the suburbs and proceeded to transfer goods to his new store. It became apparent when York barbells, which were in short supply, were found at his store and missing from the Berwyn store. Another private investigator caught that employee red-handed moving product at night in his car and he was arrested. But the charge didn't hold up as the thief claimed that he intended to pay for the goods.

To make matters worse, the thief sued The Fruitful Yield for defamation of character and he actually won about $5,000. Sometimes life just isn't fair, as this unfortunate history repeated itself much to the chagrin of Elwood and Al Powers. The Chicago area judicial system once again proved just how crooked and unjust it could be – sometimes for just the right price. A strange thing happened during this time that may or may not have anything to do with this case. Sharon, Elwood's daughter, was working one late afternoon at NOW Foods office in Melrose Park when a car drove by and someone fired a shot at the large window. She was sitting near the window and it caused quite a scare in the office. No one ever found out who did this, but it seemed a little too coincidental to be random violence.

DAVID AND DAN GET STARTED

In 1972, David Richard was a wrestler at York High School and he continually had nose bleed problems. Since wrestlers can't compete while dripping blood all over, David needed to find a solution or else he wouldn't be able to wrestle competitively. Dad suggested that he try alfalfa tea which is rich in vitamin K and would help to clot his blood properly. After some youthful skepticism, David tried the tea and it worked better than expected. But David wasn't convinced at first, so he avoided alfalfa tea for awhile and ended up with a bloody nose at his next match. After one more trial-and-error experiment, David became a believer in alfalfa tea and the effects of natural foods in general. It's a sure saying that "we are what we eat" and most people need to "feel" the effects of natural food products in order to become converted.

While Lou's children grew up working at the Fearn side of the business, Elwood's three kids took turns working as packagers at NOW or in the retail stores. I remember packaging 5-10 hours per week starting as young as ten years old, and actually setting records that the full-timers couldn't beat. Dad paid everyone eight cents per piece for a long time until a friend and I earned so much that it caused a problem with the adult workers. It was a sad day when my piece-rate was reduced to six cents per unit, although earning $3-4 per hour tax-free as a pre-teen was still pretty good money in 1974. The worst smelling products to package were autolyzed yeast powder, liver powder and spirulina powder. Any fine powder seemed to end up everywhere, so my favorite products to package were foods that also tasted good: salted soy halves, carob and yogurt-coated raisins and nuts.

Dan Richard, Doug Murguia & Elwood Richard 1986 at a convention

NOW GETS GOING

By 1972, NOW Foods was off and running with a six-page price list, over 120 products and 200 total sizes. NOW greatly benefited from Fearn's purchasing power, which enabled the fledgling discounter an advantage over other food packagers. Listed below are some of the items from NOW's October 1, 1972 price list:

PRODUCT	SIZE	WHOLESALE	RETAIL
Alfalfa Leaf Tea	18-4 oz	$5.88/case	$0.49
Alfalfa Seeds	18-1 lb	$10.68/case	0.89
Baking Soda	100 lb	$8.50	-
Bran Flakes	50 lb	$5.50	-
Brewer's Yeast Powder	12-1 lb	$8.00/case	1.00
Pinto Beans, Organic	18-1 lb	$5.20/case	0.45
Rolled Oats	50 lb	$4.00	-
Soy Protein, Pure	12-10 oz	$8.00/case	1.00
Sunflower Seeds, Hulled	18-1 lb	$9.48/case	0.79
Turbinado Sugar	12-2 lb	$6.00/case	0.75
Wheat Germ, Raw	80 lb	$11.00	-

In 1971, a friend of Elwood's named Norm Zilmer introduced Dad to the first inventory control system that was simple to maintain, accurate and low-cost. Norm was a local pharmacist and one of his vendors had provided him with the "split-box" inventory form that made ordering for stores much easier and helped to contain excess inventory. Elwood used this inventory system in his own stores and later offered it to outside customers after he found it worked so well. The Sunflower Seed health food store in Chicago claimed that this simple system helped reduce its inventory by six figures while increasing the annual inventory turns substantially.

The owner of the Sunflower Seed was Ina Walker, and she ended up being NOW's top customer for over a decade. Ina had been a charismatic and unconventional public relations worker prior to opening her own health food store. She had many unique ideas that helped her store become a success for over three decades. One time she solved her store mice problem easily enough by simply keeping cats in the store. She also sold NOW products to nearly everyone who came to her store by explaining that with labels and packaging as ugly as they were, the product inside had to be good.

One time a drunk came into her store and Ina insisted that he leave immediately. She told him that she only allowed one drunk in per month and she already had one drunk that month, so he would have to leave. That seemed reasonable enough to the drunk, so he left without any fuss or objection. Sadly, one day Ina was violently robbed at her own store, shot in the head and left in a coma. Remarkably, she recovered from the horrors of that day, but the injuries left her permanently robbed of ideal health. Her store, however, continued to operate successfully until 2005 as a testament to what hard work, conviction, value and customer service can accomplish.

INTRODUCING BOB EDWARDS

Another colorful character from NOW's early years was Bob Edwards, owner of Crystal Lake Health Foods in Crystal Lake, Illinois. Bob liked to pick up his orders and he developed an odd reputation for always spending at least one hour talking to Elwood and anyone else who would listen. He had a lot of interesting stories and was one of NOW's best customers, but Elwood was extremely busy and actually had to devise a "Bob Edwards alarm system" as a polite way to end never-ending conversations.

Bob was a super sales guy who sometimes played tricks to get a sale. He was known to call residents of Crystal Lake with a pretend survey, leading respondents to conclude that Crystal Lake Health Foods was the best place locally to buy vitamins. Another trick he played was on people who complained that the tablet size of his favorite multiple was too big. Bob kept a horse enema tablet under the counter and compared the two in size, making his multiple tablet look very small by comparison. Bob also opened a second health food store in Boulder, Colorado, which served as a personal vacation spot. Sometimes he would buy just-expired yogurt for four cents-a-cup and give it away in order to encourage customers to try the taste. He told people of the expiration date, but the price was too good for most people to pass up.

About 1974 Bob started working for NOW as the local (and only) salesman. He was very good at landing new store customers and increasing existing customers' business as well. Unfortunately, Bob developed kidney cancer at a relatively young age. He went to Mexico for some unorthodox treatments, but it was too late and a good man passed away. It's amazing how much business associates can touch other people's lives with happy memories that last for a lifetime.

NOW STRUGGLES ALONG

In 1975 NOW was selling apricot kernel pits, which naturally contain a trace component known as laetrile. Although the FDA and the American Cancer Society had declared laetrile to be useless in the treatment of cancer, many people consumed high amounts of apricot kernel pits because of the high laetrile content. One day the FDA visited NOW Foods with an armed U.S. Marshal and proceeded to seize and destroy about 200 lbs. of apricot kernel pits. When Elwood tried to retrieve his inventory, he was told that the FDA had a case against the apricot pits themselves and not against NOW Foods. Apparently the FDA declared the actual pits to be the defendant and wouldn't allow NOW to defend itself, since NOW was not accused of anything! Where was the due process of law? Elwood would still like to know.

From 1972–1976, business at NOW was pretty bleak and profits (actually losses) were even worse. If my parents hadn't inherited a mortgage-free home when Paul and Verna died, they would never have been able to get additional financing for the business. For years, our family home in Elmhurst was used as collateral in order to keep the business running. My parents didn't tell any of the kids how severe finances had become and none of us knew that Dad would go long stretches without receiving any paycheck because of NOW's financial problems.

Family finances bottomed out when David went to Illinois State University in 1974 with tuition and housing paid for by our parents. It was an emotionally shocking and depressing day for David when he was pulled from class on the first day of college because the tuition check had bounced. It is certainly a blessing for our family today to look back in the past and realize how far our business has come, enabling each of us to avoid such embarrassments both now and, hopefully, in the future. As the good book says, *"I will make them a blessing...and I will send down the showers in their season; they shall be showers of blessing."* *(Ezekiel 34:26)*

> *"I have seen the business that God has given*
> *to the sons of men to be busy with.*
> *He has made everything beautiful in its time."*
> *Ecclesiastes 3:10-11*

1978-1984

Life is full of surprises and our world marches on to the beat of a different drummer every day. In 1978, the world's first test-tube baby was born in Britain, conceived by a revolutionary technique called "in vitro." At the same time, the World Health Organization announced that the deadly smallpox disease had finally been eradicated worldwide. In Jonestown, Guyana, the Rev. Jim Jones led over 900 cult members to a mass suicide that is still known decades later simply as "Jonestown." And the Shah of Iran, America's good friend, left for a permanent vacation after being forced out by Muslim fundamentalists. The Ayatollah Khomeini seized power and held America and its diplomats hostage for 444 days, while the rest of the world watched from the sidelines.

In 1978, Elwood and Lou Richard continued to build their respective health food businesses. The time came for NOW Foods to leave the protection of its mother company, Fearn, and venture out into Chicago's western suburbs with its own facility and higher rent. Fearn, the original family legacy, peaked in these years and began sliding downhill in concert with the nation's recession. Eventually the company was sold to Modern Products under financial pressures, though part of the Richard family spirit still yearned for "the good old days at Fearn." This period was one of lean years when the retail, wholesale and manufacturing divisions were all spinning their wheels and groping for enough financial success to simply keep the door open. It was also a time when a number of key health food managers found their way to the NOW Foods family and helped to provide seed money, which enabled the businesses to keep functioning.

NOW MOVES TO VILLA PARK

By 1978, NOW Foods was still supported by the advantages of being Fearn's sister company. For years, NOW had used Fearn's purchasing power and inventory by borrowing whatever was needed and later paying for the inventory exchange. Both businesses were located next door to each other in a connected building that served each company pretty well. Fearn had leased a neighbor's building in 1972 and bridged the two so that it could expand inventory and handle expected growth. NOW's offices were originally in the unused side of the warehouse building, so both businesses gained from better use of the space.

The total space of the two buildings was about 34,000 sq. ft., which seemed immense to young kids like myself, who viewed the place more like a wonderful hide-and-seek playground. I still recall my father, Elwood, organizing occasional evening volleyball games in the Fearn warehouse. Someone would have to move quite a few skids of product each time in order to have enough room to play. Elwood and Lou knew that they operated businesses in different ways and each tried to give the other enough freedom to succeed independently. Lou was much neater than Elwood, and he always wanted the entire plant to be neat and clean and orderly. All one needed to do was view the inventory in the warehouse to see how their personalities differed. Fearn's products were neatly boxed on full pallets, which were neatly set in organized rows. NOW's inventory looked like a flea market in a warehouse, with scattered small rows of products showing much less attention to appearance. The differences in office décor were even more startling.

After years of shared inventory and warehouse space Lou decided it was time for NOW Foods to find its own home. He envisioned Fearn needing more office and warehouse space, and seemed to feel that the time was right for the companies to separate and expand on their own. Each company ended up paying a price – higher rent – as well as a less convenient relationship of inventory sharing and delivery costs. Yet what turned out to be bad for business in the short-term, ended up being a blessing in disguise for NOW. In 1979, NOW moved into a small 7,000 sq. ft. building at 721 N. Yale, Villa Park, IL. That was much larger than NOW's portion of the Fearn plant had been and allowed Elwood to introduce and stock many new products. Though NOW struggled for years and years to make a profit, the pioneering spirit of perseverance and ingenuity prevailed and Elwood found a way to make ends meet.

Below are sales for the three family businesses during this period:

YEAR	RETAIL SALES	NOW SALES	FEARN SALES
1978	$1,691,425	$472, 385	$1,192,296
1979	1,739,494	494,058	1,400,000 est.
1980	1,902,292	595,089	1,700,000 est.
1981	2,164,178	769,362	1,996,922
1982	2,121,828	862,723	1,643,068
1983	2,160,225	945,880	1,558,931
1984	2,222,130	943,182	1,400,000 est.

This period was difficult for NOW and Fearn, while the retail stores generally profited enough to keep NOW afloat. Elwood had wanted NOW to provide such good value to customers that he didn't make it a top priority to be overly profitable at NOW. Thankfully, some key employees like Al Powers and Doug Murguia worked the stores successfully and gave the company enough working cash to expand when the opportunity presented itself.

INTRODUCING DOUG MURGUIA

Doug joined The Fruitful Yield in the mid-1970s and soon became the manager of the smallest store in the chain in Downers Grove. That store was a former house and selling space was limited to about 800 sq. ft., or the equivalent of an average garage. Doug managed to grow that store's sales so fast that he set company records for sales growth and sales per sq. ft. He made a practice of having "Kelp Days" or "Lecithin Days" or "Cod Liver Oil Days" and made a big deal with displays, samples, sales and nutritional education. He taught his employees to try to sell the special product to every customer that walked through the door and was extremely successful. He became the retail chain's marketing manager and tried to duplicate his efforts at other stores, with mixed success. Some other managers were extremely independent and reluctant to change to a system that clearly worked.

Later, Doug became NOW's marketing manager and he taught me the basics of selling over the phone. Make lots of calls. Up-sell every order. Push every new product. Build good customers into better ones. Have a plan and follow through. Be courteous. Be honest. Help customers grow their business. Listen. Doug mentored me for several years and enabled me to later oversee NOW's expanded sales and marketing efforts. He was a key employee at a key time in NOW's history and provided substantial experience and leadership to myself and many others.

Doug was a very dedicated and unique natural foods enthusiast who became a Vegan, which is the strictest diet for Vegetarians. He experienced life to the fullest and often had mind-boggling stories that never failed to impress. Doug strongly believed in mind-over-matter miracles and seemed able to accomplish super-human feats. One time he shut himself into his home, turned off all electrical devices, closed all curtains and cut off all contact with the outside world. He was into Yoga and decided to fast and meditate as long as one week. He actually went without food or water for six days and claimed he could have gone on longer, but was afraid that he might become unconscious and die. Humans are only supposed to last for three days without water, but Doug proved to himself that mental and physical limitations can be expanded.

Doug was fairly normal in height, but he wanted to be a little bit taller. He started hanging upside down daily using gravity boots and actually worked out with weights while being upside down. Every morning and evening Doug would measure his height, and he told Elwood that he would literally grow one inch each morning and return to his normal height at night.

Another time Doug proved to a friend that he could improve his weight-lifting efforts without physically lifting weights. He had a contest and determined to visualize daily weight-lifting exercises and "see" himself lifting more and more weights. His friend trained at the gym regularly and was sure that he would improve his weight totals far more than Doug. However, when they competed against each other some time later, Doug's mental workouts proved to increase his weight-lifting totals more than his friend's. Though Doug was one of the best salesmen I've ever met, he often said that he never wanted to be remembered as a vitamin salesman. The potential miracles inside all people were what drove Doug to be the person he was.

GARY KLEINMAN

In 1978 Gary joined The Fruitful Yield after working as a manager for Nature Food Centers. He started in the company manager trainee program in Elmhurst and Berwyn and remembers the most disastrous day of his career. Gary showed up in Elmhurst for his very first day and Shirley Kollenburg, the manager, asked him to clean up a couple of displays to get started. The store had a huge case stack of Hain's 32 oz Safflower oil, which was very popular and packed in glass. While organizing the display, Gary managed to knock the whole stack over and a number of bottles broke. The oil ended up everywhere, including all over Gary's clothes. During lunch Gary went home, changed clothes and went back to work ready to redeem himself. He should have stayed home! His afternoon assignment was to clean up the apple juice display and Gary managed to drop about three gallons of apple juice, which were also packed in glass bottles. Juice was a mess everywhere when Denise, the assistant manager, came back from lunch and exclaimed, "I can't believe it. He did it again!" She just sat there and stared incredulously for the longest time, while Gary started cleaning the same area all over again. After twenty five years within the company, Gary more than made up for his initiation nightmare.

Gary Kleinman (center) in Downers Grove Fruitful Yield in 1980

Given Gary's initial mishaps it's a wonder that he kept his job beyond the first week at all, much less grow to be an important company manager. Fortunately for Gary and many others, Elwood had organized The Fruitful Yield and NOW Foods so that an employee actually had to work pretty hard to get fired. Honest errors are tolerated by Elwood's companies far more than normal. In Gary's case, it proved to be the right decision for both parties as Gary later built his store to be #1 in sales and eventually became a retail district manager. As one who has made many errors while trying to do too much, or deciding too quickly, I'm thankful that our company disciplinary climate is unusually friendly to our work force.

Gary also recalled a couple of humorous days when he was the manager at the Downers Grove store. One elderly customer, who seemed to be hard of hearing, walked in one day and went to the back of the store and looked through the refrigerator. Holding up a bottle of liquid Acidophilus, the customer shouted real loud, "I have diarrhea, is this good for diarrhea?" Another time the store's stock boy was dressed up as a turkey and told to walk the street out by the front of the store to draw attention to Thanksgiving specials. Three guys in a car pulled up and playfully tried to kidnap the turkey! The stock boy wasn't sure whether this was a prank or not, so he literally had to fight back and then run into the store for help.

INTRODUCING JIM ROZA

In 1980, Jim Roza joined The Fruitful Yield as another manager trainee at Elmhurst and Berwyn. Jim had originally taught science in the Chicago School System. After years of teaching inner-city school students, he decided it was time for a change. With a knowledge of natural foods and supplements, Jim became a GNC manager and learned the basics of health food retailing and management. By 1985, Jim took over the large Berwyn store and had many interesting days with bizarre customers and psychedelic employees.

Because the Berwyn store was such a well-known, super-sized health food store, many industry personalities found their way to visit Jim at the store. Franco Columbo, a body builder who was nationally recognized, did a book signing at the store and spent time talking to many customers. Dale Alexander, who became billed as the Codfather, gave talks at Berwyn as well as local radio shows selling everyone in sight on the value of Cod Liver Oil. He was quite a character with an intense message and he could really sell an audience. "Everyone should take Cod Liver Oil for a dozen reasons" was part of his regular speech. The Codfather would list in flowery language how amazingly many bodily functions could be improved by simply ingesting Dale Alexander liquid Cod Liver Oil. He was quite the showman, and everyone loved to hear him talk.

During one of the store's promotions, about 400 people came to the store on a Saturday. The store was packed! Nobody could even move within the store! Dale Alexander was on a makeshift platform and he sold cod liver oil like a carnival promoter. All of the parking spaces in the neighborhood were filled. The police even spoke to Al Powers and warned him not to do this again since the event broke the fire code for having too many people in the store. The Berwyn store set an all-time record for single-day sales and cod liver oil in particular. Eventually the lease came up for the Berwyn store and the landlord wanted to triple the rent. Although the store had been nicely profitable for many years, it was forced to move and downsize.

About that time, Jim caught his bookkeeper stealing products out the back door after some other employees tipped him off. She was fired, but not arrested, due to the store's prior problems in prosecuting employee theft. Hoping to cash in at the company's expense, she filed a complaint for wrongful dismissal, but fortunately that motion was dismissed.

After the store moved to Cicero, a drug bust occurred in front of the store that shocked the employees and customers. The employees had watched a man with a large automatic gun get out of a car going the wrong way on a one way street. They hit the alarm button and ran out the back door when they saw him walking toward their store. The Cicero police phoned after the alarm "call" and explained what was happening. "Don't worry; we know all about it. A drug bust is in progress. You have more protection than you'll ever need and it's closer than you think!" About 30 minutes later, two ATF (or similar officials) men accompanied a handcuffed man to the unmarked car and drove him away.

Jim Roza (left) with the Mayor

MORE EMPLOYEE STORIES

About 1980, Soudary Aphayavoung started working at NOW as a refugee from Laos. She became so good at packaging flours and grains that she almost single-handedly kept NOW in the low-cost natural food business. Her family had escaped communism in Laos and eventually much of her family worked at NOW, including her brothers Soudasonne and Soudasak. I had the pleasure of training Soudary in the finer qualities and quantities of food packaging when she was just getting started. Her hand speed was so impressive that later I had to challenge her to a packaging contest to see who was really the fastest. I had always been the fastest in the past and assumed that this would remain true as long as I did my best. Unfortunately for me, I was no match for Soudary, and there was no need to consider a rematch from my point of view. Soudary later developed a proud, bossy reputation because she really was the best at what she did. Nobody could come close to her talent and hustle.

One day an employee, Matt Doyle, noticed that the warehouse manager had stolen bulk inositol powder and reported it to Elwood. A brief investigation ensued and the manager was fired, but not forgotten. The manager was normally fairly laid back, but threatened Elwood at his dismissal. He showed up at work a little while later with a large Native American and was ready to do some damage to the place. I assumed he had mixed our inositol powder with some other illegal white powder and was behaving uncharacteristically violent because of it. The whole conflict ended peacefully, after Elwood talked to him at length, and that was the last we saw of him.

Another interesting associate was Mitch Blankenburg of Chase Chemical and Encapsulations. He was a very large man, about 280 pounds, who made his living selling bulk tablets, capsules and softgels to companies like NOW. He was a good sales guy, very friendly and able to get us purchasing deals that were normally better than other sources. Since he had access to unlimited vitamin samples and supplies, I asked him what vitamins he normally took. I still remember the irony in his answer: "I'm not a pill popper." It was a strange response coming from a salesman of hundreds of millions of pills every year. It's kind of like seeing a vastly overweight salesman trying to sell the low-carb diet, or a health food store owner who smokes outside the store. Something is wrong with those pictures. But then again, we all have our weaknesses, don't we?

THE SKOKIE STORE

My father is fond of telling stories and one of his favorites involved the Skokie store. Skokie is a suburb north of Chicago that has been home to a large Jewish population for many years. Of course the Jewish people are known for their exceptional negotiation skills, which were first recorded in Genesis. There Abraham bargained with God over how many righteous people were required in Sodom to avoid God's wrath. (Genesis 18) Anyway, one day a customer walked into the Skokie store when Dad was working and basically demanded a discount on a pack of chewing gum! He spent a long time negotiating for 10% off the 29 cent pack of gum and made quite an impression on my father. After finally agreeing to pay full price for the gum, the customer exclaimed, "You're not going to charge me sales tax too!"

Another time, Elwood was short-handed and needed to send an older employee named Bert to the Skokie store to help fill in. Elwood was doing inventories and working the register when a customer asked him for some nutritional help. Because he was busy, he suggested the customer talk to the other worker, Bert Gesheidle. Upon hearing the other employee's last name, the customer remarked rather slowly, "Gesheidle, that sounds like a German name." Elwood was totally embarrassed and speechless because he had never considered customer feelings like this in Skokie. Needless to say, Bert ended up being an excellent employee for The Fruitful Yield in his retirement years – at the Elmhurst store.

During the summer of 1974, Elwood was planning to close the Skokie store because it had lost money for a long time and it was again without a manager. However, my brother David was available and needed a job, so Dad sent him to that store as manager for the summer. Though this was David's first retail job, he had a natural knack for servicing customers and doing the little things that make stores successful. He filled the shelves, got customers what they wanted and went the extra mile to satisfy customers. By the end of the summer, the store had grown 20% in sales and was financially back on track. Dad found another manager to replace David, who was starting college, and the store lasted for another 30 years before closing due to lease problems.

Listed below are some interesting monthly historical numbers from April, 1978. Some of the store sizes included large back rooms or basements.

STORE	RENT	SALES	SQ. FT.	COST/SQ. FT.
Berwyn	$1,600	$55,000	6,200	$3.10
Downers Grove	$550	$27,000	1,800	$3.66
Elmhurst	$700	$25,000	2,400	$3.50
Lombard	$300	$14,000	1,000	$3.60
Skokie	$400	$16,000	1,430	$3.40
NOW Foods	$1,800	$55,000	7,000	$3.50

BACK TO NOW

By 1980, NOW's "Full Line" wholesale catalog had grown to include over 800 different sizes of natural food products. Unique niche products filled the catalog: Peanut flour, Carob Wheat Germ, Guar Beans, Carob Pod Pieces, Rosemary Leaves, Kleenraw Sugar, Uncoffee, Nucleic Acid Powder, Copper Powder, Molasses Powder and Black Currant Powder. Because NOW used such cheap (and ugly) black-and-white labels, it was very inexpensive and convenient to package many different sizes for the same product. Here's a sampling of what was offered by NOW in 1980:

- 41 different sizes of vitamin E products

- 28 different sizes of vitamin A & D products

- 28 different sizes of natural sweeteners

- 87 powdered vitamins, minerals and amino acids

- 57 different sizes of herbal teas, mostly cut and sifted

- 100 beans, grains, rice and meals - packaged and bulk

- 52 specialty flours

- Plus a lot of odds and ends that other distributors didn't handle

Elwood clearly loved to supply unusual products that mainstream distributors passed over due to low sales. His game plan was as strong as ever: Focus on providing quality products at the lowest prices and offer unique products that could only be found at NOW. Though this strategy did not produce handsome financial results for many years, the plan was in place and ready for the right circumstances. Elwood had done an excellent job of coming up with a business plan that made sense and put years of effort into making the dream a reality. With an improved label and better packaging to come, NOW was positioned to make a big move and solidify its place as a true friend to natural food enthusiasts all over the world. Elwood embodied the proverb in the good book which says, *"The plans of the diligent lead surely to abundance." (Proverbs 21:5)*

Dan Richard (center) in 1977 working at his first NNFA Trade Show

Elwood Richard (facing customers) about 1975

"My son, do not forget my teaching, but let your heart keep my commandments;
For length of days and years of life and abundant welfare will they give you.
Let not loyalty and faithfulness forsake you; bind them about your neck,
write them on the tablet of your heart, so you will find favor
and good repute in the sight of God and man."
Proverbs 3:1-4

1985-1988

Historians call a major event that changes the course of history a "watershed". In most respects 1985 was an ordinary year with no major wars, political stability in the western world and no life-changing inventions introduced. U.S. President Ronald Reagan moved to gain the upper hand in arms control and reached agreement with Soviet Premier Mikhail Gorbachov on arms reduction. A unique musical collaboration of big name artists produced a song called "We Are The World" that helped to sweep the world into social consciousness. And the U.S. was finally recovering from a recession that had affected our economy for several years.

At NOW Foods, however, 1985 easily goes down in infamy as our year of decision. No, the decision wasn't about what new labels we should consider. It wasn't about new employees, though the year did mark my initial full-time employment at NOW. It wasn't about what new products should be introduced or FDA enforcement or industry news. The big decision came to be, "Should we stay in business, or should we close 'the factory?'" By mid-year NOW's books were so full of red ink that it looked like our ship was ready to sink. Recent years of low sales, low margins, slow moving inventory and high bad debts created a situation where our future looked very bleak. Our year-end inventory had come back with shocking results and our company ended up in the red by about $100,000. With under $1 million in NOW sales for the year, this loss was overwhelming.

I came aboard the company after graduating from Illinois State in May and joined the dozen or so employees. I never knew that my years in college were preparing me to join NOW, or in what capacity. As with most students, I never even interviewed until my final semester and that was limited to a single campus interview with Osco Drug. I was so nervous that I'm sure I made a horrible impression and never did hear anything, good or bad, from Osco. Having followed my older brother, David, to ISU as well as the business field, I assumed my future would follow his to outside work, without seriously considering the family business.

That changed quickly when I came home for Spring Break and Dad offered me a position, without even needing to interview! I had already worked at NOW and our local health food store for about 10 years part time, so my rough edges were already well known to my father. What I didn't know is what aspect of the business I would take to, but I assumed I would continue working in the warehouse, picking orders, packing UPS shipments, taking inventory, cleaning up and reorganizing the mess that our warehouse had become. That all changed when my father came to talk soon after receiving the bad inventory news. His brief statement was something like, "We need to increase sales quickly or NOW Foods will be out of business."

This desperate situation was quite a shock to everyone including my father. A strange contrast is that at the time of our worst financial situation we still offered a unique employee benefit of paid basketball time in the parking lot! Most of the warehouse guys played basketball during the afternoon break while the ladies inside got an extra break, knowing the boss was outside teaching the next generation a thing or two about left-handed hook shots! Those were precious moments for warehouse workers like myself and helped to keep loyalty among staff who were likely underpaid. Our small crew developed into quite a tight family so that each worker felt part of the team and part of a worthwhile cause.

With a clear message to grow sales or else, I became a salesman overnight. My past view of insurance salesmen and similar sales jobs had to be thrown out as I was about to become one of them! Only a few months out of college, called "the kid" by the office secretary, and lacking any industry or product knowledge, I was thrown to the wolves as a last ditch effort to grow sales and keep the company afloat. Fortunately, our in-house sales and marketing guru, Doug Murguia, taught me the basics and then some to help lead the way for immediate growth. Even when our business was miniscule and losing money, Doug had the vision that NOW could be the #1 brand in health food stores. Though I thought he was crazy at the time, it did turn out that having a vision and working toward that goal helped make our success a reality. As one of the prophets said, "Where there is no vision, the people perish."

Some of the traits that make a salesman successful were needed in a hurry: Be productive, make a lot of cold calls, upsell existing customers, know and listen to customers, be persistent and offer customers something that logically will help their business. Knowing that 80% of sales are made after the fifth call is reason enough to get on the phone and make 80 quality calls per day. In those days we hand-wrote and manually priced our invoices, so I became adept at invoicing orders while calling around the country in search of new customers.

MAX EPA

About 1984, R.P. Scherer, a large softgel manufacturer in Florida, introduced a new fish oil supplement made by Seven Seas Ltd. in England. MaxEPA sales started slowly, since this type of fish oil concentrate was a new category and not yet seen in this country. The product supplies EPA and DHA, which are now commonly called Omega-3 fatty acids and still listed on all fish oil supplements. Sometime in 1985 publicity about how MaxEPA could reduce cholesterol and improve heart health spread like wildfire. National TV stations ran health reports about how new research showed amazing results with MaxEPA. It became the biggest "craze" I'd ever seen and had a dramatic effect on NOW Foods and our sales efforts. It didn't hurt that we were selling 100 softgels for under $8 retail, while all the "national brands" – as we called them – were retailing the same product for $20!

Suddenly we were able to call potential customers and offer the amazing MaxEPA for practically pennies on the dollar. It was the easiest sale in the world and I latched on to it like an animal that won't let go. We started to get a new wholesale customer every day as stores realized what a great value NOW was offering, while allowing them to compete with mail order companies that advertised in Prevention magazine. MaxEPA opened up doors to customers that might never have considered NOW because we had the right product at the right time in the right place. While some may call business breaks like this luck, I'll call it providence and count my blessings.

By 1986, MaxEPA was such a hit, and we had sold it so well, that 30% of NOW's entire business was in this new, fishy supplement. Retail health food stores, which stocked 3,000 different products, sold up to 15% of total sales in MaxEPA alone during this period. As with all great ideas and products, generic knock-offs soon appeared and NOW, also, introduced a lower cost Omega-3 softgel with the same exact potency and composition. In response, R.P. Scherer began imprinting each softgel with the name "MaxEPA" to differentiate the original, documented and researched product from generic copies. For NOW, this was a coup, because in the past competitors had claimed that somehow NOW's MaxEPA was inferior to theirs. Of course it was identical all along, made by the same supplier, but now the imprint guaranteed the quality and authenticity of NOW brand MaxEPA.

One interesting side note to the MaxEPA story is that when a generic supply of Omega-3 came out, the supplier cost was about half that of MaxEPA. As a buyer, I pleaded with R.P. Scherer to reduce its price substantially to compete with the newer offerings. It just seemed a matter of time before consumers woke up to buying a better deal, whether it had the magical 'MaxEPA' name on it or not. As with many profit centers, companies are very reluctant to reduce prices when the cost goes down or when the market dictates price competition. Fifteen years later the generic Omega-3 outsold MaxEPA by fifty to one, though it didn't necessarily have to be. Twenty years later NOW discontinued selling MaxEPA, though other fish oil supplements became very popular

Thanks to MaxEPA, NOW grew dramatically – 32% in 1986 and 38% in 1987 – with nearly 300 new wholesale accounts each year. Unfortunately, like many products that are over-hyped by the media, the bubble tends to burst quickly, sometimes for no good reason at all. In 1987, a report came out critical of MaxEPA, stating that since MaxEPA naturally contains cholesterol, it couldn't possibly reduce cholesterol and might even cause cardiovascular problems. Since the media seems to love "cures" as well as "health frauds", it picked up this story and drove MaxEPA into the ground. The product we counted on, and couldn't bottle fast enough, quickly became an inventory problem, virtually overnight. Though R.P. Scherer later introduced a cholesterol-free version, and the negative report had erred badly regarding LDL and HDL levels, the bad news was overwhelming. It's a sad thing to see bad things happen that shouldn't. Too bad MaxEPA wasn't the last important health product severely injured by the media.

I learned one other critical business lesson from the success of MaxEPA. In the summer of 1985, NOW sales were mostly natural grains and flours, condiments, teas and bulk products. One memorable product was the 100 lb. size of 'medium' bran flakes that cost us as low as six cents per pound by the truckload. Since mainstream food processors started removing the bran from wheat to make white wheat flour – without regard to the loss of nutrients and fiber – there was an excess of wheat bran available practically free. In fact, we had several promotions where NOW gave away these huge 100 lb bags of bran free to stores with $250 orders. For a cost of only $6, it seemed like a bargain promotion that cornered the local market for bran and led to increased bulk sales.

I was working in the warehouse at the time and would receive these shipments and put the stock away as space allowed. Because of the size of the bags, nearly half had to be lifted up since they always seemed to fall off the pallets. It was heavy labor largely because of the big size and it seemed like at least one bag each shipment would rip on the pallet and need to be taped. Also, since we had no walk-in cooler on site, every summer inevitably led to moth problems and bran had to be thrown away. The cheap bran was bulky, leaky, buggy and an inventory hazard that was difficult to handle. Conversely, MaxEPA was a quick, easy, clean, profitable, simple sale that pointed NOW in the direction of becoming NOW Vitamins, not NOW Foods. As an order picker, it just seemed so easy to pick and pack a case of MaxEPA, compared to all the hassles of massive bags of bran for the same amount of sales. Learning this lesson helped lead NOW to a whole new field providing vitamins, minerals, amino acids and herbal capsules in addition to still supplying our variety of natural foods. Hence the name "NOW Foods" stuck, even though food sales became a very small part of our business. Foods remained part of our genes, in our corporate blood.

CHANGING TIMES

As sales at NOW took off, it's interesting to view how best sellers changed and how natural food product cycles evolve. By 1985, NOW was basically seen as a food distributor that supplied a wide variety of unique products. Inventory was filled with unique products such as Puffed Amaranth, Carob Filberts, Carob Walnuts, Corn Germ, Yogurt Stars, Whole Dulse Leaves, Barley Bran, Kelp Flakes, Honey Powder, Eggshell Powder, Black Currant Powder, Blue Cheese Powder and Black Turtle Beans! Additionally, we sold fairly large quantities of Linseed oil softgels, which was later upgraded to organic Flax Seed Oil. Other oddities included Hunza organic dried fruits and Ceramic People Feeders, a plastic container that made you wonder what it was really for! Listed below were NOW's best sellers for this period:

1985 BEST SELLERS
#1 "Juice Packed" Bulk, dried Papaya Spears
#2 Fructose Granules, derived from beets
#3 Lecithin Granules

1986 BEST SELLERS
#1 MaxEPA (by a landslide)
#2 Vitamin E-400 d-alpha capsules (as softgels were called)
#3 Vitamin E-400 mixed tocopherols

1987 BEST SELLERS

#1 MaxEPA

#2 L-Tryptophan 500 mg capsules (new to NOW)

#3 Vitamin E (Mixed & d-alpha)

1988 BEST SELLERS

#1 Oat Bran, bulk

#2 L-Tryptophan 500 mg capsules

#3 CoQ10 30 mg capsules (new to NOW)

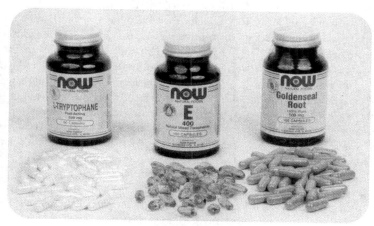

1987 New labeling ad for NOW

NOW's sales progression moved somewhat quickly into new vitamin products and away from foods, with one major exception – Oat Bran. The amazing MaxEPA craze crash-landed hard and the next craze was just getting started. For better or worse, the natural foods industry has gone from rags to riches and riches to rags due to the American public's insatiable desire for "the quick fix." When national TV broadcasts information about vitamins or organic foods, the health food industry sits on edge hoping for a positive report, while fearful of negative news. Sometimes the media seems like a big conspiracy by big business and the FDA. Other times the media is so friendly to natural supplements that you'd think they're a public relations extension of our own company! *"It seems healthy to the soul to ride out bumps in the road and not be too anxious about tomorrow, for tomorrow will be anxious for itself." (Matthew 6:34)*

With MaxEPA fading fast, several new NOW products helped to keep sales growing. In 1988, Oat Bran caught the attention of the national media and proceeded to become our top seller for the year. Oat Bran sales actually increased 1000% in one year, with Oat Bran being in such demand that we had to limit purchases and ration the new precious commodity. Suppliers couldn't make enough as even Quaker Oats had serious production shortages trying to meet their surprising sales levels. The media had, again, created this craze while rightly pointing out that Oat Bran naturally reduces cholesterol. As consumers tend to overreact using natural products, it seemed everyone, everywhere was into this new, bland breakfast food. Elwood Richard made it known at the time that

ANY good fiber – Psyllium Husks, Corn Bran, Rice Bran, Wheat Bran – would also reduce cholesterol about 10% if taken in similar amounts. Alas, the only voice heard was that of the media which had turned a normal, healthy natural food into a miracle cure. I wonder why it is that we are so gullible to accept what we read in papers and see on TV. As with other natural fads, Oat Bran sales skyrocketed for awhile only to return to its pre-hype days, moving aside to make way for the next big wave.

RISE AND FALL OF TRYPTOPHAN

The next big hit was L-Tryptophan, which gradually climbed to the top sales spot without any crazy media hype. NOW introduced L-Tryptophan capsules in 1986 and followed up with new 500 mg & 1000 mg tablets in 1987 due to strong demand. By 1988, singular amino acids had steadily grown to be widely used and L-Tryptophan grew the most because people could feel its impact quickly. Primarily used for insomnia and PMS, Tryptophan was safely used by 10 to 15 million Americans daily since 1972. L-Tryptophan is a natural amino acid found in all protein and is considered "essential" in that it cannot be synthesized in the body and must be obtained from food or supplements. The 'L' form is the natural form, compared to the 'DL' form, which is not found in protein or nature. A large glass of milk or a turkey dinner contains about 500 mg Tryptophan and this is the reason why people get sleepy after a large Thanksgiving dinner. It's natural, of course, and Tryptophan is ingested as part of every food containing protein.

Because Tryptophan is difficult and expensive to extract from protein sources, several Japanese pharmaceutical manufacturers began synthesizing it using a proprietary fermentation process. Elwood Richard had investigated the process used to make Tryptophan prior to NOW selling the product, but was unable to obtain specific details as these were carefully guarded "trade secrets." Since Tryptophan was sold in the natural 'L' form, is an essential amino acid, and had been safely sold for years, NOW began offering Tryptophan to consumers wanting a better value for a product that worked. Within only three years time, Tryptophan sales peaked at 30% of NOW's total sales and had, effectively, replaced the loss of MaxEPA.

But at, oh, what a cost. By the fall of 1989 a mysterious blood disorder spread across the nation and the common denominator turned out to be L-Tryptophan. By 1989, six Japanese manufacturers were producing Tryptophan, one starting as late as 1983. That company, Showa Denko, became the largest US supplier thanks to a new, state-of-the-art production method called genetic engineering. That errant process, plus a change in the carbon filters, produced a contaminated product that seemed to cause Eosinophilia myalgia syndrome – EMS – a mysterious affliction causing severe muscle pain, high white blood cell counts and, in about 36 cases, death. Thousands of people were afflicted with EMS, and all were traced to the same bad batch of Tryptophan made by Showa Denko. In November 1989, the Food and Drug Administration issued a rare recall of all Tryptophan products until the exact causes were known. Though the real reason became public less than three months later, the FDA continued to blame the amino acid 'Tryptophan', instead of the isolated, contaminated product made by Showa Denko, Safe Tryptophan was withheld from the marketplace indefinitely. Beyond the human losses innocently involved in this travesty, two serious issues arose. Most importantly, does genetic engineering unnaturally change foods and supplements to become health hazards? And did the FDA act in the public's best interest, or for political gain, by withholding Tryptophan from millions of consumers after the contamination was documented and isolated?

Thanks to gene splicing, pharmaceutical and major food companies have been able to genetically alter microorganisms so that they can increase reproductive rates and decrease fermentation costs. Records show that Showa Denko had introduced a new, genetically modified strain of bacteria, known as Strain V, into its production to increase Tryptophan output just prior to the EMS outbreak in the US. While the exact connection between genetically modified strains of bacteria and EMS are still subject to debate, it's clear that producers are tampering with nature with potential toxic effects. If the Tryptophan contamination was a direct result of the new gene-splicing technology, the poisonings would be the first deaths traced directly to the expanding biotech business. Because of Elwood Richard's serious reservations about genetic engineering, which is manipulation of living creature genes, NOW avoids genetic engineering (GMO) in products and tries to require vendors to guarantee non-GMO products.

Meanwhile, the FDA withheld Tryptophan from the over-the-counter market despite conclusive evidence that an isolated impurity from one manufacturer caused EMS. In the August, 1990 issue of The New England Journal of Medicine, a medical and scientific case was outlined which ran counter to FDA's thinking. It concluded that the outbreak of EMS "resulted from the ingestion of a chemical constituent that was associated with specific tryptophan-manufacturing conditions at one company." The question remains, then, why didn't the FDA release safe Tryptophan for sale to a public clamoring for the product? Health advocates point to FDA's historic anti-health food bias as reason enough to drag its feet and let the bad press doom the product forever. Indeed, the overall market for amino acids dropped noticeably in 1990 as consumers feared health problems with all isolated amino acids. In this situation the FDA enforced its case for 16 years before allowing tryptophan back into the dietary supplement market. In 2005, FDA lifted its import ban and now lists tryptophan as GRAS (Generally Recognized As Safe).

BUSINESS LESSON FROM JERUSALEM

In 1986, I was fortunate to visit Israel for the first time and enjoyed seeing the Holy Land and all the famous sites I had read about. As a history buff in college, I had studied the land of the Bible and been mystified at the Dead Sea, Masada, Sea of Galilee and many other historical-religious sites. But nothing compared to Jerusalem, the Holy City for three major religions and the city of my dreams. The Psalmist wrote, "For the Lord has chosen Zion; he has desired it for his habitation: 'This is my resting place for ever; here I will dwell, for I have desired it.'" (Psalm 132:13-14) Compared to suburban USA, Jerusalem is a world class metropolis with extreme cross cultures and a bizarre, backward way of life. A visitor gets the feeling that the clock has turned back in time as life in the Old City moves with a distinct roughness.

Shopping for goods in the Old City takes getting used to as haggling is the only way to do business. I was told early on that Arab shopkeepers would be offended if they didn't get a chance to negotiate sales of their products and I found that to be true. Walking down the skinny, dirty walkways is challenging to the senses as Israeli Arabs loudly call for your attention and literally move you into their tiny shops to see their irresistible goods. What I didn't realize at the moment is how these shopkeepers had developed an amazing science for buying and selling. Many sellers could detect I was American and some could even tell from what part of the country based on my accent. They would offer me a soft drink, invite me to sit down and then parade their wares in front of me until a sale was made. I had never seen such sophisticated service and salesmanship from such an unexpected place! Later, as I became more focused on selling NOW products to health food stores, I realized what an education I had received about true salesmanship.

An equal, and unexpected, lesson came in the form of purchasing. By 1986, my father had allowed me to purchase some products and I went at it knowing that all things are negotiable. In the past, since our purchasing power was very small, we were forced into paying full price or simply price shopping for the best deal. But I soon learned just how negotiable our raw materials were and that helped pave the way for NOW to offer even lower prices than before. One purchase from R.P. Scherer was memorable for me since it was our company's largest purchase to date, though unknown to me at the time. I ordered $80,000 in one order for only MaxEPA and Vitamin E, or over 10% of all purchases for the year. This deal was our first big purchasing discount and was only scarred by my ignorance of our bank balance, or the lack of a bank balance! I didn't think enough about paying for the bill, only what great sales we could offer with the new discount. It's important for businesses to have a balance between salesmen with dreams and practical managers who will have to pay the bills when they come due.

NEW CUSTOMERS GALORE

With a renewed focus on selling to new customers and the blessings of the MaxEPA craze, NOW products found their way to millions of new consumers everywhere. Chain health food stores like Vitamin Cottage in CO, Sun Harvest Farms (later part of Sprouts chain) in TX, Richards Whole Foods in FL, Arizona Health Foods in AZ and Boneys Markets in CA all became sales targets that sooner or later became large customers. These chains' purchasing volume was a new thing to NOW and exciting for young salesmen like me. I still have notes from our first big sale, $1,368.34, to Vitamin Cottage of Denver in January, 1986. Sitting next to my father in our crowded Villa Park office became fun as orders like this meant that the company would survive and thrive. I can still recall relaying many technical questions from customers to Elwood and back, while trying to remember the answers for next time. The natural foods business has so many different products and so many different particulars that it takes a long time to become educated in the field. Indeed, one can never stop learning as science changes, new plant extracts are discovered and new issues demand new answers.

In mid-1985, my father, Elwood, had a new idea of posting our weekly number of orders shipped and the dollars sold for the week. Prior to this sales numbers were considered confidential and most employees didn't have any clue about how badly the company was doing. After our financial situation was explained to employees, the focus became how WE could grow sales and see the results immediately. By the end of 1985, an average week would total about 70 orders for just under $20,000. By 2013, NOW would sell each day what the same company did in an entire year! Though the idea of posting sales seemed minor at the time, it was a good idea that caught on with the small circle of employees. We started to give free lunches for everyone whenever a new record was set, though that soon became too much as NOW became flooded with blessings of many record weeks.

About late 1986, NOW received free publicity from the unlikeliest of sources. The National Enquirer ran a story about a new, amazing weight loss product that would produce instant results for all types of people. It would expand in people's stomachs, giving dieters a full feeling without going hungry. The unique product was Guar Gum, a natural dietary fiber that NOW had stocked for years and was thinking about dropping due to low sales. The article noted at the end that the product was available at health food stores or from NOW Foods and it gave our address as well. We were totally unprepared for this and had no advance notice that there was about to be the greatest run ever on a product like Guar. Within hours of release we started getting phone calls from consumers as well as stores who needed the product immediately. Within days, NOW's mail peaked at up to 300 letters daily, many desperate for the amazing Guar Gum, some with blank checks and orders for a three month supply! We capitalized as best as we could, but our packagers could produce only so many bottles, and our two-person sales office could only handle so many calls. The real kicker is that we sold only one size at the time, 4 oz powder which wholesaled at $0.80 and retailed at $1.19. We soon introduced an 8 oz size and several years later added Guar capsules to supply the demand. As a salesperson, I wished we had raised the price immediately to cash in on the gold rush, but we kept to our original prices and supplied a great deal to many dieters.

By 1987, NOW had unwittingly developed into a supplier of products that were used in the drug trade. Somehow drug dealers figured out that they could cut certain drugs with inositol, a white B-vitamin powder still widely sold today for the same reason. Some drug dealers would use lactose, a natural sweetener, or some other suitable white powder for blending as well. Others would buy large quantities of empty gelatin capsules to encapsulate who-knows-what kind of drug product into them. The whole idea was abhorrent to Elwood, who had introduced six different sized empty gelatin capsules so that customers could fill their own NOW vitamin powders. By doing this, people would save money, avoid fillers and swallowing problems, and be able to take larger quantities of vitamin and mineral powders.

One noteworthy customer named Howard owned a small herb shop in Baltimore and, in a short time, became one of NOW's largest customers. It seems that he cultured sales to drug dealers and found NOW to be his best cost for the empty capsules that his customers wanted. Initially, Howard would order once a month, later once a week, and, eventually, nearly every day. Near the end this little shop was ordering over 1000 bags of 100 size capsules and requesting air shipments, something new to NOW at the time. The final straw broke when our customer was so frantic for instant profits that he requested a large order that day and for NOW to deliver it to O'Hare airport and put it on the next plane to Baltimore! That was when Elwood refused to cooperate and the customer eventually left us for some other vendor less concerned about morality and the law. Another time NOW products were shown on local TV during a drug bust and Elwood had to answer to friends who inquired why his products were involved. That's when he set up a new anti-drug allocation policy that required every order to have at least

50% non-drug potential products. That turned many customers away, including Whole Foods Market in Texas, which for some reason chose to only buy our empty capsules at one of their stores. These incidents seem humorous today, but Elwood's choices clearly pointed NOW in an ethical direction which said that profits would not prevail over doing what is right.

LABELS CHANGE COLORS

By the end of 1985, it became apparent that if NOW was to satisfy its customers, new labels had to be developed. Until this time, people who bought into NOW's concept of low prices were the same shoppers that would buy black and white private label brands at grocery stores. This market was very limited because many people perceive that a low quality label is a clear sign of a low quality product. And NOW's vitamin label was as low quality a label as possible. Elwood had come up with an excellent game plan for making healthy foods and vitamins affordable by selling direct to stores and packaging inexpensively, but marketing proved to be the weak point of his game plan. Every customer clamored for a label that would not be such an embarrassment, one that would at least be a label that would look decent on the shelves. Somehow, after years of resisting spending more money on frivolous things like labels, Elwood agreed to a more expensive label design.

The new look took several months to finalize as typesetting was done by an outside firm for the first time. In the past, Elwood considered it a cost advantage to do primitive typesetting in-house, without regard to how most customers viewed the company's labels. Starting with a clean artistic slate, a local graphic artist came up with a number of designs and we chose one that, at the time, looked as beautiful as could be. (Looking back, the situation seems similar to when a new baby is born and the only one who thinks the child is beautiful is the mother!) This beige label was a huge upgrade over the former black & white, or yellow-orange tandem that filled few health food store shelves. Most customers reacted positively, though the memory of one sticks out more than them all. Ina Walker, of Sunflower Seed in Chicago, said that the new label was almost as ugly as the old one and that was just fine with her. She had made it a practice to sell the NOW brand BECAUSE the labels were so ugly! She reasoned with customers that since the label was made to look so incredibly ugly, the product inside and the value to customers had to be exceptional. Sounds a bit like the marketing campaign for Smuckers® years later, when we heard – "With a name like Smuckers®, it has to be good." Anyway, as NOW's top customer, her response was quite a blow to my pride. But it was a lesson to listen to customers, and next time to ask them what they think before committing to something they don't want.

One final note about this period is one that affects almost all private family businesses. By the end of 1986, it was apparent that NOW would survive and growth seemed certain for years to come. At that time Elwood Richard began estate planning and was told that if he intended to pass the business to the next generation, he would need to "gift" some of his stock to family members to avoid income taxes in the event of his death. In 1986, the business had reasonably little value, so Elwood gave away about 20% of his stock to his children: David, Sharon and Dan within one year. He has continued his giving over the years and this has had a very positive effect besides saving estate taxes. Elwood always wanted more family members to work in the business and with a financial interest as a prod, family members did become interested and involved. David, Sharon and Dan continue today to be involved and thankful for this giving. In different ways, each child has made efforts to honor our father's business requests and not try to overstep our bounds, for as the good book says, *"Honor thy father and thy mother."*

*"My son, eat honey, for it is good,
and the drippings of the honeycomb are sweet to your taste.
Know that wisdom is such to your soul;
if you find it, there will be a future,
and your hope will not be cut off."*
Proverbs 24:13-14

1989–1992

People familiar with this time period will remember it for the significant changes that took place. The Berlin Wall fell physically and emotionally, allowing for Germany to be reunited. Half a million Chinese students demonstrated in Tiananmen Square, only to suffer a brutal crackdown in the end. An Exxon oil tanker spilled over 11 million gallons of crude oil in Alaska, ruining the region for years to come. And the Gulf War with Iraq significantly changed most country's foreign policies and led to U.S. involvement on the ground in the Middle-East.

At NOW Foods, this time was a tremendous growth period as NOW quadrupled in sales and expanded to fill the new warehouse on Bloomingdale road in Glendale Heights. At the end of 1988, NOW had relocated to this brand new, 12,000 sq. ft. facility which would serve NOW well, allowing for two separate additions within the span of only five years. It was during these years that customers and competitors viewed NOW as a "sleeper", meaning that the company was quietly climbing the ladder as a supplier of natural products. It was also during this time that I formalized my sales goal of having NOW sell $10 million per year, a lofty goal indeed in 1989. If we could just hit that magic number, my business career would be complete and I would see NOW as a complete success. Looking back and having passed that magic number, I can only say that NOW's overall success has been absolutely beyond my wildest dreams. In the same way, NOW's growth has likely come at the expense of competitor's worst nightmares.

It was during this period that NOW first encountered hostile competitors who were determined to spread ill will about NOW. It had happened in the past with a local lecithin supplier named Harmony, who also supplied NOW with Triple Strength Lecithin capsules. As an overly honest seller, I had told customers that our source of these capsules was Harmony, even though our prices were about 25% below the same supplier. When customers called Harmony to see if this was true, the owner lied and said this was not true and that NOW must be mistaken. I later talked to the customer and offered to send copies of invoices to prove my point, but the issue had become negative by that point. I eventually talked to our supplier about his lie and he replied that he had no other recourse since customers would change to NOW products and his line would cease to be needed in stores. Fortunately good does triumph over evil and Harmony Lecithin is a brand of the past, unable to compete with honest, low cost brands like NOW. Unfortunately, relations with competing brands have been a thorn in NOW's side for years simply because our prices cause problems for more expensive brands. Well-paid salespeople have to say something about why their products cost much more than NOW's, so libel became an unfortunate regular event among many of NOW's competitors.

In 1991, a more serious case of slander arose regarding whether NOW's vitamin E was truly 100% natural. Another low priced, small, West Coast supplier circulated a damaging assay seeming to show NOW's vitamin E was synthetic. The competitor noticed NOW's vitamin E softgels had changed color and assumed this meant that we were cheating and using synthetic vitamin E instead of natural, which costs twice as much. The competitor sent the capsules to Irvine Analytical Labs in California requesting a test for optical rotation, which determines the naturalness level. Somehow the results came back showing only 15.8, when the results should have been 24. Upon receiving this ammunition, the competitor proceeded to distribute the report to health food stores and NOW found itself at war with a terrier of an enemy.

We were 100% confident that the report was in error because NOW only purchased natural vitamin E from the three largest pharmaceutical softgel producers. Elwood Richard figured out that the testing lab had tested the entire contents of the vitamin E gel, instead of just the vitamin E content within the softgel. Since most softgels contain some filler, the filler oil should not be included in the assay for vitamin E. We also argued that vitamin E is a difficult test and we had seen two errors in laboratory testing of vitamin E in recent years. Additionally, NOW vitamin E was registered with the Natural Source Vitamin E Association and the National Nutritional Foods Association, which independently tested our products and never found a problem with NOW vitamin E. Despite our best efforts to correct the error, the damage was done. Many retailers heard the slander side of the story and never gave our side a chance or never even heard it. The ancient proverb is true, "He who states his case first seems right, until the other comes and examines him." (Proverbs 18:17) The sad part about this story is the competing company never did admit their error or the lab's error and so customers were left to wonder about who was correct.

Three years later history repeated itself with the same competitor, the same lab, and the same vitamin E test. This time the lab tested the vitamin E at only 2.27 which is far below the expected 24 for natural vitamin E. Our competitor spread the assay all over the country, and somehow a larger competitor got hold of it and made matters much worse. The larger company, from Utah, made copies and passed the assay to dozens of salespeople who showed hundreds of stores before we were able to identify the same problem in testing. In response, NOW sent the same lot tested to three different labs including Eastman Kodak, the raw producer, the vitamin E association, and back again to Irvine Labs. We requested Irvine to only test optical rotation for 400 IU worth of vitamin E and the results came back at 24.72, exactly at label claim. During this period, serious legal letters were exchanged and NOW considered suing both companies for damages and legal fees. However, as a Christian-principled company, we will do everything possible to avoid lawsuits, even when our case is overwhelmingly clear. And in this case we traded numerous letters, made similar threats and eventually, after spending enough on legal fees, dropped the whole matter. The larger competitor did, finally, issue an internal retraction, but no formal apology or explanation was ever given to our satisfaction. Among competitors, however, NOW chose to be more aggressive in competing with those brands and to introduce new products that would be better than either company's best products.

One side note to these stories is that some humor wound its way into several of these legal exchanges that are worth quoting. On November 3, 1994 a letter to our attorney stated this: "Your October 11 and 28 letters of putative refutation to Mr._____ are repetitious cant of previous self-serving, fallacious, solipsistic, specious, discursive, and at times even tawdry rant – your hallmarks. All the asinine rationalizations aside, your obdurate failure to.......do indeed bespeak quite adequately of your client's lack of verisimilitude and your own pompously meritless postulations and utter lack of intellectual and ethical credibility." Looking back at letters like this at least make the serious side of business a little lighter. The sad part of NOW's ongoing war of words with competitors is that, just like negative political campaigning, the damage can be severe and nobody seems to win. It's unfortunate, but dealing with competitors ongoing negativity has become part of our business.

STEVIA REBAUDIANA

In 1983, NOW introduced the green herb *Stevia rebaudiana* powder as a new sweetener for health food shoppers. The whole herb has a very sweet, licorice-like taste that can be used to sweeten teas, coffee, other drinks and even baked goods. Though the herb appeared to have been used by ancient South American Indians, stevia was "discovered" in 1887 by scientist Antonio Bertoni. In 1931, two French chemists named Bridel and Lavieille began to explore the secret to stevia's natural sweetness. They extracted a white compound which they named "stevioside" which was up to 300 times sweeter than sugar. Since that time, countries such as Brazil, Paraguay, Japan and China have cultivated the stevia plant and incorporated stevia into their daily food supply. Japan is the largest stevia consuming nation, using it to sweeten pickles, dried foods, fish, soy sauces, drinks and low calorie foods. In 1954, Japan banned certain artificial sweeteners due to health concerns and started cultivating stevia in hothouses. The finished extracts have been widely used in Japan to reduce sugar consumption, obesity and diabetes.

In 1990, NOW introduced stevia extract, a white powder that is suitable for baking and can be used to substitute for sugar without the licorice taste or green color. It was an instant hit as dieters, diabetics and anyone wanting to reduce sugar intake tried stevia extract and liked it. We supplied a unique niche of stevia powder, stevia extract, stevia cut and sifted (for tea) and two cookbooks using only stevia as a sweetener. Apparently our success caused a reaction from the sugar industry and/or the sugar substitute industry. Either way, the FDA became interested and came to visit NOW checking on our product labeling and literature. Shortly thereafter, in May 1991, the U.S. FDA issued an import alert banning stevia rebaudiana leaves and extracts from being imported into the U.S. Since all stevia was imported, this effectively stopped all sales of stevia, though no reason was ever given for the alert. The FDA called stevia "an unapproved food additive," which was their way of saying the product could not be consumed safely in the U.S. no matter how much the rest of the world used it. Ironically, in 1952, the U.S. Public Health Service had researched stevia and found it to be the world's sweetest natural product. The government's own researchers reported that "Stevioside does not appear to have an immediate future as a sweetener because it is difficult to see how Stevioside could compete economically with such a cheap, safe, and well-established synthetic sweetener as saccharin." And to think these are some of the same people within FDA who, comically, made policy against and even raided a company named

Stevita for supplying a healthy alternative to saccharin and aspartame! Indeed, the natural foods movement has always been counterculture to the mainstream medical, food, pharmaceutical and farming industries. In lesser ways, that continues today.

Good news came in September, 1995 when the FDA issued a revision to the original import alert and allowed stevia to be sold, as long as it was labeled "a dietary supplement." This loophole came about after the Dietary Supplement Health and Education Act (DSHEA) passed in late 1994, creating a new category called "supplements" for the FDA to look after. Prior to this, vitamins and herbs were treated by the FDA as either foods or drugs, with no room in between. The FDA now allowed stevia to be sold, though it retained the same legal status of "unapproved food additive" and not GRAS (Generally Recognized As Safe). This compromise allowed companies like NOW to keep stevia on the market, while satisfying large sugar substitute lobbies that stevia would not go into mainstream foods.

The rules changed in mid-2008 when soft drink giants Coke and Pepsi both announced the launch of new stevia products in the U.S. Coke introduced new Truvia (Stevia) packets and Pepsi introduced PureVia as the mass market titans raced to use stevia as the next "holy grail" of sugar substitutes. These companies were large enough to spend huge sums on R&D and legal fees to get their specific stevia products approved as GRAS. In response, NOW quietly launched the industry's first certified organic stevia in packet and liquid forms, now called BetterStevia®. NOW first introduced natural stevia packets in 1998, and we uniquely still operate two high-speed packet machines to keep up with demand for this best-seller.

MOVE TO GLENDALE HEIGHTS

By the end of 1988, we had determined to expand the NOW plant and move from Villa Park to Glendale Heights, about 15 minutes west. Our floor space increased from 7,000 sq. ft. to over 12,000 sq. ft. and the warehouse stocked inventory up to three pallets high. We moved into a new industrial complex where we would later double our space by taking over empty space next door. NOW's years on
Bloomingdale road were good for the company as we were able to dramatically grow into a bona fide industry contender. Sales growth for these years were:

YEAR	% INCREASE	$SALES
1989	33% Increase	$3.2 million
1990	25% Increase	$4.0 million
1991	50% Increase	$6.0 million
1992	67% Increase	$10 million
1993	40% Increase	$14 million

By the end of 1992, NOW had hit the magical sales number of $10 million and our product selection was expanding to meet the requests of supportive customers everywhere. In 1989, NOW introduced its first herbal capsules and needed to find a quality raw material supplier that could be trusted, since we did not have the herbal expertise on staff at the time. I was our supplement buyer at the time and, after contacting our usual suppliers, I called Nature's Way in Utah to see if they would sell to us. Their brand was one of the very first to put herbs in capsules and they had become known in the industry as the highest quality herbal supplier. I was very surprised to learn that Nature's Way did sell in bulk and that they had a separate sister company that handled all of their bulk and private label business. I was even more surprised to learn that their prices were more than fair and NOW could do quite well as a middleman selling a NOW brand of Nature's Way–produced products! We introduced echinacea purpurea root, pau d' arco, and goldenseal root initially, all manufactured by our friends at Nature's Way and sold at retail prices that were about 40% below that of the same supplier. Because normal vitamin and herb producers operate at margins well above those in the food business, NOW has always been able to easily discount high quality products at below–market prices.

Until recent years, NOW's game plan had always been to market to independent health food store owners, and then let that gatekeeper sell their customer our product. We had never really tried consumer advertising because that was too expensive and, besides, that's what the "nationally advertised" brands were known for. This strategy has served NOW very well over the years, though some stores just wouldn't consider NOW because our prices were too low. This meant that if they sold a bottle of NOW for $10 instead of a different brand for $15, the store would lose sales and profit and head in the wrong direction. Our answer had always been that this example would be true in the short term, but in the long term even loyal health food shoppers want a good value and will find it eventually. If stores only stocked expensive brands, then customers would move to discount outlets, mail order catalogs, grocery stores and chain drug stores – wherever the price was right. To counter this thinking I came up with an idea that seemed like a win-win situation for everybody.

In 1990, NOW introduced a second brand called "Richard's Finest Vitamins," a premium brand that would be aimed at the high-end customer who couldn't believe quality could be so inexpensive. (In some ritzy areas, stores found they would actually sell more NOW products at above retail prices, some as high as double normal retail!) The Richard's name, of course, is proprietary and did seem to fit in with other family-owned names like Carlson, Thompson, and Schiff. Several upgrades made the introductory line different including:

- Glass packaging with fancy silver foil labels
- Expanded label information included historical information on vitamins
- Potency overages of 5% on each multiple formula
- New formulas called "Special One" and "Special Two" with green food concentrates
- Food-based multi's with herbs, enzymes, fibers and all-vegetarian
- Full disclosure labeling, hypoallergenic products

The real kicker that I counted on was that stores could buy nine bottles and get three free, so some stores could sell at higher prices and make higher markups, while other stores could get great deals on a brand that "looked" more expensive to customers. The whole idea eventually failed, though the line did exist for ten years and did find a small, loyal following. One buyer in Tucson, named Richard, did quite well as he took extra pride in a brand with his name on it. I had counted on a chain called Richard's Whole Foods in Sarasota, FL to do big business with this name, but my hopes were never realized and the line became less important as years went by. I learned my lesson. Stores that bought into NOW's discount plan didn't want to stock another brand or sell at higher prices anyway. Stores that didn't like NOW because our prices were too low, didn't like the Richard's brand either because it still came from NOW. Even in business, *"there are friends who pretend to be friends, but there is a friend who sticks closer than a brother."* *(Proverbs 18:24)*

BEST CUSTOMERS AS FRIENDS

By 1990, NOW's top retail customer was a little store in New Port Richey, FL called Queen's Nutrients. Jack Queen, the proprietor, had recently retired to Florida after having a successful career in Pennsylvania. There Jack had built a little empire of four health food stores, a restaurant and even an import/wholesaler company for nuts, dried fruits and condiments. After moving to Florida, Jack's entrepreneurial skills surfaced again and he decided to open Queen's Nutrients to give him something constructive to do. The store opened in 1988 with less than 1,000 sq. ft. and was only open Wednesday through Saturday. With hours like that it's surprising that any legit retail business could survive! Jack was a sly veteran who knew his market and who knew how to build a business. Within three years of opening, the store was doing nearly $1 million in sales and the three days off had become full working days keeping the store stocked.

I recall one story that Jack told me that really helped to build his business. Initially his store sold the normal selection of products at mostly normal prices. In an average week, he would sell only about three small pints of Dannon yogurt for $0.79 each, which netted him less than $1 profit for the week in that product. Jack decided to buy a big volume of Dannon at a discount and sell at one cent over cost to build and attract regular customers. Soon, the store was selling over 150 per week, drawing many new customers, and netting the store $1.50 per week. This experiment led to discounting everything in the store by 20% off retail and rather dramatic sales growth ensued. The business was a bona fide success story, and Jack proved to be ahead of his time in many respects. Unfortunately, Jack's wife was diagnosed with multiple sclerosis and he sold his business in 1993 to help care for her. Years later both were still doing well in retirement and Wright's Nutrients has picked up where Jack left off.

Another unique customer was Michael Schwartz, who first opened Life Natural Foods in Miami in 1982. He moved to Syracuse, NY in 1985 and opened a 400 sq. ft. store called Discount Health Foods. The business was successful and grew to 800 sq. ft. in 1987 and 3,000 ft. in 1989. In 1993, another huge expansion put Discount Natural Foods in 18,000 sq. ft. of selling space, a real superstore with a deli, bakery and vast selection of thousands of different products. That lasted until 2000, when Michael had enough of big store problems and downsized to avoid employee hassles and focus on mail order and internet sales. Michael is one of NOW's all-time shrewdest, street-smart retailers that I've ever met. He knows the business inside and out and is extremely efficient in multi-tasking throughout each day. A few notes from a visit in 1997 are worth quoting: *"A visit to Discount Natural Foods is unlike any other. The first impression one sees upon entering the store is a very large and messy pile of empty boxes scattered near the register. Each box received from vendors is recycled by being used as a grocery bag, thereby saving the bag cost and the cost of disposing of cardboard. There is a Foosball table near one of three checkout lines and a five foot tall plastic bear standing nearby that seemed to have no function at all! The store would be a merchandiser's and accountant's nightmare because the inventory is so out of hand that a physical inventory is never taken.* It's really hard to separate the store's personality from that of Michael. The basement is jam-packed with another 4,000 ft. of mostly foods that came from volume deals, overstocks, close-outs and convention leftovers. Somehow Michael manages to run the register himself while doing much of the ordering 'from the cuff' and answering customer's questions all at the same time. Overall, it's no surprise that this is NOW's top individual store and growing rapidly."*

Another special customer is Mastel's Health Foods in St. Paul, MN, which has operated in the same small location since the mid-70s. Mastel's opened in 1968 and moved six years later to the current location which John Mastel bought. The store has an organic garden growing in the backyard, an impressive feature not available to most health food stores. This store features a thorough level of customer service and really seems to go out of their way for customers. I visited the store in 1993 and noticed that the store had almost as much inventory downstairs as back stock, compared to what was on the shelf. John explained his counterculture inventory build up as a hedge against inflation. He adopted this plan when inflation was a problem and kept to it as a way of always having what customers wanted in stock.

Loyal, long-time customers are what real business is all about. Customers like Zephyr and Kemper Isley of Vitamin Cottage, Barry Tauch of Wings of Health, Michael Dworkin of Parkade Health, Bob McGrath of Discount Health Foods, John Roher of Richards Whole Foods, Don Forsbender of Lincoln Health Foods, Gary Dodson of Dodson Nutritional, Dave and Henry at Harvest Health, Joe Bassett of Bassett's Health Food, and so many more helped make business a pleasure when NOW needed customers the most.

DELIVERY CHALLENGES

Since the mid 1970s, NOW had made local deliveries to health food stores in company owned trucks. Having our own little trucking company, (mostly one van and one driver) was necessary to expand the Chicago area business, but delivering orders was never smooth. In the early days, Elwood would use his family station wagon to haul 100 lb bags of flour and up to 380 lb drums of soybean oil. Elwood himself was a regular backup driver for years whenever a driver would quit without notice or fail to show up. Building a business takes many sacrifices and our family "suffered" through many wagons that got beat up making deliveries. I got my chance to make deliveries one summer and enjoyed the freedom quite well, despite the Chicago area traffic. I still recall the day I lost my wallet in a bad part of town where I had stopped the van to fill

---

*Michael claims that retailing guru Danny Wells starts off his seminars with a picture of this store and he tells aspiring retailers what NOT to do.

up with gas. After discovering my problem, I was scared to death knowing I had filled my tank with $20 worth of gas and I had no cash to pay. Fortunately, I left as collateral a two-wheel cart until I could borrow some money at the local health food store and drive back for an exchange.

From 1980 to 1988 it seemed like NOW went through a couple of dozen drivers as well as several horrible trucks. Many employees worked stints as drivers, notably Matt Doyle and Dave Lendy, both NOW employees in better positions thirty years later. One driver came back from his route drunk, and that was the end of him. Another decided, on the first day on the job, to go hang out at a Lake Michigan beach and skip most of the day's deliveries! But as bad as our delivery failures got, not much compared to the day Bill Palumbo drove our 24-foot truck full speed under an overpass bridge that was about two inches too low. The truck's top peeled back like a metal lid and Bill drove our ruined truck back to the plant. It snowed that day and we had to remove an entire truck's contents over the top, since the back door couldn't ever open again! In 1988, Bill Smith was hired as our driver and his experience helped make local deliveries normal business, and no longer an adventure or nightmare waiting to happen.

SHARK CARTILAGE

In 1992, Dr. William Lane, Ph.D. wrote a book called "Sharks Don't Get Cancer" in which he cited new evidence that ingesting dietary shark cartilage might reduce the incidence of cancer in humans. His brand at the time was Cartilade, and sales soon took off and a new health category was quickly established. In response to requests, NOW introduced our first Shark Cartilage product, which was extracted in Japan and retailed at $36.95 for 100 capsules. (Years later the source and process are different and the retail price is down to $14.99). The timing of our introduction proved to be divine, as unknown publicity was about to make Shark Cartilage the biggest product of the year.

Near the end of 1992, 60 Minutes on CBS ran a news story about claims made in the new shark cartilage book and included an interview with Dr. Lane. The author answered tough questions very well and the reporter seemed sold on the potential for the new supplement. The next day at work, the Shark Cartilage craze had begun and consumers everywhere were clamoring for the new cure that had just been legitimized on major network television. Because very few brands sold Shark Cartilage at the time, every bottle produced could be immediately sold. Our timing couldn't have been better because suppliers of raw shark cartilage powder ran out of supplies quickly and a brief shortage kept new competitors from the marketplace. Within a few months, NOW introduced a second, pure product from New Zealand in capsule and powder form that proved to be close to the original Cartilade product. It's interesting how some products get major media attention and others, even better ones, don't. Freedom of speech is a great part of our country, though sometimes the media has more influence than it should.

A NEW DIVISION - HEALTHCO INTERNATIONAL

In 1991, Elwood had the idea of starting a related company that would supply small competitors with our raw materials and help leverage our purchasing and increased production. NOW had sold to some companies, such as Solaray, niche ingredients that they were unable to find elsewhere. But when NOW became a larger competitor, branded companies didn't want to buy from us because we were a feared competitor with too-low pricing. Our aim in starting HealthCo was to sell to these same type of accounts, while hiding behind a separate identity. Initially, HealthCo was run by Shirley Kollenburger, a veteran health food manager who had owned her own store in Lisle, IL previously. She also happened to have been my first boss at The Fruitful Yield health food store in Elmhurst, IL in 1979. Shirley was a natural manager and saleswoman who initiated new business and serviced customers quite well. By the end of 1991, HealthCo's first year, sales hit $149,000 and the new venture was off and running.

In 1993, David Richard left the Glendale Heights Fruitful Yield store and became co-manager of HealthCo, initially sourcing raw materials direct internationally. David helped obtain New Zealand Shark Cartilage direct, when the market was oversold and short on supply. He later found a connection in England that helped to import panax ginseng, siberian eleuthero herb, royal jelly, bee pollen and propolis direct from China. Then he found direct sources for French green clay and Moroccan red clay powders. David was also instrumental in lowering costs of products such as evening primrose oil by sourcing the imported seeds directly and then negotiating contract processing runs. These purchases were done under the HealthCo umbrella in an effort to truly make HealthCo international. These deals also provided salespeople with lower costs that beat the market prices on each of the items noted. Prior to one purchase, David had one lot of Propolis tested for heavy metals and found out that lead was quite a problem. He brought this up to the Bee Products Association, an industry trade group, and apparently no other company had been testing for this. Within a short time, most other brands of Propolis had to issue a formal recall due to lead contamination, but NOW's propolis was safe from all heavy metals.

In 1994, HealthCo Brokerage was launched as an attempt to broker sales direct from farmers and growers to retail health food stores. David hooked up with companies such as Aloe Farms, Zumbro, Aspen, Nutri-Pak, RyVital, Vitality Works, and Indian Wells, who would bypass traditional distributors and ship directly to retailers at discount prices. This did create some conflict within NOW, as we found ourselves competing internally for the same wholesale dollar, from the same customer base. The major problem with phone brokerage was that no major brands would switch services to HealthCo, since no representatives were actually selling inside stores. Our plan was to operate as telemarketers at a reduced fee for manufacturers, but that never seemed to take hold and the entire brokerage division was discontinued within a few years.

A NEW SYSTEM

By mid-1988, David had rejoined the family business after 10 years in corporate America, mostly as Systems Analyst. His initial project for NOW was to purchase and implement our first computer system. That system served us well for several years and enabled billing to be automated. However, a new Comptroller named John Wallis joined NOW in 1991 and proceeded to work toward a new system that would take NOW to the next level. In the first system, our code numbers had included one letter and four numbers, but this caused problems with similar sounding letters. The new system solved that problem and many others and served NOW very well until 2002 when our Oracle era began.

Prior to 1991, salespeople hand-wrote orders and gave them to order entry workers, who would input orders throughout the day. A big change occurred when I was told salespeople would have to type orders in directly, a new part of the job that I was not keen about. I was concerned that salespeople would stop trying to sell on the phone as they would be required to do the jobs of two people. My negative bias probably had more to do with my failure in college to survive writing Cobalt and Basic computer programs. "Once burned, twice shy" the saying goes. In a short time, however, NOW's sales group learned the system, led by Nick Rana, who was the first to figure out how to use our new toy.

Many significant new products were introduced during our years on Bloomingdale Road. Listed below were the top selling new products for these years:

1989 Chromium Picolinate Caps, Echinacea Caps, Goldenseal Root, Pau d'Arco, Barley Grass, Deodorant Stones and Evening Primrose Oil

1990 Essential Oils, Richard's Line, Prescription for Nutritional Healing book, Silymarin and Pycnogenol

1991 Ester-C, 4x6 Acidophilus, Tea Tree Oil, CoQ10 60 mg, and 23 more Essential Oils

1992 Liquid Herbal Extract Line and Shark Cartilage

By the end of 1992, NOW's best sellers had changed significantly, again.

1 Prescription for Nutritional Healing Book

2 CoQ10 30 mg

3 Goldenseal Root Capsules

4 Evening Primrose Oil Softgels

Due to our tremendous growth over the past five years, it became clear that it was time to move again. The warehouse was far too full, production had squeezed out every ounce possible and our offices were in dire need of space. As we prepared to move again, we could only count our blessings for having such problems. Elwood's original strategy was paying off and we were making many right moves, but, as the good book says, *"God gives the growth."*

*"And on the banks, on both sides of the river,
there will grow all kinds of trees for food.
Their leaves will not wither nor their fruit fail,
but they will bear fresh fruit every month,
because the water for them flows from the sanctuary.
Their fruit will be for food, and their leaves for healing."*
Ezekiel 47:12

1993–1996

Four years can be a long or short time depending on one's perspective. In 1993, the first terrorist attack on U.S. soil took place when New York's World Trade Center was bombed in the underground parking lot. In Washington, Israel's Yitzhak Rabin and the PLO's Yassir Arafat shook hands outside the White House, sealing a breakthrough peace agreement that was supposed to end the Middle-East conflict. And 85 cult members died in Waco, TX after a 51 day siege by our government.

At NOW Foods, business couldn't have been better during our 25th anniversary year celebration. Lou Richard joined NOW full time to help prepare for our biggest move yet, as NOW had totally reached its space limit at 2000 Bloomingdale Road. Many new products helped drive business along and loyal customers made daily suggestions that led to continuous product and process improvements. In 1994, NOW made the big move to 550 Mitchell Road, where, amazingly, our unfettered growth continued. Elwood, Lou, David and I all found ourselves in a profitable family business that was growing substantially, helping people's health, and lowering costs to consumers. Life was good.

UNCLE LOU RETURNS

In 1985, Elwood, Lou and Bill Richard sold Fearn Soya Foods to Modern Products in Milwaukee. Fearn had dropped in sales in recent years and had two disasters doom the company at once. In 1984, one third of Fearn's major distributors went bankrupt, leaving the company with serious debt that couldn't be collected. This was unexpected and caused a great strain on Fearn's finances. At about the same time, Fearn's only recall ever occurred and, basically, brought the company down. Fearn had been buying brown rice flour and quick-cooking brown rice from Nieman Brothers (manufactured by Riviana Foods), not knowing that ethylene dibromide (EDB), a grain fumigant, had been added during the process. The company received a letter from the New Jersey Department of Health requesting a recall after this showed up in lab testing. Fearn did conduct a very expensive recall that it expected would be covered by Riviana Foods, but that company claimed it was not responsible for the recall because it was not required by the FDA, only requested. Fearn sued and won a small settlement, but the tide had already turned and Fearn was forced to sell at an inopportune time.

Sadly, our beloved Fearn company, which had been in our family ownership for 36 years, was forced to sell and moved abruptly to Milwaukee. Lou continued working for a year or so under Modern Products ownership, but disagreements arose and the time came for Lou to move on to greener pastures. From 1987 to 1993, Lou worked as an engineering consultant for a variety of large food companies (Nabisco, General Mills, American

Maiza) doing contract food processing jobs. This helped him immensely when it came time to help NOW automate jobs that had been done by hand for years. So it was that Uncle Lou, as my generation affectionately calls him, joined NOW as a project engineer in charge of planning our big move to Mitchell Road. A zillion details go into planning and executing construction for such a large building. Lou designed and worked with the builder to make sure the new plant would be ideal for food processing and packaging. I still recall Uncle Lou making a very big deal out of the type of doors to be used in the new building. He traveled to the door manufacturer in Wisconsin just to make sure that the new doors would last into the next millennium! "There are doors, and then there are doors," he said.

As with any family business, relationships can be helped or hindered by having so much personal contact. I was a little nervous when Uncle Lou started at NOW, somehow fearing that his efforts might impose on my own accomplishments. But soon Lou was solving problems and finding new equipment to help automate bottling production and, later, encapsulation of powders. He quickly found a home at NOW and hundreds of employees came to see Lou as a vital part of NOW's growth and success.

MITCHELL ROAD

By the end of 1992, we reached an agreement with the landlord who owned the entire block of future buildings on Mitchell Road in Glendale Heights, IL. However, David Richard became concerned about the location because the back of the building was located within 50 feet of overhead electric power lines. A number of discussions ensued about the potential danger of electromagnetic fields and whether any damage could occur to employees through the building. We got expert opinions and even had a measuring test taken at the site to see how much of an issue was really at hand. In the end, our Board of Directors voted to build across the street instead, even though this meant a contract penalty of almost $40,000. We decided that NOW Foods is in the health business as a first priority, and that the health of our employees is something that should not be compromised.

In 1994, one of the salespeople suggested a new way to pay commissions for "add on" business. For years, as with any good sales company, salespeople would take orders and service customers on the phone and then try to add on additional sales. I recall that when we introduced Natural "Caroguard" Beta Carotene in 1987, I was able to add on to every one of the first 16 orders, just because we were the first to market. Over the years we held informal contests to see who could "add on" the most dollars, but all without added compensation. This was partly because we didn't want to become pushy to the point of being traditional "salespeople". Also, nobody had figured a way to handle commissions by hand without a great deal of effort. Once a simple structure was set up, everyone found it easy to sell. Customers got a great discount, salespeople made extra money and NOW was able to sell new or overstocked products almost automatically. It's a good lesson to listen to workers who are "on the line" as they usually have the best ideas for improving their areas of expertise.

MELATONIN CRAZE

By the start of 1994, a new supplement called Melatonin was widely sold as a replacement for banned L-Tryptophan. Melatonin is naturally produced in the pineal gland of mammals and has been researched extensively since 1959. For most people, Melatonin helps solve insomnia, and it also acts as an antioxidant without side effects or chemical dependence. Initially, NOW decided against selling Melatonin because of concerns that the product is a synthesized hormone. From March through December, Jim Roza, NOW's Quality Manager, searched for answers about the toxicity and safety of melatonin. Meanwhile, our competitors were selling this "latest cure" in increasing quantities and customers were pressuring NOW to introduce this latest product. Finally, in December, 1994, we introduced a 3 mg capsule after receiving authoritative assurances from the research godfather of melatonin, Dr. Russell Reiter. This leading authority on melatonin research called NOW on his own to inform us about the numerous studies he had performed regarding the safety and efficacy of melatonin. The new capsule quickly became a best seller and helped fill the void lost when Tryptophan was banned from the market.

Once again, it seems, our timing was providential. In 1995, Newsweek Magazine ran two articles on melatonin, including one full cover story highlighting the main benefits: insomnia, anti-aging and jet lag. The first article was published in August and immediately suppliers ran out of inventory and the price tripled. We were aware of four European manufacturers who made the product and tried everything possible to get more than our share of the scarce powder. While we battled suppliers for more inventory, customers clamored for instant relief from everything possible under the sun. The more we tried to squeeze product out of Europe, the more customers ordered, and the higher the price rose. It's really amazing how much business can be affected by a positive nutrition article. In this case, we were selling tens of thousands of bottles of melatonin per month and actually had to allocate sales so that we didn't sell out. In December, Newsweek ran a follow up article that also stirred up business substantially. Again, the same flurry of sales and the same flurry of buying scarce product followed.

One result of every health fad is that other potential manufacturers make plans to join the supply chain and capitalize on the new growth market. Inevitably, too many suppliers start producing the same product about the same time and the shortage very soon turns into a supply glut. In the case of melatonin, Chinese pharmaceutical factories figured out how to make the product and today the powder costs about 90% less than it did when it was "priceless." The irony is that the European producers who gouged the market in a bidding war can't compete today with lower cost competitors and have lost the market that they once owned. The saying is true, *"He who loves money will not be satisfied with money; nor he who loves wealth, with gain: this also is vanity."* (Ecclesiastes 5:10)

NATURAL INFERTILITY

When I married my wife, Beth, we were told that we would be unable to conceive children. In fact, Beth had been told that at an early age by her doctor. Typical with most young couples, we determined to try to have children after a few years and visited a couple of doctors to see what they could suggest. In the end, we went the medical route (along with prayer) and today have three wonderful, healthy children.

However, as part of the process, I was required to submit sperm samples to give the greatest possible chance of conception. About that time, I was reading quite a bit of literature about infertility and I came across some insightful information about Royal Jelly and Panax Ginseng. It just so happened that, in 1994, NOW introduced a new capsule with these two ingredients, as well as a separate liquid Royal Jelly in honey. As with any male in the position of being tested, I wanted my numbers to be the highest possible for success in conceiving, as well as impressing the doctor! I began heavy dosing with both products and was tickled each time when the doctor reported near record sperm counts and motility levels. It was a prideful and happy moment that helped me survive the unexpected invasion of my privacy.

During this period a number of big sellers were introduced. They include:

1993　Saw Palmetto Complex, ChromeMate®, Antioxidant Caps, NAC, Body Balm and Deodorant Stones in a stick

1994　Grape Seed Extract 60 mg, Sucanat®, Glucosamine Sulfate, Saw Palmetto 160 mg gels, Ginseng & Royal Jelly, Bone Calcium, 8 Billion Acidophilus & Bifidus, Melatonin caps and Esiak Tea Concentrate

1995　Boswellin®, Esiak Caps, (later Ojibwa) Cat's Claw, Creatine Powder, Pygeum & Saw Palmetto, Glucosamine 1000, Joint Support™, Citrimax®, Stevia Extract, CoQ10 100 mg and Sublingual (chewable) Melatonin

1996　Stevia Liquid Extract, EcoGreen Multi tabs, Echinacea Drops, KidVits™, Ginkgo Biloba 120 mg, Alpha Lipoic Acid and Acetyl-L-Carnitine caps

During this period, NOW tried to sell as many trademarked name brands as possible as a way of assuring high quality. We had learned a lot from MaxEPA and tried to find other "MaxEpa's" that would fill a niche of quality name products at low prices. In the summer of 1994, a new product called Citrimax® was launched at a major convention with more hype than I had ever seen before. NOW wanted to offer the trademarked product and approached the vendor, with whom NOW was already a customer. Because NOW's pricing is so low, it tends to make competitors and, sometimes, suppliers nervous. In this case, other vitamin brands had already told the supplier that they would not introduce the new Citrimax® product if NOW was allowed to sell the same thing at 40% lower cost. This is a part of business that is really distasteful. I suppose it compares to when a Wal-Mart store wants to open in a small town and every business feels threatened, even though Wal-Mart would bring efficiency and savings to the same people as consumers. In this case, with no good short term options, NOW went to a competing supplier of the same raw material under the trade name Citrin®. That product was launched quickly, and apparently drew notice from the makers of Citrimax®. Within a short time, we reached an agreement to sell the Citrimax® product also, though the original snub lingered for years.

Another brand that turned NOW down was Tonalin brand CLA. In 1997, we had contacted the office that sold Tonalin and requested to become one of their branded distributors. This is quite normal business, and it's basically unheard of for growing companies to turn down new customers. At the time, Tonalin was only sold by a few brands and their goal was to sell to brands that would advertise the name Tonalin. Since NOW is a small advertiser, due to cost constraints, the supplier viewed NOW as more of a problem than a solution. If NOW introduced Tonalin at 40% off the price of other Tonalin brands, it would discourage advertising by those other brands and dilute the growth of the product. That was their thought anyway. What the producer of Tonalin didn't consider is that there are other options and NOW soon introduced a non-patented form of CLA (Conjugated Linoleic Acid), with the same basic composition as Tonalin at 40% off. Within a couple of years, CLA became a very big seller for NOW and the new owners of Tonalin were soon calling on us to switch to their original product. "Once burned, twice shy" goes the saying, and that has remained true as far as CLA to this day. Once the supplier burned their bridges with NOW, it was hard to start a new business relationship after being rejected.

Sales at NOW continued brisk growth through these years, amazing our bankers, auditors and accountants. Listed below is the sales growth at NOW during these years:

YEAR	% GROWTH	$SALES
1993	41%	$14 million
1994	43%	$20 million
1995	60%	$32 million
1996	28%	$41 million

MULTI LEVEL SALES SPURTS

Pycnogenol® is a standardized pine bark extract that acts as an antioxidant many times more potent than vitamin C or E. In 1995, the French company that made Pycnogenol®, Horphag Research, ran into supply problems. A multi-level seller in the U.S. had done such a good job of promoting Pycnogenol® that production was caught off guard and expanded manufacturing was unavailable until 1996. This caused a shortage of Pycnogenol® and led some companies to look for alternative sources of the precious pine bark extract. Soon a generic pine bark extract became available in addition to grape seed extract, which is nearly identical in polyphenols and proanthocyanidins, the active measurable components. A problem surfaced when several major vitamin brands began using the trade name Pycnogenol on labels, but with generic pine bark or grape seed extract within the product. We had asked the only authorized distributor about the other brands and were told that legal proceedings were being initiated against some of the largest brands on the market who were cheating. It is ironic that consumers generally put the most confidence in the largest brands, perhaps because their marketing is so persuasive, and their image of quality so sure. My experience is that the largest vitamin companies are often the ones who cheat the most, not because of quality control standards, but simply because they choose to do what it takes to make the highest profits.

By mid–1996, another great wave drove a product called liquid colloidal minerals. At the time, a tape had been circulating called "Dead Doctors Don't Lie," which made extensive claims about the benefits of taking colloidal minerals. A multi-level company, again, did such a stupendous job promoting the product that many customers went to health food stores to find a lower priced, comparable product. Soon, NOW's store customers were demanding a NOW product and we responded with a product called "77 Colloidal Minerals." Sales started so strong that we sent out for a full, independent assay to make sure everything claimed by our vendor proved true. At the same time, a paper by Alexander Schauss, Ph.D. was circulated claiming colloidal minerals were unproven and contained unsafe levels of aluminum. While supply problems and quality issues were being addressed, customers kept ordering more colloidal minerals than we could stock. Eventually a trip was needed to help clear the air.

On December 4, 1996, I visited the original Clark mine in Emery County, Utah to try to get more supplies from our vendor. It was also an opportunity to get a firsthand understanding of colloidal minerals and the factual history from "the source." The Clark family had sold "Miracle Water" as early as 1926, naturally derived from humic shale deposits. The product sold slowly in early years, but received so many unsolicited testimonials that the business helped Thomas Clark survive the depression years. Apparently, all humic shale colloidal mineral products come from the same area in Utah and, after processing, the by-product is used by local farmers as a natural fertilizer. The visit to the mine was quite an experience and showed what vast mineral resources are available in places like Utah. Unfortunately, our alliance with the Clark family ended when we were able to source low–aluminum colloidal minerals elsewhere six months later. It was a good business move, but a sad day for me to walk away from my new friend, Bret Clark.

Another wonder product peaked about that time called Klamath Blue-Green Algae, a whole food concentrate similar to spirulina. Another multi-level company, Cell Tech, did an outstanding job (again!) promoting the health benefits of a specific microalgae that grows in Klamath Lake, Oregon. Due to some negative publicity about a potential toxin in the lake, NOW sent Nick Rana to visit and get a first hand look at how our product was being processed. Nick took a boat out on the lake, collected pictures and talked to the suppliers about processing techniques and cleanliness. We were able to tell a true story firsthand about NOW selling a safe, quality product that was independently tested free of toxins. Klamath Blue-Green Algae had its dedicated followers who took the algae religiously, though like many good products it has had its heyday and now is on the mature side of a product's life cycle. I wonder why good products have to have down cycles. It seems that if a product works, it should never decline, but always grow at least by word of month. If only life were so simple! A poor crop and concerns about pollution caused NOW to drop this product in 2012.

ODDS AND ENDS

In 1996, NOW became involved with the Autism Research Institute in San Diego. We were donating money and decided to start officially giving 1% of 12 different B vitamin and mineral sales. The institute had been doing research using particular vitamins in search of a cure, or at least some help for those with autism. At least 18 studies have been published since 1965 showing that high doses of vitamin B-6 (preferably with magnesium) provide many benefits to about half of all autistic children and adults. Additionally, extensive testing has been done using DMG (mistakenly called vitamin B-15), niacin, and pantothenic acid to combat autism, each with varying degrees of success. Being involved with a serious ailment like autism reminds people in the health food business exactly why we do what we do. Natural foods and vitamins are part of the solution for people's health problems. Usually not a miracle cure, but clearly on the right side of health.

In 1995, NOW hired a large kick boxer to do telemarketing and he was extremely confident that he could do the job. Kick boxing is a pretty rough sport, so confidence is a basic requirement to be successful. At first, the boxer-turned-salesman looked like he would be a good fit and be able to aggressively go after new business. But after a couple of months, it was clear that this was not the job for him and he was not the friendly type of employee we wanted. Just before he left, it became clear that because his fingers were about double the normal thickness in size, he was basically unable to type, and therefore made far too many errors. Ken Spear, our head of Human Resources department, had the very unpleasant task of letting our new employee go. We were all quite relieved to see that the final conversation went smoothly, as this guy was sizable enough to do some serious damage.

In 1995, David Richard began writing a book on Stevia that would help promote sales of NOW stevia products. We had been selling another Stevia book before the import alert, but that book seemed to disappear when we wanted to reorder. David tried to find someone else to write the book, but no one else was interested, so he did it himself. The success of that book led to a new division within the company called Vital Health Publishing. A couple of years later, David bought that company and has since published quite a few books that are available in health food stores and elsewhere. About that time, the FDA raided a stevia products company in Texas called Stevita and threatened to destroy David's book, which was considered "adulterated food labeling." As ridiculous as that was, it was a real threat and David teamed up  with Dr. Julian Whitaker to fight back. They threatened the FDA with a first amendment lawsuit and, eventually, the FDA dropped the matter about David's book. Later, they both filed a formal petition to the FDA for rulemaking, which became a matter of public record and kept the FDA from overstepping its bounds regarding stevia and books in the future.

Finally, this period ends with the death of Fran Kalve, January 31, 1996. Fran had worked at NOW since 1983 and had become a Grandmother of sorts to employees and customers alike. Fran was rarely sick, though very heavy in weight, and had developed into our top inside sales add-on performer. Thirteen years earlier, Fran was the entire sales department, receptionist, secretary and customer service department. She continued to service the Chicago delivery area and call on many customers that grew to love her. She had a rough way about her, yet was baptized in her mid-50s and really enjoyed telling people about her faith. Those that knew her couldn't help but be touched by her. She had a certain way about her. Her friends and family miss her, but haven't forgotten. As the good book says, *"We believe that Jesus died and rose again and so we believe that God will bring with Jesus those who have fallen asleep in him."* (1 Thes 4:13-14)

"A cheerful heart is a good medicine,
but a downcast spirit dries up the bones."
Proverbs 17:22

1997–2002

The end of a millennium is a landmark division of time. Historians reflect back on the past 1000 years, futurists look ahead to the next 1000 years, while a billion people are simply trying to avoid hunger each day. In 1997, Japan hosted a Global Warming Conference that included 150 nations who agreed to reduced greenhouse emission levels. The movie Titanic became the biggest box office hit of all time. And U.S. President Bill Clinton, the most powerful man on earth, faced impeachment over a very public and messy affair with Monica Lewinsky.

At NOW Foods, we prepared to move one more time as sales, again, exceeded expectations and a contingency plan with the landlord fell through. This would be the fourth move in 15 years, by far the biggest challenge due to the increased size, expanded manufacturing equipment and complex software needed to run the new warehouse. By early 1997, Lou Richard and Jim Emme, our Plant Manager and future president, began making plans to build from scratch the first building the company would ever own. The challenge was huge, but prior moving experience and dedicated efforts prevailed and helped the company move in July, 1998.

1998 New NOW facility

Initially a search committee looked in the local area for vacant land that was zoned for industrial use. One site was ruled out because we thought the street noise would be a problem. Another was discounted because it was within one mile of a recycling transfer plant and may have been a source for small rodents. We finally found, and agreed on ten acres of land just three blocks away from the current building for the ridiculously high price of $2 million. The new building would be 203,000 sq. ft. and include enough space to allow Elwood to make all of his dreams come true. Lou, particularly, was very involved and tenacious in making sure that the new plant would be rock solid and custom suited for food manufacturing and distribution. The production area, alone, would total nearly 80,000 sq. ft. and plans allowed for expansion in future years if capacity became an issue. A new Quality Control Laboratory was greatly expanded with all of the latest testing equipment, and a small army of chemists and technicians were hired to run the never-ending assays. When reviewing our year-end costs, I'm always shocked to see that we spend so much more on Quality Control than we do on Marketing. Most vitamin brands spend at least 5-10% of sales to market their products. NOW has always spent under 2% of sales on marketing, and well over that for Quality Control. I'm pretty sure that no other natural brand of vitamins, foods, teas or cosmetics can legitimately make that claim.

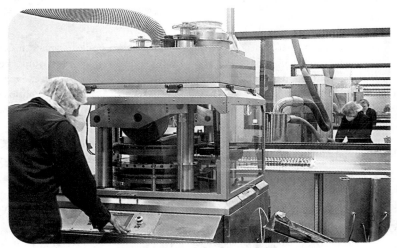

NOW high-speed capsule manufacturing

1997 NOTABLE NEWS

NOW's amazing growth continued into 1997 as the company increased sales by 38%, totally maxing out the Mitchell Rd. location. Some of the new products driving sales were Elder-Zinc lozenges, Joint Support cream, Lycopene, MSM 1000 mg, 5-HTP, CoQ10 50 mg gels, Omega 3-6-9 and Alpha Lipoic Acid. Overall, stores and consumers kept buying more and more NOW products, leading the company to question whether it could sustain the same rate of growth in the future. From 1986 - 1997, NOW grew an average of 43% each year, which far surpassed the industry average and helped turn NOW into an industry force to be reckoned with.

In the fall of 1997, an unnatural disaster hit and made business as uncomfortable as possible. United Parcel Service (UPS) went on strike, leaving most of the country with no short-term options for shipping business packages. At the time, NOW was fortunate to have been using DHL for air service to stores and, in some ways, that did help save the day. DHL had been carrying about 25% of NOW packages and we tried to divert as many packages as possible to them. But that company quickly reached its peak and was unable to accept truckload amounts that we needed to ship. We also tried to ship larger orders by common carrier trucks, but these soon became so backed up that the best solution seemed to be to wait and pray for resolution to the strike. After more than two weeks of virtually zero UPS deliveries, the national union agreed to terms with the company and all seemed to be back to normal. Unfortunately, we didn't realize that the Chicago district had its own union and contract and that did not get resolved for several additional days. Business disasters like this don't seem quite as bad several years later, but it's also hard to forget which shippers were part of the problem and which ones were part of the solution. As the proverb says, *"a man of many companions may come to ruin, but there is a friend who sticks closer than a brother."* (Proverbs 18:24) Shortly after this NOW switched shipping to FedEx, in part because it is a worker-friendly, non-union delivery company.

DR. JAMES BALCH

During this time, Dr. James Balch, a urologist, board surgeon and co-author of the book, *Prescription for Nutritional Healing*, approached NOW with the idea of becoming a spokesman for the company. Prior to this, Dr. Balch and his wife, Phyllis, owned a health food store in Indiana that bought products from NOW. Dr. Balch had become familiar with our line of products and corporate personality over several years and he felt that we had enough in common to forge an alliance. Until that time, NOW had never sought out a national personality like Dr. Balch to act as a spokesman, because we were always concerned about the cost. But because Dr. Balch liked our company we were able to make a deal and introduce a line of products called "Dr. Recommended" with Dr. James Balch's picture on each bottle. By 1997, Dr. Balch was as famous as one gets in the natural foods field, on his way to over five million books sold. He was well known at health food conventions, on weekly radio shows, speaking internationally and even in demand within the medical community. Dr. Balch helped put that seal of approval on NOW as a company. By being a Christian–principled company, we had caught Dr. Balch's attention and had an advantage over other suppliers who would have liked to have had Dr. Balch in their corner. Although Dr. Balch and NOW parted ways in 2005, the partnership was a great experience and we will always wish him the best.

And so we came to the fateful month of July, 1998 when our dreams, and nightmares, were about to unfold. One thing the company had learned from the 1993 move was that you can never over prepare. Our plant manager, Jim Emme, did an outstanding job of coordinating the physical move, so that most of the entire business was moved within three days. I recall being totally shocked, because our last move, with far less inventory and equipment, had lasted over a week and ended in a total mess. The 1998 move appeared to be a miraculous event, with everything in place and business ready to resume on Monday. But a major problem soon erupted that caused shipments to be delayed for up to three weeks and employees' patience to be tried far beyond reason. The problem was that we installed a new $1 million order picking/packing/distribution system that was driven by the company's computer system using new software. The new "pick-to-light" system, which is computer driven, wouldn't work for nearly three weeks and the new warehouse was not set up to handle our old fashioned picking style. Those were dark days at NOW and I'm still thankful for loyal wholesale customers who somehow put up with the company when we were barely able to put up with ourselves! Perhaps the memory is too recent, but it seems stressful to even try to remember those days in detail, even today. Thanks to very long and critical hours by our IT staff (Ed Cuttle and John Wallis), we made it to the end of the tunnel and the picking system has become a cost-saving necessity just as good as promised.

One of the primary goals in moving was to expand manufacturing production into areas that we had been outsourcing. Since 1968, NOW had been fairly successful in packaging grains, flours, teas, liquids, vitamins, herbs and anything else sold in health food stores. By 1997, the company had fairly high-speed equipment and a well-organized warehouse that was simply outgrown. The new building would include multiple high-speed encapsulators, three pharmaceutical-style bottling lines, new tableting equipment, a packet machine dedicated to stevia alone, high-speed food bagging, blending, liquid filling, tea bagging equipment, a huge freezer and refrigerator, the latest and greatest picking system and some extensive warehouse fixtures. With a low-cost manufacturing base, very low marketing and sales costs, nearly zero debt and a brand new building, we were ready to take on the world and improve our business several steps beyond our wildest dreams!

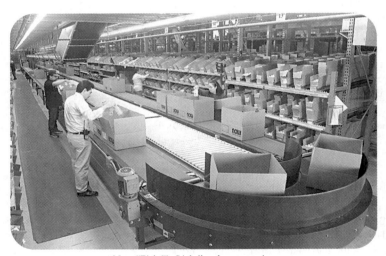

New "Pick-To-Light" order processing

VITY AWARDS

A trade magazine called *Vitamin Retailer* had been running a survey for several years which tried to determine the best-selling brands among products in health food stores. This was an issue that was very exciting to employees at NOW because the results legitimized our efforts and showed how far the company had grown. The survey was sent to independent natural food stores across the country and the results were tabulated and announced in the magazine. In 1999, the results were so favorable to NOW that many joked that because we were near Chicago, we were the best at stuffing the ballot box. (Of course, Chicago is famous for such political tricks in the past only!) Anyway, I think the results did skew in NOW's direction because the small, independent health food store is our primary customer, while other large firms sell more to national retail chains or mail order houses. Here are the results published in early 1999:

First Place Gold Award	Second Place Silver Award	Third Place Bronze
CoQ10	Alpha Lipoic Acid	Antioxidant Caps
Ginkgo Biloba	Bovine Cartilage	Bee Pollen
Grapeseed Extract	L-Carnitine	CLA
Heart Support	Chromium Picolinate	Echinacea
MSM	Evening Primrose Oil	Melatonin
Pycnogenol	Goldenseal Root	Panax Ginseng
Respir-All™ (Allergy)	Joint Support	Saw Palmetto ext.
Shark Cartilage	Omega 3 1000 mg	Silymarin extract
Stevia	Omega 3-6-9	Super Enzymes
Vitamin C	Phosphatidyl Serine	St. John's Wort
Vitamin E	Vitamin A	

During 1998, another slew of good-selling new products were introduced, the best ones being Whey Protein, CLA, Prostate Support, Glucosamine & MSM, Stevia Packets and a line of liposprays. Sometimes it's obvious which new products will sell well, though other times our best guesses aren't even close. Liposprays are, perhaps, the best example of a product line that should outsell traditional tablets and capsules, but don't. Liposome technology is simply a scientific method for increasing the quality and speed of absorbing internal and external supplements. Liposomes have been used for several decades in the cosmetic and pharmaceutical industries, mainly to increase the effectiveness of skin applications. Liposomes can increase the absorption of nutraceuticals by 50%, require less active potencies and can be slowly released over time for a more balanced effect.

Given the above advantages of liposomes and liposprays, we decided to introduce a line of lipospray products that would offer the highest bioavailability of each product. Initial products included B-12, Echinacea, Ginseng, Kava, St. John's Wort and Total Wellbeing, my favorite! Each of these sprays tasted great, was reasonably priced and gave a standardized dose in every spray. Each product had vast advantages over comparable products we sold in capsule or tablet forms. Yet, despite all these advantages, liposprays still haven't caught on and seem destined for small sales long-term. As I see it, Americans love to pop pills and get some instant feeling, like one gets when taking aspirin for a headache. We love convenience and the perception is that powders, liquids and any other non-pill form is inconvenient and for "health nuts." Years later only B-12 Lipospray remains in NOW's line-up.

INDUSTRY SLOWDOWN

By 1998 the health food industry was riding a huge wave that saw explosive growth for most of the nineties. Many of the trade magazines reported annual growth between 10-20% each year for the trade as a whole for that period. The times were good and the future looked even better. I had been watching the stock prices of competitors like Twinlab and Nutraceuticals and decided to put some of my 401K money into these stocks to have a little fun and watch the price go up and down. I also planned to take advantage of receiving competitors' annual reports delivered right to my doorstep without even asking!

Shortly after buying into these industry stocks, GNC announced a new discount strategy that it hoped would boost sales and increase its already dominant market share. Unfortunately, Wall Street didn't take kindly to the discount plan, fearing reduced profits, and punished the stock price badly. At the same time, other public health food stocks crashed in the same wave and soon my 401K money dropped in half and the game wasn't quite as much fun as I had planned. "Buy low and sell high" has been true throughout the ages, and I learned my lesson the hard way about investing in public stocks.

To make matters worse for the industry, raw material prices were dropping and this led to increased price competition from mass market stores. NOW, itself, has been a leader in reducing prices on products such as Ginkgo Biloba, Glucosamine, Melatonin, Creatine, and Saw Palmetto. In fact, over the years, NOW typically drops as many prices as it raises to show customers that not all companies perpetually raise prices for no good reason. With deflation for vitamin prices came pricing pressures for suppliers and soon many companies found themselves vulnerable to a downswing in the market. As chain drug stores, grocery stores, outlet stores, mail order and online businesses all jumped into the vitamin business, the long-term viability of the independent health food store came into question. Would the independent health store become like so many other industries' independents – mostly wiped out and replaced with discount supermarts and super sections in bigger stores? Or could the independent health store survive with superior service, better quality, selection and nutritional education against the onslaught by the masses? This was the question of the day as companies bet their futures by picking the retail market that was expected to survive and grow nutraceutical businesses.

Thankfully, another media blitz launched a new product that helped to offset some of the above losses. In March, 1999, Newsweek magazine ran a brief article touting a new supplement that might help relieve depression and help arthritis as well. SAMe (Sammy) is a pharmaceutical amino acid that was sold only in Europe for two decades prior to its introduction in the U.S. The original article quoted research which showed SAMe provided relief to 70% of depressed patients, roughly the same percent that benefit from traditional drug treatments. In July, Newsweek ran an expanded follow-up story on SAMe that detailed how SAMe works within the body, plus other benefits as well. Initially SAMe was very expensive and available only in relatively low potencies. But after these articles hit, volume skyrocketed and other manufacturers started making SAMe. This led to fairly dramatic price decreases, which allowed for higher potencies at similar prices. SAMe landed in the health food market and within a short time established itself as a best-seller in stores of all types. Once again, the media had a huge influence in launching an unknown product and driving it home to mainstream America.

During these few years of famine, NOW may have been the only national vitamin brand to continue growing in sales. Between 1999 and 2001, the company grew in single digits each year and easily outperformed the market. Surveys showed that the overall consumption of vitamins dropped by 5% in 2000, but NOW could at least hold its head high by increasing sales above all public suppliers within the health food industry.

At the prodding of Elwood, NOW started working directly with researchers to support their clinical efforts with nutrition. In 1997, NOW supplied cranberry capsules to the University of Calgary's OPTIMUS Programme, which "conducted the first randomized, double-blind, placebo-controlled, longitudinal trial of cranberry supplements ever conducted." The research centered on treating multiple sclerosis patients with cranberry supplements to control urinary tract infections. Another study, supported by NOW, was with the MCP Hahnemann University of the Health Sciences in Philadelphia. NOW provided the amino acid Glutamine as a potential treatment for cocaine and alcohol abuse as well as a placebo for control. This study involved 100 patients who ingested between two and eight grams of Glutamine per day for 12 weeks. In January, 2000 NOW supplied SAMe double strength tablets to NNFA (later NPA) for submission to the newly formed UCI Center for Complementary and Alternative Medicine. This double-blind, randomized, crossover trial involved determining the effectiveness of SAMe in the relief of knee pain due to osteoarthritis. Thirty patients took 600 mg of SAMe for six months, with some controls modified during the trial to determine effectiveness. Finally, in 2000, NOW supplied NNFA with a custom Folic Acid tablet that would be given to the Hispanic Women's Initiative Program (HWIP), a division of March of Dimes. Four major U.S. cities were involved in the distribution, with the goal of reducing neural tube defect pregnancies This grass roots project proceeded well and NOW was later recognized as one of the contributors during a Chicago event.

THE MYLES LIPTON STORY

A unique NOW customer was Myles Lipton, who owned a small mail-order business called "Dial and Save." Myles was not the humblest person I've ever met as I recall he once told me, with all seriousness and without bragging, that he was the most knowledgeable source in the world for vitamin sales over the internet. Apparently he devoted from 4 a.m. to 8 a.m. every day for several months to search and study what products were being sold online, and at what prices. As a mail order company, Myles was keenly interested in gaining whatever possible advantage might exist for his business. Myles was also a dreamer who had several simultaneous ventures in the works, some of which were definitely better than others.

One day Myles called me and insisted that I come down to St. Louis the coming weekend to discuss something so big that he wouldn't even hint at it over the phone. With a pregnant wife and two small children at home, I was very reluctant to go off on some wild goose chase and I repeatedly tried to politely turn the invitation down. Finally Myles offered to pay for two nights for my family at the St. Louis Ritz Carlton hotel, insisting that I meet with him within days. Since being frugal runs in my family, I couldn't turn down Myles' final offer and started making plans to drive to St. Louis for a big Friday evening dinner meeting.

After supper together, Myles suggested that we go to the top floor of the Ritz to talk about whatever he felt was so important. After some brief small talk Myles leaned over and whispered softly, "I'm about to become a billionaire!" Now that's a conversation starter that will get anyone's attention. Apparently Myles had federally incorporated his business name "Dial and Save" to cover all classes of trade and he had recently discovered a multi-level marketing phone company with the exact same name. The MLM phone company had expanded quickly and was close to having total sales of about $1 billion. Myles attorneys had told him that because the phone company was using his properly registered name, he would be due a huge windfall from that business. Myles claimed that he actually "owned" the phone company since their name was his name and their total value would all be his! In short order Myles devised an interesting strategy for investing his expected billion dollars. He wanted to buy a retail drugstore chain with at least 1000 stores, and then buy NOW Foods and Source Naturals/Threshold Enterprises to supply the stores. This would reinvent nutritional education via nutritionally educated pharmacists.

Predictably, Myles dream never turned into reality and I tried to convince him at the time not to count his marbles so fast. I also told him that NOW Foods was not for sale and that my father would not be interested in selling the company at any price. This only raised the purchase price in Myles' determined mind and he chased his billion dollar dream with a legal team for over a year. Sadly, Myles' wife called some time later to say that Myles had accidentally killed himself and all of his financial dreams seemed quite unimportant. I lost a quirky business friend, NOW got stuck with a large bankruptcy debt from Dial and Save, and Myles lost the most priceless possession he owned. It reminded me of a tragic irony Jesus spoke about when he said, "What shall it profit a man if he gains the whole world yet forfeits his own life?" Myles may be gone, but he touched many friends in the natural foods business and will not be forgotten.

Y2K ISSUES

As the millennium approached, more and more genetically modified or engineered foods came on to the market. Because this is disturbing to the natural way of growing foods, NOW more actively opposed the use of genetically modified organisms (GMOs) in our food supply. We've argued that, at a minimum, genetically engineered foods should be labeled as such so that intelligent consumers can make informed decisions about what they put into their bodies. NOW has funded and supported Mothers for Natural Law, Citizens for Health and the Campaign to Label Genetically Engineered Foods in an effort to influence the battle for our food supply. NOW has also supported an industry task force, which includes Whole Foods Market and Wild Oats Market, to validate analytical tests for detecting GMOs in various foods. Because this is a relatively new issue, more education and support is needed to change the way our country grows foods, before it is too late.

The end of 1999 saw many companies and consumers stocking up and taking inventory. NOW was well prepared, having spent large sums on computer and phone system upgrades 'just in case.' In preparation, many customers and suppliers had sent NOW letters explaining their own situation, with some requiring NOW to provide assurances that business would go on as normal. When the clock ticked midnight and the computer world hadn't ended on January 1, 2000, I had to wonder if all of our expensive preparation had been unnecessary. One of our customers had taken extraordinary pains to prepare for the new millennium. E C O Foods in Honolulu, our best store customer in Hawaii, decided to close up shop and move to Nevada, where he opened a new store. Somehow, the owner thought that life in the desert would be safer and more insulated from Y2K damage. Unfortunately, the move proved to be in vain and the new store went out of business within a year. It's sad to see formerly successful businesses fail and even sadder to see longtime business friends disappear. Hopefully Bobby, the owner, will return to the Big Island and resume the successful business he had led so well.

In 1999, NOW negotiated exclusive importation and distribution of a deodorant cream called Lavilin. The product had been sold in the U.S. for a number of years, but the Israeli manufacturer was disappointed with sales and chose to deal with NOW due to our expanded health food store distribution. The Lavilin product is amazingly unique for a deodorant, as it naturally kills bacteria, which cause body odor, for up to seven days. I didn't really believe this until I tried it and found it to be true. Even after basketball and a shower, the product continues to work far beyond what most people would think possible. Unfortunately, in 2004 NOW lost this exclusive line back to the former U.S. importer and five years of promotion and effort seemed wasted. Some years earlier NOW had replicated the active ingredients in Lavilin and still sells "Long Lasting Deodorant" in stick form. As an ongoing user, I can vouch that our generic version actually works and lasts for up to a full week with just one application. Really!

Dr. Cassista, NOW's microbiologist

QUALITY MATTERS

In June, 2000 NOW underwent an intensive three-day independent audit by NNFA to see if NOW qualified for GMP (Good Manufacturing Practices) status, a new industry program designed to improve quality. The auditor was a 37-year FDA veteran who followed raw materials from the time they reached our dock, through manufacturing, into the warehouse and out the door. Areas such as identity testing, stability, potency and product formulation were all closely scrutinized to assure that NOW adhered to proper GMP protocol. We had been preparing for this visit for some time and had made significant paper trail changes to assure that our auditor would be satisfied. On July 6, we received official notice from NNFA that NOW received an "A" rating as a manufacturing and distribution facility. This was the highest possible grade given and allowed NOW to 'toot its horn' to the world. Later, NNFA required a disclaimer for every use of their GMP logo on labels because "the quality of individual ingredients has not been certified." We were told a small competitor complained and threatened legal action because the new logo would give an unfair advantage to companies, like NOW, that manufactured their own products. Maybe so, but the GMP program has been a huge step in the right direction for the industry, by requiring companies to guarantee full potency of each product at the end of the expiration date. Better quality supplements is a goal that suppliers, consumers and the government all agree upon. By 2008, FDA adopted formal GMPs and began implementing site inspections of vitamin manufacturers with even greater strictness for product safety and quality control.

About this same time, NOW decided to apply to become a certified organic manufacturer and distributor of organic foods and food supplements. Products like barley grass powder, alfalfa seeds, flax meal, vanilla extract, lavender oil, flax seed oil, and spirulina are a few examples of organic products that have been third-party certified from the ground up, requiring three years of no synthetic preservatives, chemicals or fertilizers. NOW applied to Quality Assurance International (QAI) for certification as it seemed this company was preferred by many of our vendors and seemed to be one of the largest certifiers. We soon learned that certified organic products require much, much more documentation and assurances than non-certified or wildcrafted products. A new, organic section of our warehouse was required so that non-organic products wouldn't 'contaminate' the organic goods. An internal organic tracking number needs to be assigned to each lot of organic product to allow for a comprehensive audit. Testing by gas chromatograph and mass spectroscopy are also required for any possible pesticide residue contamination. Additionally, NOW requires that every new organic shipment must be frozen for three days and then tested for micro levels. Since NOW is one of the very few natural food brands to have an in-house microbiology lab, we are able to determine results as quickly as possible. Finally, all procedures used on organic products must meet the Organic Foods Production Act of 1990 (Recommendations to the Secretary of Agriculture) and the Guidelines for the Organic Food Industry, which is produced by the Organic Trade Association. Organic products are the wave of the future for good reason: our bodies work better and live longer without artificial preservatives, chemical additives, fertilizers, fumigants and pesticides.

A final quality frontier was passed in 2002 when NOW became certified Kosher for a limited number of products. Kosher regulations are very strict and require manufacturers like NOW to do an incredible amount of paper chasing to verify vendor claims and assure proper processing methods. The whole Kosher system stems from an odd verse in Exodus 23:19 which says. "You shall not boil a kid in its mother's milk." Over thousands of years Rabbis have expanded the interpretation of this verse and it is still not agreed upon today. Basically, the idea is to keep any meat products separate from any milk products so that an animal is not cooked or consumed with milk. Within the Jewish community today there are different levels of Kosher certification, some more strict than others, on production equipment, sanitation, documentation and processing. NOW chose to be certified by the strictest branch, Circle U, which is accepted as Kosher by all Jews. To the average Gentile, this merely means that NOW's Kosher products are the cleanest possible products, having passed the highest levels of Kosher laws.

GOING INTERNATIONAL

As NOW grew to be a larger concern in the early 1990s, international sales started to become a major area of growth for the company. Initially, NOW didn't have the manpower to reach out to international markets, so customers somehow managed to find us. As early as 1992, NOW sold to customers in Canada, Israel, Japan, Norway, Philippines, Poland, Singapore, Taiwan, and the UK. Ten years later exports have increased many-fold and dozens of new countries have opened their markets to NOW products. International sales are NOW's biggest growth potential simply based on population and the newness of supplements in many countries. Selling to many international markets makes one appreciate the nutritional freedoms we have in the U.S. Countries like Canada had regulated products like vitamin C and vitamin E as drugs and required Natural Product Numbers (NPN's), which means much higher costs of doing business. Other countries, like many in the European Union, have such difficult trade barriers that it becomes very expensive to do business with them.

On the flip side, NOW is a huge importer of nutritional products and buys nearly half of all its products produced overseas. Psyllium Husks from India, dried fruit from Thailand, Tea Tree Oil from Australia, Lycopene from Israel, Organic Stevia from China, Hoodia from South Africa, L-Carnitine from Switzerland, and Pycnogenol from France are some of the better known imports NOW sells in health food stores. What is less known is that many more traditional products are now produced in far away places, particularly China. Did you know that most of the vitamin C consumed in the U.S. is produced in China? Same with Royal Jelly, Evening Primrose Oil, Chlorella, Glucosamine, Creatine and many teas. There's just no escaping the fact that today's business world is international in scope and many distant countries are better suited for growing or manufacturing certain types of natural food products.

In December, 1998 our Vice President at the time, Al Powers, made an official visit to China to solidify a customer relationship and promote the sale of NOW lecithin products. Al had been NOW's Vice President for many years and Elwood's choice to succeed him when he retired. So in response to the Chinese customer's insistence that NOW send over its highest official, Al agreed to go and had a very unusual visit to China.

The plan was for Al to be part of a media blitz to help educate the masses and sell more lecithin. NOW's importing customer was very well connected within the government and he had arranged for a press tour involving about 10 speeches in both Beijing and Shanghai. Al's speech, which was repeated identically ten times, had to be submitted to the government for screening and approved for public use before an assembly could be legal! Many cameramen and dignitaries attended these speeches and some were broadcast on national TV and radio. Each speech was constantly interrupted so that an interpreter could explain every word in Chinese as well. In Beijing, a huge neon sign had been put up that said, "Welcome NOW Foods!" It looked a little like Times Square in New York City and NOW was made out to be a U.S. brand similar in size to Coca-Cola or McDonald's. Al was able to accomplish his own personal goal of citing NOW as a "Christian Principled Company" and mentioning the name of Jesus Christ on communist television. In the end, the Chinese customer wanted NOW to pay for these extravagant marketing expenses – after the fact – and our relationship soon crumbled when we couldn't agree on a seven figure marketing fund without purchasing guarantees. Perhaps to recoup promotional losses, the customer found a loophole in the next letter of credit payment and a container load of lecithin sat somewhere in China, unpaid, while we tried to make a deal with the customer. Eventually, the customer bought the container load at public auction, probably for pennies, and NOW was left holding an empty bag, while the customer continued to pirate NOW's name on lecithin products all over China. We learned an expensive and bitter lesson in international business, something like, *"Put not your trust in princes, in a son of man, in whom there is no help." (Psalm 146:3)*

In 2002, NOW made a deal with Galilee Herbal Remedies, a kibbutz in Israel, to sell a co-branded line of vegetarian, kosher and organic herbal formulas. The paperwork required to consummate this deal was extraordinary. Galilee Herbal Remedies (GHR) had a line of products that needed NOW's marketing muscle and NOW is always looking for opportunities that can offer value to customers on quality products. After nearly a year of discussion, certifying, and sourcing issues, the new line launched in 2002 with production and distribution provided by NOW. The resulting premium line is the very type of business that NOW seeks to provide: Superior quality, unique products, alliances with leading suppliers throughout the world and excellent value. Though the line did not sell well, and was dropped three years later, NOW is committed to improving many existing products to be vegetarian, organic and possibly kosher.

In June 2001, NOW sponsored the International Association of Biomedical Gerontology conference in Vancouver, B.C., Canada. Forty-seven internationally prominent researchers presented current research regarding aging with the goal of increasing public awareness of aging research. This was expected to lead to dietary and lifestyle changes, which would allow people to live longer and healthier lives. Dr. Denham Harman, MD, Ph.D., the originator of the Free Radical Theory of Aging, was the host and driving force to put the conference together and work with NOW to try and make extremely technical research understandable to the average reader.

Elwood Richard has long had an interest in anti-aging research, especially since he turned 70 years old! His own theory about aging is similar to Dr. Harman's and goes all the way back to the Tree of Life in Genesis. If the Genesis account is historical and factual, then it may be that the original Tree of Life was some sort of an antioxidant tree. Since we age largely because of oxidation, much like an apple oxidizes quickly when cut open, a powerful antioxidant may have acted in a physical way to keep Adam and Eve alive indefinitely. After all, they seemed to begin aging only after being removed from the Garden in Eden and away from the Tree of Life. The first humans may have needed to consume the antioxidant tree daily, in order to counteract the natural effects of being human. (Interestingly, the book of Revelation talks about a tree of life reinstituted in the end time, which may explain how people could be immortal once again!) In the meantime, folks are advised to consume more antioxidants like vitamin C, vitamin E, Alpha Lipoic Acid, Glisodin and Grape Seed Extract, and refrain from oxidized foods such as fried chips that cause oxidation in the body.

DREAMS DO COME TRUE

On February 7, 2002 Elwood received a phone message from Bill Walton, former National Basketball Association player and late NBC basketball commentator. Our future President, Jim Emme, had sat next to him on a recent flight and told him that the owner of NOW still plays basketball weekly at 70 years of age. Apparently, Mr. Walton decided to make Elwood's day, because he called the next week and left a very inspirational and humorous message. Listed below is a copy of that message, a call that made my Dad so giddy it was a day to remember.

"Elwood Richard, my name is Bill Walton and I'm not calling to ask for anything. I was given your name by Jim Emme, Director of Marketing and Distribution. I ran into this fine gentleman on an airplane. He said that you are an outstanding basketball player, even though you may have lost that explosive quickness just a week or two ago. But, still very, very tough. I'm in the Basketball Hall of Fame and with NBC sports and I'm on my way to the All-Star game in Philadelphia this weekend. There's been some injuries and we need some players who we can rely on. If you get a chance, if you have confidence, ability, poise, competitive greatness, physical fitness, skill level and commitment to the team, we're looking for some really good players. There's a big game in Philadelphia Sunday night and we don't want a junk game, we need really solid players and I heard that you are one of the most solid players in the country, even though you have that nagging back injury. Please call me at .... I'm not calling to ask for anything. I'm just calling to thank you for making this country and this world a better place. Keep shooting every time you get it. You can miss as well as the next guy. Congratulations. Be safe. Be quick, but don't hurry.

Don't play defense with your face down, it's not a good idea. And never mistake activity for achievement. Good health to you Elwood. Chase that ball down. Remember, failing to prepare is preparing to fail. Good day sir."

Looking back, this era was one of the most exciting and fulfilling chapters in the story of NOW Foods and our family. Our successes up to this point exceeded everyone's expectations and my wildest dreams, yet it turns out there was even better to come. Who could have foreseen that by the end of 2002 NOW would employ more than 500 people, own a 203,000 square foot warehouse that we built, sell over $100 million annually, and be one of the top health food brands in the United States? I'm still amazed at the bountiful blessings bestowed upon us. From our very humble beginnings, and against all odds, NOW Foods has succeeded by filling a needed niche in a growing industry. It's not because we're smarter or harder working than our competitors (although we do try). It's because our business has been blessed with exceptional customers and employees who have bought into NOW's game plan to make quality natural products affordable. To future generations the good book says, *"Let this be recorded for a generation to come, so that a people yet unborn may praise the Lord"* (Psalm 102: 18). NOW had achieved everything our family hoped, but now it was time to start preparing for the challenges that come with being one of the top natural product brands in the nation.

> *"But as for you Daniel, conceal these words,*
> *and seal up the book until the end time;*
> *Many will go back and forth,*
> *and knowledge will increase."*
> **Daniel 12:4**

2003-2005

Recent years hardly seem to qualify as history. Yet every year brings a multitude of surprises, disasters, discoveries, wars and hope. On March 23, 2003, the United States launched a preemptive attack against Saddam Hussein, the Butcher of Baghdad, in an elusive search for weapons of mass destruction in Iraq. A new disease called SARS afflicted countless Asian travelers, as well as our neighbors in Toronto. Atkin's low-carb diet peaked as one in every 10 Americans lost weight with the widely promoted fad, though it turned out to be short-lived as Atkin's declared bankruptcy in 2005. Finally, the entire world worked its way out of the shadows of international terrorism that had erupted on 9/11.

At NOW, these three years were largely spent gearing up for the next great sales wave and future acquisitions, in order to keep up with public competitors' growth. NOW installed a new Oracle ERP (Enterprise Resource Planning) system in June, 2002 and became internally divided about the benefits of a bigger and better system. The health food industry seemed to 'discover' NOW as we received a number of prominent awards including Manufacturer of the Year by one trade magazine in 2003. Vitamin consumption in the U.S. sunk to the low single digits as the Coral Calcium fad slowed and negative publicity on Vitamin E hurt sales of that category by up to 40%. And my father, Elwood, formally retired January 1, 2005, leaving the company in the hands of a very capable management team that he had molded over the previous decade.

INDUSTRY CONSOLIDATION

Every business student knows that it is a natural progression for growth industries to eventually mature and consolidate into fewer, larger and stronger competitors. Industries such as hardware stores, drug stores, book stores, toy stores and more have seen the number of independent businesses shrink in favor of large, usually public, consolidators and category-killers. These giant retailers and brand names are changing consumer shopping choices as more and more family businesses fail to survive the spiraling competitive landscape.

At NOW, our first company acquisition in June, 2000 was a big one: Puresource (www.puresource.ca), Canada's largest wholesaler with over 100 employees. Puresource had grown very quickly in only 10 years and had been NOW's preferred importer to sell NOW products into Canada. Our part-time sales rep in Canada, Doug Finlay, was also a business real estate broker and he suggested this marriage and helped to make it happen. Puresource had a very successful sales and marketing team, but a weak financial side that caused the company to be sold. Our primary objectives for this purchase were to accelerate NOW product sales into Canada and to test the waters to see how profitable and practical distribution of third party brands to health food stores could be. Ten years after this acquisition, NOW has become one of the leading brands in Canada exclusive to health food stores, in small part helped by including the Canadian maple leaf in our main logo! NOW sales grew by over 2,000% in just 5 years as Puresource focused on distributing NOW brand to independent stores. Our management team learned much about nationalism north of the border, which is alive and well, and all U.S. employees needed to learn on-the-job how NOT to offend Canadians with American bravado.

In June 2003, NOW opened a distribution depot in Sparks, NV to improve our service levels and shipping times to West Coast customers. Previously, NOW either shipped ground orders by UPS or FedEx and air shipments by DHL. But this was either slow or expensive, so we made plans to build a distribution facility that would be able to support our most distant US customers. The new building is 29,000 sq. ft. and features a simplified picking system that is lower in cost and easier to use. The manager instilled a high level of service among her employees and she had an interesting personal example of superior customer service. One Friday, she was at home on vacation and the office called to say that a very large order had been shipped to the wrong customer and the trucking company couldn't deliver it for several more days. The order was very big, so she rented a local U-Haul truck and drove nine hours with her family in tow to pick up and make a special Sunday delivery near Los Angeles. The customer was very grateful and our manager even made a Herculean effort to get back to Sparks in time for the Monday rush of orders. That's the kind of effort that makes a difference between good companies and great ones.

Later in 2003, another opportunity came our way when the owners of Nature's Apothecary, a brand of liquid herbal extracts, called offering to sell us their small business. The business had been in decline for several years and came crashing down when a deal with GNC fell through. Nature's Apothecary had over-extended itself and produced vast quantities of unusual liquid herbs, which could not be sold through normal store channels. The line was conceived using wildcrafted "fresh" herbs, which had to be harvested, transported and processed for extraction within 72 hours. Despite the production challenges inherent in "fresh" liquid extracts, the line grew to over 250 different products, including aromatherapy inhalers and room sprays. A nominal herbalist would be humbled by lack of knowledge of herbs in the line such as Blood Root, Figwort Leaf, Hydrangea Root, Poke Root, Squaw Vine, Stone Root and Toadflax. Unfortunately, Nature's Apothecary never took off and NOW discontinued the entire brand in 2007.

In May 2005, NOW purchased Burnham Labs, a cosmetic manufacturer in Niles, IL that gave NOW expertise to add new personal care products. John and Soo Chang had owned the company for about 10 years and it seemed to be an opportune time for them to cash out and for NOW to cash in! NOW had been a customer of Burnham for over 5 years as Burnham made products such as MSM lotion, Long Lasting Deodorant Stick, Celadrin® Lotion, Joint Support Cream and Wrinkle Rescue™ Cream. Burnham only had about 15 employees, which NOW easily absorbed and needed to run the existing business. This prompted one big change within NOW as quality and production departments needed to gear up to become OTC (over the counter) compliant. This involved some substantial changes such as added documentation, longer stability studies, FDA notices, additional product testing and some process changes. The extra costs give reason enough to be thankful for living in the U.S., where supplements are protected by law and not subject to excessive pharmaceutical costs.

In August 2005, NOW purchased another Canadian distributor, Produits Biologiques Himex Inc. (www.inari.ca) in Montreal, Quebec to support our existing Puresource efforts. The former owner was dying and had been in prolonged negotiations to sell his business. Unfortunately, he passed away before a deal was complete, but NOW did purchase the company from his estate and kept a solid business afloat that likely, otherwise, would have gone out of business. Himex imports many certified organic foods and sells a brand of packaged foods called Inari, largely to stores in Quebec. The goal is for Himex to leverage Canadian house brands (Herbal Select) and to establish NOW as a dominant brand within French health food stores. Politically, we can only hope that unity will prevail among the provinces as Quebec retains its distinctly unique home within Canada. As the good book says, *"Behold how good and pleasant it is when brothers dwell together in unity." (Psalm 133:1)*

THE ORACLE AGE

Early in 2001, NOW management began discussing the need for a much larger computer system to drive future growth. We anticipated making many acquisitions, expanding into foreign countries, opening multiple distribution centers and needing a world-class warehouse system for GMP and better efficiencies. A consultant recommended that we look at a super-duper, new, all-encompassing system known as ERP (Enterprise Resource Planning). Until that time, NOW had used a very simple, low-cost system known as FACTS, which did not have any bells or whistles and was very easy to operate and fix. It lacked many of the options that we wanted and so management decided to move forward with the purchase of an Oracle system.

Initially, our board approved the sticker-shock cost of $3 million to buy, build and install an entire system in order to fulfill all of our company goals and dreams. This was quite a step up from our last system that had cost under $100,000 only 10 years earlier and included all software, hardware, printers, one year warranty and 15 terminals! Somehow, we pressed forward and hired an outside consultant company to review our processes and set up Oracle to fill our needs with customized software. The consultants 'lived' in NOW's offices for over a year and they seemed to be more learners than teachers for this latest-and-greatest Oracle 9i system.

In June 2002, NOW went live with Oracle and the company practically shut down. For several weeks we were unable to ship many orders, unable to answer the deluge of phone calls and unable to conduct many basic business functions. Our sales phone service levels plummeted to under 20% (# of calls answered within 45 seconds) compared to our norm of 85%+. Basic actions like entering orders took, and still take, much longer than our former, simple, low-cost system. The lure of Oracle's superior reports and information turned out to be a major problem because our expensive new system operated at a crawling pace compared to what we had before. In order to support our amazingly patient and kind customers, NOW shipped overnight air for many months and ended up wasting over $500,000 in FedEx air charges. In the end, we figured that implementing Oracle ended up costing the company about $10 million total in extra labor, consultants, lost sales, excess freight and more. Below is a quote from internal reports later that summer:

"June 2002 was probably our worst month of sales service to customers ever... The speed of Oracle continues to be a problem. It is not OK currently. Every function (log-ins, searches, screen changes, set-ups) is frustratingly too slow. It is making productive employees unproductive and frustrated. After 10 weeks, we remain handcuffed in many ways."

Fast forward three years and Oracle is a well-adjusted, cost-saving tool that is helping NOW in many ways. It took a lot of in-house learning to figure out how to use the system to our advantage, and today it all seems worthwhile after all. Oracle provides excellent reports and the system is extremely stable and functional for years to come. It also provides NOW with the ability to purchase additional outside companies and link systems in ways that are optimal for financial reporting. I wish we didn't have to go through all the pain and hard work of changing to Oracle, but at least the system works today and does provide many advantages that competitors lack. But let's never change systems again, life is too short!

AWARDS & MORE AWARDS!

A flurry of industry awards arrived at NOW during this time period. Below are the highlights of how NOW stopped being a 'sleeper' company and started earning industry and peer respect:

- In 2003, *Nutrition Industry Executive* magazine awarded NOW its Manufacturer of the Year award. This was a pleasant surprise and came with a feature article to the health food trade about NOW's history. It included the statement "NOW's hard-earned position as an example for others to follow persuaded the staff of Nutrition Industry Executive to name the company Manufacturer of the Year for 2003."

- In 2004, NOW was recognized by Consumerlab.com, an independent testing business, for being "the top ranked brand in health food stores based on customer satisfaction." This resulted from a consumer online survey of 6,300 shoppers showing all major vitamin brands and asking regular users of dietary supplements to rank their level of satisfaction in various areas. When the results were in, NOW was at the top of the list!

- In 2004, the U.S. Department of Commerce gave NOW an Excellence in Export Achievement Award for our stellar sales growth in many markets overseas.

- *Vitamin Retailer* magazine continued to honor NOW with multiple VITY award winners each year. In 2004, NOW gained eight 1st place awards as best-selling products in health food stores.

- NNFA presented my father, Elwood, their Crusader Award in 2004 at the national convention. This award is similar to a Lifetime Achievement award and honored Dad for his lifelong industry efforts.

- In 2005, *Nutrition Business Journal* presented Elwood another Lifetime Leadership Award. They noted his hard work, vision and commitment to inspire a large company and entire industry in areas of retailer support, overall quality and taking proactive measures toward environmental preservation.

- In 2005, NOW's analytical scientists gained industry respect when our newly developed method for HPLC testing of glucosamine was approved by the non-profit AOAC (American Organization of Analytical Chemists). This means that a method that NOW created was accepted by AOAC, after a 2-year validation process, to become the official standard test for the industry.

BILL RICHARD LEAVES HIS MARK

After years of being passive stockholders, two of Bill Richard's progeny joined the NOW team as full-time employees. After eight years with EVEREN Securities, daughter Beth Pecenka left her position as Senior VP, Equity Research covering the Specialty Retailing and Supplement Manufacturing sectors, for an all-too-short break to have three healthy, energetic boys. During this so-called break, Beth also worked as a NOW consultant to provide industry and competitive analyses. Since August 2003, Beth provided expertise in strategy and business development, as well as later leading our marketing group. Unfortunately, a messy problem caused Beth to leave the family business she loved in 2015.

Bill's son, Mike Richard, finally took Elwood's advice to retire from the U.S. Navy and return to the business. Mike served 25 years, rising through the enlisted ranks and obtaining his commission as a Naval Officer. Mike's experience in operations & logistics, personnel, and administration has already had a positive impact on the company. Easygoing by nature, Mike was extremely happy to learn that we no longer hand-pack desiccated liver powder like he did in his teens.

Sadly, just as Mike and Beth were settling in to their roles at NOW, their father, Bill Richard, passed away April 25, 2004 after fighting a battle with cancer. I truly feel that Bill would have listed his children's increased participation in the family business as one of his proudest accomplishments. Their decisions to join the company full-time was a result of "talking shop" with Bill often about NOW and his vision lived on through them.

CHOLESTEROL BE GONE!

Having become a 40-something in 2004, I had a blood test at our local health food store in May, 2004 to check up on my health. I had not been tested like this for at least 10 years since I am normally in very good health and almost never visit a doctor. I expected a very clean bill of health because of my healthy lifestyle, regular basketball, multitudes of vitamins and immersion into health foods from a young age. The report shocked me when it showed my total cholesterol was at a surprisingly high 269 and LDL (bad cholesterol) was at 195. Though every other part of the test had very healthy results, I had never anticipated any trouble with cholesterol, especially at my age. Fortunately, there is so much information available to naturally reduce cholesterol that nobody needs to get hooked on statin drugs, which warn of many negative side effects.

I started a regime of a variety of NOW nutritional products. I knew from many customer reports to expect a very significant improvement in cholesterol. Without any lifestyle changes I took another test three months later and was quite pleased to see my total cholesterol had dropped from 269 to 180 and my LDL levels dropped from 195 to 113!!! As a final bit of good news, my liver scores for GGT, AST & ALT all improved thanks again to my nutritional program, which is aimed at supporting a healthy liver. My ALT (GPT) liver enzyme number made the biggest improvement from too high at 46 to just right at 29.

Interestingly, I had another blood test one year later to see how my cholesterol levels would be. After I had reached my goal for lower cholesterol levels, I reduced my program to a low maintenance level. My test in August, 2005 showed my total cholesterol increased slightly to 208, but was still much improved over 269. LDL levels were moderate at 134. With this helpful information, I'll go back to an intermediate nutritional program and test again regularly to continue my guinea-pig experiment!

CHANGING OF THE GUARD

After many years of promises to retire, Elwood stepped down as our President January 1, 2005. He had publicly declared Al Powers to be our next president for many previous years and always made a point at our annual Christmas dinner to let everyone know that he really would retire one day soon. After hearing the same story for so many years, many employees felt that he would actually continue indefinitely because he just couldn't pull himself away from the day-to-day business. After all, he was the one with the vision for NOW, at one time the only employee, and the 'boss' for 37 years to so many varied workers. Additionally, those who know Elwood understand that he is a workaholic and enjoys working with health food products, chemistry, research and health food retailing. He still works more hours than many of our managers, but he moved his office down to a normal cubicle in a remote part of our office without any direct reports or specific day-to-day responsibilities.

This process of stepping down and giving up authority is typically painful. Most family businesses endure great stress working through the many decisions involved in the changing of the guard. Who will lead the company? How can we assure long-term financial success? How can we avoid estate taxes that might sink the ship? How involved will/should the founder remain? What about going public or ESOP's (Employee Stock Ownership Plans)? How to pass on the company mission to family members and managers who often don't share the same business passion? As the richest and wisest man (Solomon) in the world said in his old age, *"So I turned about and gave my heart up to despair over all the toil of my labors under the sun, because sometimes a man who has toiled with wisdom and knowledge and skill must leave all to be enjoyed by a man who did not toil for it. This also is vanity and a great evil."* (Ecclesiastes 2:20-21)

In our family's case, this act of succession went off without a hitch. It was very well planned out in advance, future leadership was established, estate planning was in effect for over 15 years and Elwood had many, many plans that he wanted to do. The real key was Dad's humility and willingness to disengage from management, while Al Powers' duties increased. Fortunately for all, the company enjoyed a double-digit growth year and record profits in 2005, so the honeymoon period allowed Elwood the opportunity to not worry or become overly involved in daily work matters. Elwood does remain NOW's Chairman of the Board and is very involved in directing board activities and many other matters of interest to him. He is a board member of Citizens for Health (www.citizens. org) and the driving force to start the National Health Research Institute. Elwood enjoys going to technical conferences (American Oil Chemists), promoting educational e-mailings, biking in good weather, and visiting many retail health food stores. He's found himself working more than he had thought previously, but has found more time to do things with the family, and especially his grandchildren.

CHARITY TO THE WORLD

As NOW's profits grew over the years, so did NOW's charitable giving. The primary owners each had their own favorite charities to support and we had to discuss the ground rules at first to determine how we would divide the pie. We agreed to donate funds for "basic human needs", which mostly means food, water or vitamins, and often in destitute areas. We also give some support for conservation and agreed that we don't want to donate to any charity that might offend any of our owners. We require financial statements from each non-profit and aim to give to those that give the highest percent funds to the cause, and not to overhead. This has been a wonderful benefit to having a successful and profitable business. Roughly, 32% goes to local needs, 32% to world needs, 22% to disaster relief and 14% to conservation.

Mother and daughter helped by Vitamin Angel.

CHARITIES THAT NOW HAS SUPPORTED IN RECENT YEARS:

Autism Research Institute   www.autism.com

Compassion International   www.compassion.com
 – Helps children's needs.

Conservation Foundation   www.theconservationfoundation.org
 – Land and river protection organization.

Feeding America   www.feedingamerica.org
 – Help fight hunger.

Feed My Starving Children   www.fmsc.org
 – Feeding God's starving children hungry in body and spirit.

Hephzibah Children's Association   www.hephzibahhome.org
 – Supports children's care.

Hill of Hope   www.hillofhope.org
 – Helps unfortunate in India

Life Center Elgin, IL   www.tlcpregnancyservices.com
 – Provides pregnancy support.

Marklund Children's Home   www.marklund.org
 – Supports severely handicapped children and adults.

Meal-A-Day   www.cmadfa.com
 – Provides basic food and services.

Natural Health Research Institute   www.naturalhealthresearch.org
 – Informs consumers and officials on health research.

People's Resource Center   www.peoplesrc.org
 – Local food pantry.

SCARCE Environmental   www.scarce.org
 – Inspiring people through environmental education.

Vitamin Angels   www.vitaminangels.org
 – Gives supplements to those in need.

Williamsburg Christadelphian Foundation   www.wcfoundation.org
 – International needs.

World Relief   www.worldrelief.org
 – Gives support to refugees.

MANY GOOD THINGS

As 2005 ended, NOW had accomplished many great things. Our corporate name changed to NOW Health Group, in order to reflect NOW as the lead brand in our growing lineup of brands and integrated companies. NOW's slogan changed to "Nutrition for Optimal Wellness" in order to take advantage of our acronym and to better identify what it is that we do. Our famous orange NOW colored labels were tweaked with an extra slice of purple and a bit more design depth to produce a trendy, feature-rich package. And NOW teamed up with Marcia Zimmerman, CN to help endorse NOW products, lead training sessions and utilize her decades of experience in product formulation and nutritional education.

Yes, life at NOW had been good to this point, and many great things were yet to come. It's a good thing for a business to provide rewarding work for its employees, healthy nutritional products for its customers, and a reasonable profit for its owners. NOW wears this Triple Crown proudly, and as 2005 wound down we were reaping the rewards of this labor and gearing up to continue it. *This will bring health to your body and nourishment to your bones. Honor the Lord with your wealth, with the first fruits of your crops." (Proverbs 3: 8-9)*

> *"I am going to bring it recovery and healing;*
> *I will heal them and reveal to them abundance*
> *of prosperity and security."*
> *Jeremiah 33:6*

2006-2009

It's good to be thankful in bad times as well as good. But it's certainly easier in business when there's more to celebrate than to mourn. In 2006 the debate about global warming was heating up thanks to former Vice President Al Gore's movie "An Inconvenient Truth". Iran and North Korea were two rogue nations saber-rattling threats of using nuclear arms. An E. coli outbreak in spinach, which killed three people in the U.S., caused spinach salads to disappear from the market, including restaurants. And Time magazine boldly proclaimed their Person of the Year to be none other than You!

At NOW, the company continued to grow and receive many additional awards. From industry magazines to government proclamations, NOW racked up some amazing business accomplishments. We completed a major building expansion in 2008, and became fully compliant with current FDA Good Manufacturing Practices (CGMPs) by mid-2009. A new brand called Protocol® was launched in 2007 to sell exclusively through licensed health care practitioners. This would utilize NOW's excellent manufacturing facility and lab capabilities while tapping the fast-growing doctor market. And NOW's Richard family members organized the first Family Council in order to better communicate to management family wishes.

MORE AND MORE AWARDS

Company recognition from peers and press accelerated in these years. In 2006 NOW won six more VITY product awards from *Vitamin Retailer* magazine, an award for educational initiatives regarding NOW University from *Nutrition Business Journal* and an Earth Flag for Business as NOW became the first for-profit business in our county to earn this award. My father, Elwood, also received a Natural Legacy Award from *t* magazine. In 2007 NOW claimed eight more VITY awards, a Business Achievement Award for efforts on behalf of the industry and recognition for Outstanding Business Recycling Program. These were all significant and greatly appreciated, but nothing close to what came in 2008. In 2008 NOW was fully recognized and rewarded in five significant ways:

Nutrition for Optimal Wellness.

BEST FULL LINE OF SUPPLEMENTS

The trade magazine *WholeFoods*, which is unrelated to the Whole Foods Market stores, gave NOW this honor in an article titled *The Time Belongs to NOW*. This was the first time we received this award, which recognizes full-line brands for overall performance.

MANUFACTURER OF THE YEAR

This was a repeat award winner, though from a different source. *Vitamin Retailer* magazine's editorial staff picked NOW among many possible brands. They wrote that "NOW stood apart in areas of quality, leadership in science and innovation, and dedication to retailers and the industry as a whole." This significant, repeat, public acknowledgement is humbling – as it should be! Hopefully it reflects *"he who is lowly in spirit will obtain honor." (Proverbs 29:23)*

CHICAGO'S 101 BEST AND BRIGHTEST COMPANIES TO WORK FOR

The National Association for Business Resources picked NOW in 2008 thru 2012 for this prestigious award. This annual competition honors companies that recognize employees as their greatest asset. An extensive array of professional criteria is used to determine the top 101 best companies, including communication, community initiatives, compensation & benefits, diversity & multi-culturalism, employee education & development, employee engagement & commitment, recognition & retention, recruitment & selection, and work-life balance. NOW's mission, values, culture and leadership are all focused on the company's commitment to its employees.

NOW FOODS NAMED "CORPORATE HERO"

A new book by Ellis Jones called "The Better World Shopping Guide" listed NOW as the only 'Corporate Hero' in the section on vitamin brands. This was the highest honor given and came from NOW's significant waste reduction plan, environmental and sustainability efforts, donations to food banks, and recycling efforts. The real surprise is that no one at NOW even knew about this book, or the great news, until a friend from church showed me what she had found at the bookstore. NOW had no input or insights into this book at all, but we did start to distribute the book and have found it to be a great 3rd party reference to our way of doing business.

PRESIDENTIAL "E" AWARD FOR EXPORT EXCELLENCE

In May, 2008 NOW's International sales manager Philip Pittsford and CEO Al Powers toured the White House with other NOW employees to receive this award. NOW was one of only 21 U.S. companies to earn the award this year. Philip and Al actually spent private time in the Oval Office with President Bush, who congratulated our managers on their efforts. Created by President John F. Kennedy in 1961, the Presidential "E" award is the highest honor that the federal government can give to any American company or organization that has made significant contributions to the increase of American exports. NOW publicized this event on our website with a photo-op and splashed the news across the natural foods industry. One day I received a phone call from a troubled consumer who was very upset that we would mix politics with business by showing President Bush on our homepage.

While I tried to explain that our PR efforts were non-political, and that I personally was apolitical, he just couldn't understand or get over seeing the Commander-in-Chief so prominently on our website. He was so rattled that he told me he would have to throw away all of his NOW products, because he couldn't support such company politics. The real kicker is he admitted to being a Republican, but apparently not a big fan of that Republican President!

Al Powers (Left), President George Bush, (Center) Philip Pittsford (Right)
Photographed by White House Staff Photographer

NEW PRODUCTS

NOW's sales engine has always been driven by new products and we managed to introduce over 280 new skus in these four years alone. Customers and suppliers call us all the time with good suggestions for new introductions. In 2006, our best new products were CoQ10 600 mg softgels, Citrulline caps and B-12 Energy Packets. The B-12 product is very unique and is a tasty, small powder packet that can be used by bikers, or anyone, direct into the mouth or in drinks. We constantly aim to introduce quality new products like this that are new to the market and that make sense nutritionally. In 2007, our best new products were: Mangoni™ Liquid Concentrate, Ultra Omega-3 and L-Tryptophan (again). We formulated Mangoni as a superior, yet comparable, product to XanGo®, which is a multi-level marketing product. XanGo® started the mangosteen beverage market and with 1 million distributors helped to make Mangosteen a known name among health enthusiasts.

In 2008, our best new products were: AlphaSorb-C™, Vitamin D-3 5,000 IU, Ubiquinol CoQH-CF™ and Easy Cleanse™ pack. Our scientists spent over a year developing AlphaSorb-C™ as a replacement for Ester-C®, which was no longer available to NOW. We filed a patent for AlphaSorb-C™, which includes buffered vitamin C and threonic acid, plus we added alpha lipoic acid to enhance the body's absorption and utilization. Initially we labeled this product "Superior to Ester-C®", but soon removed that claim from labels and brochures after NBTY, the new owner of Ester-C®, warned us of legal action certain to come!

In 2009, another product surge hit the natural foods industry and this time the source was none other than Oprah. The talk-show host had discussed a new antioxidant berry called Açai with Dr. Perricone, and tied it into her own diet regime. Almost instantly, internet firms started offering super diet Açai products "as seen on Oprah." Several fly-by-night web companies ran into legal troubles with the FTC and the Better Business Bureau over excessive dieting claims and auto-shipment scams. Meanwhile, NOW responded to this supercharged demand by supplying an organic, freeze-dried Açai in capsule form, in addition to our Açai drink. We avoided all references to dieting and Oprah because the value we found in Açai is as a whole food antioxidant. In the first two months of selling this product we sold out quickly and were unable to keep up with demand. It's just amazing how much influence public figures like Oprah have, affecting millions of people and even suppliers like NOW. Six months later we added an organic Açai pure powder and Açai liquid concentrate as market demand kept this good-tasting berry in the news.

INTRODUCING PROTOCOL FOR LIFE BALANCE™

As early as 2004, NOW's strategy team looked at vitamin sales through doctors as an attractive market. NOW had already sold to many doctors for many years, but we never really tried to do this because we viewed doctor sales as time-consuming, quite small and not really profitable.

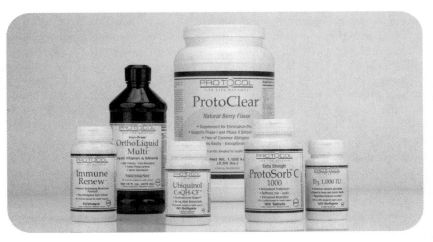

Our views gradually changed as we found doctor sales of supplements growing in double-digits each year. We noticed that the practitioner channel was starting to enter the M & A (merger and acquisition) phase, which could be an opportunity for us. By 2005, our board had approved entering that market with an exclusive doctor brand and our preference was to find an existing company that we could purchase.

I volunteered to search for a brand that would fit within our company culture and be interested in a sale. I called more than a dozen doctor brands and eventually narrowed the field to three potential suitors who seemed to be a possible match. I visited each of these and was surprised at what wouldn't work for NOW. Synthetic Vitamin E, DHEA, artificial sweeteners, DLPA and other blacklisted items at NOW were too abundant in the brands we looked at. If we purchased one of those companies, we'd inherit products that we didn't allow in NOW brand and that would be costly to change. In the end, we were unable to find a brand that met our acquisition qualifications, especially our quality standards. So we proceeded to plan B to build a brand with healthy and natural ingredients which we would want to use ourselves.

In 2007, with the help of industry veteran Evan Zang, we came up with the brand name Protocol. We added the 'For Life Balance' part in order to have legal claims for our future doctor brand. (www.protocolforlife.com) We proceeded to lay out a game plan that would enable us to realistically and eventually become the # 1 brand sold to doctors. Protocol For Life Balance was launched in July 2007 with about 100 products. We quickly expanded our sales force, attended many physician conferences and aimed to introduce innovative and proprietary new products exclusively for Protocol for Life Balance™. Our flagship new product, ProtoClear™, was introduced in mid-2008 and quickly became the door-opener we needed. ProtoClear™ is a unique, high-protein, pea protein-based, detox powder mix that tastes better than competing brands. We fortified the product with many extra ingredients and managed to keep the finished product hypo-allergenic, instant and non-GMO for a superior elimination diet supplement.

MAP PRICING STRATEGIES

Every business sets prices in a strategic manner. Costs have to be covered and pricing has to be viewed as acceptable or fair to customers. Certain margins need to be made for any for-profit business or it won't be able to survive. The practice of picking prices is a delicate matter with much expertise in each business. Just search for an airline ticket at various websites and you'll see how much energy goes into setting the right price for the right flight.

In the U.S., the laws regarding how manufacturers price their products to consumers have changed. Until 2007, it was difficult for brands to require retailers to sell at their suggested retail prices. They might withhold shipments from retailers who discounted too deeply, but the brands didn't have full authority to set retail prices. This changed in June 2007 when the Supreme Court ruled 5 to 4 to make it easier for manufacturers to require retailers to stick to their "suggested" prices. This is known as Manufacturers Advertised Price or MAP strategies. This ruling overturned a previous anti-trust statute that said MAP agreements were illegal. Suddenly, brands such as Sony, Cisco, Samsung, Black & Decker and thousands more began implementing and enforcing MAP policies in order to control prices to consumers. The brands often hire outside companies such as NetEnforcers, MAPtrackers, Cyveillance and others to police their policies to help enforce their pricing plans among retailers. Within the natural foods arena it soon became apparent that many supplement brands were instituting MAP pricing of their own. Brands such as New Chapter, Garden of Life, Flora, Renew Life, Solgar, Enzymatic Therapy, Nature's Way and more initiated retail pricing controls so that online retailers could not discount too deeply. Their idea seems to be that websites can discount very deeply and too low prices might affect consumer brand perception and, I'm guessing, their profits. The challenge they face is with so many independent retailers selling their products, enforcing MAP is like herding cats. It seems like every time I look I see another retailer who is violating known pricing rules and the manufacturers end up being price cops.

At NOW, we determined that as a value brand we would do a disservice to our end customers by putting MAP in place. We also found that many of our successful store customers resisted MAP because it becomes another form of unwanted regulation. Because our mission is to "provide value in products and services that empower people to live healthier lives", we opted to avoid MAP policies. We let our natural foods market set fair prices and believe this is what's best for our consumers, store customers and NOW. The rulings are still being challenged and some states (Maryland 1st) are currently enacting laws banning MAP pricing, so we'll see how the courts determine the outcome.

Interestingly, in March, 2000 I was personally sued, along with NOW, for this very issue by an online vitamin retailer. At the time NOW did not sell to web retailers and actually had a policy against selling to that class of trade. Unknown to us, our web customer claimed that I had enacted discriminatory pricing when I simply asked them how they could be profitable when selling at wholesale prices. Initially, the customer had bought and sold at the same price in order to grow quickly, which I knew was not sustainable. In the end, we cut off wholesale shipments, they sued, we counter-sued and the whole mess ended up settled out of court and wasting everyone's time. The web retailer thought that it would win a landmark internet pricing suit, but we knew that our pricing policies were fair, time-tested and legal. The saying is true, *"make friends quickly with your accuser, while you are going with him to court." (Matthew 5:25)* Eight years later their same CEO and new CFO both contacted me repeatedly in order to buy our products again, but the memory of being sued was still too close. I had to tell them that our new sales policy is that we don't sell to any customer who sues us!

FAMILY BUSINESS 4TH GENERATION

Every leader needs to make preparations for the next generation to take over. Failing to do good succession planning is one of the main problems for family businesses today. At NOW, my father, Elwood, had done this for many years regarding Al Powers as the next CEO, as well as for future family members to join the business. One hurdle he didn't expect to encounter was from his own management team, which had reservations about preferential hiring of Richard family teenagers. Elwood found that he had to personally step in and lean on managers in order to get his grandchildren jobs at his own company!

Family businesses face this unique challenge in different ways compared to large public companies. With over 500 employees, nepotism can threaten the workforce as they may see unfair favoritism and think that future advancement is limited. At NOW, Sarah Wong became our first family teen worker of the 4th generation in 2004. After a rough first summer and a satisfying second summer, the family created a Family Council to help develop and mentor teens, while interacting with management. I had attended an expensive but helpful Kellog family business seminar and learned the value in organizing the family side of business. In time, the Family Council developed expectations and guidelines for hiring both teen students and future professional family members. We needed to become more formal in our planning because three more grandkids started working at NOW in the summer of 2009. Nathan Richard, Michelle Wong and Maddy Richard joined the workforce part-time, and we found our advance preparations paid dividends. The next generation better understood their role and how they needed to work harder than other employees to honor their family name. For *"a good name is to be chosen rather than great riches." (Proverbs 22:1)*

In order from left to right: Mike, Dan, Elwood, Beth

THANKFUL TO MAKE A DIFFERANCE

After growing for ten good years at 395 Glen Ellyn Rd. in Bloomingdale, IL, it became necessary to expand our production capacity just to keep up with demand. The original 203,000 sq. ft. building was built with this future expansion in mind, as we hoped to continue our growth curve. By 2007 the company determined that we would expand by building out within our existing walls and add 54,000 sq. ft. of two-storied production space. NOW had subleased part of our building for ten years and this helped to reduce our original construction costs while providing some rent income. The expansion would make total production space 98,000 sq. ft. and the entire plant 250,000 sq. ft. Effectively, this expansion allowed NOW to double sales, which we hoped to accomplish within seven years.

NOW's chief engineer, Dan Mirjanic, took on this project and, with much help, accomplished the task on-time and close to budget. The entire cost of $4.5 million was paid in cash as the company is blessed to operate with no real debt. This is a huge advantage and is very apparent when times are tough and other companies are forced to sell their business because of some misfortune. NOW is also able to go to many bankruptcy auctions and pay cash for expensive machinery. With our build-out complete, much new additional equipment was purchased to make more capsules, tablets, liquid blends, powder blends and packaged goods. One extra reason we needed to expand was to help meet new federal Good Manufacturing Practices (GMPs). For companies our size, the new rules kicked in June 25, 2009 and suppliers needed to either comply with all requirements or eventually go out of business. Our new build-out included 4,500 sq. ft. of additional lab space for significantly more product testing, including many tests above and beyond those required by FDA. We test for heavy metals to parts-per-billion levels to assure safety. We test for allergens, including gluten, and label products gluten-free when appropriate. Using a new specialized instrument, we are now able to test and detect when products have been irradiated. We do these to provide for the safest and healthiest products available. We've increased hiring of new analytical and micro testing staff as our lab runs 24 hours per day doing dozens of sophisticated chemical analyses and microbial tests per day.

At NOW we were thankful to be part of the 5% of thriving companies as sales continued to grow above our projections into 2009. We gained largely because NOW is a value brand and our entire mission is to make quality natural products more affordable. It's ironic that after decades of defending our value business model, it took another recession for consumers to realize that high prices don't necessarily equate to high quality, and that there are still companies out there such as NOW that value quality and people over quantity and profits. Thanks to our sales and production growth we actually added 28 new jobs in 2009, which was about 5% of our total workforce at the time. At a time when jobs were scarce it was amazing and wonderful to be able to help people by providing useful and important jobs. We all need to *"labor, doing honest work with our hands, so that we may be able to give to those in need." (Ephesians 4: 28).*

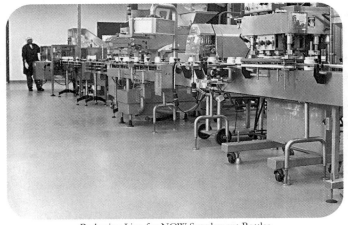

Packaging Line for NOW Supplement Bottles

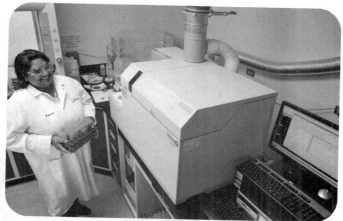

Inductively Coupled Plasma Mass Spectrometer (ICPMS)

High Performance Liquid Chromatograph (HPLC)

Microbiology Laboratory

Bottling Line

Encapsulating Machine

"The earth has yielded its produce;
God blesses us.
That all the ends of the earth may fear Him."
Psalm 67:6-7

2009-2013

2009 was a year of important political and economic change in the U.S. Barack Obama was elected President, and former First Lady, and one-time foe, Hillary Clinton became his Secretary of State. America was burdened with two expensive foreign wars - Iraq & Afghanistan - which were becoming less popular with the public. General Motors filed for bankruptcy as the entire auto industry teetered on edge. Pop icon Michael Jackson died suddenly and the world population increased to over seven billion mouths to feed.

At NOW, history repeated itself with more sales growth, more sensational media hype, more facility expansion and more thievery. NOW became more politically active with personal visits with Senators McCain and Durbin, while building support for the Congressional Dietary Supplement Caucus. Dr. Oz started a daily show in 2009 and has been one of the best advocates anywhere for a natural, healthy lifestyle. When he recommends specific supplements, brands like NOW listen closely and enjoy the windfall. Record sales at NOW led to extensive hiring, new facilities and a guessing game for long-term planning. NOW's board of directors made the decision to put foods back into NOW Foods, so there's been a renewed focus to build our food category up to 25% of our total volume. Finally, while NOW continues to be family-owned and operated, the natural foods industry continued to evolve with consolidation, acquisitions and mature companies going public.

POLITICS & MORE POLITICS

In early 2010, former Republican Presidential nominee, and Arizona Senator, John McCain introduced a bill called the Dietary Supplement Safety Act of 2010. While this bill sounded innocent and reasonable enough, it was a dangerous and unnecessary threat to our industry once again. The bill, which was supported by the U.S. Anti-Doping Agency, NFL and MLB, aimed "to more effectively regulate dietary supplements that may pose safety risks unknown to consumers." The problem was the bill overstated the safety issue in supplements by requiring companies to report non-serious adverse events to FDA and provide for immediate recalls of unproven products. It would also create a regulatory climate similar to the burdensome and bureaucratic system in place in Canada, which kept many healthy products off the market.

NOW's Neil Levin (see www.honestnutrition.com) and Al Powers arranged to meet with Senator McCain while he was in Chicago February 12, 2011. They were able to visit briefly and discuss the bill, and the Senator was agreeable to at least read our position paper about the faults in his bill. Meanwhile, industry groups such as the Natural Products Association (NPA), Council for Responsible Nutrition (CRN) and American Herbal Products Association (AHPA) all issued statements criticizing the bill and calling for it to be rejected. After hearing from these groups and many voters in his own state, Senator McCain abruptly rescinded his support for this bill and the matter died in less than one month.

Dick Durbin (D-IL) was the second ranking Democrat in the Senate, with over 30 years of political service, and an arch-enemy of the natural foods industry. Senator Durbin first challenged the natural foods industry when he introduced the misleadingly named Dietary Supplement Safety Act of 2003. That burdensome act would have made many vitamins regulated like drugs, which would raise retail prices and likely put many small supplement brands out of business. This proposed amendment was defeated, but Senator Durbin would continue to re-introduce proposed regulations on vitamins for many years.

In a friendly gesture, NOW invited Senator Durbin to visit our main facility and showcase our people and equipment. Since we are located close to Durbin's Illinois office, he agreed to visit on January 24, 2011. We had a positive, but brief, tour and parted ways hoping that Senator Durbin would better appreciate our industry and quality controls. Unfortunately, the next year Senator Durbin proposed another anti-supplement amendment, but it was soundly defeated in the Senate 77-20 with help from Senator Harkin.

Senator Durbin (left) with NOW CEO Al Powers

NOW also welcomed the following politicians who toured our plant from 2010-2012: US Senator Mark Kirk, Congressman Peter Roskam, Congressman Randy Hultgren, Congressman Joe Walsh and Congresswoman Tammy Duckworth. Nevada Governor Sandoval also mentioned NOW in a February speech in 2012 regarding NOW hiring 100 new workers in Sparks, Nevada.

TOO MUCH DEMAND!

In early 2011, NOW experienced too much demand again, but this time in an illegal way. Since the company had built a Western distribution center, daily truckloads were shipped from Chicago to Nevada in order to keep that warehouse stocked. This daily allotment was fairly smooth for about ten years until one day a full truckload of our products was missing. Someone actually stole a full truckload of our products! We contacted the local police, who investigated and were unable to find the crooks. Imagine my surprise when the FBI called about six months later (November 16, 2011) saying that they had found our missing truck in Miami as part of a drug bust. Many of the boxes had been opened, but almost all of the original containers were still in the truck. Unfortunately, the products had been stored unprotected in the heat of the summer in Florida, and we had to rely on our insurance to cover this loss. *"Do not trust in extortion or put vain hope in stolen goods; though your riches increase, do not set your heart on them." (Psalm 62:10)*

After this experience, our shippers began hiding a tracking device in each truck so that if this ever happened again we would be able to find the truck quickly. Well, guess what happened next? Somehow history repeated itself and another full truckload of our products went missing less than a year later. Our trucking vendor immediately notified the police and began tracking the lost truck. The next day we received some hope when the tracking device was located and the truck was pulled over in Indiana. Unfortunately, the thieves turned out to be professionals who knew what they were doing, and they had found the tracking device and moved it to another truck. It seems that some criminals spend a lot of time staying one step ahead of the law! Later, our inside sales manager, Marymae Lorenzo, found these same products being sold on Amazon at far-below-cost by the case. We did our own investigation and discovered that the seller was less than 20 miles from our warehouse and had never bought from us. We gave extensive information to the local police, but they didn't do what we expected and so we had to write off another large loss.

THE GREAT AND POWERFUL OZ

Dr. Mehmet Oz is more than a trendsetter. He became an icon. He was born in 1960 in Cleveland, Ohio and earned an undergraduate degree from Harvard in 1982, MD from University of Pennsylvania School of Medicine and MBA from The Wharton School in 1986. Oz was both class president and student body president during medical school. He is a renowned cardiac surgeon who has written or participated in over 400 research papers and has several patents. To say that he is qualified to be "American's Doctor" would be an understatement.

Thanks to his wife who is a producer, Dr. Oz started a health series for the Discovery Channel and that's how he met Oprah Winfrey. Oz became the medical expert on her top-rated show from 2004-2009 and claims that Oprah taught him how to talk to audiences and win them over. Dr. Oz started his own spin-off show in 2009 focusing on medical issues and personal health. He has been wildly successful as a TV host and built up an extremely loyal following. When Dr. Oz talks, people listen and take action.

In 2011, Dr. Oz began recommending various nutritional products to help people improve their health. One show was entitled "Flat Belly Supplements" and the # 1 recommendation was a fiber called Apple Pectin. NOW was one of the few brands that had this fairly obscure product in stock and it soon jumped from being a mediocre seller to # 1 virtually overnight. Dr. Oz then talked about another fiber called Glucomannan and an antioxidant called Astaxanthin, helping to turn both of those products into household favorites.

Dr. Oz unleashed his full marketing power in early 2012 when he talked about six separate NOW products. 7-Keto® became the headline product for his big show called Best Belly Blasting Supplements, and this instantly became the top seller (short-term) in NOW's history. Oz also talked about Black Currant Oil, L-Carnosine, Relora®, Red Mineral Algae and Rice Bran Oil – causing each product to jump well over 1,000% in sales. The sales deluge was so extreme that NOW's overall inventory service level dropped enough to be our next major corporate problem! Our biggest challenge with these crazy fads is how to meet demand quickly, something that is easier said than done. But as the good book says, *"You will eat the fruit of your labor; blessings and prosperity will be yours." (Psalm 128:2)* Below is a poem that I sent to Dr. Oz that year in an unsuccessful effort to make contact with him.

Thank you, thank you – good Doctor Oz
Here at NOW Foods we give you applause
For you helped sell our vitamins for a diet
Created demand to cause a near riot

We love how you talk – no need to veto
Relora, Carnosine and 7-Keto
CLA, Red Algae and Rice Bran Oil
Selling these products we no longer toil

We owe you great thanks for teaching the masses
About healthy products, yes this surpasses
We'd like to send samples of these and more
Products found at the local health food store

We'd like for NOW to be of those you call friends
We'll share research, data, products and trends
Feel free to visit, call or e-mail
We'd jump through hoops for you, this we avail

ANOTHER KIND OF TIDAL WAVE

March 11, 2011 was a very bad day in Japan. A record 9.0 earthquake rocked the Pacific Ocean and caused a massive tsunami to hit Japan's east coast. Over 15,000 people died, 100,000+ were made homeless and over 100,000 buildings were destroyed. People all over the earth gasped in shock and horror at the damage that was inflicted on that island nation. An additional problem soon erupted when, as a result of the tsunami, a major nuclear plant suffered a meltdown and released radioactive poisons. Soon, trace amounts of radiation were detected throughout the entire planet and people everywhere became concerned about their own health and radiation poisoning.

Almost immediately customers started calling NOW and asking for Kelp (natural source of iodine) and Potassium Iodide, which is often used during radiation poisoning. While we sold out of Kelp quickly, we determined to supply as much Potassium Iodide as possible. We had never produced or sold Potassium Iodide before, but with the emergency scare in full force, all departments at NOW worked together to quickly research, test, purchase, manufacture and bottle 75,000 bottles within just two weeks of the nuclear accident. This amazing effort helped soothe the worries of thousands of customers and was very rewarding to those who helped make this happen so quickly. Interestingly, an Amazon.com buyer called us during this time and said that Jeff Bezos, famed CEO of Amazon, wanted to quickly buy a lot of Potassium Iodide tablets and donate it to Japan. Price wasn't really a consideration, but we were unable to produce enough bottles fast enough and so we missed out on that opportunity.

EXPANSION IN NEVADA AGAIN

By December 2010, it became apparent that NOW would need to expand production facilities again in order to keep up with ongoing double-digit growth. This time we determined to expand our Sparks, Nevada distribution center to a large manufacturing and distribution plant. The decision to move away from our home in Illinois was fairly simple. We needed to diversify in case of a natural disaster or some other work stoppage. The state of Illinois is relatively unfriendly to businesses, in huge debt, and a recent 50% state tax increase was the final straw. Because NOW already had a second home in Nevada, it made sense to expand in that area and enjoy the benefits of location, climate, low taxes and friendly government.

NOW purchased land in Sparks and began to build a 165,000 sq. ft. building in 2011. By spring 2012, our distribution center relocated and construction continued for full-scale manufacturing and lab testing. In addition to producing tablets and capsules, the Sparks plant would be our first time to manufacture the softgel form of vitamins. It takes very sophisticated pharmaceutical equipment to make softgels, and it's quite interesting  to watch. It also takes experienced technical people to run the lines. Compared to making dry capsules, softgels require some art as well as science and are much more difficult to master. NOW plans to add more softgel lines in future years, which will help our supply chain and overall quality control.

The Sparks plant mirrors our Illinois facility in many ways including labs. We duplicated most of our Illinois lab equipment and now operate two ultra-modern, full-scale laboratories. Combined, NOW has 24 HPTLCs (High Performance Thin Layer Chromatography) testing units, which is an incredibly large number. NOW also has four GCs (Gas Chromatography for fatty acid analysis), three ICPMS machines to test for minerals and heavy metals, two SOLERIS systems, one PPSO to test for irradiation and much more. Our labs conducted 16,000 separate analyses per month in

2013, while utilizing 100+ quality department employees, including 12 holding Ph.D. degrees. In 2011 NOW hired a key QC manager named Aaron Secrist, who had been a GMP auditor. He helped to raise the bar in our testing program, while sharpening our overall quality program. As a result of all of these quality efforts, NOW's formal FDA audit in 2012 ended with zero "observations", meaning that our production facility is fully compliant.

Due to the new plant and extra production needs, NOW added over 240 new full time jobs in 2012 alone. This meant that we had over 1,000 employees for the first time! This was a challenging number of employees to hire, train and absorb into our culture in a fairly short period. We also had developed a top-priority for employee safety, after having a period of unacceptable safety results. This started in 2007 when NOW's injury record was more than double the national average and management became very concerned. NOW engaged Milliken Consulting to help improve our safety record and eventually our DART (Days Away, Restricted or Transferred) measurement showed fairly dramatic improvement. Milliken taught the company how to involve employees and focus on avoiding injuries. Senior managers made employee safety the company's top priority and the emphasis filtered down to all employees. By 2012, NOW's injury record declined so that we became more than twice as safe as the average U.S. manufacturer.

PUTTING FOODS BACK INTO NOW FOODS

Although NOW began as a food company, we migrated to supplements over the years due to a variety of factors. By 2010, our non-Stevia food business was under 5% of our total sales and declining. NOW's board determined that food sales needed to be increased in order to act as a hedge against potential negative supplement legislation. A long-term goal of 25% food sales was set and we began investing in ways to enlarge our food business. One of the first things we did was to hire a dedicated food brand manager, Food Dave, who came from Whole Foods Market. He analyzed our strengths and weaknesses and helped to determine a plan of action to put the 'foods' back into NOW Foods! One obvious first step was to improve our packaging. It's amazing how much effect packaging has on sales, and NOW food products always had that generic look and feel to them. We changed the graphics, labeling and zip seal to be much more user-friendly. Below shows our before and after look:

Old packaging until 2012   New packaging 2013

A bigger change was that all of our foods would be divided into sub-categories, which would help highlight the different aspects of each food product. Below is how NOW foods are currently marketed:

NOW Real Food® – This is the majority of our existing food products and includes all of our staple flour, grain and nut products. Packaging is attractive, yet simple and clear. By 2013 every item in our food line is non-GMO and most new products are certified organic.

NOW Real Tea® - By the end of 2013 we had 20 great-tasting teas that we manufactured in tea bags. Dr. Oz had talked about Hibiscus Tea several times and this became our # 1 seller due to taste and nutrition benefit.

BetterStevia® – NOW's Stevia is actually better than every other brand of Stevia we've tasted. An outside flavor company told us the same since our Stevia is processed with enzymes to buffer the bitter aftertaste. It also helps that our Stevia is certified organic.

Living Now® – This is a new branding of gluten-free products now packaged in a certified gluten-free and allergen-free facility. Each year we'll be adding to this line to help supply healthy products to people who need to avoid common allergies.

Ellyndale Foods®– This is an entirely new food brand that features our finest gourmet food products. The name came from our main plant being on Glen Ellyn Road in Bloomingdale, and, hopefully, will become a household name.

MERGERS AND ACQUISITIONS

In the good old days, family businesses easily and naturally passed from one generation to the next. If the father was a carpenter, then the sons would normally follow suit and inherit the family tools. If the father was a fisherman, then the chances were very good that the children would inherit the boat, tools and way of life as fishermen. However, today succession planning is one of the most difficult and, yet, critical aspects for businesses to be sustainable. The biggest challenge today is how parents of family businesses can cash out with the least amount of taxes applied at death, or in a sale. Within the U.S., this became much more problematic in 2013. Estate taxes leaped to a maximum of 55%, which can cripple most small businesses which try to pass to the next generation. The changes in our tax law, and other factors, have caused many natural food companies to change ownership as a way to survive. Below are some of the recent changes among brands found in natural food stores:

- In September 2009, Atrium Innovations purchased **Garden of Life**, which has become quite popular after launching in 2000.

- **Sprouts**, a natural foods supermarket chain that began in Phoenix, purchased the large Henry's chain in CA, Sun Harvest in TX and then Sunflower Markets in CO. By mid-2017 Sprouts had grown to have 270 stores and growing quickly.

- In February 2012 the pharmaceutical giant Pfizer bought **Alacer**, maker of Emergen-C packets and other products since 1972.

- In June 2012 **New Chapter** made news by selling itself to Proctor & Gamble. This was a major move for the industry as many observers feared that New Chapter would soon become a mass market brand.

- **Vitamin Cottage**, with 140+ stores in the Southwest, went public in mid-2012 in order to provide succession and capital to compete with other retailers with deeper pockets.

- **Super Supplements** retail chain, based in Seattle, sold to **Vitamin Shoppe** in early 2013 as part of major retailing consolidation. It won't be the last big retail deal, either.

- **Schiff** was a pioneering industry brand that started in 1936, but has now had several owners, gone public, and recently sold again to Reckitt Benckiser, a massive multinational British company.

While many firms make drastic ownership changes in order to survive, NOW has been richly blessed to have same-family ownership into our fourth generation. Thanks to foresight and selfless planning by Elwood Richard, NOW has been able to prepare for succession and survival of the family company. "A good person leaves an inheritance for their children's children, but a sinner's wealth is stored up for the righteous." (Proverbs 13:22) May the blessings we have received for 45 years continue, and allow for the next generation to continue with the ongoing mission established by Elwood: *"To provide value in products and services that empower people to lead healthier lives."*

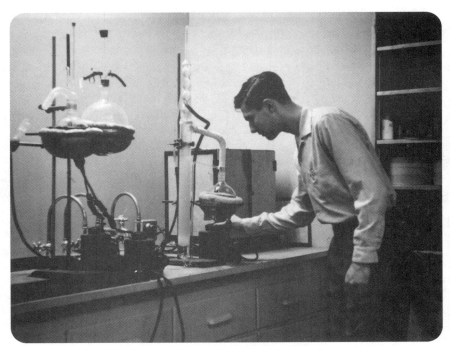

Elwood working in the lab about 1960

> *"Look! God's dwelling place is now among the people....*
> *'He will wipe every tear from their eyes. There will be no more death' or*
> *mourning or crying or pain, for the old order of things has passed away."*
> **Revelation 21:3-4**

2014-2017

It's strange how history tends to recall mostly bad news. In 2014, a new virus called Ebola erupted in West Africa and, with good reason, scared travelers worldwide. Starting in Ferguson, Missouri, "Black Lives Matter" became a national movement following video recordings of black men killed at the hands of white policemen. ISIS took control of parts of Syria and Iraq and ushered in a new era of violence and cruelty. Russia took advantage of regional unrest to seize Crimea in Ukraine and annexed the territory, stunning the western world. Finally, the ALS ice bucket challenge swept the nation as millions raised awareness and participated in this charity.

2014 was a year of major change at NOW. A new CEO, new CFO, new COO and new Chairman of the Board were significant changes for a family business used to longevity and continuity. Our CEO, Al Powers, retired and was replaced by Jim Emme, former COO. Al continued to work as a company ambassador to the industry, working part-time for the Natural Products Association and Vitamin Angels especially. Several senior managers were let go for various reasons and Elwood Richard, our founder, stepped down from his position as board chairman. One would think that business would suffer from so many changes, but actually sales and profits continued to grow. From 2011-2016 NOW's total sales increased double-digits every year, and profits exceeded expectations.

AN INTERESTING AWARD

On December 3, 2014, the website selfstorage.com ranked the top twelve power suburbs in the country. What is a "power" suburb is anyone's guess! Ratings were based on population size, per-capita income, unemployment rate and poverty level compared to the same info from 2010. We're still not at all sure why, but our home city of Bloomingdale, Illinois was chosen as #10 on the nationwide list. It helps that NOW is the largest employer in Bloomingdale and we have received repeated awards for employee care. Here's what the site noted, happily and surprisingly, highlighting our company:

"Not quite 30 miles west of Chicago, Bloomingdale scored especially well in two categories: the reduction in poverty and unemployment. NOW Foods, a major manufacturer of products for health food stores, is based in Bloomingdale." (http://moving.selfstorage.com/top-suburbs-in-us)

In April 2017, NOW received a new employee award from the *Daily Herald Business Ledger* and five other Illinois business groups. NOW was named as one of only 21 large Illinois businesses for the 2017 "Best Places to Work in Illinois" award. More info is at www.bestplacestoworkinil.com. This was on top of NOW earning a fourth consecutive national award as "Best and Brightest Companies to Work For" from the National Association for Business Resources (NABR) in 2016. We also won our tenth consecutive award as one of the "101 Best and Brightest Companies to Work For" in the Chicago area. Amazing and humbling actually. We do try to live by the good book when it says

"Do not take advantage of a hired worker who is poor and needy, whether that worker is a fellow Israelite or a foreigner residing in one of your towns." (Deuteronomy 24:14)

SNEAK ATTACK

Business is always evolving, but it's hard to prepare for unreasonable government actions. On February 3, 2015, the New York Attorney General Eric Schneiderman inflicted serious damage to the natural products industry, and four large firms in particular. GNC, Walmart, Walgreens and Target were caught by surprise when Schneiderman declared that a new and unknown testing method, DNA barcoding, is the new standard for testing herbs. He put out a media blitz featuring 390 total tests by a barcoding expert, which showed most herb products by these four retailers failed to either contain the herb listed on the label, or included undeclared contaminants. Schneiderman basically went to war with the natural products industry.

Very public cease-and-desist letters were sent to these large retailers demanding that they stop selling their house brands of Echinacea, Ginseng, St. John's Wort and other herbs. The Attorney General claimed that 79% of products failed testing and major news media picked up and ran with the story. Schneiderman did a marvelous job marketing how *"Mislabeled Consumer Products Pose Unacceptable Health Hazards"*. He cited support from a New York State Senator, a New York State Assembly Member, a Senior Nutritionist at the Center for Science in the Public Interest and a Professor of Pharmacological Sciences at Stony Brook University. Initially, the attack looked like a scientific slam-dunk win for consumers, and Mr. Schneiderman in particular.

As the industry prepared to defend itself, DNA barcoding experts came forward to shed new light on the subject. It turns out that DNA fingerprinting (barcoding) definitely helps to identify the right herbal species being tested, but it has very limited use for herbal extracts. The DNA test is just too new to work for extracts, and those were the products tested by the Attorney General. FDA itself issued a statement noting that the agency neither uses nor requires DNA barcoding and considered it not yet validated for herbal testing. It also came to light that Mr. Schneiderman's chief DNA barcoding expert, Dr. James A. Shulte of Clarkson University, is not really an expert at all. Dr. Schulte has a background in evolutionary biology and reptilian zoology, but is not considered an expert in botany, pharmacognosy, or natural product chemistry. Finally, the Attorney General, himself, has come under the microscope for his true intentions with this unscientific attack. Various media questioned his methods for gaining public exposure for this and other investigations, and whether his real intentions are more political in nature.

Regardless, companies such as GNC suffered financially from this witch hunt. GNC, alone, experienced significant sales declines in the herbal category and overall from lack of consumer confidence in supplements. GNC's share price fell dramatically from $48 in February 2015 to only $7 just over two years later! A black cloud affected the entire industry and lawyers lined up like sharks with new lawsuits. At NOW, we were only glad to be spared the direct negative exposure that hit GNC, as the entire affair seemed wrongly intentioned, unfair and untrue.

ESSENTIAL OIL DIFFUSERS

In 2013, NOW introduced our first ultrasonic essential oil diffuser. Our essential oil category had grown about 40% every year in recent years and customers began asking for a diffuser to help use the oils. Little did we know how big the market is! Initially NOW introduced one diffuser in 2013 and sales reached $600,000 in only four months. Not bad at all, and well above expectations. In 2014, NOW sold two different diffusers and sales leaped to be about $6 million. In 2015, with five diffusers available, NOW sold $16 million in this new craze. How did this happen so suddenly? And could this growth continue?

It turns out that multi-level marketers helped create and drive new markets and big sales. NOW first started selling essential oils in 1990, but sales really took off when the Young Living company became a significant seller. Young Living focused entirely on promoting essential oils and claiming that their very expensive oils were the "best essential oils on the planet". What else could they say given their seriously high prices! Young Living was the first big marketer to reach millions of consumers through a vast "distributor" network of consumers. Their pyramid-shaped commission structure tends to drive sales growth, but also forces high prices. In any event, the entire market boomed as people discovered how amazing and helpful essential oils can be.

Another MLM brand, dōTERRA, branched off from Young Living and started selling essential oils in 2008. In just two years, the company sold $100 Million and reportedly reached $1 Billion by 2017. Amazing growth, truly stunning. dōTERRA invented slick marketing terms like "therapeutic grade" essential oils to make it appear to be selling higher quality products, but NOW's comparative testing showed no differences in competing products. MLM brands often grow fastest by making claims that most brands know are illegal. dōTERRA received a warning letter from FDA in September, 2014 for marketing its products as possible treatments for cancer, Ebola and autism. In 2017, NOW essential oils continued growing to be the # 1 selling brand in the natural store channel, while diffusers began declining due to new competitors and mass markets.

RUMORS OF DEMISE...

The independent health food store has declined for years. Mass grocery, drug and chains like Walmart, Target, Walgreens and CVS gradually took the lion's share of vitamin business. The good old days of health food stores selling a high percent of vitamins in their market is long gone. GNC recognized this shift in 1998 and started opening over 2,000 stores within Rite Aid drugstores. NBJ (Nutrition Business Journal) reported in 2016 that 58% of the entire nutrition industry is now sold in mass markets. Costco stated in 2017 that it is the largest seller in the world of organic foods. And then there is Amazon. Who would have guessed that Amazon would exceed Google for product searches? Or that 36% of all Black Friday sales would be on Amazon? Or that Amazon is raking in more than 50% of all online sales growth! Independent health food stores would seem likely to follow the death of independent pharmacies and independent book stores. Except not really.

The *percentage* of vitamins and organic foods in independents has definitely declined as consumers have found more availability of natural products in their traditional grocery store, chain drug store or Walmart. Independents have also faced fierce competition from natural food chains such as Whole Foods, Vitamin Shoppe, GNC, Sprouts, Natural Grocers, Earth Fare and Fresh Thyme. These massive chains have collectively opened about one new store per day in recent years, putting the squeeze on the local independent store. To be sure, the number of independents have declined in recent years, but the survivors are stronger, smarter, more flexible, and better suited for long-term survival.

It helps that organic foods, natural supplements, sports and personal care products – the natural foods industry – has grown consistently for decades. Compared to other industries that squeak out 2% growth per year, the natural foods industry has been extremely blessed. Especially within the USA. NOW's percentage of sales to small, independent health food stores has declined significantly over the years, but our dollars sold to independents continues to climb. That's because the strong survivors have adapted and many of them are doing "brick & click" combo retailing. It's not easy for independents, and they need your support now more than ever, but many stores are doing quite well by providing a great combination of excellent service, superior quality, healthy products and good prices.

A REFUGE FOR REFUGEES

In 2017, NOW is home to just over 1,400 employees. Most of these workers are long-term employees who come from areas near our facilities, or who are drawn to our type of business. Having decent jobs to support a large family is life-changing for refugees, or anyone else for that matter. It has been a wonderful privilege to see the successes of former refugees, who develop into upstanding citizens and lead safe, healthy and fulfilling lives.

While Americans have struggled with the issue of refugees and security, Canadians have largely taken a different approach. Canadians have historically been more welcoming to immigrants and refugees, based upon the number of people Canada accepts relative to the total population. The country also has a private sponsorship program that allows private citizens to bring in refugees if they pay for their expenses. In 2016, NOW's Chairman of the Board was Jim Estill, CEO of Darby Appliances in Guelph, Ontario. Jim became wealthy as CEO of EMJ Data Systems and SYNNEX, while serving on various boards. As a result of the humanitarian crisis in Syria, Jim determined to put up $1.5 million of his own money to rescue more than 200 Syrian refugees. He organized a support system in his area that provided job and language training, healthcare, housing and all personal expenses for their first year in Canada. This made the news across the globe and is a wonderful example of a practical way to help strangers. As the good book says, "Do not neglect to show hospitality to strangers, for by this some have entertained angels without knowing it."

PIRACY

In 2017, NOW's international team developed significant business selling essential oils to Saudi Arabia. This was a nice surprise as we had never sold to the oil kingdom and had always been limited by regulations, labeling and the high cost of doing business. One day our partners there discovered pirated products that NOW doesn't even sell. They found five different NOW Solutions bar soaps, even though NOW does not sell bar soaps. Our logo, brand identity, labeling and images were perfect copies of our carrier oils, but the products were totally bogus. I suppose this is the price of success. Someone sees something that they like and simply decides to take what they want. Unfortunately for NOW, everyone in the world does not abide by "Thou shalt not steal." NOW was forced, again, to defend itself legally and call in the lawyers to address this trademark infringement.

DEATH OF OUR FOUNDER

Elwood Richard was our founder and patriarch. Unfortunately, Dad died April 7, 2017 and this was an emotional drain on the entire family and business. He was 85 years old and lived an incredible life. Elwood developed mesothelioma, a form of lung cancer that develops from asbestos exposure and is too well known today. He researched this condition and knew that this cancer would be terminal. After discussing conventional treatments, he started regular vitamin C injections of 50 grams and this seemed to help significantly. In his last year, Elwood wrote the following public article as advice to others, entitled: **Malignant Pleural Mesothelioma: My Personal Story and the Marlboro Men.**

Recently I have been diagnosed with mesothelioma, a disease caused by exposure to asbestos. My only exposure was 60 years ago when I used asbestos to insulate a lab furnace. I can't remember if I was warned to use a mask when working with asbestos, but did not. Mesothelioma has hampered my activities to where at the start of my treatments I was only able to walk 100 yards at a time. With a lot of time to think about why this happened to me, I thought of the Marlboro Men. Like me, they made choices with serious health consequences. I also thought about other health choices that we all need to consider.

Marlboro Men were rugged cowboy types who appeared in ads smoking Marlboros. At least four of those who appeared as Marlboro Men died of smoking-related diseases such as lung cancer and emphysema. Several relented of their association with Marlboro and became involved in anti-smoking campaigns. More information about them can be found by googling "Marlboro Man" and "Death in the West" — a 1976 documentary about the ailments in Marlboro Men.

Critics may wonder why the Marlboro Men were not aware of the association between smoking and lung cancer. After all, since 1953 the UK had required warning labels on cigarettes sold there. And certainly by 1964 when the Surgeon General declared that smoking increased the risk of lung cancer, this should have ended the discussion. However, the majority of Americans did not really believe this.....Don't dismiss possible threats to health that are life-threatening. Hoping this will lead to better health for you.

It is impossible to acknowledge what our founder meant to NOW. He was everything – literally – and then some. Elwood started NOW as a simple idea and a small dream. He worked tirelessly for almost 50 years, always generating left-field ideas, experimenting in business as if it was one big laboratory. And Elwood was always a true scientist at heart. He loved to work in the lab and find out what was new. He was always critical about what we could be doing better, whether in our labs or in sales or in production. Elwood Richard was truly one of a kind and we miss him dearly.

50 YEAR CELEBRATION

2018 is NOW's 50th golden anniversary and a significant achievement. There aren't many independent American family businesses that survive successfully for 50 years. Our industry is littered with family businesses from the past who couldn't do what NOW has done. Virtually every large natural vitamin company or organic food brand is owned by a different corporation than the family who started it. Business just isn't that easy, which is why we count our blessings every day.

We had fun brainstorming big ideas for how we could celebrate 50 years and make a big splash. Our marketing team came up with a variety of ideas and our board of directors came through by agreeing to provide $5 million in total funding! This is really amazing considering our history and struggles. Our board directed that these funds go towards four different areas: 1) NOW's charitable donations were up to about $2 million in 2017 and we planned to increase this to $3 million in 2018. 2) NOW will do some significant bonuses and gifts for employees. 3) NOW will provide extra marketing and discounts for health food store customers. 4) NOW will spend close to $2 million for consumer promotions and events – all extraordinary budget plans.

One big idea we had would be to spend roughly the full amount on a 30 second Super Bowl commercial. That would be as big of a splash as possible, but we decided pretty quickly that we didn't want to put all of our eggs into one basket. We also could triple our normal advertising, but that wouldn't be much fun and likely wouldn't generate the kind of excitement, or higher sales, that we were aiming for. We did come up with a lot of great ideas and here's a couple that, God willing, will reach customers in 2018.

Who doesn't remember and love Willy Wonka? Remember the golden tickets and what a craze that started? One idea we had was to market various significant prizes within our products and promote this on packaging and social media. Think $10,000 would get much attention? We did and looked into the legal rules for giving away prizes within our products. You've probably seen "No purchase necessary" signs by other brands for similar contests or sweepstakes. "No purchase necessary". Why? For some illogical reason, the U.S. does not make it easy for companies to give away prizes when a purchase is required. Does that make sense? Why does our government have rules for how to give away something for free after a purchase?

Another interesting idea was to promote independent, positive videos about NOW on YouTube. We discussed ways to engage consumers in a contest to get the most views on individual videos about our products. Again, the company could give substantial marketing rewards for videos that go viral with anything good about NOW! The company would need some approval process in order to avoid legal or safety concerns, while making sure the message is truly positive. What fun! What a great way to celebrate a rare golden business anniversary! What a way to ride off into the sunset. *"Consecrate the fiftieth year and proclaim liberty throughout the land to all its inhabitants. It shall be a jubilee for you."* *(Leviticus 25:10)*

"So then neither the one who plants nor the one who waters is anything, but God who causes the growth. Now he who plants and he who waters are one; but each will receive his own reward according to his own labor."
1 Corinthians 3:7-8

2018-2020

Just a few years seems like an eternity. While school shootings and hurricanes captured many headlines in 2018, nothing could compare with the world's dramatic changes that took place in 2020. No one could have imagined the effects that the coronavirus Covid-19 would have on the entire world. No nation was spared from the health crisis, nor the financial costs. People everywhere changed how they shop, when and where they travel, how they worked from home, how they social distanced and how life will never be the same. Amid the pandemic, NOW's 50th Anniversary capped a half-century of struggles, survival and success.

Life was good for NOW as 2018 began. The company had averaged 15% annual sales growth in the prior seven years and was well positioned to continue. Despite political concerns about tariffs from China, sales and profits kept increasing. We continued to win annual awards for employee care and continued to emphasize quality and safety as unbending top priorities. One family member left the family business and several more joined to get started. Change remained constant, either from new products, new equipment, new sub-brands, acquisitions and some big deals. For better or worse, NOW was beginning to feel and act much more like a big business.

WALMART COMES TO VISIT

In October 2018, NOW welcomed a special visit to our plant by eight executives from Walmart. We had been in discussions to sell some private label products, thanks to Bill Scaife, our broker, who used to work for Nature's Way. He was connected with Walmart buyers and helped with arrangements and introductions. We were quite surprised and impressed when their team flew in for the day in their private jet just for this meeting! We learned that Walmart's quality standards were higher than we expected and they were in process to remove objectionable ingredients such as magnesium stearate, artificial colors like titanium dioxide, tri-calcium phosphate and more from their Spring Valley private brand. Walmart also requires specific lab testing for potency, micro, heavy metals, disintegration, traceability and other things such as testing methods.

During our discussions, it became apparent that Walmart was also interested in buying some NOW brand products. Until this time, our NOW brand was always exclusively sold to natural food stores and prohibited from mass stores like Walmart. But the marketplace had become complicated as NOW sold to some store-within-a-stores such as HEB in Texas and Hy-Vee stores in Iowa. Also, Amazon moved mountains by becoming the world's biggest open market, and NOW had been selling direct to Amazon for nearly a decade.

So what's the difference between selling our brand to Amazon vs. Walmart? NOW brand was already widely sold on Walmart.com, even though that was not our intent. Well, for decades NOW had declared that our products were exclusive to the natural health food store channel and we had good reason for that 'line in the sand.' This caused internal debate about whether NOW should allow our brand to be sold in Walmart, including among our board of directors. Eventually, we decided to take baby steps and try limited skus, with differentiation such as custom sizes, to avoid direct comparisons with our independent customers. Two years later, mass sales like this remain well under 1% of NOW sales and we still prefer dealing direct with small store owners who are educated and passionate about natural products.

JIM EMME HEADS TO DC

In 2018, U.S. President Donald Trump called out China for unfair trade practices and intellectual property theft. A trade war began and both countries imposed tariffs ranging from 5-25% on each other. The U.S. imposed three separate tariffs in 2018 and another in 2019, affecting over $500 Billion of goods per year. China responded with its own tariffs at over $100 Billion per year and cut significant food imports from the U.S. The two global superpowers continued to publicly negotiate while the rest of the world anxiously watched and waited for a resolution to the problem.

Our company had a big interest in avoiding tariffs and keeping worldwide trade open. NOW exports to China are significant, and our purchases from there are critical. Products such as vitamin C and many other vitamins are made almost 100% in China alone. Every brand sources Vitamin C and most B-vitamins from China, since that is the only viable source worldwide. So when our CEO, Jim Emme, was invited by our trade group, Natural Products Association (NPA), to go to Washington regarding tariffs, he went without question.

Jim soon found himself regularly attending phone meetings and in-person meetings in Washington as part of an industry-tariff group. Some meetings included lower-level staffers, but other meetings included the very top levels of our government. One meeting from November 20, 2019 included three House Representatives and five Senators including two former presidential candidates, Rand Paul and Mitt Romney. Those are some serious movers and shakers and Jim found these meetings to be helpful to keep our natural products with as few tariffs as possible. At one phone meeting, President Trump himself joined briefly and Jim was quite surprised to be an insider at a meeting with such dignitaries!

Above Senator & former Presidential candidate Mitt Romney. Right photo is Senator Rand Paul with Jim Emme in both meetings in 2019.

TROUBLE FOR RETAILERS

As Amazon has grown over the years, many retail chains went out of business, unable to compete in the new retail world. Chains such as Toys-R-Us, Blockbuster Video, Borders Bookstores, Sports Authority and Radio Shack were mostly replaced by web suppliers who could deliver larger varieties at lower costs, and at amazing speeds. Other chains went bankrupt, but managed to stay afloat at least for the time being. This was the retail world before Covid-19, which knocked many retailers out of business for good.

Until 2020, the larger natural food chains were mostly immune to this type of trouble. Retailers such as Whole Foods Market, Sprouts, Natural Grocers and Fresh Thyme continued to grow and take market share from independents. Then over-expansion, debt and failing profits moved in to really affect these organic grocers. In early 2020, three major natural chains fell hard and fast. Fairway was a successful New York chain with 15 volume stores and over $600 Million in sales, but too much debt forced it to go Chapter 11 in May 2016 and again in January 2020. Earth Fare, based in Asheville NC, had 50 stores at its peak, but, suddenly and without notice, closed all stores in January 2020. Some stores did re-open under the same name, but it's hard for a retailer to overcome the stigma of being bankrupt. Then Lucky's Market announced it would close 32 stores and keep seven open with a different ownership group. Lucky's had been partners with Kroger to grow stores, but that marriage fell apart after too many losses and Lucky was also forced to declare bankruptcy in January 2020. What a bad month for the natural foods channel!

The biggest chain to fall was GNC, which declared bankruptcy in June 2020. GNC's first store opened in 1935 and it grew to become the dominant vitamin retailer with over 8,000 stores worldwide. But many stores were located in losing mall locations with high rents, causing GNC to sell 40% of shares to the Chinese Harbin Pharmaceutical Group in 2018. Covid-19 was the final knock-out blow as GNC couldn't weather the storm that no one could have predicted. The retailer may come out of bankruptcy leaner and stronger, but only time will tell. The most obvious lesson from almost all failing businesses is to stay out of debt. Investor money must look irresistible up front, but it's a common theme and biblical directive to avoid debt. *"If you have nothing with which to pay, even your bed will be taken from under you!"* (Proverbs 22:27)

NOW TESTS AMAZON-ONLY BRANDS

Generic brands are winning on Amazon and it's not always good. In our industry, we started noticing many vitamin brands that we had never heard of landing in top-spot search locations on Amazon. Many pseudo-brands launched "Sponsored" products, which are paid advertisements. These new marketers understood how to win on Amazon, with slick claims, paid search terms and optimized content. They are able to gain a profit despite amazingly low, actually too low, prices.

I suspected fraud when I noticed the expensive supplements seemed too good to be true. I found a number of brand-less products offerings of CoQ10 400mg potency in dry capsule form and knew that high-speed machines could not run this potency due to how sticky the ingredient is. These brand names were also foreign to me, so that was a second red flag. The third red flag were the prices, which were too-low-to-be-legit. So with a lab full of testing equipment, we decided to purchase a number of questionable products and assay these to find out.

Our first round of testing was completed in August 2017 and we found products as low as 30% in potency, some with excessive heavy metals and others with high microbial contamination. This was shocking, but not surprising at all. We reported the results to our Amazon buyer and tried to contact the brands directly, though this proved hard to do. We followed up with another round of testing in March 2018 and found that 7 out of 9 CoQ10 no-name brands failed potency tests. Some were close to label claim, two were above label claim (200 mg) and four brands had less than 30% of labeled potency. Clearly 'buyer beware' was appropriate for these unknown brands.

Later in 2018, we also tested a round of acetyl-l-carnitine and lavender oil brands, because we could guess through pricing that brands were cheating. We found about what we expected, and again reported all results to Amazon directly in hopes that it would take action to stop brands that mislabel or misrepresent natural products. On February 28, 2020, we conducted another round of CoQ10 testing and this time found five out of ten brands had potencies under 20% of label claims and every brand tested was below label potency. Two brands actually contained less than 1% of label claim! We decided to send our complete data to industry trade groups and the FDA directly, but still could not get the attention this deserved. We finally went public to various trade magazines and found several willing to report on this "exposé" using our data. You can find these results if you search online for articles in May 2020.

Although some of our family owners thought this was reckless and an invitation to be sued, we went public with all of our info because cheaters don't deserve to prosper. Low-potency, mislabeled vitamins harm everyone, including legit brands like NOW. As an industry leader, we also have a responsibility to help keep our industry clean and legal. While researching these brands, we stumbled on to a class action lawsuit (www.truthinadvertising.org) against most of these same brands for the product SAMe. Apparently it was becoming known that some new brands on Amazon were cheating, and lawyers were starting to become interested. So we decided to test these same brands of SAMe ourselves, assuming, again, that foul play was involved.

On March 10, 2020, NOW reported that ten different brands of SAMe tested at very low potencies and two actually contained zero SAMe. This is an expensive product, which people pay $30 or more per bottle. It's also an important supplement that people buy for a real benefit. How sad is it that some business people with no integrity can cheat and get rich quick? How sad that it is so easy to get away with too? And how sad that this continues long after we made our results public and shared the info with the FDA.

In July, 2020, we decided to test a new round of unknown brands on Amazon for the brain supplement phosphatidyl serine. This time we bought three bottles of each and did three different tests on each brand, two by our labs and one by an independent lab. We initially found that many products seemed to be intentionally mislabeled by implying higher potencies on the front of the label, but on the side stating "per 2 capsule serving size". Next, we found confusing labeling within the Supplements Facts panel, in order to deceive and yet defend against potency testing. Some brands also claimed to be 60-90% lower priced, per gram, than NOW brand on Amazon, so we were certainly suspicious from the beginning.

We tested 40 samples in total and found 42% of no-name brands contained less than 10% of label claim! That's shocking and sad. Yes, less than 10% potency and yet still widely sold on Amazon. 90% of these samples contained less than 85% of label claim and only two of these brands passed 100% label potency test. Once again, NOW shared these assay results with Amazon, the FDA, supplement trade group NPA, and the media to try to force changes and shut down these cheating brands.

Meanwhile, what should a consumer do who doesn't have resources to test potencies like NOW does? My recommendation is "buyer beware" and avoid unknown brands of supplements that you don't find in natural food stores.

COVID-19 CHANGES THE WORLD!

On Dec 31, 2019, China reported to the World Health Organization (WHO) a cluster of pneumonia cases in Wuhan and this was later termed the novel coronavirus. The WHO named this new virus 'Covid-19' because it is genetically related to the deadly SARS virus from 2003. The WHO next declared on March 11, 2020 that this new problem is a worldwide pandemic, a term rarely used. It was last used, and overused, in 2009 regarding the H1N1 swine flu, which proved to be not as deadly as the WHO predicted. Within this context, many world governments were intentionally slow to aggressively take action, assuming that this virus would just go away soon enough on its own.

The natural foods industry had a seismic shock on March 2, 2020 when the Natural Foods Expo West show cancelled just two days before it was to start. This convention in Anaheim was typically a gigantic event with about 80,000 attendees, including many from overseas. People were in shock that our business lives could be so unsettled, and so quickly. This was before virtually anyone in the U.S. wore a face mask or even limited their travel. Boy did we underestimate the changes that would come!

A few days later we learned that our business would be one of the main beneficiaries from this epidemic. Monday March 9, 2020, started a dramatic shock in demand that we could not handle. Demand for that week more than tripled, with many products like zinc, vitamin C and elderberry selling up to a year's supply in one week. What happened in such a short period of time to cause so much change? On March 1, 2020 there were less than 100 total cases of Covid-19 in the U.S. On March 9, the U.S. reported over 700 cases and 26 deaths. America was changing by the hour and there was no end in sight. When the NBA suspended the basketball season on March 11, everyone knew that life was not about to be normal anytime soon.

One of NOW's senior scientists, Dr. Rick Sharpee, proved to be very valuable because of his past experience with coronavirus. Rick had written his thesis decades earlier at the University of Nebraska as part of his discovery of coronavirus in cattle. He had also published an article in the medical journal Lancet predicting coronaviruses in people. Unfortunately, his predictions proved to be true and Rick shared his extensive knowledge with NOW customers on February 19, 2020.

By the end of October, eight million people in the U.S. had the virus and over 200,000 died. Worldwide the numbers were much worse, and still accelerating. Who could have guessed that global commerce, healthcare, daily work, travel and personal habits could change so much, and so soon? Who could have guessed that every customer at the local Walmart would be required to wear a face mask and keep proper six-foot social distancing? Who could have predicted that most office workers would change to work remotely at home or that churches would only offer online services? The effects on national debts are staggering, but the loss of lives is even more irreplaceable.

Like many "essential" businesses, NOW struggled mightily to meet the new demand. We asked our employees to work overtime and even had office workers on the line in both production and shipping. We outsourced nearly two billion caps and tabs to approved vendors to help make more needed supplies. We hired as many new workers as possible. We changed our production plans to make long runs of "immune-related" products, but soon found that we had hundreds of products with crazy demand. Customers started making more homemade sanitizers, so our pure almond oil and vegetable glycerin leaped in sales. For whatever reason, our dried milk powder went up about ten times normal amounts. America was on a buying binge of toilet paper, hand sanitizers, hand soap, thermometers, baking goods and home office equipment. Customers also wanted any kind of product that might increase their immune system.

It feels bad to celebrate our growing successes while so many people were laid off from work and struggling to make ends meet. But part of our company's mission is to help people to live healthier lives, and this was a time when our products could really make a difference. Some product demands were incredible. Amazon placed a single order for over 100,000 bottles of N-Acetyl-l-Cysteine tabs and we were not remotely capable of making so much product with so little notice. We didn't anticipate at all that this particular product would be in such demand. As different supply countries shut down, we found it difficult to source products from India, China and elsewhere for months. Our maple syrup vendor even ran out of supplies and had to scramble. Our total demand basically doubled overnight and stayed that way.

For sales and profits, these were the best of times at NOW. For service, supply, stress and fill rate it was a disaster. Our corporate goal is usually to ship 96% of what customers order and most of 2020 ended up closer to only 60%. Even though we managed to manufacture 40% more goods than in 2019, we still could not catch up to the insatiable customer demand. We did make longer-term plans to increase production units, but not in time for the 2020 Covid-19 gold rush. No one knows how long this will last, or what to expect in 2021 and the future. The folks at NOW aim to continue supplying as many health products as possible, and at our usual great values.

BIG & BIGGER

Crain's Chicago Business published an interesting list of "Chicago's Largest Privately Held Companies" on April 20, 2020. Each company submitted 2019 sales numbers, which are generally private and not well known. Some top well-known brands in Illinois included Aldi in Batavia, Ace Hardware in Oak Brook, Jewel-Osco in Itasca, and True Value Hardware in Chicago. 353 companies were highlighted, with information on each including sales, sales growth in 2019, number of employees and type of business. Imagine our surprise to find NOW at # 106, especially since this was the first time we had ever provided our sales data. We still like to think of ourselves as a small, Mid-west supplier, but the numbers say otherwise. NOW reported sales in 2019 at $634 Million and 11% sales growth.

The real shocker is how NOW compared to more famous companies that are smaller in sales. The Chicago Cubs baseball team listed sales at $471 Million and 4% growth. The Chicago Bears football team reported $453 Million, the Chicago Bulls basketball team $301 Million and the Chicago White Sox baseball team $285 Million. NOW not only was revealed to be much larger than all of these famous sports brands, but our sales growth rate doubled the best of these. To top it off, NOW's sales were more than the Bulls and White Sox combined, which is really eye-opening. While we are excited by these numbers, we also remember many warnings about pride, including *"When pride comes, then comes disgrace, but with humility comes wisdom." (Proverbs 11:2)*

FAMILY EXPANSION

By the end of 2020, a number of 4th generation family members started working at NOW or Fruitful Yield stores. This is a direct result of Elwood Richard's legacy of encouraging family members to work in the family business. He thought it would be a good way to keep kids busy, and what better place to work than the family business. This has worked very well, similar to an internship, as a way for our young people to learn how to be productive. Our Family Council helped to set up hiring rules, which guides fairness issues in hiring and promotions. Young family shareholders are offered temporary jobs during school years and are basically treated the same as other workers. We've been happy to include Sarah, Maddy, Gina, Michelle, Nolan, Max, Sam, Tim and Faith with part-time work. We also have a professional route for those who intend to make working at NOW their long-term career. In 2020, Adam and Nathan both started full-time work at NOW after working part-time for several years. Below is a picture of shareholders at a meeting in 2019.

NOW ARENA!

There is an 11,000 seat arena in Hoffman Estates near NOW's Illinois facilities that opened in 2006. Sears corporate offices were located nearby and bought the naming rights for this venue to be called "Sears Centre." In 2018, Sears declared bankruptcy and we had the vision of taking over the naming rights of this building. I contacted the Village and pursued this as a project because it was more and more obvious that Sears would not be around that long to keep their name on the building. In 2019 and 2020, Sears continued to decline and the Village began warming up to NOW as a viable naming partner.

We began seriously negotiating in early 2020 and received Village legal approval at a public meeting on June 23, 2020. The deal was very agreeable and the Village never even sought out competitive bids for naming rights. NOW paid a fair price for up to 15 years to have our brand name all over this building. Our employees will certainly benefit by getting free tickets to many types of entertainment. We hope that this deal will be a 'win-win' partnership, but of course this all happened in the middle of Covid-19 when no one was attending any big group events. The Arena has hosted about 500,000 people per year to all kinds of sporting events, entertainment, motivational speakers and graduation ceremonies. What happens in the future is still unknown, but our long-term business plans include the NOW Arena and we think this public notoriety will be good for our brand. *"Let this be written for a future generation, that a people not yet created may praise the Lord." (Psalm 102:18)*

POEMS
BY ELWOOD RICHARD

The poems on the following pages were written by Elwood Richard, the founder of NOW Foods. Many of these poems are based on familiar children's nursery rhymes. They are meant to be humorous, but at the same time are intended to illustrate a point about health.

Elwood officially retired as president of NOW at the beginning of 2005, but he was still highly involved in the industry and NOW. El's passion continued to be health and he lived an active life while carefully watching his diet. He had more time to travel with his wife, Betty, and be involved with his five grandchildren.

El hopes you enjoy the poems and keep in mind the good-natured fun he intended.

Elwood Richard 2003

TV advertising affects all of us, but hopefully we can put it into a rational context. It doesn't pay to advertise wholesome, unprocessed, low cost foods as the margins are too low. It is the junk food with sweet treats, salty snacks, and fluffed up cereals with a special prize in the box that have enough margin to carry the cost of advertising.

Generally we know what is involved in a good diet, but we are drawn into the idea that somehow we are missing out on something wonderful and absolutely necessary in order to have a full life. A few, like Mary in this poem, will listen to good advice for their health.

MARY, MARY, NOT QUITE CONTRARY

Mary, Mary, quite contrary,
Why use those junk foods so?
With fries and pies that supersize
And greasy things all in a row?

Then said Mary, quite contrary,
"I saw their ads on TV.
I'd have no fun 'til I'd begun
The junk foods that they made for me."

But Mary, Mary, quite contrary,
You've got things in reverse.
What fun is there when you compare
Your health when it's very much worse?

And Mary, Mary, quite contrary,
Junk foods will make you sad.
For they create such excess weight
You'll rue every bite that you've had.

Mary, Mary, not contrary,
Went to her health food store.
She bought the things that Nature brings
And now she has good health galore.

For many years our former IT director had smoked three packs of cigarettes a day. His family, including his little girl, saw an anti-smoking message on TV in which a little girl asked this question of her father. Later his own little girl got in his lap and asked him the same question. He told her he was quitting and wasn't going to die. He threw out all his cigarettes and has never smoked since.

DADDY WHEN YOU GONNA DIE?

Copyright ©2000 Elwood Richard

A smoking message on TV
Had a small girl on her dad's knee.
This little girl 'bout three feet high
Asked, "Daddy, when you gonna die?"

And later on in that same day
My own girl came, I thought to play,
Sat on my knee, asked with a sigh,
"Oh Daddy, when you gonna die?"

I only could look helplessly
When my small girl looked up at me.
I couldn't think of a reply
To "Daddy, when you gonna die?"

I started back when in high school.
We thought "safe-to smoke" the rule.
I never thought I'd be a guy
To answer "Dad, when will you die?"

And later on when I knew more,
I realized the chance in store,
But thought it would to me apply-
Not one who asked, "When will you die?"

I'd thought about it quite a bit.
For many times I'd tried to quit.
The question now was real close by
'Bout "Daddy, when you gonna die"?

I knew that I could smoke no more.
There was no other answer for
The look in my child's solemn eye
And question, "Dad, when will you die?"

Later when inclined to smoke.
I'd think of how my daughter spoke,
Then firmly could this thought deny
Remembering. "Dad, when will you die?"

When friends that smoke will try and fail,
They need a thing to help prevail
A thing on which they could rely
A thought like "Daddy, will you die?"

Quite a bit of research has been done on using xylitol products to reduce tooth decay. An article in The Journal of Dental Hygiene, Vol. 76, Fall 2002 contains this information.

"Xylitol is a naturally occurring sweetener which is essentially not fermentable by the caries-inductive oral microflora." (This means that decay causing bacteria can't use it) .. " the oral health benefits of xylitol can most easily be attributed to its interference with the metabolism and adherence of S.mutans and other cariogenic bacteria" (This means that xylitol disrupts the chemical reactions in decay negating bacteria and their ability to stick to the teeth). "With habitual xylitol use there is a shift in the bacterial flora to a xylitol-tolerant population... (which) tend to be harmless." (This means that the amount of decay causing bacteria becomes less with regular xylitol use.)

XYLITOL TOOTHPASTE
A POEM YOU CAN SINK YOUR TEETH INTO

Most of us seek to have good teeth
So bright on top and strong beneath.
We can assist you in your quest
To share a smile that looks its best.

Yes, we have one that's good for all,
It's fluoride free with xylitol.
Just use it carefully each day
To help prevent your teeth's decay.

Xylitol makes a deadly schism
In every oral microorganism,
And they're the ones that activate
The stuff that makes tooth health abate.

Xylitol toothpaste does the trick
To help a smile through thin and thick.
So run down to your health food store
For healthy teeth and smiles galore.

Many believe that the modern way is the fast food way, and those that abstain from this are "health nuts". The movie "Supersize Me" shows what can happen to those on a fast food diet.

FAST FOOD GUY

Copyright © 2000 Elwood Richard

Big fast food guy, each day walks by
My fruit and yogurt hut.
Says to my face, "You big disgrace,
You are a health food nut."

And when I say that's not okay,
It makes him pleased as punch.
He says it's rude to spurn good food,
Like Taco Bell for lunch.

He says "health nut" is slander but,
Appropriately applied.
For each one knows all food that grows,
Is better deep fat-fried.

He is so bad, it makes me mad
To call my food so funky.
So next day I make my reply
"You big bad fast food junky.

"Your stomach noise can scare small boys.
A mess is your complexion.
Your body weight is much too great;
Your mind a vast perplexion."

"I'll bet you if, you great big stiff,
You use my food ten days,
Your stomach would feel twice as good,
And clear your brain and gaze."

I thought the guy would never try,
My smoothies and my diet.
He said to me if it was free,
He'd be the first to try it.

Now each day we contentedly,
Eat yogurt, nuts, and fruit.
The guy that I gave my reply,
Became a health recruit.

The way the average person looks at things is a continual puzzle. People are so careful to look at the label on pet food to be sure it contains everything needed for pet health. They also look after plants carefully with pruning, special pest controls and fertilizers. Their car is well maintained too. They know to check fluid transmission levels, use quality oil and change it regularly, and to use a good grade of gasoline.

People do this because they know this preserves the health of their plants, pets, car, etc. You would think people would see a pattern in this and apply this same concept to personal nutrition. Instead they listen to commercials that tell them to "go for the gusto" and that if indigestion results, they can take a pill for that.

Somewhere along the way (like Babe Ruth at the end of his career) one needs to take care of oneself. Often it is too late, and one reaps the health one has planted.

REAPING WHAT IS PLANTED

Copyright ©2000 Elwood Richard

We drive with care and check the air
In tires and use the latest
Oil that's high test and buy the best;
We really want the greatest.

When planting plants, we take no chance
With cheaper fertilizer.
We really try the best to buy
Because we think it's wiser.

We don't forget to ply each pet
With foods, they think suspicious.
And spare no care to fuel their hair
With elements nutritious.

But we all choose fast foods to use
All sugar, salt, and greasy,
And dare to say, this is okay
Because it is so easy.

But when our health requires some wealth
Were kind of slow to try it.
Most earnestly, we hate that we
Are limited by diet.

No use to whine as we decline
That fairness wasn't granted.
Though cars are swell; and pets excel;
We've reaped what we have planted.

WEIRD STUFF

When visitors stay at our house
And see the cooking of my spouse,
They think within, "It's as I feared.
The stuff these health folks serve is weird."

The first thing that they often see
Is that we offer herbal tea.
We appetitze with stone ground chips
Accomp'ned by her yogurt dips.

The salad has a wild array
Of colored greens put on display.
The dressing from a recipe
That my spouse has designed for me.

And when they try to make more sweet
The food they shortly plan to eat,
The sugar bowl's not there to see
Just syrup from a maple tree.

The main course could be lentil soup
Great for a late incoming group.
With this, I favor cakes of rice
The soy sauce flavor is quite nice.

If rolls are served, they can't be white.
Whole wheat the kind that seems just right.
The spread my wife selects will oft
Be mixed with oil to keep it soft.

The rice will have a shade of brown
And tends to cause our guests to frown.
Dessert could be her pumpkin bread
Or fruit with yogurt served instead.

The visitors don't understand
This weird stuff which my spouse has planned.
But when they try it they relate
That my wife's weird stuff's really great.

My wife was working at our health food store in Lombard and did wait on a customer who bought large amounts of supplements for his dogs. Although my wife (I substituted "counter guy" in the poem to make it rhyme) did raise the points in the poem, the pet owner actually walked out of the store shaking his head at the idea of using those items that were good for his dogs. The poem shows how things should have turned out. Items that local dog breeders and owners have used to improve pets health have included kelp powder, alfalfa powder, bone meal, yeast, lecithin, soy granules, wheat germ and many others.

At the start of the health industry, by-products were used by farm animals including blackstrap molasses, whey, lecithin, bran, and wheat germ. Because these were by-products, the price was very low. As farmers began to appreciate the value of these items, the price went up and eventually researchers found that they had nutritional values that were helpful to humans too.

THE WONDROUS WISE MAN
Copyright © 2000 Elwood Richard

There was a man in our town,
We thought was wondrous wise.
He went in for health foods galore
Where he bought health supplies.

It made you smile to see his pile
Of powders, pills and such.
The counter guy let out a cry,
"How can you use so much?"

The wise man said with face quite red,
"How stupid can you get?
The stuff you see is not for me,
It's only for my pet.

I must relate, my dog looks great
And thrives on what you see.
He goes to shows, the town all knows,
And earns a lot for me.

I use a plan with kelp and bran
To make his coat to shine.
This photo shows how my dog glows;
Are other dogs so fine?

He has a feast on brewer's yeast
Which fills my dog with pep.
One can't believe or quite conceive,
How sprightly is his step."

The counter man again began,
"Because your dog looks swell,
So likely you use health foods too,
To help your looks as well."

The man we all thought to be wise,
Said, "Everybody knows
I own the pet and don't forget
I don't compete in shows."

"I must pursue my point of view,"
Replied the counter guy,
"If it puts pep in a dog's step,
It should be worth a try."

And when he saw what he had done,
With all his might and mane.
The man grew wise, got more supplies,
Since now the facts were plain.

SPROUTS

In 1999, there was an outbreak of sickness from alfalfa sprouts in the Madison, Wisconsin area. Herb Bostrum, Director of the Bureau of Communicable Diseases, was in charge of gathering information that led agricultural officials to recommend that people should not eat sprouts. Fearing that sprouts could be banned, we wrote Mr. Bostrum to recommend a method for producing safe sprouts using a citric acid rinse. We furnish free information about sprouting safely and recipes available at your health food store.

USDA information shows that sprouting increases the total food values in mung beans as follows: Vit A 102%, thiamin 175%, riboflavin 400% and niacin 147%. Vitamin C increases from not detectable in the seeds to more than many fruits and vegetables including apples, beets, carrots, sweet corn, and peaches. Depending on the time harvested, the seeds increase in weight about 800%.

The herbivores at Lincoln Park Zoo in Chicago were once fed a supplement to their diets by sprouts which the zoo raised, to assure that their expensive animals would remain in good health.

SPROUT DOUBT
Copyright © 2000 Elwood Richard

When Mr. Bostrum had his doubts
That benefits occurred from sprouts,
We had to send a note to say,
"You should not take our sprouts away."

Though his reports showed sprouts were bad,
We sent the best info we had.
It showed a rinse with mild citrate
Made sprouts look good, and tasted great.

Sprout cost is small you must agree;
Their use is great economy.
Fresh vegetables are rarely found
At merely pennies to the pound.

Sprouting raises values in
B-1, B-2, and niacin
In seeds you can't find any C
But when seeds sprout, the C will be

There's not another food that could
Be fresh and wholesome and so good,
And we know sprouts are useful to
The herbivores at Lincoln Zoo.

Please note the things we have to say,
And do not take our sprouts away.
We hope that we have said enough
To show how much we need this stuff.

HUMPTY DUMPTY

Humpty Dumpty sat on a wall.
Humpty Dumpty had a great fall.
All the kings' men were surprised when they found
Humpty unbroken. He rose with a bound.
Humpty was careful and used every day
NOW Bone Strength pills to prevent shell decay

JACK WAS NIMBLE

Jack was nimble, Jack was quick
Glucosamine had done the trick

CHLOROPHYLL

Why reeks the goat on yonder hill
Who daily dotes on chlorophyll?
I think that I can tell you how.
The brand he ate was not from NOW.

One of our managers used to go to grade schools and give a talk about the problems with the high sugar intake in the USA. Including the corn sugar sweeteners, it is over 140 lbs. per person per year.

Part of her demonstration was to pour level teaspoons of sugar into a clear glass cup and ask the students to raise their hands when the level in the glass reached the amount in a standard Coke and a Twinkie. She found that it was 22 teaspoonfuls, or about 3 ounces (85 grams). The students had all raised their hands well before she reached this amount. The little boy in the poem really did throw out his lunch. He had been sent to school with only a Coke and Twinkies for lunch.

TWINKIES AND A COKE
Copyright ©2000 Elwood Richard

One speaker we would often send
To grade schools so she could extend
Nutrition they could comprehend.

She used a cup to demonstrate,
In hopes that they'd eliminate
The sugars in the food they ate.

With just a Twinkie and a Coke
She'd demonstrate the things she spoke,
And made it clear to those small folk.

She wanted all the class to guess
The sugar content of this mess
'Twas eighty grams, but all thought less.

She said the people living here
Will eat two thirds of their weight each year
And cause good health to disappear

One boy stood up, so far from trim
He left the room; his smile was dim.
This was the same lunch given him

The little boy came back to say
He would not be at lunch that day,
He just had thrown his lunch away.

TIES (BRAIN CIRCULATION)

The main problem with neck ties is that blood flow to the brain is reduced because the tie and collar press on the arteries to the brain. The best solution is not to wear a tie or to make certain that it is not too tight.

Especially as we get older, we need all the support we can for our brains and some supplements can be helpful. Gingko biloba will increase blood flow to the brain and bioflavonoids increases the circulation through small capillaries. Lecithin, at a level of 10 grams per day, and ginseng at 1000 mg per day can also be helpful.

TIES

We use man's ties to put in place
Some quite nice patterns 'neath his face.
We think the habit is okay
Because it will high style convey.

But now the facts have been made plain.
Ties slow the blood-flow to the brain.
I used to wear ties all the time.
But now it's like white-collar crime.

However did this habit start?
Was it a clothier very smart?
What likely made this habit grow
Was excess cloth and greed for dough.

Except for show, it has no use;
At least not one we can deduce.
Ties cannot open foods that's canned
Or help to clean a dirty hand.

Ties won't hold parcels on a bike
Or anything athletic like.
The only thing they're useful for
Is making wearer's necks get sore.

In summer when it's very hot
Ties do not cool you off a lot.
That is a time a man soon finds
He really knows that tie that binds.

Now to conclude ties don't make sense.
They slow blood flow and add expense,
What wearing ties now really means
The wearer reads men's magazines.

Visit our family of websites

nowfoods.com
nowfoodsinternational.com
nowsportsproducts.com
protocolforlife.com
betterstevia.com
fruitfulyield.com
puresource.ca

The Peaches Dann Mysteries
by Elizabeth Daniels Squire

"HOW CAN PEACHES BE A DETECTIVE IF SHE CAN'T REMEMBER ANYTHING? The feisty but absentminded sleuth is . . . practical, funny, charming, middle-aged—and memorable!"

—Sharyn McCrumb

Who Killed What's-Her-Name?

When Peaches discovers her Aunt Nancy's body floating in a fish pond—and suspects that she herself was the intended victim—she must commit the clues to memory . . . and find out who committed the deed . . .

Remember the Alibi

It looked like a series of suicides. But Peaches notices a suspicious pattern—and fears that her own father might be next on the list of victims. Now she has to make sure this clever killer doesn't make dear old Dad nothing but a memory . . .

Memory Can Be Murder

A nasty young man with a penchant for verbal abuse is found dead. It's up to Peaches to figure out who took confrontation a fatal step further . . .

"ELIZABETH DANIELS SQUIRE HAS A REAL WINNER HERE. TIE A STRING AROUND YOUR FINGER AND REMEMBER HER NAME!"

—Margaret Maron

MORE MYSTERIES FROM THE
BERKLEY PUBLISHING GROUP . . .

DOG LOVERS' MYSTERIES STARRING HOLLY WINTER: With her Alaskan malamute Rowdy, Holly dogs the trails of dangerous criminals. "A gifted and original writer." —Carolyn G. Hart

by Susan Conant

A NEW LEASH ON DEATH   A BITE OF DEATH
DEAD AND DOGGONE   PAWS BEFORE DYING

DOG LOVERS' MYSTERIES STARRING JACKIE WALSH: She's starting a new life with her son and an ex–police dog named Jake . . . teaching film classes and solving crimes!

by Melissa Cleary

A TAIL OF TWO MURDERS   SKULL AND DOG BONES
DOG COLLAR CRIME   DEAD AND BURIED
HOUNDED TO DEATH   THE MALTESE PUPPY
FIRST PEDIGREE MURDER

CHARLOTTE GRAHAM MYSTERIES: She's an actress with a flair for dramatics— and an eye for detection. "You'll get hooked on Charlotte Graham!" —*Rave Reviews*

by Stefanie Matteson

MURDER AT THE SPA   MURDER ON THE SILK ROAD
MURDER AT TEATIME   MURDER AT THE FALLS
MURDER ON THE CLIFF   MURDER ON HIGH

BILL HAWLEY UNDERTAKINGS: Meet funeral director Bill Hawley—dead bodies are his business, and sleuthing is his passion . . .

by Leo Axler

FINAL VIEWING   DOUBLE PLOT
GRAVE MATTERS

PEACHES DANN MYSTERIES: Peaches has never had a very good memory. But she's learned to cope with it over the years . . . Fortunately, though, when it comes to murder, this absentminded amateur sleuth doesn't forgive and forget!

by Elizabeth Daniels Squire

WHO KILLED WHAT'S-HER-NAME?   REMEMBER THE ALIBI
MEMORY CAN BE MURDER

HEMLOCK FALLS MYSTERIES: The Quilliam sisters combine their culinary and business skills to run an inn in upstate New York. But when it comes to murder, their talent for detection takes over . . .

by Claudia Bishop

A TASTE FOR MURDER   A DASH OF DEATH

MEMORY
CAN BE
MURDER

Elizabeth Daniels Squire

BERKLEY PRIME CRIME, NEW YORK

MEMORY CAN BE MURDER

A Berkley Prime Crime Book / published by arrangement with the author

PRINTING HISTORY
Berkley Prime Crime edition / June 1995

ISBN: 0-425-14772-X

Berkley Prime Crime Books are published
by The Berkley Publishing Group,
200 Madison Avenue, New York, NY 10016.
The name BERKLEY PRIME CRIME and the BERKLEY PRIME CRIME
design are trademarks belonging to Berkley Publishing Corporation.

PRINTED IN THE UNITED STATES OF AMERICA

10 9 8 7 6 5 4 3 2

Acknowledgments

I'd like to thank everyone who has contributed to the further empowerment of Peaches Dann. Sometimes I think she has more friends than I do; what's done right in this chronicle is due to those helpers. Whatever may be wrong is probably due to the fact that Peaches or I couldn't remember.

Special thanks to:

Bonnie Blue, talented sculptor, poet, and puppeteer, who created a wizard puppet that inspired Ann's wizard.

The North Carolina Crime Writers, who organized a trip to the state crime labs, where I learned some criminal ins and outs about plastic bags.

The New York Zoological Society herpetologist who, several years ago, put a rattlesnake through its paces while I took notes. This was originally meant to be used in a short story, but wound up between these covers.

My neighbor Dan Harwood, for mountain snake stories.

Tom Morrissey, former sheriff of Buncombe County, for material about marijuana growers.

Detective Pat Hefner of the Buncombe County Sheriff's Department, for material about cults.

Carrie Lovelace (whom we shall miss), for mountain herb lore.

Lisa Franklin, for her rosemary recipe, and lots of other help.

Dershie McDevitt, Peggy Parris, Geraldine Powell, Virginia Sampson, and Florence Wallin, my much-valued writing group, for wonderful suggestions.

Robert and Yana Livesay, who also gave useful suggestions.

Worth Squire, the poet, who can always supply the right word.

Pat Dunton, for a few ideas about Jungian analysts.

Monika Wengler and Sue Kensil, who can spell.

Sis Cheshire, my cousin, who has endless memory-trick suggestions.

Laura Gilman, my editor, and Luna Carne Ross, my agent, without whom this book might not have been.

And Chick Squire, my husband, mainstay, and fountain of good ideas.

CHAPTER

1

"I'm scared." The voice on the telephone wavered. "Maybe I'm losing my mind."

Actually, how not to lose things is something I know a lot about. That and how to find them. Learned the hard way. But I mean objects, like my glasses. Lost minds are not my field of expertise.

"Go away," I wanted to say. "I haven't had my coffee. It's 8:30 in the morning. I have plans for the weekend."

I'd just waved goodbye to my ever-loving husband, Ted, and sat down at the kitchen table. I looked forward to a leisurely cup of coffee and then, after that, I planned four undisturbed days to put the finishing touches on my book: *How to Survive Without a Memory.*

You see, after fifty-five years with unpredictable spaces between my little gray cells, I'm an expert. I have a coping trick for every occasion. I have a publisher and I'm just doing the last rewrite. I want to finish.

Out the kitchen window a robin pulled a worm from the

green lawn, which was great for the robin, but not so hot for the worm. Life is like that.

"You do remember me, don't you?" the frightened voice begged. "I'm Cousin Clothilde's daughter Anne, from Winston-Salem. I did a puppet show when you came to visit, back when I was a kid."

The fog lifted a little: I saw a pretty child and puppets that made me laugh, though Cousin Clothilde, this girl's mama, was fierce uptight.

"What makes you think you're losing your mind?" I asked. "You sound sane."

"I hope it's just me being foolish," she said, "but I think someone wants to kill my Sam with black magic." Could I have heard that right?

"I'm Mrs. Sam Newman now." I needed to remember her new name. With her New Man Sam, should she be on the lam or they'd get in a jam? I visualized that. I could remember his name that way. Pictures, rhymes, and puns are a gal's best friends.

"I'm here in the mountains," she said. "Not far. Do you know where Bloodroot Creek Road is?"

"Yes."

"I'm staying at the place right at the end. I'll meet you out on the road by the mailbox. Please come quick."

"I will," I said, "because it sounds to me like I need to hear about this in person." If she was out of her mind, I could tell it better with my eyes helping my ears. Why can't I just say no?

I took my pocketbook with the shoulder strap off the hook where it lives when it's not on my shoulder. (See *Hang-Ons* chapter in *How to Survive*.) I felt for my key ring, which stays snapped inside the pocketbook except when I'm driving. You have to be crafty if you're totally absentminded or else you spend your whole time looking for stuff. At least it was a lovely day for a ride, sunshiny with blue sky and the mountains shimmery green.

I found Anne standing nervously by the road in a yard full

of huge old trees, in front of a strange Victorian house. Half of that house glowed fresh-paint white. The other half was gray with peeling paint. The dividing line was vertical. Even the funny Victorian tower on top was half gray, half white. The front door was bright red with brass carriage lamps on each side. Something wild was certainly bound to happen in a place like that.

Anne was unusual, too. A pretty girl with almond-shaped eyes and arched eyebrows that lifted up at the outer edge. She had long brown hair and an unpainted oval face, like my grandma in her wedding-day picture, and wore a long skirt and a long-sleeved, scoop-necked blouse that would have looked right on Grandma. She put her fingers to her lips and said, "Wait."

She pulled me off into an old springhouse at the side of the driveway. Dark water filled a long stone trough along one side. Thick stone walls were waist-high, with square-cut logs notched together above that. A fine place for secrets. No windows. Slits of bright light shone through the narrow spaces in between the logs. Otherwise the room was shadowy, and cool for June here in the Carolina mountains. Through the wall slits I could smell honeysuckle baking in the sunshine. Nice.

Ted would have asked, "What's going on?" right off. But I figured Anne was shy. The creep-up-on-the-subject type. Glad of the shadows that made her face hard to read.

"I called you," she said softly, "because my mother said that you might help out if we got in any kind of trouble up here. I don't usually do what my mother says. I'm nineteen, and I'm married." She raised her chin as she said that, with plenty of ginger. "But, you see," she said, going minor, "I'm prone to catastrophes. I just naturally have bad luck." She said that with drama, with both hands open as if she held an invisible ball of trouble. "But I was so sure things were going to be better after I married Sam, and they have been—until now. . . ."

"Does Sam think something is wrong here, too?" I said, encouraging her to get to the point.

"Oh, that's part of the problem," Anne said, hugging herself like she was cold. "That's why we can't leave. Sam thinks the greatest chance of his career is here. Sam's an artist, and he wants to paint Revonda Roland. That's the woman we're working for. And I want Sam to have his chance." She raised her chin again. There was spunk in this girl, scared or not.

"Where does black magic come in?" I had to know that!

"Revonda's son, whose name is Paul, has books about magic." Anne's voice wavered again. "He told me so, though I haven't seen them. He keeps his room locked. Plus he told Sam something bad would happen if we stayed here. He said this place killed people."

Well, a girl with imagination would certainly see black magic in all that.

I noticed two large black spiders lurking in webs in a corner as if to give the right atmosphere. Another ran across the floor. I try not to be scared of spiders. Scared. Did Paul want to scare off Anne and Sam?

"Sam's a genius." Anne's eyes shone with pride. "He just hasn't been discovered yet." She paused and stared at the spiders. "Sam paints what's wrong with the world. He paints the kind of portraits that show what people are really like, how they're trying to impress other people—stuff like that." Anne began to walk nervously up and down, making the springhouse seem even smaller than it was.

"So they don't like his portraits?" But certainly nobody would threaten death because of that.

"Oh, sometimes they do like his portraits!" she cried. "Because Sam paints so exactly what they're trying to pretend to be that they don't see what's wrong with it. It's only if they find out what other people think of the portrait that they get mad."

She stopped. "There's Sam."

I heard footsteps on the gravel drive outside, and somebody whistling gaily.

"Anne," a man's voice boomed, "where are you?"

She smiled like Christmas morning, stood tall, stuck her head out the door, and called, "Right here, Sam."

Almost immediately a large, cheerful man exploded through the doorway, and I thought Aha! Exhibit Number One. The black-magic target. Maybe. Sam was stocky, about six feet tall. Muscular, not fat. Casual, in jeans and a white T-shirt. His reddish hair and beard burst forth with wild exuberance. The springhouse seemed five sizes too small for him.

Sam reached out his hand and beamed. "You must be Cousin Peaches." I liked him right away. Charm, I thought. He turns the world golden as soon as he walks in the room. Even for a fifty-five-year-old cousin on his wife's side.

"This is Sam," Anne said, in a tone that said, "This is my darling." He put his arm around her shoulders, and I could feel electricity shoot through her. Feel attraction between those two till it crackled.

He turned his whole attention to me. "I understand you've written a book."

"How to Survive Without a Memory," I told him. And felt foolishly important. Well, of course I was pleased that my book was going to be published, but he made me feel like Margaret Mitchell and Agatha Christie rolled into one. Such a nice man!

"We all need a book about how it's absolutely O.K. to be imperfect. I'm for that," Sam said.

I was startled. "I never thought of my book that way," I said. "But I guess it's about how to get around what you're *not* good at by using what you *are* good at, like remembering things by rhymes and other tricks if you can't just remember them neat. I guess that *is* about the art of being imperfect." We laughed together. I felt a little drunk. Super-charm affects me that way. And as for Anne, her eyes were full of hero worship, like an actress in an old silent-movie love scene.

"That's wonderful, to accept being imperfect," Sam cried, "because the bad thing is to lie to yourself. This rotten world is full of people who do that!" He beamed and brushed away a swinging spider.

"And you paint people exactly the way they lie to themselves—that's what Anne tells me. I'd love to see your paintings," I said. Was it Sam's paintings that enraged this Paul until he implied threats?

"I'd love to show you my work!" Sam led us out into the blinding sunlight, waving toward a small weathered building across the driveway from the big house. "Come over to my studio!"

"We have a great deal here," Anne told me. "We get a studio and half the day for our own work, and the other half of the day we work for Revonda Roland. She grew up around here, then went off and made it on the Broadway stage. Now she's come back and is fixing up this place."

Revonda Roland, I thought. Vonda was a little like wander with a German accent. I pictured Hansel and Gretel wandering. They were German, right? I put the witch in the picture—scary things are easier to remember. And Revonda was vondering again: revondering. I'd get the last name next time.

Sam pointed toward the house: "That's my first job here."

"I can imagine!" I said. "I never saw a house half-painted quite like that."

"Paul did it that way," Sam laughed, "and then announced he wouldn't finish the job. That's part of why we're here."

We crunched down the white gravel driveway. On the left, before the curve to the house with its wide front porch, stood the studio, with a two-car garage downstairs—a bright red car in one side and a white pickup truck in the other. A brown van was parked beside the building. Above the garage the studio had big windows. A huge old tree on one side of the building drooped branches around it like protecting arms. Sam led us up the stairs on the side of the building and into a room paneled with pine.

He strode past a small table with four bentwood chairs around it, and past a big worktable with puppets sitting at the back: a red-haired grouch, a wizard in a pointed hat, even a goldfish. Sam hurried us past an empty easel, set just right to catch the light, and led us to the end of the room where paintings leaned against the wall.

"Here's one I like," he boomed. He picked it up and set it on the easel.

My first thought was: What perfectly lovely colors. A beautiful design. Then I realized it wasn't an abstract design but a trash dump. On the edge of a pond, oozing some poisonous-looking green stuff into the water. I felt tricked.

He threw his arm around me. "Gotcha!" he cried happily. "Some of my things are not that subtle." He pulled up a painting of a circle of scrawny, hungry-looking children with large frightened eyes. "I started to call this *Hunger*," he said. "But I decided to call it *Eyes*."

I could see what Anne meant about his pictures. I wouldn't want that one in my house, with the hungry eyes following me around. How could the man who painted that picture be so cheerful?

"This one is my mother," Anne said in a voice like a challenge. "It's not finished yet."

I was shocked. I know Cousin Clothilde pretty well. Pop, my eighty-five-year-old father, is fond of her. She drops by when she comes to the mountains. And there was the time when my first husband, Roger, and I went down to the beach and spent the night at Clothilde's house in Winston-Salem on the way. That's when we'd met Anne as a child.

Cousin Clothilde's house looked like a photo spread from *House Beautiful*. Except more elegant and less practical. The living room was all in shades of white and gold. Pop said that Cousin Clothilde's father was a pig farmer, and she was working to get away from the pig image. It made me feel tired, just looking at her, with her every hair teased into place. Somehow Sam had got that into the picture. He caught her attitude by the way her lips were pursed: Only perfect would do for Clothilde.

It was the only portrait I ever saw that I wanted to talk back to. Listen here, I wanted to say, who gave *you* the right to decide how I should behave?

"Does your mother like it?" I asked Anne.

"So far," she said, "it's the only thing she does like about my marrying Sam."

I was amazed.

"Mother felt I should marry a rich man who could look after me." Anne made a face like she had a bad taste in her mouth. "She doesn't think Sam will ever be rich." She threw Sam a loving glance, and he threw his arm around her and gave her a bear hug. "But Sam *is* rich. He enjoys life. We enjoy life."

I knew I wouldn't want the judging eyes of that portrait of Anne's mother in my house any more than I'd want the eyes of the starving children hanging in my kitchen. I'd get an ulcer.

"Really remarkable pictures," I told Sam. "They get me in the pit of my stomach."

"Because they are about the state of the world." He threw his arms wide with enthusiasm. He seemed too large even for this big, bright room. "My pictures are about the way we pretend that everything is beautiful while the world falls apart."

"But we don't!" I couldn't let that pass. "Don't you watch television? We constantly criticize. We carp at every little thing any public figure does. Why—"

He interrupted. "But that's the same thing. The opposite side of the coin. We tell ourselves we all ought to be perfect so any little flaw should be magnified and pecked at. The world has cancer, and we carp about zits." Why did he radiate joy when he was telling me that?

"I believe I have talent." He paced around the room, pleased with himself. There was even something naive and charming about that. "And I have a great opportunity here. I am painting Revonda Roland's portrait, and it's going to be the best thing I've ever done."

"Why?" I asked.

But he looked at the clock over the worktable. "It's noon!" he cried. "I have to run. Revonda gets upset if I'm late. Cousin Peaches, it was great to meet you!" Sam gave me a quick hug, then exploded out of the room with as much speed and energy as he'd exploded into the springhouse when he first appeared.

"Do you have to go?" I asked Anne as soon as I caught my breath. She was standing by the picture of her mother. I noticed they had the same bow-shaped mouth. But Mama's was rejecting. Anne's was merely tense.

"I can be a little late," she said. "It's Sam that Revonda likes most. Here, sit down." She waved at the bentwood chairs by the small table, then pulled one out for me.

"You called me," I said, "because . . . ?" She walked over to the worktable and picked up the wizard puppet in his pointed black hat. He was a large puppet, with a head that was almost life-size. She slipped her hand into the body, held him in front of her, and suddenly he grabbed my eyes. Anne all but disappeared.

"Revonda *is* trouble," the Wizard said in a deep portentous voice. "She's a retired actress who never retired." He nodded wisely. "She wants what she wants. She wants Sam. That can pull Sam and Anne both into danger."

"But she's seventy-five years old," Anne's voice said as she reappeared, frowning. "She doesn't want Sam for a lover. She wants him for a protégé, almost for a son. She can help him. What's wrong with that?"

"She already has a son," the Wizard said darkly. "And a twisted bad relationship. Be careful of the son. He wants to hurt."

Anne slipped her hand out of the puppet, and suddenly he was only cloth on the table again. "I'm sorry," she said, "but

I think better if I talk with the Wizard. It's silly, but it works." She patted the empty black puppet.

I'd never been warned of danger by a puppet before, I'll say that. But Anne did look upset. Kind of pinched around the face. "Could you meet Revonda and Paul and tell me what you think?" she asked. "When I'm so scared, without any real reason, it makes me feel crazy. But," she added quickly, "don't go now. Revonda doesn't like surprises. I'll work it out for you to come when she expects it." She smiled. "I feel so much better knowing you're going to help."

"O.K.," I said. "Call me when I can meet them. I'm mostly home working on the book." I gave her a hug. "I like your Sam," I said.

I drove home feeling lonesome. Ted and I usually handle things together. We're a new team, only married for a year and a half. But when you work with somebody who just naturally pings when you pong, whose strengths and weaknesses dovetail so well with yours, you get spoiled. And since I had this ominous feeling, I wished he was here to talk this strange situation over with before things got worse than just the premonitions of a nervous cousin.

Ted was only away for a few days at a newspaper symposium down east. But I knew from experience that all hell can break loose in a lot less time than that.

CHAPTER

2

I got back to my own work—rewriting the chapter on machines that help memory. Funny the simple bits you don't think of unless somebody tells you. Like the answering-machine trick. If you're out and you have to remember to do something first thing when you get home, what's the best way? Why, call yourself up. Leave yourself a message on your machine. Actually I insulted Ted by mistake the first time I tried that out. He picked up and I said, "I don't want to speak to you. I want to speak to the machine."

The phone by my desk rang. It was Anne. "I haven't called you back," she said, "because Revonda's son Paul has been away. He had a big blowup with his mother and stalked out. Not long after you were here. Revonda's been too upset for you to come meet her. But now"—her voice got more intense—"Paul's been gone for two days. Nobody knows where. He simply vanished. Revonda's in a terrible state, but she won't call the sheriff. Perhaps if you could offer to help Revonda find him . . ." Her voice trailed off.

"I've never done missing persons," I said. But by now I was so curious that I said, "I'll be over later this morning, as soon as I check on my father. He's not in good health." I didn't add that Pop always bore watching because he could make more trouble sitting still in a wheelchair than three-year-old quintuplets in a china shop.

"We'll be in the big house," she said. "The room on the right with the door onto the front porch. That's Paul's room. Revonda is getting us to paint the woodwork while he's gone."

What? Painting woodwork didn't sound to me like a thing you'd worry about if you were in a terrible state about your only son. It made me even more curious about this Re-wonder Revonda, who went to pieces and thought about woodwork all at once.

Pop would know something about Revonda if her people came from these parts. I could kill two birds with one stone when I went by to make sure he was O.K. I would not mention magic. Pop's imagination could take off enough without extra help.

But Pop wasn't O.K. He was bored. He'd rolled his wheelchair over to the glass door that looked out on the garden, where the phlox and roses and foxglove were in full bloom, and was staring into space. He turned around balefully when I came in from the kitchen, where I'd stopped to speak to Bessie, his new housekeeper.

"Even the birds hide in the woods," he said accusingly. He managed to look so frail under his fine white hair that I might have let myself forget what a force he can be. I knew he was angry because his favorite sitter had married a rich Texas oil man and quit her job. Fortunately, Pop is loaded and can afford sitters around the clock. But he couldn't compete with a Texan who was rich, young, and sexy.

"I have a puzzle for you," I said. "What do you know about a woman about eight years younger than you named Revonda, who grew up in Bloodroot Creek and went off and became an actress?"

"Revonda Glenn," he said. "Her married name is Roland. Hot dog! She did what she pleased." He rolled his chair back over to the round mahogany table where he usually sat and waved a hand for me to sit, too. "She wasn't an actress when I knew her. But she knew how to get people to help her out. She did summer theater when she was only fourteen. That's how I met her. Some gal! Folks like Revonda and me made a point to know the summer people. If you want to make money, it helps to know money." He winked at me. "Later she went off and worked for one of them after her father drank himself to death. Her father was talented and no good."

"Talented how?" I asked.

"He could carve little animals that almost came alive. But mostly he just drank."

"What became of Revonda?"

"I heard she married a summer person's rich cousin and got to be a star on Broadway but under some other name. Elvira Lane, I think it was. She was a second-string star. That was in the fifties and the sixties."

Pop was having one of his good days, remembering all that.

"I'd like to see Revonda again," he said. "She was never dull. Have you met her?"

I was glad I could say no. Pop getting in touch with Revonda while trouble brewed was not what we wanted. I said a friend of mine had asked about her, then managed to change the subject. A little later I set out for Revonda's.

It's strange and wonderful how every single mountain valley is unique. Bloodroot Creek Valley is long and broad with low mountains along both sides like the backs of sleeping dragons, and far mountains visible beyond that. The fields by the road are a patchwork: row-crops, tall grass, cows, and a bigger patch where new houses seemed to grow in rows, too. In one field a tractor was cutting hay, and children waded in the creek by the road. Revonda's place was at the far end of the valley. Beyond her house the road took a new name and rose sharply toward the pass over to Mitchell Creek.

I drove in her driveway, past the springhouse on my left, up to the big, old Victorian split-personality house. I heard dogs barking, but nobody came to the door to check out why. The red car was missing from the garage. I went straight to the room on the right with the door that opened directly off the front porch, where Anne said she and Sam would be painting woodwork.

I knocked and Anne called, "Come in." I walked right into a cracked mirror—or at least that's how it felt. There were mirrors in front of me, above me, to both sides of me. Mirrors of all shapes glued to cover the wall and, in between them, black. Except around the door at the far side of the room. Sam and Anne, each with brush in hand, were busy painting that woodwork white. They stopped and said, "Hi."

I wanted to say, "Let's get out of this place." There was something about that room that made me dizzy. I get quite dizzy enough with no help at all just trying to work some strange machine, like a new computer. Or having to fill out a tax form. But this was much worse.

The mirrors were all sorts of odd shapes, as if Paul got them from a junkyard and then made a crazy quilt to cover the walls and ceiling. All I could see in every direction was me, reflected from every angle and in every size. I'm not bad looking, but once is enough! Actually, it wasn't just me, but me and everything around me. I felt queasy.

"I feel like these mirrors could swallow me up," I said. "How do you stand it?" Mirrors and more mirrors reflecting mirrors. "When one of us moves," I said, waving my arms to see the effect, "everything moves like we're all inside a dern kaleidoscope."

"It helps if you deliberately look at something else," Sam said. "Look at one of us."

I looked at him, and it did help. He was the same as the day before, hair and beard still electric, grin still enthusiastic.

"This room could be helpful if you forget what you look like," I tried to joke. To keep my balance. "Except I'd like to remember myself right side up, not upside down and sideways and every which way."

"We never came in here until yesterday," Sam said. "Paul never invited us in, and he'd lock the door when he left."

"Revonda says he used to be a stage-set designer and a costume designer, and I can believe that," Anne said, rolling her eyes. "Maybe for horror films. Revonda went off to the liquor store. She'll be back."

Just looking at this room made me feel drunk. At least the floor didn't reflect. It was black and bare.

The French doors I'd come through didn't reflect because they were curtained on the inside with some white opaque stuff. Paul didn't want anybody to see in. Paul has kinky sex here, I thought. That was it! What a place for an orgy. Well, evil is in the eye of the beholder. Remember that. But this room encouraged the eye to expect something bizarre.

I noticed the poster on the door from Paul's room into the rest of the house. That door was closed, all but a crack, and hanging on the back of it was a picture of a naked man, about half life size, spread out on a five-pointed star. He seemed to be standing in the air between Sam and Anne.

"What did you say about strange books?" I asked.

Anne pointed to a bookcase. "Mostly about Medieval magic. We were looking at his books yesterday, after we measured to see how much paint to get." She folded her arms across her chest and hugged herself. "I'll tell you, those books make me nervous. Some of them have curses in them."

"But some of those books have magical cures, and some of them are very funny," Sam said. "I opened one book at random, and it said that in order to cure a cold you should kiss a mule." He began to laugh.

Anne's smile was forced. "I guess I feel like if you're prone to bad luck, then curses are more catching," she said.

I noticed she had picked a spot to paint that was far from the bookshelf.

Suddenly I was grateful that all I have to fight is a bad memory. Hardly ever has it occurred to me that I was prone to bad luck. "It seems to me," I said, "that to a large extent we make our own luck by looking life straight in the eye and doing whatever has to be done."

"I guess when I'm in a place like this," Anne said, "I half believe in demons."

Demons. I didn't even like hearing that word in this kaleidoscope room. This was not a room to be rational in. This was a room to foster dreams—no, not just dreams. Nightmares. Be sensible, Peaches, I told myself.

I started over to look at the books, to see for myself what could be in them that scared Anne. I kept my eyes on the black floor so the mirrors wouldn't make me dizzy. Whammo. I bumped into a chair. And what a chair. It was a dark wood rocker with a grotesque face carved in the back. Because I'd bumped it, the chair began to rock, and the face looked up, down, up, down, almost alive. I looked away from that grotesque face into the mirrors, and I saw the face on every side leering at me, and moving this way and that. I was seized with terror. I screamed, and shut my eyes to stop seeing that demon face. This place really got to me.

Sam rushed over and put his arm around me. Anne cried, "What is it?"

I pulled myself together. "I suppose there is some little corner in me that half believes in demons, too," I said shakily, "especially when that dern chair face rocks and I'm already feeling dizzy."

An angry voice said, "Only a fool ignores demons." I knew it must be Paul. He stood in the doorframe where the poster of the star-man had been a minute before.

He clicked on the light by the door, making the room twice as bright. Paul was odd enough to fit the room. He wore black jeans and a black T-shirt and a pair of scuffed high-topped hiking shoes that looked like they'd walked a long way. And yet he didn't look like a man who'd like to hike. He held a cigarette in the long pointed fingers that would have seemed just right for a pickpocket or a saint, except his fingernails were bitten. A curl of smoke wafted past his face. He was good looking, with dark curly hair and even features and a sensuous mouth. He had intelligent eyes. Around his neck a medal hung on a black cord, a strange antique medal with letters and numbers on it glimmering in the light. Paul, the costume and stage set designer. I made myself remember that.

He raised the cigarette to his lips, took in a puff, and blew a perfect smoke ring in Anne's direction. "You have absolutely no right to be in my room, but you assume you have the right to read my books," he rasped. "And to condemn them." He looked Anne up and down as he said that, as if he liked her bra size and had contempt for her soul. He was so contemptuous he was like a burlesque of himself. He fascinated me and made me angry.

I wondered how long he'd been listening at the door. He turned toward Sam. "After a single glance you feel you have the right to laugh at my books."

Sam said, "Why do you care so much?" He was so eager I suspected he was composing Paul into a picture.

Anne was flushed with anger. She tried to answer Paul back. "I was interested in what you like to read, Paul. I wondered why you stay in this place you seem to hate, why you come back." That was a challenge. Good for her.

"Why I come back?" His voice hit two notes at once, like a kid I used to sit near in the sixth grade. "Where would I go? I can't live forever in the woods." A vein stood out on his forehead. "What did you think I'd do—work for an old woman like you and Sam do? I'm not like you." Now he was shouting at Anne, ignoring me. "You came here for my mother to use against me. You and Sam." He swept them both with hot black eyes. "Where did my mother know you before, Sam?" he demanded.

"Your mother? Revonda never knew me. We came here through an ad in the Asheville paper."

Paul's sneer reflected round and round and round us. Very ugly. "An ad? Bullshit. My mother never hired anyone without fifteen references. She never asked Sam for a reference, did she?" He wheeled on Sam.

"Or me," Anne added.

"You?" Paul laughed. His teeth were shiny white. "Revonda doesn't care about you. You are an appendage. My mother knows Sam from somewhere"—he glared at Anne—"and she lies about it." Paul was trying to upset and scare Anne, I was sure of that. Anne was wide-eyed. She seemed dumbfounded.

I heard a car in the driveway.

"You know why my mother wanted to hire you?" Paul snarled at Sam. "She did it to make me look bad. Because I don't finish things fast enough to suit her. She did it to prove I do a bad job of whatever I do and you can do better." His face was bright red. "Why the hell do you think you have the right to paint my room without my permission," he demanded, "even if she told you to do it? I damn well ought to have the right to say O.K. or not O.K."

He turned to me. "You don't have any excuse for being in my room, whoever you are." This was not a man who would be easy to like.

His words had run together so fast nobody had a chance to say who I was. "What the hell happened to privacy?" he demanded.

I heard the outside door of the room open, and there stood a white-haired woman in a bright red pantsuit, a great deal of skillfully applied makeup, and gold jewelry by the ton.

"When you leave and don't tell anyone when you're coming back, what do you expect?" she said archly. "I say you lose your rights, Paul. This *is* my house."

She turned to me, smiled with great charm, and said, "You must be Anne's cousin she said was coming over. I'm Revonda Roland."

"Now you're going to ignore me, aren't you?" Paul cried out. "You get upset when I vanish, or so you say, and when I'm here you treat me like shit." There was anguish in his voice, as if he were a child and his mother had rejected him.

"Paul, dear," Revonda said condescendingly, "we'll discuss whatever upsets you later, when our guest is gone." Her red and gold stood out in the mirrors.

"No," he said. "That won't make it right." He turned and his eyes hit Anne. The paintbrush was still dangling in her hand. She seemed to have shrunk. He held her in his gaze and said: "So you've noticed there are curses in my books. There are, and I'd like to put a curse on all of you." He scanned us all with his angry eyes. "Because you're putting a curse on me by the way you treat me."

Revonda laughed like ice cubes tinkling. Just listening made me cold. "But you've told me what to do about a curse, Paul," she said. "I know what it says in your books and that you believe it. If a man or woman refuses to accept a curse, it boomerangs and hurts the sender. If we all refuse to accept your curse, it will come threefold back on you."

I thought: When this Revonda is angry, she doesn't know how destructive her words sound.

I watched Anne. She seemed too upset to hear what Revonda said. Still worried by Paul's threat.

I thought: This Paul has spotted Anne as more vulnerable than Sam. He's spotted her weak point. Her fear of bad luck. He's going to use that against them. Because he doesn't want Sam *or* Anne here. He wants his mother to himself.

"Get out, all of you!" Paul yelled.

Anne started toward the outside door. The mirrors must have confused her. She walked briskly toward what she must have thought was the door, and crashed head on into a long piece of mirror.

She let out a small cry, staggered back, and Sam rushed to put his arm around her. "You'll be sorry for this, damn you!" he said to Paul. His voice was calm but strong. I

would not have wanted anybody to look at me with the rage
Sam had in his eyes as he looked at Paul.

My intuition told me this was not the time for me to learn
more about these people. This was the time for me to get
out.

CHAPTER

3

SUNDAY, JUNE 30

Ted called Saturday night, and I told him a little bit about the wild family my cousin and her husband were working for. But not much. Why worry him? He wouldn't be back till Monday afternoon.

Revonda called and invited me to lunch at noon on Sunday. I figured she was as curious about me as I was about her and her son. If she was embarrassed about the scene I'd witnessed, she didn't say so.

"I've heard so much about you," she said when I arrived. "How you've almost been killed several times and so cleverly managed to outwit the killer. I understand you've also written a book."

She was dressed to the nines in a tiger-print pants-and-blouse outfit and tiger's-eye earrings. I don't mean that semiprecious stone they call tiger's-eye. Her earrings were made out of glass eyes, which must have come from a taxidermist. They looked smashing, as if Revonda had taken on the spirit of a big cat. Her own green eyes were just as bold, which fit with what my father said about her as a young woman: "She did what she pleased."

But her manners were super-civilized. She shook my hand and welcomed me and said how she enjoyed meeting a cousin of Sam and Anne's. "They are so talented," she said. "They answered an ad. But I had hardly hoped to find such high-quality young people who I'd want for friends as well as helpers."

She ushered me into her living room, where light streamed in from windows on two sides and brought out the vivid colors in this great big red-and-blue Oriental rug that covered the whole floor. In the middle of the room were two red cushiony couches, back to back, as if to dramatize that sometimes there were people in that room who didn't want to speak to each other.

Big fringed red-and-blue pillows were plumped just right on the couch facing us. Polished silver ashtrays sat on the coffee tables. No newspapers or books out. I felt as if there ought to be a velvet rope in front of the whole sitting area, like a museum.

Tiger Woman strode right over to a bar, where she poured us both glasses of sherry. She led me around the couches, past some chairs, past a stool with a coat of arms in needlepoint, and stopped by a group of pictures on the wall.

"That's where I came from." She waved toward black-and-white photographs, all enlarged. They were out of place with her rich-actress furniture, but I could see by her high head that she was proud of them.

In one photo a mountain man in an old felt hat and high work shoes held the hand of a little girl. She had Revonda's determined face and sharp deepset eyes. The man reminded me of some of my folks on Pop's side. In another picture the same man had on Sunday clothes and stood by a tree with a tired-looking woman and the little girl. A third picture showed the man, still in felt hat, holding a dead snake by the tail. He had to hold his arm high to show the whole length. The man had angry eyes like Paul's.

Revonda leaned against the back of a high-winged oversize, overstuffed chair with a jungle print on it: red and blue tropical flowers plus a lot of lush green leaves. The colors were so electric I'd have almost been afraid to touch that chair. Something might crawl out of the leaves and bite me. But Revonda leaned and pointed to another part of the wall in back of it.

"You saw where I came from. This is what I was able to do!" she crowed as she waved at framed theater posters. Here was Revonda grown up, but still young and pretty, playing all sorts of parts. I could recognize Joan of Arc with her sword and Lady Macbeth staring at her damned spot and Queen Elizabeth with her ruff.

I noticed a silver-framed picture on a dark wood table next to the jungle chair: Must be Paul, at about ten, dressed up in a suit and a necktie and holding hands with his mother. Paul and Revonda smiled as if they didn't need a thing but each other. "I was a good mother," Revonda said. "You can see that. You must forgive Paul his temper tantrums. He has such an artistic temperament."

My eyes couldn't find a picture of her husband. Why did she care if I, a newly met stranger, thought she was a good mother?

Queen Revonda Elizabeth of Arc led me through a dining area with huge Audubon prints on the wall, through a pleasant kitchen with a stone fireplace, out onto the side porch, where Anne was setting a table for lunch, putting wineglasses on a glass-topped table surrounded by five wicker chairs. Revonda nodded. Not a lot of warmth between those two.

Then here, to ruffle the peace, came Paul around the corner of the house. His black eyes under his tousled dark hair said he still thought we were rats carrying plague. He was smoking just as he'd been the day before. Mephistopheles complete with his own hellfire smoke, I thought, that's what he meant to look like. Complete with hounds of hell. Twin black rottweilers came running down the porch behind him, growling. I backed up and bumped into Revonda, who had lingered behind me.

"It's all right," Revonda said loudly, stepping forward. She patted the dog nearest to her. "You can see they're good watchdogs. They obey. They are friendly as long as I say, 'It's all right.'" She smiled encouragingly at me, but my left leg was thinking about the time a dog bit me in the third grade.

"This one is Hound," Revonda said, continuing to pat the dog. "The other is Baskerville. Baskerville likes Paul better than she likes me. Hound obeys me better. She's a good dog."

Paul glared at her. "I don't answer your commands fast enough."

I could see he had come to lunch in order to be difficult. I began to suspect that was what he enjoyed most in life.

"You remember Peaches Dann," Revonda said to Paul.

He bowed. "How could I forget the interloper friend of your new helpers, who will replace me." So friendly.

Sam was coming up the porch steps to join us. Revonda turned and smiled radiantly at him while Paul plunked himself down at the glass-topped table.

Paul shrugged. "You'll all learn to hate this place as much as I do." He still wore the strange antique medal with numbers and letters in a spiral on it, which swayed against his black T-shirt. He glowered at his mother, ignored the rest of us, and smoked.

Revonda just went on with the next act: elegant lunch. She got Sam to carry it out on a tray from the kitchen at the end of the porch: crab salad and chilled white wine and rolls and butter.

She slipped into a seat next to Sam and looked up into his face and fluttered her eyelashes. "My son is very talented." I figured she was saying that for Paul's benefit. "He's tried painting, not to mention designing stage sets, and tried real estate."

"And failed at all of them—at least, by your standards."

Paul blew a cloud of smoke. My eyes watered. I was sitting next to him. Anne was in the seat at the end of the table between Paul on one side and Sam on the other. Sam watched us all like he enjoyed the show.

Revonda went right on sipping her wine and acting like everything was O.K.

"Sam is painting me," Revonda turned to me, smiling. I refrained from telling her to watch out. Certainly he'd catch that predatory look she gave to Paul. Like no matter what Paul did, he was still her possession. Perhaps she'd be blind to the truth.

Paul is disappointed in us, I thought. He hasn't managed to make us miserable or furious. But he'll keep trying.

Anne was fidgeting. She put her fork down, reached into a black bag she'd brought with her, and pulled out the Wizard, black pointed hat, black robes, and all. "How do you do," he said, bowing, "I am at your service." He wore white gloves, and Anne's hand was in one of those gloves holding a big book marked *Spells*.

"Ask me a question," he said, "any question. I know everything. It's all right here in my book of spells."

Revonda raised an eyebrow, which said the Wizard had not been invited.

Paul laughed. Not with us but at his mother. "Ask the Wizard what to do about snakes, Ma. You haven't told these people about killing two rattlesnakes the day before they came, have you, Ma? You haven't told them this is a big year for snakes. Maybe you need a spell to keep these people safe."

I shivered. I'm afraid of snakes.

Anne must have been, too. She let the Wizard's book slip. Her wineglass teetered on the edge of the table, then plunged. I gasped. Revonda cried, "My Waterford crystal!"

But Sam had already caught the glass in midair and put it back.

The Wizard waved his wand and said, "My magic can do anything. I can even make a wineglass fly."

I laughed. Anne was trying to break the tension.

Revonda did not laugh. "Perhaps you have a puppet that deals with reality. I might like that." She looked at Paul. "I don't care for magic."

Paul jumped up in his cloud of smoke. "You don't care for magic because it interests me," he snarled. "You don't care for anything that interests me. You'd like to throw out all my books. And don't start telling me how you gave me braces and piano lessons and my own shrink. To hell with that. I'm leaving. Just give me some money, damn it. It's my money."

Revonda put her hand to her throat, and I thought: Mary, Queen of Scots, sentenced to beheading.

"I won't give you money to use for drugs and liquor, or to spend on that girl. I won't help you to destroy yourself the way your father did."

I was embarrassed to be sitting there sipping from her Waterford crystal, looking out over the blue-green mountains and hearing all that. Paul began to yell so loud the neighbors could probably hear, too, and the nearest neighbors were out of sight.

"You got your money from my father. Who drank because he hated you. His money will curse you."

Revonda stayed calm, chin high. "Weak people shout."

Paul stalked off the porch and around the house. I noticed Anne had put the puppet away and turned pale. She'd meant to help.

Revonda looked sick, and a tic by her left eye made it appear to keep winking. Her hand on the table clenched. "I'm so sorry about this," she said to me. "I simply get so upset at Paul I'm not myself." She said that without humility. Her head was still high. She can't help acting proud, I thought. My mother used to say, "Pride goes before a fall." I read somewhere that the Greeks called it hubris, which brought the anger of the Gods.

Maybe if Revonda actually saw herself in Sam's portrait,

she could begin to change. Maybe Sam would be doing her a favor after all.

Maybe you're lucky in this life, I thought, if you have some very obvious fault that helps you to avoid hubris!

"I hate to leave you folks, but I promised to go pick up some plants from Revonda's friends who're moving," Sam said calmly. Good moment for an exit! He thanked Revonda for the delicious lunch, which he'd eaten in double time, winked at Anne, and went off down the porch steps. He drove off, waving goodbye. I thought he was lucky.

Anne and Revonda and I finished our crab salad in uncomfortable silence. Then Anne took the plates into the kitchen, and Revonda showed me where the bathroom was. She led me back through the kitchen, dining room, and living room to a small hall with doors off both sides. A bookshelf stood against one wall of the hallway, with all sorts of knickknacks on it. My eye fell on an old-fashioned pearl-handled pistol. That didn't go with the family pictures on the wall. Wrong style. Just beyond the shelf a door on the right was painted black and had a brass door knocker on it. I thought: That's Paul's room. It must be.

Revonda hesitated by that door as if she wanted to look inside, and I was curious myself. Was Paul in that room, raging? Or had he taken off again? But she raised her head even higher and didn't look. She led me to the end of the small hall and pointed out the bathroom door.

Like every other room in the house, the powder room was eye-catching with wallpaper that had wonderful dreamlike birds and animals among green leaves. The venetian blind matched the leaves in the wallpaper. I pushed it aside and looked out the window and saw a young boy wandering past the house. I didn't think much about it. Country people wander through each other's yards, looking for lost dogs, taking shortcuts, or whatever. I put the blind back squarely in place. Revonda's house had that effect. You felt everything had to go just so. I got my lipstick out of my shoulder bag and touched up my face. Then I returned to the table where Anne and Revonda were waiting.

Anne left us and in a little while came back with a chocolate cake. We made polite conversation. Anne said her family were going off on a cruise. Leaving that afternoon, in fact. Her mother had finally persuaded her workaholic father to take a few weeks off and go to Bermuda.

Revonda told us how this house had once belonged to her great-grandfather. It had passed out of the family, and she'd been so pleased to be able to buy it back. Maybe that was Great-grandpa's pistol on the whatnot shelf.

We spoke politely. We had the air of three people in remission from an illness; Paul's outburst was still with us. Finally Revonda got up and asked if I'd like to see her theater scrapbooks.

She opened the white door across from Paul's black one and led me through into a small study with blue and red flowered curtains, blue and red flowers on the wallpaper behind an old-fashioned rolltop desk. Cheerful.

Anne joined us shortly, and we all three ended up looking at scrapbooks together. We spread them out on a table and drew up chairs.

That was the first time I saw a picture of Revonda's husband. Always in pictures of her. At after-performance parties and such. He was a moody-looking man, pale with brown hair. Generally looking at his drink, not at Revonda.

Finally I glanced at my watch and was surprised to see it was three o'clock. I thanked Revonda for the lovely lunch and was standing just inside the front door saying goodbye when the doorbell rang.

Revonda opened it to a woman who could have been in that theater scrapbook, done up for a comedy. She had inch-long false eyelashes, hair piled up like a modern sculpture, a swishy flowered chiffon dress, and three-inch heels. She had on enough makeup to frost a cake, which didn't hide the fact that she must have been about seventy years old. Funny, the effect was kind of nice. Now, how did she fit in?

"So here I am," she said to Revonda, "cheering myself up with a new dress. My godson doesn't answer when I knock on his door, but you have some nice company for me to meet." She stuck out her hand to shake with me. "I'm Marvelle Starr," she said. "Actually I'm both Paul's godmother, and the theater's gift to Bloodroot Creek. Because I'm too old to do face-cream commercials any more, and those were the best parts I got. So I'm retired. Sometimes it depresses me that I'm retired. I come down to talk about old times with Revonda here."

Paul had a godmother! That didn't fit any better than the pistol. But, hey! I thought: Marvelle Starr. What a stage name—designed so you'll remember not just the name but what she wants to be!

"This is Peaches Dann," Revonda said formally, keeping her hand on the doorknob. "She and Anne are just leaving."

I wanted to go home and jot down my impressions. As we started down the gravel driveway, Anne turned to me and begged, "Don't go. Come by the studio for a minute," and I remembered how I'd wanted to look at her puppets.

I spent about two hours, admiring her handiwork and talking. I sensed she was nervous and wanted company. The air was heavy. Even indoors. I walked over and looked out the window toward Revonda's house. Marvelle Starr in her swishy chiffon was just getting into her silver Ford and saying goodbye to Revonda. She zoomed out the driveway. "That Marvelle doesn't let this heavy weather keep her down," I said to Anne.

I picked up a puppet in the shape of a mischievous little girl with red hair. "That's Me Too," Anne explained. "About all she says is 'me, too.'" My watch caught my eye. I said, "Good grief, it's after five, I'll have to go."

That's when the scream hit us. I was so startled I dropped the puppet. Yet some part of me wasn't surprised. The scream seemed to come from Paul's side of the house. Anne and I both rose instantly and ran toward the porch of the big house. We dodged through the white rattan porch furniture so fast Anne knocked over two chairs. She seemed O.K., so I ran ahead, around the corner of the porch, drawn by the scream.

Revonda stood in the outside door to Paul's room, mouth so screaming wide I could see down her pink throat. Not like herself. Not like Joan of Arc or Queen Elizabeth. Her eyes were round with fear, and she was clutching the doorframe.

She grabbed me and pulled me into Paul's room among the crazy mirrors, Anne following close—the three of us reflected every which way. Revonda pulled me into a small room off the mirror room—Paul's bathroom. The walls in here were black. Against them were a shining white sink, a bathtub, and something strange sticking out from the wall.

Revonda kept on screaming. She waved wildly at that whatever-it-was built in the wall. And then my eyes grasped it. It was a pull-out laundry bin. My grandmother had one like that with a chute right down to the basement. A pair of bare feet stuck out the top, seeming totally unreal, like monster flowers. Clear plastic ruffled round them. Only, the flowers were two hairy legs and bluish bare feet sticking out of rumpled black pants. Also a hand, twisted so you could see the gray-white palm. Black spirals were painted on that palm and the soles of those feet—spirals like the one on that medal Paul had been wearing.

"Help me pull!" Revonda begged. Then I understood why she hadn't pulled this body out alone. It was stiff. Stuck in the bin. As I pulled, I asked myself: Could this awful wooden thing be Paul? We'd seen Paul alive and angry just—I glanced at my watch—five hours before.

CHAPTER

4

We tugged the body out of the laundry bin and laid it on the black-and-white tile bathroom floor. Paul's face was blue and moist, with the thin plastic stuck to it, like plastic wrap over something hot that had cooled. A black spiral was painted in the middle of his forehead. Green leaves were inside the bag, stuck to his face. Something thin and hairy that could be dill. My grandmother used dill for making pickles, but, dear God, not in the bathroom. Not as decoration for the dear departed dead. And near the dill some other green I didn't recognize, with little pale flowers on spikes.

Revonda cried out, "Oh, Paul!" She sank down onto the floor next to him and began to sob so hard I was afraid it would tear her lungs.

I felt sick, but I also felt a kind of awful calm. Because I was sure I was looking at some deliberate and terrible creation. Something devised to send a message, either by Paul if he killed himself or by the person who killed him. I searched for a suicide note, scanning the black-and-white floor and the white enamel fixtures. Nothing in the room but Paul wrapped in plastic and a white washcloth and towels hanging on a rack and a cake of white soap on the white basin.

Through Revonda's sobs I could hear Anne in the next room on the telephone. "Come quick. A man is dead." I heard her describing the way we found Paul. Surprisingly calm.

"You must come sit down," I told Revonda. "You need to keep your strength to help when the sheriff comes." That galvanized her. She raised herself up from the black-and-white tiles. "That Harley Henderson's an old fool!" she cried out. "I've known him all my life. He won't know what to do."

I heard a car outside on the gravel. I heard Anne say, "Oh, Sam! Thank God, you're here," and then a mumble I couldn't make out. Revonda pulled herself up to her feet, holding on to my arm, still shaky, makeup running all over her face, but her voice was suddenly firm: "Sam will know what to do."

I reached in my pocketbook and handed Revonda a tissue to wipe her face before helping her into Paul's room, where Sam took her arm and led her toward the face chair. I went back and reexamined every inch of the bathroom, beginning with poor Paul. I put on the reading glasses that always hang around my neck on a chain and looked more closely at the feathery herb near his poor blue face. Yes, definitely dill. I took out my notebook and made a sketch of the dill and the other herb or whatever it was. I read the words on the dry-cleaning bag, which was what was over Paul's head and body—an ordinary flimsy-looking dry-cleaning bag. Three winter dresses in my closet were stored in bags like that. Down a side of that twisted bag, small white letters against Paul's black shirt said WARNING: TO AVOID DANGER OF SUFFO-CATION, KEEP AWAY—I had to lean around sideways to see the rest—FROM BABIES AND CHILDREN. DO NOT USE IN CRIBS, CAR-

RIAGES, OR PLAYPENS. THIS IS NOT A TOY. I shuddered. Not a toy.
I wrote the words in my notebook.

I looked down into the laundry bin. The bottom was
narrower than the top. In the very bottom a black hole
opened onto the cellar floor below. It was not wide enough
for a body to fall through.

I tried to imagine Paul stuffed into that bin with plastic
stuck to his face. His arms would be pinned to his sides. He
must have struggled violently to get loose. Blacked out
before he could get out. Or suppose he deliberately dived
into that hole, deliberately stuck himself there. I had to be
calm and keep my mind clear.

The top of the bin was pulled as wide as it would go and
splintered where we had forced Paul's stiffened body out.
Nothing else in the room seemed to be out of the ordinary.

I left the bathroom and entered Paul's hall of mirrors.
Revonda was sitting in the chair with the face carved in the
back, rocking. Sam was kneeling next to her. I thought how
the darned chair face must be sticking out its tongue at the
middle of her back and almost began to laugh, but this was
not the time. At least Paul's wooden face wasn't reflected all
around us. Revonda's face was bad enough. It had col-
lapsed. She looked a hundred years old.

Sam's broad artist's hand was covering her long slender
hand on the arm of the chair, and he was saying, "I'm right
here," just like my mother used to tell me when I was scared
of the dark.

Anne was still holding the phone. "They want me to stay
on the line till someone gets here," she said to me. I was
getting used to the mirrors, more able to ignore them, to
treat them like television wallpaper.

"I'm alone now." Revonda's whisper was hoarse and
forced. She turned to me.

I said, "I understand," because I could see she needed me
to so badly. I didn't understand this kind of being alone.
Alone with ugly memories of fights. Alone with sad
reflections. The mental kind. In some of the real physical

reflections, she must be able to see Paul's body, as I realized I could, through the bathroom door. I wished I hadn't noticed that.

Poor Anne, anchored to the phone, was watching Revonda with tears in her eyes. I could see Anne felt she had to say something, to do something. She couldn't bear the pain that radiated round Revonda. Revonda hardly moved except to rock. The pain crackled. I could feel it, too. Ungrounded.

Anne said, "Revonda, we'll help all we can. We'll be here with you. We won't leave you. I promise."

Because Revonda looked so low, I was glad Anne said that. Or at first I was. Then it worried me. I looked at Anne's gentle, old-fashioned face. She was the kind to keep a promise. What if something more was wrong here? If poor Paul was a symptom of something out of whack? In his family? In the valley? Whatever. Then Sam and Anne ought to get out.

But now, I suspected, it was too late for that. So what next?

I needed somebody to talk about this with, to try to unravel what was happening here. Somebody who was not mixed up in the horror. I needed my journalism professor husband back from his symposium. He's good at facts. I'm good at intuition. Oh, how I missed Ted.

CHAPTER
5

LATER SUNDAY AFTERNOON

The sheriff's deputies didn't take me seriously. But they didn't let me leave, either, on the chance that I might be more than I seemed.

There were three men: tall, medium, and short. Those men must have been used to some chilling sights, but they looked at Paul and his mirror room with wide eyes. "By damn," said the shortest one to the tallest. "Don't this beat all?" He pulled himself straighter in his tan uniform, as if he was remembering to be as professional as possible. He pulled up a chair next to Revonda and began to ask her questions. Her face was blank, as if she didn't hear. Her eyes were red rimmed and glazed.

Meanwhile, Medium-Sized had detached Sam from Revonda and was towing him out of the room. "I wasn't even here," Sam was saying loudly. "I need to know what happened, too."

The tall deputy made sure Paul's outside door was locked, then asked Anne and me to go with him. He walked briskly, with shoulders thrown back, indicating he wanted us to go in front of him. "All the better to see you, my dear," the Wolf would have said to Little Red Riding-Hood. Why did I feel like he was a wolf? Because I knew his job was to suspect us all. Because he had a spring in his step like he enjoyed suspecting.

He led us down the hallway from Paul's room, through one end of the living room with its big couches and pictures of the past. I turned my head and saw Sam and Medium-Sized sitting at the far end of the room in two chairs. Sam was talking, and the deputy was taking notes.

I would have loved to hear what Sam was saying, or what the other deputy was asking Revonda. But I was so glad to get out of that mirror room, reflecting Paul's body, that nothing else seemed crucial.

The tall deputy told us his name was Ron Brank. Ron, I thought. I'd like to *ron* away from this place. I pictured that, with him running after, waving a gun. Vivid pictures help. Brank? Well, you might say we were at the brink of being suspects, and *brink* is almost like *Brank*. Or you might say that *Brank* rhymes with *yank,* and he wanted to yank us in for questioning. Also he was a lawman who would never rob a *bank,* which rhymes with *Brank*.

"I'm actually a neighbor," he said, neither chasing nor yanking, but leading into the dining room. "Revonda didn't recognize me, so she must be in a bad state." He shook his head. "Of course." His brown-black eyes seemed kind, at least at that moment, even if his black curly hair put me off. His hair was as coal-black as Paul's. He glanced at his wrist. He wore one of those watches with circles and hands to tell everything: tides, seasons, day, month, altitude, pulse. Expensive. He was obviously willing to pay to know. His wrist under that watch was thick and muscular. Sexy.

Anne is going to confuse him, I thought. Precision & Muscle meets Imagination & Grace, and—let's face it—my cousin Anne seemed spacy in her state of shock. But charming. Maybe more charming because she looked so helpless.

Precision & Muscle was polite. He held a chair for me at the dining room table. He told me to sit there and wait, then he took Anne into the kitchen to question her. He left the door open, to keep an eye on me, I suppose. I couldn't hear exact words. This Ron what? Ron-on-the-brink, yank me to the bank, Brank.

Sun shone in the kitchen window, turning Anne's hair blonder. Better than that eerie mirror light in Paul's room. Ron seated Anne at the table in front of the fireplace at the far end of the kitchen. Her back was to me. He sat on the opposite side of the table, holding his notepad and a small black tape recorder. Boy he didn't take a chance on forgetting. I could see his mouth moving.

More men arrived, including an extra-tall gangly one. I'd seen his picture in the paper. He was the sheriff. I'd never dealt with him because we live in the city. We deal with the Asheville police. But in the county, he's in charge. "What have you found out here?" he boomed at Sam's interrogator.

The next thing I knew, Revonda appeared with her deputy trailing behind. His mouth was half open in surprise. The deputy gripped his notes and followed close, as if he wanted to make it clear that Revonda was his witness to question even if she did seem to be getting away from him.

Revonda marched right over to the sheriff. He was standing near her theater posters. Even compared with Lady Macbeth, the real Revonda looked haggard, but her head was back at that proud Revonda angle. "Harley," she said hoarsely, "I've known you a long time." She didn't say it like a compliment.

"I've known you just exactly as long." He spit out the words and clenched his oversize hands into fists. Not friendly. These two had fought before.

"Somebody killed my son," she said, "and I expect you to find out who." She said that like a challenge.

All it took to pull Revonda together was rage. Rage that

this man, whom she did not respect, was in charge of finding out what happened to her much-loved son. Rage was her tonic. She was going to be all right. I wasn't so sure about the sheriff. His face turned red, and I hoped he wasn't prone to heart attacks.

"I intend to investigate every angle," he said. "Murder, suicide, and accident."

I almost laughed, except this was so grim. How could you possibly suffocate by accident in a plastic bag with spirals painted on your hands and feet and forehead, and sprigs of herb beside you?

"My son did not kill himself!" Revonda thundered. More noise came out of her than I would think could fit inside. Short Deputy and Medium Deputy opened their eyes wide again. Ron Brank in the kitchen glanced up briefly.

"If you don't discover who killed my son, I will." She was hissing. What versatility. "I have a friend," she said, pointing to me, "who has solved two murders, and I'm going to get her to help. This is Peaches Dann."

The sheriff looked me over. "This is no place for anyone who thinks solving crimes is a hobby."

He had a nerve! I didn't say anything. I wanted to help Anne out. If Revonda thought I was working to help her, fine. The sheriff was a paper tiger. Revonda was a real leopard. Ready to sneak through the bush, so to speak. She leaned on that chair with the jungle print. I half expected her ears to grow pointed and a lashing tail to appear on her rear. Given a choice, I was better off on her side.

CHAPTER
6

"What was it that you didn't tell the deputy?" I asked Anne as we drove along. She bit her lips.

"What makes you think—"

"Maybe I can help you in this mess," I said, "but not if you don't level with me."

So, O.K., I had jumped to a conclusion. If you can't remember details, you have to do that. Develop your intuition. Maybe my intuition somehow feeds on those details I can't retrieve. At least not when I want to.

The deputies had let the two of us go, saying they might have more questions later. Someone was still interrogating Sam, and the sheriff himself was working on Revonda. I had suggested that Anne and I go for a ride and maybe get something to eat at McDonald's back nearer town. I was hungry. Anne had said she wanted to go to the studio and wait for Sam. So I'd whispered, "I need to talk to you in a secure place."

She wrote a note to Sam and fastened it to the door at the

bottom of the stairs to the studio. Upstairs, lights were on. The deputies must still be searching. Her note said we'd bring back chicken sandwiches.

I imagine some of the crew swarming over the place had already searched my car because they let me take it. Also, it seemed that my usual in-case-I-need-it junk was better organized than when I left it! Anne and I rode past the springhouse, out of the driveway, in silence. We rode down the long valley with the green mountains on both sides, green fading to blue dusk.

"I trust Sam," Anne said tensely. "I know he tells me the truth. But he does things that other people don't understand."

I waited for her to tell me more.

"That man rattled me," she said. "I mean, Ron Brank. First, I felt better because I could tell him all the awful things that happened. He seemed to understand that it felt like being dipped in poison. Like maybe it *was* part of some curse. He made me feel safe."

At best, Precision & Muscle is a balance for Imagination & Grace.

"And then," Anne went on, "he began to ask questions about where I came from. He asked me where I met Sam."

Long silence. She held her hands clamped tight together. The feel of rigor mortis came back to me.

"Why were you afraid of that question?" I asked.

She gave me a nervous glance, but she'd gone too far to stop. "I told him I bumped into Sam in Boston, which was true. I was living there and doing kids' parties with my puppets. I was doing O.K. even if my family didn't think so. But I just naturally get into trouble. One day I took the wrong subway and ended up in a tough part of town, and I was thinking about how I might do a puppet show about a character who got lost in a dangerous place. And there, right next to me while I was looking the other way, a girl was stabbed."

She turned her eyes to me, amazed. Those green eyes under the lovely curved eyebrows. Somehow those eyebrows added to a haunted look in the eyes. Not good.

"In a dangerous part of town was that so strange?" I asked. "But I admit getting lost and ending up in a dangerous place would have rattled me."

Anne went on reliving Boston. "I never saw the girl"— she sighed—"until she brushed against me as she fell. She lay so still on that dirty sidewalk, bleeding. The knife was still in her back. A kitchen knife. I don't like to remember that. It's like I'm right there again. Near trouble. Like always." She hunched her shoulders.

"What did that have to do with meeting Sam?" I asked.

"Afterward, when the cops let me go, I bumped into Sam on the police-station steps." She paused, looked at me searchingly, crossed her arms, and hugged herself.

"Look," I said, "I know what it's like to get lost and feel dumb about it. And I've come across several bodies, though I don't feel jinxed like you say you do. What happened to me was part chance, part knowing lost souls and maybe, partly, that after you do something once, it's more likely to happen again. People pull you into it. The important thing is to figure out why it happens and do something to try to stop whatever is wrong. So, now you need to talk. I'm here to listen."

She took a deep breath. "I got to talking to Sam on the street in front of the police station. I told him I'd been questioned as a witness to a crime. Sam told me he'd been questioned as a suspect in a crime that hadn't happened and would I like to have a cup of coffee." She gave me a pleading glance. "There's just something about Sam that made me know he was O.K."

It seemed to me I'd heard somewhere that was the way a number of women had reacted to that famous Victorian Englishman who drowned them in bathtubs. On the other hand, Sam did seem as trustworthy as a great big puppy.

Anne sat up straight, uncrossed her arms, and smiled. "It never occurred to me that Sam had committed a crime. He isn't the type. He's too alive."

"What was he accused of?" I asked. We had arrived at McDonald's. Good. I could see the time had come when I needed to write down any names or dates she mentioned. We each got some chicken fajitas and Anne got an orange juice and I got coffee. We parked, and between bites she told me the rest of the story. Trouble didn't hurt her appetite.

"Sam and I went to a coffee shop, and he told me he'd worked for a ninety-year-old woman named Margaret Lansing, a real honey, he said." Anne took a gulp of her juice. "Sam promised this old woman he'd let her die at home in bed, not in the hospital on machines." She bit into her fajita, swallowed the bite, and went on: "He sat with her and held her hand while she died." She turned to me. "There was nothing wrong in that."

We were parked, windows down, next to a small dogwood tree with thin leaves. A brown bird sat on a branch near the top and watched us. Anne threw him a crumb of tortilla, and he jumped down to get it. She went on slowly.

"He said the woman was in pain and ready to go. I guess I'm good at listening. Sam needed somebody to listen and to believe him."

"Who was it who didn't believe him?"

"The police," she whispered. Then she raised her voice. "Because it turned out she'd changed her will to leave Sam six hundred thousand dollars." She frowned and sighed. "She'd cut out her only nephew, who never came to see her." Oh, boy! She finished her fajita and her orange juice and wiped her hands on the napkin. She went on in a sudden rush. "So the nephew accused Sam of using undue influence to get her to change her will. He accused Sam of deliberately letting her die of neglect in order to get the money sooner." She turned to me angrily. "You know Sam would never do that! He told me he didn't care about money except for enough so he can paint what he pleases. Sam didn't want to waste good painting time in court."

"And so?"

"That's why he offered to let the nephew have the money if he wouldn't press charges." She sighed. "Just like that. Six hundred thousand dollars, gone. I'm not sure I could have done that. But Sam didn't care."

"I bet your father was horrified," I said and then wished I hadn't said it. Anne's father was an accountant. Losing even a dime struck him as a mortal sin. I lost some change once when I was visiting him years ago. He made me keep looking till finally I found it where I'd dropped it out on the lawn. I spent an hour and a half looking for thirty-five cents, which was considerably less than the minimum wage.

"We didn't tell my father about it," she said. "I couldn't tell this deputy Ron Brank about what happened in Boston. So I told him Sam wanted to paint me, and that's how we met. Which is partly true. Only that was later."

"But what will happen if Sam tells about the woman who died in Boston?"

Her eyes filled with tears. "I had to guess what Sam would do," she said. "I think he'll follow my grandmother Ott's advice."

"Why?" How did her grandmother get into this?

"My grandmother loved Sam right away. She was the only one I told about what happened in Boston. She stood there right by her window box full of red, white, and blue petunias. She's a flower person. She said, 'You and I know Sam is a wonderful, irresponsible artist who doesn't care about money, but most people wouldn't be able to understand that.' Mainly she meant my parents. 'So I just wouldn't tell anybody about that money,' she said. 'It's none of their business.'"

"Let's hope," I said, "that Irrepressible Sam remembered

that. Your grandmother may have been right, but it's easier to tell the truth. You have to remember yourself every minute to tell successful lies or even half-truths, which I guess is what you've done. *I* couldn't carry it off." I gave her a hug. "I'll cross my fingers for you."

CHAPTER
7

Ted called late Sunday night. He said he'd been worried when he couldn't get me on the phone. I told him the whole ugly story. "I'll have to tell Pop what happened to his friend Revonda," I said to Ted, "or else somebody else will make it sound worse. I tried to call him just now, but he was asleep already."

"I can't imagine how anybody could make what happened sound weirder than it was," he said grimly. "The papers and the TV will have a field day. I could start home now," he said, "if that'll help."

If I knew Ted, he'd listened so hard and taken so many notes and networked so long at his conference that he was exhausted. "I'd rather have you home later, rested and full of good ideas."

"Good," he said. "I'll get home early tomorrow afternoon."

Amazingly, I was able to sleep. Paul's strange death left me feeling stunned, but I had to be on my toes the next day.

Anne was going to need moral support. Pop was going to need calming down.

I was at Pop's before he woke up. I found Ella Marie, the sitter on duty, in the kitchen reading a romance novel with the door into the hallway open so she could hear Pop call. Ella Marie: blond, about thirty-five, with blue baby-doll eyes and plump hands.

"It's important for you to keep your voice down when I tell you something that may upset you," I said quietly.

"What?" she whispered. Her eyes seemed to double in size.

"There's been a strange murder near Bloodroot Creek," I said. "The victim had books about magic, and he was the son of an actress. The television and the newspaper will be playing this up. Have you brought in the paper yet?"

She shivered with anticipation. She licked her upper lip. With all the Ella Maries out there, of course the media would be playing it big.

"The dead man's mother was a friend of my father's when they were young."

"A friend of your father's!" Ella Marie cried out as loudly as if she'd been stuck with a pin and won the lottery at the same time. I could see a personal connection with the murder really got to her.

Pop rang his bell. He has radar ears.

"I'll go," I said firmly. "Stay, please, and cover the phone."

I hurried through the dining room into the living room, past the sliding glass doors overlooking the garden and down the short hall into Pop's room.

"What's happened?" he asked hopefully. "What's wrong?" He looked so innocent, lying there under his fleecy white blanket which matched his silky white hair. Innocent as dynamite.

No point in putting this off. "You remember we talked about your friend Revonda Roland?"

"Of course. She was never dull. What trouble is she in

now?" He clutched the blanket, like he was ready to throw it off and jump up.

"Yesterday she found her only son dead."

"Oh, I'm sorry," he said. He eyed me thoughtfully. "You're mixed up in this somehow, aren't you? That's why you asked me about her the other day!" He sounded triumphant to have figured that out.

"Our cousin Anne is staying with her," I said resignedly. "Cousin Clothilde's daughter from Winston-Salem." Keeping him out of the middle of this was going to take all my ingenuity.

"Tell me what happened!" he demanded, and I did, trying to play down the dramatic parts, like the eeriness of that mirror room. "You were there!" he cried. "You have a talent for these things, Peaches!" Pop just loves to be in the thick of things, which is hard for a man who can't walk and occasionally is not even sure where he is. "We must call Cousin Clothilde and offer any help we can give!" he said eagerly. "Call Ella Marie. I want to get up right now!"

"Cousin Clothilde and her husband are off on a cruise," I said firmly. "Anne has asked me not to bother them till they get back, no matter what."

He began to ring his bell again.

What Anne actually said was that she was grateful her parents were away. They tended to get hysterical when she got in her messes. I would hardly have called this Anne's mess, myself. It was Revonda's tragedy.

Pop rang his bell like the house was on fire. It's a brass bell with a wooden handle that makes enough noise to wake the dead. We couldn't wake the dead. But maybe we could find out what it was the dead man knew. Pop might actually help with that.

Ella Marie arrived, waving the newspaper and smiling happily to be called where the action was. "It was a man named Paul Roland they found dead—right?" She handed the paper to me, and I was surprised how little the paper had discovered by press time. None of the lurid details, except that Paul was found dead in a plastic bag. Good. That gave me time to regroup. I left fast and got myself a cup of coffee from the pot in the kitchen. Pop didn't like family members hovering while he dressed, anyway. He liked his most helpless moments to be private except for the sitters. He couldn't manage without them.

I took my strong hot coffee and sat down at Pop's table in the living room. He had a shelf of his books and mementos behind him if he sat on one side of the table and, if he sat on the other side, the glass doors onto the garden right where he could look out.

In nothing flat, Ella Marie wheeled Pop's chair next to me on the side of the table where he could look out on the roses and lilies. "A good day for action," he said. Ella Marie hovered hopefully, hungry for details.

That gave me an idea. "Let's get Ella Marie to go buy some Danish pastry from the Blue Moon Bakery," I said. The Blue Moon down the mountain in Asheville had ovens imported all the way from France, and Pop couldn't resist their baked goods—I knew that. Ella Marie would be gone at least three quarters of an hour.

"Get a loaf of raisin-pecan bread," I told her. That was her favorite. I could see she was near mutiny to be sent off while we discussed Paul's death.

"What do you think is going to happen next?" Pop demanded as she disappeared out the door.

I told Pop about the sheriff and how Revonda didn't trust him.

"The sheriff thinks it could be suicide or murder or an accident?"

"I think he put in that accident part to upset Revonda," I said. "Though I did read about a man who apparently hanged himself by accident because he found it sexy to almost hang himself, and one day the *almost* didn't work."

Pop considered that with relish. "People are very strange. What can we do to solve this case?" He leaned back in his chair importantly. He calls me the Absentminded Detective, and I think he figures that means that if I can be a little bit like Sherlock Holmes, he can be like Watson. Of course, once you get the reputation for being able to help when something goes wrong, you get called. Especially by relatives. Because we claim kin in these mountains, we have enough to sink a battleship.

"I think the sheriff is leaning toward murder," I said. "He may suspect Anne and Sam. Sam is Anne's new husband."

"The bastard!" Pop said. I could tell he meant the sheriff, not Sam. His eyes sparkled with anticipation.

"So the more I know about where Revonda is coming from," I said, "about anything in her past that could be related to this in any way, the better. After all, this happened after she came home to the valley where she grew up, and where you knew her."

"Revonda liked me," he said, then sipped his coffee. "She liked anybody who looked like they were going to have the gumption to get off the farm and get over being poor. That was in thirty-three, when we were both in this amateur theater group. I just moved the scenery, but she was in some of the plays. She could see I was going somewhere." Pop preened. "She was right, too!"

Pop was born in 1910. He would have been twenty-three then. He used to be a looker. "Just how close were you and Revonda?" I asked.

He smiled enigmatically, sipped more coffee, and went on. "She had this grandfather she talked about a lot. He was rich. People saw him coming, and they smiled. He was generous. He told Revonda she was smart and she'd marry a rich man." He stopped and considered. "Maybe she was being kind, letting me know it wasn't going to be me. Because I wasn't rich in those days."

Good grief. Imagine if Revonda had been my mother! Thank God Pop hadn't been rich. But if Revonda had been my mother, I wouldn't have been me.

"Her grandfather died in a fire and didn't leave anything. He'd spent it all. Her father was dirt-poor. He drank.

Revonda said she was glad her grandfather never knew how bad things got."

"Revonda has pictures of relatives around the house. Nobody looks like a grandfather. That's odd."

Pop shrugged. "He died when his house burned down, and maybe the pictures burned. Revonda's father wouldn't let her mother have a picture of the old man. They hated each other, Revonda's pa and grandpa."

"Not a happy way to grow up," I said.

"The fire was set," Pop said. "Somebody getting revenge. Her grandpa was a lawyer, you see. Maybe somebody thought he didn't get them off when he should have. Or he got their enemy off when they wanted revenge. His house burned with him in it when Revonda was a kid."

In some families, tragedy stalked from generation to generation. Somehow it seemed to happen a lot out in our mountain coves, where the hard times and the fierce family loyalties had meant revenge was O.K., even to later generations.

"You must have known her well for Revonda to have told you all that," I said.

He gazed out at the garden. "She was some gal."

"So what happened after her grandfather died?"

"Revonda asked me not to tell," he said defensively.

"Pop," I said, "it must have been over sixty years ago when she asked you not to tell. Unless her son was murdered and it's relevant, I'll keep mum."

He poured milk and sugar in his empty coffee cup and stirred them up.

"I won't tell you what I know if you don't tell me what you know," I said. He sipped the sweet milk. I waited.

"Her father kept drinking and he beat her," Pop said.

I whistled. "Revonda wouldn't want anybody to know that, even now. She's too proud. If you hit her, she'd hit back. But I suppose as a child she couldn't stand up to a grown man."

Pop nodded. "He only beat her when she tried to take his

whiskey away. So she stopped trying. She told me it made her feel bad that she couldn't do anything to help him. He drank himself to death. That's one reason she left the county. She couldn't bear for everyone to know. You see, she found him down on his knees, leaning over the privy. Maybe he went there to puke. He was dead, with the bottle still in his hand."

I could see him. "How did anybody know?"

"In a valley like Bloodroot Creek, news travels," he said airily. "The sheriff had to know, to rule out foul play. He was the father of the sheriff they have now—the one you met. As soon as Revonda could, she left the valley. Damned if I can see why she came back." Pop paused and thought. "To show us, I suppose, that she wasn't like her pa, that she was like her grandpa said she'd be: Rich. Damn it, I'd like to see her. We need to go offer to help."

"Pop," I said, "the last time you decided to get mixed up in what looked like foul play, you were poisoned. Thank God you're so tough you're still here. Trust me, this is not an appropriate time to visit."

Pop mixed up with Revonda and maybe black magic was more than I could cope with, I was sure.

"Like it says in your book, it's important to do it now!"

That stopped me. Pop had asked to read my manuscript. That meant, of course, that he got a sitter to read it to him. He's legally blind, even if he can recognize people and see colors and movement. The fact that he wanted to hear my book had amazed me. He doesn't believe anybody should admit a fault.

"I do have a chapter called *Do It Now*," I said, grudgingly. "It certainly does not apply to rushing off half-cocked to see Revonda."

"Yes, it does. I just read it," he crowed and reached in back of him and took the top chapter off a facedown pile. He thrust it at me.

"Read the part about putting off what really matters. Go on, read it!"

O.K., I thought. Get it over with.

Don't put off a thing that's crucial. Do it now. *By doing something right away, you leave less chance to forget.*

"But—" I began.

"Keep reading," Pop thundered.

I ought not to have to use my own book to testify against myself. The Constitution should outlaw that. I read:

I like the Serenity Prayer: Dear God, grant me the serenity to accept the things I cannot change, the courage to change the things I can, and the wisdom to know the difference.

(I'd never change Pop, for sure.)

What that has to do with Do it now *is this: If you always did everything you meant to do immediately, you'd be either compulsive or a saint. So I find it helps my wayward psyche to put off a few things that don't hurt. Then I feel better about remembering to do the things that really matter. The trick is, like the prayer says, to know the difference.*

"Exactly," I said, "and therefore . . ." Pop glared at me. I went on reading.

If you put off doing the laundry and forget to do it until you need the clothes, that may not make a difference. If you put off storing the winter clothes until the moths eat them, that does.

If you put off calling a friend who is twenty, she'll probably forgive you. If you forget to call a friend who is ninety-seven, she may have departed for the Promised Land before you call. You'll feel bad. That's a difference.

* * *

"A-ha!" Pop cried out. "And Revonda and I aren't spring chickens!" I ignored that.

If somebody could get hurt if I don't do it, I do it now. Immediately.

I made that rule after I read the newspaper story about the coed who got raped. She wasn't sure if she locked her door. While she lay in bed debating, she fell asleep. In the morning there was a man in her room, who said, "If you scream, I'll kill you," and proceeded to rape her. She needed that rule the night before. Do it now.

I had thought about deleting the rape bit—it didn't really fit with the upbeat quality of the book. Naturally, Pop loved that part.

"Now, you'll admit," Pop said, "that someone may have been murdered at Revonda's house under very strange and suspicious circumstances. If you ask me, a crazy man did it. He may be about to murder Revonda and Anne and her husband at any moment. We need to get there right away!"

After that outburst he leaned back in his chair, out of breath, and shut his eyes.

I reached over and touched his hand. "You look exhausted from the strain. Let me go right now and come back and report to you about what happens," I said.

He sighed—hating to give up, I figured. "I guess that's best. If you're sure you'll tell me *everything*."

"In the meantime," I said, "I wouldn't talk about this too much. I think it will bring us good luck if we just keep it to ourselves."

"Of course," he said. "And in the next few days, we'll have Revonda and Anne and her new husband over to lunch. It's the least we can do, don't you think?"

Ella Marie arrived with a bag of wonderful-smelling baked goods before I could answer. God bless her.

I left quick before she could ask questions, leaving her and Pop happily eating fresh-baked Danish. I went down Pop's front steps, past the boulders my mother had made into a super rock garden, to my car, waiting in the driveway. At least it was a lovely day. The road side of Pop's house faced woods and a near mountainside, cool and shadowy.

I was not even out of the driveway when a van came careening up and Anne jumped out. She ran to the window of my car.

"I went to your house. . . ." She was breathing hard. "Your neighbor said you might be here. Something terrible has happened. A folder of Sam's sketches has vanished."

That didn't sound so terrible, compared to finding Paul dead.

She clutched my arm. "That folder could incriminate us."

CHAPTER

8

MONDAY, 10:45 A.M.

"Sam copied magic marks out of Paul's books, and he copied some pages, too," Anne told me. We'd pulled our cars into an overlook on the Blue Ridge Parkway and sat on the low stone wall to confer. "Those things were in a folder of Sam's sketches in our studio before . . . you know . . . and the folder was gone when we got back after . . ." She kept hesitating, trying to decide how to describe Paul's death. "The sheriff's people searched our studio before they let us go back there." She looked out across the valley of trees to the far mountain, swallowed, and went on: "The sheriff asked us questions this morning. I think he's decided Paul was murdered."

"He told me it might be murder or suicide, or even an accident. How can you tell he thinks it's murder now?" I asked firmly.

"It's not what he said. It's just a feeling I have."

Two buzzards were soaring out in the valley in front of us.

"While the deputies were searching our studio, they must have looked at Sam's pictures." She flushed. "If my father was shocked, what did the deputies think?"

"Describe the pictures you think would have shocked them most."

"The worst is the one of the old man's body under ice. Sam didn't show you that picture. My father said you'd have to be crazy to paint something like that." She sounded hurt.

"Actually, it's a beautiful picture if you don't look close. There's a lovely pattern, silver and white, with other colors glinting through." She hesitated as if she wanted to stop there, swallowed, and went on. "But if you keep looking, you see what's actually there." She frowned. "You know how Sam says he likes to paint man's inhumanity. And, boy, did he hit the jackpot in that one." She got a faraway look, as if she were seeing the picture in the distance.

"And what's in the picture?" I nudged her to go on.

"You see, this old man lived by himself, and he ran out of stove wood, and by the time his neighbors noticed there was no smoke coming out of his chimney, he was lying on the floor frozen. The pipes near him froze and burst, and then the pipes thawed and gushed water all over him. His body froze again, all covered in ice. That really happened. The newspaper clipping that told about it was part of the painting." She turned troubled eyes to me. "And when the sheriff's men searched our studio, what do you suppose they thought when they saw that picture?" She stared into the distance again, and then her voice thinned to a whisper. "They didn't *say* anything, but a dead man under ice is almost like a dead man in a plastic bag. And furthermore, right now, while he's upset, Sam is painting something else that has a real plastic bag in it. I can't be sure what it is yet."

I put my arm around her. She needed the warmth. "We must focus our minds on what we can do to find out what really has happened."

She nodded. "Yes. I know. I'm trying. That's why I came to get you."

"Here," I said, "we're getting cramped. This wall is too low to sit on." I walked her up and down the stone-walled overlook, as she pulled herself together.

"Yesterday, you told me you were afraid Sam told the deputies one thing and what you said didn't match," I reminded her. "What happened? Did Sam tell them he'd been accused of helping an old lady to die in Boston?"

She winced when I asked that. Then she broke into a smile. "No! He didn't tell them. And, of course, he didn't do it!" she said hotly, but then she broke into an even bigger smile and stood straighter. "Thank God he didn't mention it, and neither did I."

I prayed they'd done the right thing and the accusation wouldn't come back to trip them up later.

"So," I said, "things often turn out better than you expect!" But that bit about Sam even then painting a picture with a plastic bag in it did bother me.

"Sam just doesn't think about appearances," she said.

She was so right.

"And I trust him completely," she said, "but when I'm scared, I'm not positive I trust myself in who I pick to trust."

Maybe I'm lucky. If you have a bad memory, you *have* to develop a good sense of who to trust. Because you often need to ask someone what happened. I thought I trusted Sam, but I wasn't absolutely sure.

"Let's go talk to Sam," I said.

CHAPTER
9

We passed an old woman walking down Bloodroot Creek Road, dressed in about five shades of red: skirt, socks, blouse, overblouse, and even a cloth hat, all swearing with each other. In the sunshine she positively shimmered. She wore high-topped work shoes and clutched a bunch of wild flowers. She waved with her free hand. When we got out of our cars near the studio, I asked Anne who Ms. Mismatched-Reds could be.

"That's Knowing Agnes." Anne frowned, as if this Knowing Agnes didn't make sense to her. "Revonda says she wanders up and down the valley and goes to visit wherever she wants to, and people look out for her. They got her to wear red so the cars won't hit her."

"That sounds kind."

"You have to be careful when she's around," Anne said. "She repeats what she hears. Without even knowing what it means. Otherwise, Revonda says, she's harmless."

Interesting, that they let her be. Town people would have

locked her up, maybe had to. But how intriguing—that she could repeat what she heard and not know what it meant. I wondered if people used her to repeat what they wanted heard. Well, this was not the time to worry about Knowing Agnes. It was the time to worry about Anne and Sam.

We found Sam at his easel, painting away at something I couldn't make out, except there was a glint like clear plastic or ice in it. I asked what it was, but he said he was just fooling around to see what would come. He began humming to himself some spiritual I half-remembered. "Nobody Knows the Trouble I've Seen." Not his kind of song, I would have thought. I felt a dent in his confidence. His movements were tighter. He wasn't laughing, even with his eyes.

"Let's go for a walk," Sam said, giving me a significant don't-talk-now look. Did he expect the place was bugged? He cleaned his brushes and put them away while Anne and I each ate some cheese crackers and drank a glass of milk. Instant early lunch.

The three of us walked up the road past a field of cows, past several houses, and finally we came to a field that appeared empty. Sam spread the rusty barbed wire, and we slipped through the fence.

"There's a nice private nook, where we can talk." Sam led us around a big boulder set against the side of a hill. A lower rock was almost like a bench. I was just about to say he'd found a great place when a brown bull with a white face appeared.

He came out from behind a clump of bushes on the other side of the field and lowered his head and stared at us. His tail swished.

"Not to worry," Sam said cheerfully. "Bulls aren't fierce like they used to be. They've bred them to be milder."

Sam sat back on our rock, perfectly at home. He turned to me, and without any preamble he said: "What would Paul be trying to hide in that room with the doors locked except for what was in his magic books? He had place markers in them! I figured if he had any crazy idea that could be dangerous, the books would have a clue to it." His eyes were eager for me to agree. But I waited.

"If there was any real kind of danger here, I didn't have any right to ask Anne to stay here. So I needed to know. Paul might have come back before I had a chance to look over his books."

"He did it all for me." It was the first time I'd heard Anne be sarcastic. Her eyes glinted with anger.

"Did what?" I asked.

"On Friday," he continued, "when we measured his room for paint and went out to do errands, I put the marked books in a bag and took them with us."

"And copied the marked pages at the library." Anne's eyes were still angry. "I didn't realize what he was doing." One of her hands was picking bits of grass nervously, though she kept the rest of herself still.

"I knew Paul would be mad if he found out," Sam said, throwing his arm around Anne, "and I didn't want you mixed up in something like that."

She pulled away. "I'd rather know all along what we're mixed up in," she said in a low voice and ducked her head.

"I put the copies of magic stuff in one of my envelopes of sketches where no one would ever have a reason to look."

"You thought," Anne said unhappily.

"All on Friday?" I asked.

"Yes. Then I was busy and didn't have a chance to look at the stuff, and on Sunday we found Paul's body, and when we got back to the studio after the sheriff's people searched it, the envelope of magic stuff was gone. If they found those magic spells, they must be wondering why we had them." He stopped and frowned. "I had even copied a page with marks like the ones we saw on Paul's body."

Bingo. We'd come to the jackpot.

Annie winced. I whistled. "And you think the deputies found your stuff and took it?"

"This morning they don't act like they took it," Sam said

in a hopeful kind of way. "People like that think of magic as like strange kinds of sex," he said, becoming more cheerful. "Off-limits and therefore fascinating, and dirty at the same time. The thought of it tends to make them smirk. They're not smirking."

Anne nodded.

"So," I said, "our best hope is to explore the possibility that you somehow misplaced the stuff." The bull raised his head and ambled toward us. I made myself sit still. Bulls chase what moves.

Sam stared at his feet and said, "Oh, hell, I didn't mean to make trouble." He looked as glum as Annie did.

"O.K.," I said, "if you lost something, you came to the right person. I happen to be an expert at losing things—in fact, I have a whole chapter in my book about it. I may know more ways to do it than anybody else you ever met." I made myself sound cheerful. I had to rev them up.

Sam threw his arms around me. "I knew we could count on you!" He acted as if I had announced I could turn straw into gold. "Let's go over all the ways of losing things you know and we'll see what fits." A strange way of looking for Sam's envelope—but why not? It's always pleasanter to talk about something you know well, than to get up and walk past a bull of doubtful disposition.

"Obviously, this was more than *elementary losing*," I said, slapping a bug that bit my arm. "It wasn't just that you put it somewhere and you don't remember where."

Sam shook his head. "We'd have found it by now if that was all."

"And *wrong-size losing* is out? You didn't look for a large envelope when you should have been looking for a small envelope because you forgot you moved the stuff?"

He shook his head no.

"Did you put it in a dangerous place, like on the kitchen counter where one of you could sweep it into the trash with an elbow and not notice?" I seemed to remember a tan trashcan next to the counter. "I think of that as *two-stage losing*, and maybe it should be three-stage or even four-stage, because it isn't serious unless you put out the trash and the trash man takes it to the dump."

"*My* envelope was too big for the wastebasket," he said firmly. He slapped a bug, too. This field was not my favorite place after all, except it smelled good, like new-mown hay. The bull began to rub his back against the apple tree. Two small apples fell.

"I specialize," I said, "in *sandwich losing*. I'm usually smart enough to find something if I've merely dropped something else on top of it. Know thyself, they say, and I know myself well enough to know I may have put my sweater on top of the cookbook. Though you might call that *open-faced-sandwich losing*."

I knew myself well enough to know I was mainly putting off passing that bull. "But *sandwich losing* can be sneaky," I continued. "You put a paper down on a pile of papers the same size, then later absentmindedly put another pile of papers on top of that. Especially dangerous for writers.

"And then there's *purloined-letter losing*," I said. "That fits with Poe's famous story about the blackmail letter carefully hidden in plain sight. Suppose the envelope you've been looking for has been altered to look exactly like something you would hardly notice, like a grocery list. Perhaps you inadvertently wrote on the back of it. Ted and I have an expression when we find something we lost that way. We say we Edgar-Allan-Poe-'d it. But again, your envelope sounds too big for that."

"I have searched every scrap of paper the right size, believe me," Sam told me earnestly. Anne shrank more into herself as if she was cold. The sun had, in fact, gone under a cloud. The mountains around us had turned from green to blue-gray.

"We haven't run out of possibilities," I said. "Stop looking hopeless. Next, we'll try a variation of what everybody's mother always tells them."

Anne glared at me. "You mean: 'Stop and think where

you had it last'? We did that. But we can't remember *where*."

"Let's try an expansion of that." I felt I was on to something. "Go through the day. Because we want to remember what else you may have done that may have contributed to some complicated or compound way of losing." Hey, that might work.

"We'll try anything," Sam said. He picked a long piece of grass and began to chew it.

"We can make a schedule of everything that happened even if we don't find those papers," I pointed out. "We may find other clues to what killed Paul so soon afterward." That revived them a little. "O.K.," I said, "you got up on Friday morning. Then what?"

"We had cornflakes and orange juice," Anne said, almost belligerently.

"And you said that we were running out of food and toilet paper and we'd better go to the grocery store," Sam reminded her. "Then Revonda knocked at the door."

"You see, it was right after you left on Thursday that Revonda had a big fight with Paul, and he ran off," Anne said. "She acted like it was the end of the world and went to her room, sobbing. So on Friday morning we were relieved to see her asking for something and acting more like herself."

"That's when she told us that she wanted to paint Paul's woodwork. I was curious to see Paul's room." Sam's voice came alive.

"Revonda gave us the key, and we went over and measured to see how much paint we'd need," Anne said. "At first that room seemed more bizarre than anything else. I thought what a great scene the Wizard could do with a backdrop like that. Wow!"

"I was the one who went and looked at the books first, but Anne looked, too," Sam said. "Then we knocked off to do errands, but we went back to the studio, and Anne fixed us some sandwiches for lunch before we left. I said I'd forgotten something in Paul's room. I parked the van in front of Paul's door and put the marked books in a canvas carrying bag in the van for us to take with us."

"You should have told me." Anne gloomily waved away a fly.

"No," he said, "you would have talked me out of it. You'd have been afraid I would get in trouble."

"And you have!" she cried.

"Not yet," Sam said. "And if we find the copies of the pages Paul marked, I'll bet they show us what went wrong, and why he died." Sam raised his chin as if he dared us to disagree. The sun came back out from under the clouds, lighting his lion mane.

"So you put the books in the van," I said, "and then what?"

"When we went to do errands, I took along one of my big envelopes that has sketches and clippings for picture ideas."

"While I went for groceries for us and for Revonda and to get some things for Mert next door," Anne said, "Sam went to copy something at the library. Something for his idea envelope, I thought."

"Anne didn't notice when I took the bag of books out of the van." Sam glanced at her sheepishly. "I was a little sneaky," he said with a wink.

"You used the library copying machine, I assume," I said. "Anybody see you?"

"I doubt it," he said. "You see, there were a lot of schoolchildren having a story hour, and the reader was making noises like all kinds of animals. Moo, baa-baa, bow-wow. Attention was on her.

"Then," Sam continued, "I put the magic pages in between the larger sketches, in the hopes that if anybody ever looked in my envelope they'd only see the sketches. Because Paul would have had fits if he knew. After our errands I put the books back in Paul's room."

"While Sam was copying pages, exactly what were you doing?" I asked Anne.

"I was off getting some birthday wrapping paper for our neighbor Mert at Roses. One of her grandkids is about to be three."

"What kind of a bag was the wrapping paper in?" I asked.

"Oh!" Anne cried. "It was in a big flat brown paper bag. It was the size of Sam's manila envelope." Her face lit up with hope. "And after he got in the car, I threw that bag, which had been in the front, into the back of the car." Her eyes became huge. She pressed her fingers over her mouth, then pulled them back. "I could have picked up that bag and the envelope together. I've done that before. Picked two things at once by mistake when my mind was on something else and not even noticed. I could have taken them both together into Mert's." She caught her breath, then broke into a big grin. "So maybe the sheriff doesn't have that stuff!"

"Pickup-and-delivery losing," I said. "I hadn't thought of that."

Sam grinned, too. "Sometimes it pays to make mistakes."

Then Anne frowned. "Mert would have noticed. She doesn't miss a thing. And she calls herself Mert the Mouth!"

"Did you take anything else into her house?" I asked.

"I picked up her newspaper in the driveway," Anne said. "Sam went right back to the studio, and I took the bag to Mert. I carried the bag and paper together."

"Now try to remember every move you made," I said.

"I stopped on the front porch a minute and talked to Mert. I pulled out the paper and Mert said she guessed the paperboy left her two newspapers because she already had one. She said that boy was so vague she wondered why he didn't walk off a cliff. I guess I gave her the bag of her stuff and came home."

"Didn't you wonder what happened to your envelope?" I asked Sam.

He threw out his hands. "I thought it was between two canvases that I brought in." He laughed. "I was so busy not calling anybody else's attention to the envelope that I didn't check it myself." He raised an eyebrow at me. "Revonda called me and diverted me. She can be demanding."

Now, there is another way to losing I hadn't thought of: *Super-hiding.* I've done that. In fact, I never have found the wallet I got to surprise Ted for Christmas last year.

"Maybe I was foolish to take those books and copy those pages," Sam said. He didn't say it like apology. He was smiling like a friendly pirate. "But now that something or somebody killed Paul, we absolutely need to look at what he marked in those books."

He had a point. Anne sat up straighter and said, "I'll go see Mert. She called this morning and asked if there was anything she could do to help. I'll tell her I need to talk. She'll be dying to know what I saw yesterday." She jumped up, ready to start. Thank goodness the bull's back was turned, tail swishing flies. I stood up, too, ready to get out of there. Anne turned to me. "You come, too, Peaches, and help look and listen. There's not much that happens in this valley that Mert doesn't know—and tell."

"If that envelope is at her house, Edgar-Allan-Poe-'d, or sandwiched or whatever," I said, "the two of us will find it."

"Say, this could all be a lucky break." Sam jumped up and threw his arms wide. He rushed over and hugged Anne, who hugged him back this time. Then he hugged me again. Which was kind of nice.

The bull was still hind-end toward us, but he flicked his ears. "Please," I said, "can we sneak out of this field while the bull is busy?"

CHAPTER

10

"Notice Mert's lilies," Sam called after us as we set out across the road.

"Yes," Anne said to me, "she has the prettiest double yellow lilies I ever saw, all in bloom at the side of the house. That's like Sam," she added. "If he was about to be hanged, he'd notice yellow lilies." She said that with rueful pride like maybe it was a mixed blessing. What? No hero-worship?

Whoever built Mert's house liked to make wood paper dolls. Near the lilies was a wood cutout of the rear end of a woman leaning over, presumably weeding. Around the top of the porch was the kind of fancy scalloping that people call gingerbread. The waist-high rail around the porch had fancy-cut spokes, too, and the supports at the corners of the porch roof had the cutout silhouettes of birds. Even the front door had a cutout of a soaring eagle applied at eye level. To the left of the door, a large plastic throw covered a pile of something Mert evidently didn't want the rain to blow onto.

Before I had time to look underneath the plastic, the front door opened.

"I saw you coming!" cried a small woman with freckles, her gray hair pulled back in a bun. She threw her arms around Anne and cried, "Oh, Lord, I've had you on my mind!"

She turned to me and said, "And you must be the smart cousin who is helping out!"

"Peaches Dann," I said. "I hope I can be smart."

"Well, come right in." She grabbed us both and pulled us inside. She led us right through the living room past a brown couch and a recliner and a coffee table with a bunch of the yellow lilies and some blue irises. Except for the flowers on the table, all the surfaces were bare. No manila envelope. She led us on into a bright kitchen full of strawberry smell, talking all the time. "Just imagine. Just imagine me, yesterday when you found Paul, me taking all the neighbors to a revival. And it isn't even the usual time for revivals." Her broad mouth twisted up into a wry, kindly grin. "We went off just when you might have wanted to yell for help. And now what can I do? Besides pray?"

Anne said coffee would help.

"I'm freezing berries," she said. "You won't mind if I finish."

She sat us in two chairs at the kitchen table, handed us each a cup of coffee from an electric pot, and sat down to hull more strawberries. "Have a few from the master supply," she said, and I noticed she'd also put a saucer of powdered sugar on the table to dip them in. She picked up a particularly plump red strawberry by its green cap, dipped it in the sugar, and held it out for me to bite from the cap. I did and we all laughed.

"Good, huh?" she said, and then shot us a searching glance. "Now let's get serious. You know, the sheriff treated me like we went to that revival yesterday just to spite him. Every outside witness gone when you found Paul. And imagine me missing the only murder I may ever have across the street, if it was a murder. The folks I've talked to are fifty-fifty on whether it was." She cocked her head. "Now," she said, handing Anne a strawberry, "I want to hear the whole story."

Anne told it well. She got across the feel of what happened. How, in a way, it seemed unreal and, in a way, predestined. She even told something I hadn't heard yet—Revonda had persuaded the Reverend Moore, who had known Paul, to give a memorial service right away, even before the medical examiner gave back the body, in order to lay to rest all the talk that Paul was a heathen. I wished Revonda luck. Of course, Anne left out the part about Sam, and how he kidnapped magic books.

"I suppose they asked you a lot of questions," Mert demanded. She'd left the strawberries to get herself a cup of coffee.

"That deputy named Ron Brank asked and asked," Anne said. "He said he lives just up the hill."

"And sharp as a tack." Mert sat back down. She took a sip of coffee and peered at Anne over her cup. "Likes excitement. And likes the girls. Watch out."

While we talked, I'd been busy looking around the kitchen, trying to see any place where a big manila envelope might be. But the counters were bare except for a mixer and a few canisters.

"Do you think those marks on Paul were coiled snakes?" I turned back to hear Mert say that.

Snakes! In my mind I saw those whorls again through clear plastic, and in my mind they came alive, and they were snakes about to strike. My imagination is almost as good as Anne's.

Anne looked spooked.

Mert leaned forward across the table, eyes narrowed. "Some folks say those marks were magic, meant to call the devil." She closed one red-stained hand into a fist. She stared at the fist like it surprised her, opened her hand, and laughed. "If you ask me, this magic stuff is silly, just a lot of playacting to pretend to be important. That's what I think." She said that like a challenge. "Some people around here see the devil everywhere. They found a satanic cult at the high school last year. Maybe you heard. Just kids trying to say: 'Look at me.' That's what I think," she said scornfully.

So if Mert found Sam's copies of the spells and stuff, she might not take them too seriously. But the people she told might.

"If you ask me, what hit Paul had to do with Revonda," she said. "Somebody getting even with Revonda. Lord knows they couldn't pick a better way. Revonda is strong. What that woman's been through would fell an ox. Paul was the lost one. I wonder if anybody would bother to kill Paul, just for himself—if it was murder."

Mert turned to me. "I suppose you know about the preacher who mailed Revonda a snake?"

"Revonda?"

"In a shoebox," Mert said. "A dead copperhead. There are a lot of good Christian people in this valley, but there are a few nuts. Jeeter Justice, up the hill, is one. Jeeter sent a note with that dead snake, calling her the snake temptress, coming back to this valley as a bad example to the young'uns. They put him in the state asylum at Broughton for a year."

"For mailing the snake?" That sounded extreme.

"Well, not just that. He took to going into banks, and he'd yell and harangue about how they were lairs of greed all full of sinners. When he was on trial for trespassing and disturbing the peace, he began to scream at the judge and call him a sinner and a hypocrite, and the judge had him committed to Broughton. Now he's out, and if he takes his pills, he stays calm. His wife is a fine woman. Related to most folks in the valley."

Anne was bug-eyed. "Revonda has never said a word about anybody mailing her a snake!"

"Revonda won't say what makes her look bad." Mert began cutting up the strawberries she'd hulled. She looked first at Anne, then at me as if she was about to say something important. "I'm truly sorry for Revonda. I'm sure she is really a good Christian woman, but she brings trouble on herself." Mert tucked the loose hair back in the bun at the nape of her neck as if she wanted to set the world right. "Revonda likes to own people." She shook her head. "Paul got away from her into craziness. That's what I think. Like Paul's father got away into drink. And finally drove into a tree, poor man, and that killed him."

"When?" I asked.

"A couple of years ago. Just after they moved back here. I never did see the man sober."

Mert stopped with a strawberry in one hand and small knife in the other. Her fingers were red with juice, which reminded me of blood. But her face was still kind. "I knew Revonda when we were kids. She had a hard time. Then she's had a bad time with that boy. Even when she got back here. But she didn't want to throw Paul out. If Revonda could just try not to put on such airs, not to be so arrogant right out in front of God and everybody. Then she'd have more real friends." Mert still paused, knife in the air. "And now Paul's gone."

"You say the vote is fifty-fifty suicide or murder," I said. "You believe Paul could have killed himself? You think he could have marked himself and put that bag over his head and jumped into that laundry chute?" I had my doubts.

"I do." Mert said that firm and clear.

"Ron said it was possible," Anne said, eating another strawberry, "because of the way thin plastic bags cling. I asked him about that. Except I noticed there wasn't a marker by his body. And there were those whorls"—she squirmed—"or maybe snakes."

While I sat there and tried to sort out suicide and snakes, Mert got up and began to sugar the cutup strawberries. "Never waste time," she said. "Our pioneer ancestors in these parts were Scots-Irish. I guess the Scots stuck on me. Now, Revonda's grandfather came here from South Carolina. A three-piece-suit oratorical county lawyer. No way Scots. He died in a fire."

"I understand Revonda grew up dirt-poor," I said.

"Her father was a charmer with a run-down farm. All that piece of land was good for was to hold the world together. And like I said, he drank. She found him dead of it, frozen solid in the privy. She'll not tell you about that."

But Pop had.

"Of course," said Mert, "her father spoiled her best he could when he was sober. He let her act like a boy. She was the first girl in this valley—and I guess the only girl—to win the Fourth of July contest to catch a greased pig— greased with lard. We don't do that now. We think it's cruel to the pig. She was a sight when she finished, but she won. She always won. Except with her men.

"Revonda went off bitter. Her father insulted people when he was drunk, and he wouldn't let Revonda's mother go to church. When he drank himself to death, the folks in this valley didn't come to the funeral. Revonda resented that."

"It seems like too much," I said. "And her husband killed in an accident. Now this with Paul."

Mert nodded. "Otherwise she's done so fine. It's a study."

"You mean on the stage?"

"And marrying money. But money didn't help Paul." Mert put a freezer container of sliced strawberries in the refrigerator, and began to fill another.

When I was a girl," Mert said, "we knew families that feuded. Mostly over in the next county. Mostly related to making whiskey. Bad blood lasts a long time in these mountains. Some said Revonda's grandfather got in the middle of that, as a lawyer. Some will be saying that there's bad blood down to now. I don't hold with that."

Bad blood and bad luck. We had to allow for both or either. But above all, we needed to find the envelope with the magic symbols in it.

"This is a wonderful house," I said. "I love the way the shelves have Victorian curlicues to hold them up. Could you show me the rest of the house?" Mert took me into the two bedrooms, one with a sewing machine set up and pieces for a quilt on the bed. But no stacks the envelope might be in. The closet door was standing open, but the shelf stood empty except for a black straw hat and a pair of black medium-heel shoes. I'd left Anne back in the kitchen where I counted on her to look in every cabinet and nook.

The second bedroom was full of pictures of grandchildren. "I stay in here," Mert said. "The front room is for kids who spend the night." I opened the closet door and said, "Oh, that's the wrong door," as if I'd opened it by mistake.

No sign of our envelope.

I asked to use the bathroom. At least I could search there with the door shut. A brown bathrobe and a plastic shower cap hung on a hook on the back of the door. The bathtub was a nice old one with claw feet. Nothing under it. But don't give up, I warned myself. A pencil and a shopping list lay on the counter near the toilet. The list said, "recycle newspapers." Hey! That was it! The tarp on the porch covered newspapers! A sandwich-loss possibility.

I came out of the bathroom and found Sam had arrived and was telling Mert how he loved her kitchen. He had his arm around Mert, like she was his long-lost mother.

While Mert was diverted, Anne shook her head at me. She hadn't found anything. I smiled and winked at Anne.

"I couldn't help seeing 'recycle newspapers' on your Do-It list," I told Mert. "Sam tells me he's about to recycle his and Revonda's. Should we take the ones under the plastic on the front porch for you?"

Sam hardly even blinked. "Yes," he said. "Revonda called and wanted me to take the dress she's going to wear to the memorial service to the cleaners. And we're going to recycle papers on the way." He was so casual. What an actor.

I prayed to God my guess was right and our envelope was in that pile. Where else was left?

Mert led us to the porch, took off the plastic throw, and reached to help us move those papers into the van. "You girls just relax," Sam ordered. "Let me show you how strong I am." He picked up a big bundle of untied papers from the top of the pile.

We couldn't stop Mert. "I'm used to being handy. I didn't grow up to sit," she said. But Sam and Anne and I worked so fast, we moved most of the papers. Nothing odd in my piles. We got in the van, me in the backseat and Anne with Sam now in the front. He didn't say a word until we were way down the valley. He whooped: "Hooray. You were right! I found it!" What a break. What a relief.

"Anne, I know what you did with that stuff. You must have put the bag and envelope down on top of Mert's pile of papers." He laughed and turned to me. "There must be a whole category for people who have a special talent for creative ways to lose things." He turned back to Anne. "You absentmindedly handed Mert the bag and put the newspaper down on top of the envelope. Did the phone ring? Obviously something diverted Mert. She left that paper there because she already had another one."

Anne laughed. "Mert or one of her neighbors put more papers on top and didn't notice. What incredible luck."

Sam turned and winked at Anne. "The best mistake you ever made. So now we can study the stuff Paul marked in his books, even while the sheriff has the books."

They both began to sing: *"We'll recycle all the papers when we come, when we come."* And then: *"We'll study all the magic when we come, when we come."* Singing to celebrate.

"Sam," Anne sang, "you *are* changing my luck!" That look of worship was back in her eyes. She loved him partly because he sang all-out like a mad pirate, or a mad saint.

To make everything fit our fib, we went back to Revonda's to get her papers to recycle. One of the sheriff's department cars was there, and a deputy, who seemed to be studying Revonda's front door, nodded at us. Because I needed to visit the plumbing, I went into the studio. (Last bathroom visit had been research.) Sam carried the precious envelope hidden in a newspaper. He carried in some other stuff from the backseat. I wasn't paying too much attention to what. Anne went ahead of us, so she didn't notice, either.

I heard him open the closet door and the rustle as he hung something inside. I turned and saw him put the envelope flat on the closet shelf, still under the newspaper.

I noticed a glimmer behind him. I heard Anne start to scream and shut her mouth on the sound before it could get out and be heard outside. She leaned on the round table as if she could hardly stand. "Sam. There's a plastic dry cleaning bag in that closet. With something black in that bag. It wasn't here before."

"Oh, yes," he said. "Not to worry. I just put it there. It's only Paul's black suit. Actually, I already got the cleaning while you were at Mert's."

"Paul's suit is in a bag like the bag that killed him!"

"I should have thrown the bag away," he said casually, "but to tell the truth, I want to paint it. I can do it by memory but not as well." That was Sam. If it upsets you, paint it. I could see Anne wanted to burn the thing.

He pulled the hanger out of the closet, whipped the bag off the suit and folded the plastic bag up. She just stood stunned as he put the bag in the top bureau drawer with his socks.

"Paul wore this in a dinner-theater play, and someone spilled soup on it. One reason Revonda wanted me to go right to the cleaners was to get this suit. She's comforting herself by being picky."

"And the detective let you walk right in with a bag like the one that killed Paul?" Anne had her hands on her hips, outraged.

Sam seemed surprised. "They don't care what we bring in, only what was here when Paul died."

"Why get Paul's suit today, for him to be buried in, when there's only a memorial service coming up. Why bring the suit here?" she asked.

"I know you won't like this." He pulled on his beard and looked sheepish. "But this is important to Revonda. This suit isn't for Paul. Revonda has asked me to wear it to the memorial service. He and I are the same size."

Anne gasped, and her eyes went so large they hardly seemed to fit in her face. "Why would she want you to do that?"

I wondered myself.

"She's obsessed," he said, "by wanting to be sure each of us will look right at the service. And you know I don't have a suit."

Anne shook her head no, but Sam ignored that.

"Revonda's friend Marvelle is finding a black dress for you, Anne," Sam said. "Revonda needs any comfort we can give her. And just because Paul owned this suit doesn't mean we have to be superstitious, does it?"

He should have known Anne *was* superstitious. Even I could remember that.

"It's a dead man's suit. It could be a murdered man's suit, a haunted suit. Please don't wear it!"

I wished that girl didn't have such a good imagination. I wished Paul hadn't said he'd put a curse on us. I'd repressed that. It had gone right out of my head. It came back now.

Anne deliberately straightened herself. "Maybe I'm being silly," she said. She clenched her fists and took a deep breath. "If I'm hysterical, that won't help."

She forced her face into a tremulous smile. "At least Sam won't walk in Paul's shoes," she said, turning to me and trying to joke.

Now it was Sam who looked horrified. "Did you have to put it that way?" he said slowly. "Because now I've promised and I really can't go back on my promise." He picked up a brown paper bag from the closet floor. Slowly he opened the bag and took out two black shoes, both glowingly shined, and with the laces neatly tied in bows.

CHAPTER

11

MONDAY, 5:30 P.M.

I came home to find Ted's car parked in front of the house, and hurried inside so fast that the door banged shut. I ran through the living room and found him in the kitchen leaning on the counter near the electric coffeemaker, leafing through the mail, and waiting for the coffee to finish dripping.

I threw my arms around him. He felt so normal. He felt like the center of the familiar world. And our nice sunshine-yellow kitchen was a part of that world, No mirrors. No black candles. No paintings of disasters. Nobody saying Help! I kissed Ted like he was the most wonderful man in the universe.

"Bad stuff you're mixed up in, huh?" he said into my hair, hugging me back hard, then holding me out where he could see my face. His eyebrows were raised in a what-now? expression.

"I sure do need you to bounce this around with. I need you to be sane like you always are," I said.

"That bad?" he said. "Let's get some coffee and go sit down. Boy, I never learned so much in four days. Really good stuff about computer reporting for my journalism classes. I'll be telling you about it for weeks, but let's hear the disaster now."

We went and sat in the two big armchairs that are catercorner in the living room. I started at the beginning, to make sure I told all. I explained how Revonda had been with her friend Marvelle, and how Anne and I had been together most of the time—but not all—during which Paul either killed himself or was killed. But Sam had no one to vouch for him. And how that could be bad because he had been accused of murder in Boston, though the sheriff might not know that since charges weren't pressed. I told Ted about Sam kidnapping Paul's books, and about the sketches that vanished and how we'd just found them, and I even threw in the bit about Sam having to wear Paul's shoes at the service.

Ted ran his fingers through his hair: sign of deep thought. "You realize," he said, "that you've allowed family loyalty or whatever to put you in a bad spot. You've kept things to yourself that you should have told the sheriff, and probably you'll continue to keep mum, if I know you."

"But Anne *is* my cousin," I said. "And those two kids don't know diddly-squat about taking care of themselves."

"Which means," he said, "that they are even more likely to let the cat out of the bag about your part in this."

He was right. I'd been thinking so hard about helping those kids I hadn't thought about myself. Old One-Track Mind.

"I'd advise you to get out of this and stay out," he said, sipping his coffee thoughtfully. "But I know you'd rather spend a year in prison than stop now."

"That's true. I have a feeling Anne and Sam are going to need all the help they can get."

"Be very careful," my husband said, grinning like that was a joke. "I'd miss you."

"We need your logical mind in this," I said, encouraged by his grin. "You need to come look at these copies of the pages Paul marked. I told Sam I had to come home and ask for your help. He suggested we come back this afternoon."

"One of us mixed up in this is already too much," Ted said. He drummed his fingers on the arm of his chair, considering. "But I certainly don't want you in trouble by yourself." He was good at logic, but he was also good at rationalizations. We finished our coffee and set out before he even unpacked.

As we got into Ted's car, I felt drops of rain. By the time we reached Bloodroot Creek, the rain almost overwhelmed the windshield wipers. Thunder boomed. Revonda's house looked pretty dramatic in the lightning flashes. Especially the tower. There's something horror-movie about a tower on a dark house. The electricity was evidently off because both Revonda's house and the studio were dark except for one flickering light in each—a candle or an oil lamp, I figured.

We parked, ran through the rain to the door, and felt our way up the dark studio steps. We called out, and Anne opened the upstairs door for us, holding a candle. "Sam's over with Revonda," she said. The candlelight made her lovely face downright exotic. She had on a caftan of some wine-red Indian fabric with a big paisley print—comfortable, no doubt, but adding to the exotic effect. Underlining her natural grace. I introduced her to Ted, and I could see appreciation in his eyes. Ha! I thought. Gotcha! Ted wouldn't pull out and leave such a pretty girl in the lurch.

She took our wet raincoats and hung them on a peg to drip. I could tell by the way Ted immediately darted his eyes around that he was itching to look into every corner of the studio and especially at Sam's paintings. But Anne waved her hand toward the bentwood chairs around the round table and made it clear, as she hurried us to them, she wanted us to sit right down and look at the magic stuff.

We sat in three chairs, and Anne put a large envelope on the fourth chair. She pulled out some papers and held the top one in the candlelight. She knocked the others on the floor, said, "damn," and picked them up, nervous, as if she was afraid they'd fight against her.

"Sam and I have had a chance to just glance through these," she said. "I'll begin with the only place he says was marked with a red ribbon, which must be the one Paul thought was most important of all."

She held out a picture of a round-headed, half-bald man wearing a loose overblouse and a shirt with a ruff collar. His right hand was on the handle of a sword with a word on it: *Zoth*. Behind the man was a window, and through the window were books and manuscripts scattered on the ground near a tiny human head, which seemed quite cheerful considering it had no body. Strange. "And here's the opposite page." Anne pointed. I read Mr. Ruff-and-Sword's name: Paracelsus, 1493?–1541.

"A physician, astrologer, mystic, and magus," Ted said, studying the text. "His motto was *'Be not another if thou can'st be thyself.'*"

"Well, I'm for that," I said. "That's not magic."

Ted was already digesting what the page said. Talk about reading fast. "Because Paracelsus thought for himself, he made enemies and discovered things, it says here." He read further. "Paracelsus discovered a cure for syphilis that worked."

"Yes," Anne said, "and because he laughed at the bigwigs and went by what he saw with his own eyes, Sam thinks he must have been great. That article about Paracelsus explains how he thought magic worked."

Good grief, on this one page could there be an explanation of magic? No wonder Paul put a red ribbon there.

Ted read aloud: "'Imagination is like the sun, the light of which is not tangible but which can set a house on fire.'" Did he mean like the sun's rays could set fire through a magnifying glass?

"'All depends only upon a man's imagination to be sun—that is, that he wholly imagines that which he wills.'"

"That doesn't seem so strange," Anne said. "Giving a good puppet show works the same way—imagining wholly." She glanced at the puppets hanging against the wall, shadowy in the candlelight. "Which is why I'm glad I have a good imagination." Her face softened. She glanced back at the page, and her frown lines deepened again. "So why did Paul need black woodwork and crazy mirrors if plain imagination does the trick?" she asked. "Why did Paul put his red ribbon to mark this place?"

That was a good question.

"Perhaps the other pages Paul marked tell more about how he thought," Ted said. "How did he mark them differently?"

"Sam says all the rest were marked with scraps of torn paper, like he just did it on impulse," Anne said.

We passed the pages around between us. There were all sorts of strange charms, even one for becoming invisible. Oh, come on!

But these charms were all knocked right out of my mind when a black symbol caught my eye: three marks, a little like a Chinese word. Points of ink made parts of the symbol rise like flame. It was labeled "Charm used in cursing an enemy."

Revonda had said Paul was into *good* magic. A curse couldn't be good magic. I shivered and turned to the next page—and that knocked my socks off, too. "Here's the charm with lines in a spiral and magic symbols like that thing that Paul wore round his neck!"

Anne nodded. "Yes, I know," she said. "Paul told me it was a charm to bring him protection."

"So what did Paul need protection from?" I asked.

"From his own imagination, perhaps," Ted guessed. "Or maybe from someone who wanted to manipulate his imagination to scare him to death. Or maybe from someone he suspected wanted to kill him."

"But who?" I asked.

A throaty dramatic voice answered from the doorway:

"Someone wanted to destroy him, and they succeeded!" I jumped an inch. Revonda! There she stood, holding a folded umbrella. She was so white her makeup was like a wrong-color picture painted on her face. She wore a white shirt and black pants. Sam was a dark shadow behind her. I hadn't heard them come up the step—maybe due to the storm noise or maybe because we were concentrating on the pages. And, oh, boy, what would she think when she saw we had them?

"I saw your car," she said to Ted. "I'm Revonda Roland—you must be Peaches' husband." She came forward and held out her hand to Ted, who stood to meet her. Even her hand was unnaturally white. Yet, in her despair, she could still look up at Ted through her eyelashes, almost like a flirt. "If you've come to help, I thank you. I don't expect much help from the sheriff."

Sam came in and stood behind Anne's chair with both hands on the bentwood back. His hair was pointed with wetness.

"You see," Revonda said, "Harley was once a shy kid who asked me to marry him. He was a lot younger than I was, so I thought it was funny. I laughed at him. I was too young to understand how that could hurt his pride. Now our sheriff will do whatever is guaranteed to hurt me most."

"But certainly he'll have to behave like a professional," I said. "He is the elected sheriff of the county."

"I wouldn't trust him as far as I could throw a two-ton truck full of lead weights," said Revonda. "He's slippery as a greased snake. We're on our own."

Then Revonda turned to Anne. "Those are pages from Paul's books, aren't they?" The Paracelsus picture was faceup on the table in front of Anne.

"I copied pages before Paul died," Sam spoke right up, "the ones he'd marked. I was afraid that something was wrong here. I wanted to know what he was mixed up in. And now we *need* to know."

I waited for Revonda to get mad. But she went around to

Sam and put her arm around him. "Thank God you did," she said, hugging him. "Because the sheriff has taken Paul's books, and we all need to look at these for clues." She took the envelope of papers off the fourth chair and put it on the table. She sat down in the chair. "I've looked through Paul's books," she said, "but not at a time when I thought . . ." She hesitated. "I didn't expect to find him dead."

She took a deep breath. "There's a lot about mirrors." Revonda's voice was hoarse, but she began to read us about some man named Pretorius in the seventeenth century, who said a boy could see the future by staring at a mirror in a basin of water.

Sam was looking over her shoulder: "He thought the devil helped, of course."

Revonda bristled.

Sam patted her arm. "Why should the devil have to help?" he asked. "Look, here it says a person can stare into a shiny shield to see the future. Or stare at a shiny fingernail. If anyone stares at something shiny long enough, he can hypnotize himself, right?"

"You mean"—I leaned forward—"you could hypnotize yourself into seeing the future? Listen!" I was getting excited. "In Paul's room I could almost feel demons and until I got used to those crazy mirrors, I did feel hypnotized. So the members of a cult trying to raise demons could certainly have stared themselves into some altered state of mind." I felt the hair on my back and arms rise.

Revonda leaned forward. "And that altered state of mind could lead to murder."

She put her hands over her face. "I can't look at these anymore now. I can't stand the strain. Tomorrow I'll look, after we pray for poor Paul. But don't think for one minute," she said, raising her chin, "that because I'm not studying these now I won't do everything in my power to find the killer."

I wouldn't want to be a killer that Revonda decided to track down. She had the most determined eyes I ever saw in my life. Even candlelight didn't soften them. "We *will succeed*," she said, seeming to beam her whole will through her eyes.

I had the oddest feeling that some kind of magic was on her side.

CHAPTER
12

So Sam wore Paul's black suit. I almost laughed. The suit was so strange with Sam's lion-mane hair. He was like a mad, long-haired scientist dressed to win the Nobel Prize. But I could see Anne struggling desperately not to be superstitious about that suit—to say nothing of those black shoes.

We were all in Revonda's living room, ready for the service, though we didn't have to leave for fifteen minutes. Revonda had put on black with pearls and held her head high. Trembly brave. She sat in her jungle chair, sipping a Scotch for the road, the dogs at her feet. Sam sat close beside her in his mourning suit. I was on the other side. Anne looked at a bunch of red roses and blue delphinium. "I like these best," she said, looking at the card. "From Tam."

"Let me see," Revonda demanded. She examined the flowers. "My cousin Mat could have afforded better than that," she said in a prissy schoolteacher voice. "He's a lawyer."

Ted winked at me. Yes, Revonda was uptight. Ted had just come back from taking something out to the kitchen to the cousin in a too-tight dress who was rearranging the fridge, fitting in the offerings of food that friends and neighbors brought.

Someone knocked hard on the front door. The dogs began to bark, and Revonda had to shush them. The sheriff opened the door and stuck his head in. The rest of him followed uninvited. This was hardly the moment we needed for him to turn up, with those half-closed, speculating eyes. He walked in so determined, yet light and quiet on his feet: a stalker. "I have something important to tell, Revonda." He stood tall on her oriental rug in his fancy boots.

Sam got up to give the sheriff his seat next to Revonda and stood behind her, leaning on the back of her jungle-print chair. I bit my lip. By gosh, Sam was like an Amish elder rising from a dreamscape—like a guardian angel in deep mourning. But he didn't seem funny to Anne. Her scared eyes kept repeating: Sam in a dead man's suit.

"Revonda, honey," said the sheriff, pulling his chair around to face her, not far from me but ignoring me. "I know you don't want to see me right before the service. But the media people have been after me so hard. I need to tell you what I told them before you hear it on the news." He shifted in his chair, leaning toward her. "I think I owe you that." He turned and stared at the rest of us. "I'd like to be alone with Mrs. Roland."

Revonda held her head like a statement: A woman with real pearls gets what she wants. "I want my friends to stay right here. They can be helpful." She reached up toward Sam behind her, and he put his hand over hers and patted her hand.

The sheriff's square jaw firmed up even squarer. But he also squirmed, all gangly six-feet-plus. Queen Revonda had him pinioned with her magic stare. Whatever he'd come to tell half stuck in his throat.

He began to talk about the ways Paul could have died. He

kept waving with those big, clumsy hands. Medium-wide-apart when he said: ". . . rumors of a cult." Wider when he said: "It could have been a crazy person." Twisting together when he talked about drug killings. Revonda had told me she thought drug dealers could buy him off. Harley Henderson wouldn't even charge much, she'd said—he didn't have enough sense.

Revonda spoke: "You said you'd come to tell me what you told the media. You said you let yourself be pressured into a statement. Well, I'm waiting."

Ted was watching her with a little pleased smile. He likes a woman who knows her own mind.

Even the rottweilers saw something was up and sat at attention, ears perked.

The sheriff leaned forward and paused. "Now, Revonda"—his eyes were steady on her, but his hands held each other as if he was nervous—"honey, you're not going to like what I say."

"I never have."

"The coroner found cocaine in Paul's system. That didn't kill him. But it sure could have twisted his thoughts. And as for his body, there were no lumps. No broken bones. No sign of a struggle."

"And so?"

"And, honey, the most likely thing is that Paul killed himself."

I was relieved. That meant the sheriff couldn't possibly suspect Sam or Anne.

But the jolt hit Revonda like she'd been shot. She pressed back in her chair. She blinked.

The sheriff just plowed on. Either that man was thick, or else he really meant to hurt. "If there'd been a note, we would have decided right away. But people don't always leave a note."

"Cowards kill themselves. I didn't raise a coward." Revonda was rigid as glass. Her eyes glittered. Maybe the glitter was from tears, but she didn't let them fall.

"Well, honey, there were no latent fingerprints in his room from anybody but you and Sam and Anne and your friend Marvelle—and your play detective here." His voice went heavy with sarcasm when he got to me. "No recent footprints from anybody we couldn't account for. First, we thought there were, but, Revonda, you have so many kinds of shoes, we found a match for the extra prints by studying your closet." He managed to make it sound like it was all her fault for liking shoes. Like maybe she was Imelda Marcos in disguise. That big mouth half smiled, like he was glad it was her fault.

"Now, about the plastic bag. The bag that killed Paul was next on the roll from the one on a dry-cleaned pair of pants in Paul's closet. Little faults in the plastic matched. That bag must have been from the same batch of cleaning. You might say he had the means right at hand to kill himself."

Revonda seethed with fury. I could practically feel the heat from where I sat. The sheriff had reactivated her. Pushed the emergency button. "So you're too stupid to catch a killer in gloves," she hissed, "or a killer who borrowed a pair of my shoes."

I had visions of a crazy Killer Cinderella. We'd catch her with Revonda's slippers.

The sheriff shook his head slowly, as if he didn't know what to do next. "We'll keep looking, honey. Good Lord, we go way back, you and me. I'll do all I can." Mock soothing voice. "But I still believe Paul killed himself."

"Why?"

"He was depressed, honey. When Henry Williams at the Box Elder gas station told him to have a good day, Paul told Henry it was a good day to be dead. Now I ask you! He killed himself."

"I suppose you think the devil made those marks on Paul. Some fools think so. I hear Jeeter up the hill says that. And it's his daughter, Jinx, who ran after Paul. Told the world she loved him. Little fool."

Jeeter. Mert said someone named Jeeter mailed a dead

snake to Revonda. The name was so odd it stuck in my mind. And his daughter was after Paul? And named Jinx? How horribly appropriate! To love Paul would sure be a jinx. Revonda said this Jeeter's name like poison.

Revonda was practically breaking her pearls from twisting them. But still pink-furious. "You know there was nothing in Paul's room that matched those marks on his body. Nothing he could have used to paint himself like that. You told me that yourself."

"But you didn't see him come in, did you, Revonda, honey? He could perfectly well have put the marks on someplace else and then come home and killed himself." Now, that was far-fetched. We'd seen him just a little while before he died, and the sheriff knew it. But the sheriff sounded pleased he'd thought of it.

Revonda's fingers pressed into the chair until I thought the fabric might tear. Sam reached down over the chair back and put a hand on each of her black shoulders. "We have to get to the church," he told the sheriff. "The service is at one, and it's ten of one now." Sam was almost holding Revonda down. But it didn't work.

She jumped up and screamed at the sheriff: "You don't know about Paul. All you have is a mouth as foul as a garbage truck. You don't care who killed Paul. Or somebody has bought you off."

The sheriff turned bright red, and his eyes became even narrower. He stood up, too, so he looked down on her: "Revonda, honey, if you want to talk murder—why, our best suspects are right here in this room." He pinned each of us with his eyes so hard I felt like shrinking back.

"Of course, you all say you were with someone when Paul died. Except Sam Newman here." The sheriff smiled like he could see through all our alibis. He straightened taller. "And remember, Revonda, if you stir things up too much, you might even get people to wondering about you, honey. Because Paul had life insurance made out to you."

She stared him down. He was taller, but she had more

presence. Circe about to turn Odysseus into a swine. "We—were—life—insurance—beneficiaries—for—each—other. Neither—one—of—us—had—anybody—else." She said that like she was spelling it out for a child.

"Two hundred thousand dollars," the sheriff said dryly.

At least *that* insurance wasn't made out to Sam.

"You get out of here!" Revonda began shouting. "Harley Henderson, you're a jackass. I knew it back in school. Harley Henderson, I wouldn't spit in your ear if your brain was on fire!"

Revonda turned to us as soon as he was gone. "I don't know what that man is trying to cover up. But I don't trust him as far as I could throw a house."

CHAPTER
13

The phone rang just as we got to the front door, ready to leave for the church. Cousin Edna came running from the kitchen, shaking her head from side to side as if to say "No, no, not that."

What she did say was: "Revonda, I'm so sorry, Reverend Moore had one of his attacks. Asthma so bad he can't do the service. But Reverend Phillipson will do it for him."

"Phillipson's an old fool." Revonda just stood there in the white doorframe, glaring. "First, that damn fool sheriff, now this."

As we rode along in the funeral-parlor Cadillac, Revonda said, "The killer will be there to watch me while I listen to that old fool preach about how good can come even from evil. He'll preach right for idiots or babies or hypocrites. Not for me."

"How do you know what he'll say?" Ted asked.

"That's all he ever preaches, no matter what he says the subject is. When that nincompoop says God can work through murder—and he will—how can I not get up and scream?" She'd screamed enough.

"Remember, you're not alone," Sam said. "We're with you."

There was a mob at the small stone church a couple of miles down the road. A staring mob. Some people had given up the idea of being able to press into the church. They were standing outside church windows in the hot sun, saving themselves look-in places, waiting for the service to start. One man even had a little boy on his shoulders so the boy could see in the window better. They swiveled around to stare at us.

Revonda was the main attraction. A television reporter with a camera and a backpack spotted us and began to shoot. Was Revonda that famous as an actress? About medium-famous, I'd thought. No, it must be stories going round that brought those people and the TV man. The talk about magic, drugs, Satanism, suicide, or murder.

We hurried in the back door and were ushered through to a front row, reserved for the immediate family. I studied the congregation for a moment or two when we entered the church. I spotted the sheriff and that deputy called Ron, standing up at the back. On the far right Mert in her brown Sunday dress nodded.

Knowing Agnes was just a few seats away. She sure stood out because she had on the same red skirt and unmatching red blouse that she wore when she wandered up and down the road and picked wildflowers. She actually held a bunch of Queen Anne's lace. Revonda's friend Marvelle Starr, all done up in black and diamonds, almost eclipsed Revonda. Revonda stage-whispered: "That Jinx is here." Jinx. The girl Revonda said ran after Paul.

The front of the church was banked with red and white roses.

Revonda, one seat over from me, couldn't keep her hands still. Her right hand kept moving from finger to finger of the left, as if she were counting. There was a small rustling in back of me. The whole congregation was on edge, couldn't keep still. I held Ted's hand to steady myself. I was glad the organ was playing.

Standing up front, the Reverend Phillipson—the one Revonda said was a fool—looked more like an eighty-year-old baby in horn-rimmed glasses. His white hair was soft and fuzzy with the pink scalp showing. His smile was trusting as a baby's. I liked him. But he was as out of place at that service as the heads of the people staring in the open church windows.

"In whatever happens, however terrible, we must find some good for the future." He swept us with his gentle brown eyes, encouraging us to agree. "Paul's death is telling us we need to pray for each other more." I glanced at Revonda. Her jaw was set as if her teeth were glued together.

"Paul was a young man searching for something. Once in a while he talked to me when I was out weeding my garden. He was angry at the world for being so imperfect. That happens to us all from time to time. But he found it extra hard. He needed our prayers. And now he is taken from us violently in a strange way that we do not understand. He is now in the mercy of God, who sees more deeply and understands more deeply than any of us."

He held up a bunch of twigs. Revonda whispered: "The old fool has to act things out."

"This is a bunch of twigs." He took one and snapped it. "See how easily one breaks. We are like that. But when we pray together we are strong." He tried to break the whole thick bundle of twigs. He beamed. "Together, we can't be broken. We must pray together for strength and understanding."

Revonda hissed: "He used that line on the kindergarten." Sam patted her hand.

Reverend Phillipson didn't notice her glare. His gentle smiling face was like a cherub's on a valentine. More rustling in the congregation. His cheerful faith was adding to the edgy mood in that church—I guess they didn't think it fit in with possible black magic. But I thought he made a nice change.

He blessed us all and told us to pray to God for positive thoughts and quickly finished the service.

Revonda leaned heavily on Sam as we walked out. Anne still kept glancing at that eerie black suit as if she'd like to rip it off of Sam and burn it. Not the thing to do in church. Revonda stopped in the back doorway. She turned and looked up at Sam. She stood back and smiled at him. Like he was a long-lost friend who'd just come in the door.

"Thank you for wearing Paul's suit, Sam. It looks right on you." I thought: She's cracked under the strain. Then she repeated back what he'd said to her. "I am not alone." She clutched his arm again. "Sam, you are a son to me now."

Anne watched that with a set face. Like she was scared her face might misbehave if she just let it relax and do what it pleased. I wondered if she was seeing Paul again the way I was. Complete with sneer. Paul asking again, "Where did my mother know Sam before?"

Then Anne came forward and took Sam's other arm and squeezed it, as if to say, *He's on loan to you, Revonda, but he belongs to me.*

And I thought: It's dangerous to love a man with great charm.

CHAPTER
14

AFTER THE FUNERAL

"I will receive people until three o'clock," Revonda pronounced as we drove back to her house after the memorial service. "I will show them all that I can't be cowed. I survive."

We drove up to her big old Victorian house, still only partway painted, though I noticed Sam had managed to finish the front porch. The rottweilers, who'd been inside when we left, were out on the porch. They both came running toward us, their short ears flapping in the breeze, stumpy tails wagging. They didn't bark because they knew us. "It's all right," Revonda told them and took them inside.

As soon as she freshened up, she stalked over to her jungle-print chair and sat down, head high, ready to take on the world. Her hands were clenched into fighting fists. I didn't like it. I felt quite sure she was going to do or say something unwise.

Sam went off to get extra ice, which we were somehow lacking, and Anne went out into the kitchen to help put out food and drink. I asked Revonda if there was anything special I could do, and she told me to take her glass and fill it. "Scotch," she whispered. "Anne knows where it is. Don't bring me that nasty iced tea the rest will want."

When I brought the glass back, she said: "Now, go listen to what people say." She didn't need to tell me that. I walked over to the pictures of Revonda's family, specially studying the one of her father. He had a stubborn jaw but reckless black eyes. Like Paul. From there I could watch the front door and pick the people I'd drift near to.

What I was able to hear didn't seem like a help. A large woman with a belly that hung over like a shelf was telling a thin woman, "I'm bringing peach cobbler to the Fourth of July picnic."

A small stringy man was saying, "My tomatoes are doing good, but my corn is looking sickly." Nobody seemed to be gossiping here in Revonda's house. In a way, I was glad of that.

I saw Mert and enlisted her as a who's-who agent. I knew Paul had a girl named Jinx, and I wanted to meet her.

"She'll come," Mert said. "She knows Revonda hates her, but she'll come to any place where folks might talk about Paul. Paul was real mean to that girl. She had it bad, and he didn't. They say she still does."

"Who else is here who might have been close to Paul?" I asked. She pointed out Marvelle, who was just making an entrance in her black and diamonds, and hugging everybody. "Marvelle was Paul's godmother," Mert explained. "Revonda arranged that. They got on so well, Paul and Marvelle—why, that woman in her fancy clothes gets on with everybody. She just loves her neighbors, so they like her. She's vain as a peacock and nice at the same time."

Marvelle the peacock went to talk to a dark-haired woman in gold earrings like coiled snakes. How did she have the nerve to wear them so soon after . . . Mert squeezed my arm. "That woman is a psychologist. They say Paul went to see her. Didn't do much good, if you ask me."

Marvelle went out to the kitchen and came back with a glass of what must have been Scotch. Sam came back, whispered something to Revonda, and took her glass out to the kitchen for a refill.

"That's one of Paul's dinner-theater buddies," I heard Mert saying, pointing to a fidgety red-haired man with a mustache who was standing next to Lady Macbeth. "Paul was in one of those groups that act while people eat dinner. But they only did it once in a while. Revonda said they were playacting boys. Not serious."

The young man with the mustache avoided Revonda's glance, perhaps because he wore a black T-shirt, of all things, with black jeans. The T-shirt said, TO BE IS BETTER THAN NOT TO BE—ASK WILL.

Revonda was all hollow eyes, watching who came. Paul's picture was at her elbow. Somebody had floated one perfect rose in a silver bowl next to that picture. Of Paul, who fought with his mother. Who was cruel to the girl who loved him. Who threatened Sam. Who laughed when Anne walked into a mirror, and sneered at me. Who nice Reverend Phillipson said was lost and needed help. So who was he?

A young woman with tear-swollen face, in a dowdy black dress, came in the front door. She stood at a distance and stared at the silver-framed picture of Paul next to Revonda. Mert nudged me: "That's Jinx."

I thought how pretty Jinx was—with her shining red hair and those wide-set green eyes—even with her face shiny and swollen from recent tears. And how much she looked as if she were waiting for somebody to hit her in the face. From across the room Revonda glared as if she'd like to be the one to hit her. Revonda's hand holding her glass trembled. She turned and nodded at Anne, who took the glass for a refill. Oh, dear, I thought, it's not going to help if Revonda gets drunk.

While my head was turned, Mert had gone to get Jinx and bring her to meet me. When I turned back, there she was. "This is Anne's cousin Peaches," Mert said. "She'd like to help find out what happened to Paul. She'll want to talk to you, Jinx, I know." Mert the Mouth. This was not the time to question this poor girl except to tell her I was so sorry about what had happened.

But Jinx took hold of my arm with a cold hand. "I have to talk to you." There was not enough breath behind her voice. I had to work hard to hear. She pulled me away from the others into the corner near the entrance into the dining room.

"I have something to show somebody who wants to know about Paul." She was one hundred percent intense, quivering like a hummingbird, and still smelling of tears. "Not the sheriff," she said. "He wouldn't understand." I noticed Revonda staring at her angrily. "I don't have to stay here—not if you'll come and see me," the girl said. "Mert will tell you where to find me." She ran out the door, edging past a startled white-haired woman who was just coming in.

Marvelle had moved over toward the hall with the door to Paul's room off it. Moved that way with glass of whiskey in hand. Paul's door was surely locked, but I could see that the door to Revonda's room was open, undoubtedly so guests could use the bathroom. I drifted over near the entrance to the hall, and when I saw Marvelle come back out of Revonda's room, I walked over and stopped her. "When you get a chance, I'd like to talk to you about Paul," I said.

"Good." She reached over and grabbed my arm as eagerly as Jinx had. Except her hand was bonier. Did they think I'd run away?

"Paul wasn't a monster," Marvelle said dramatically. "Some people are unhappy and they don't have any imagination about it. He was unhappy in extremely original ways." She reached out with her free hand and touched the wall, steadying herself. She was a little high. Not quite solid on her feet, but not gone enough so she couldn't navigate.

"When did you see him the last time?" I asked. If she was willing to talk, I might as well find out what I could. We had the hall to ourselves. Behind us was a backdrop of interwoven chatter, like any get-together.

Marvelle let out a long quavering sigh. "I saw him just before whatever happened." She stopped and stared at his black door. "Behind that door." She pointed with amazement. "Because it was just after lunch." Her face contorted into pain, and I half expected bits of makeup to pop off. But she smoothed out her face immediately.

"The day before, he'd asked me to come over to see him." She spoke clearly, like she was reading lines. "He wanted to show me something. But when I came, he said please to go away, he needed to be alone. He needed to think. I believe we each have a right to live our lives in our own way." As she said that, Marvelle's voice broke. "So I left." She took hold of one diamond earring and squeezed hard. "I wish I'd stayed. But he was my friend because I let him be himself." She squeezed her other ear so both hands were occupied. Unbraced, she swayed slightly. "I do not let myself cry over what's done," she said loudly and took off into the living room. I followed, worried that she might trip on the rug and fall, or bump into somebody.

Marvelle stopped not far from Revonda in her jungle chair. She said loudly to no one in particular: "He had a right to kill himself if that's what he wanted." I tried to get to her, to restrain her. But I couldn't get there in time.

The room had fallen silent. "We'd talked about suicide," Marvelle said. "Sure. As the final option when life becomes unbearable." Then she seemed to notice everybody staring at her.

Revonda had heard. "Come here, Marvelle," she ordered angrily. Marvelle didn't move. It was Revonda who stood up there in the center of the room near her favorite chair, holding on to it to keep steady. She turned slowly around to make eye contact with every single person in the room. From Ron drinking iced tea next to the picture of Joan of Arc, to Reverend Phillipson eating a sandwich by the fireplace, to Mert by the window to the porch. The room positively throbbed with surprise and waiting. I thought, Oh, brother! Revonda will give it to them.

She didn't shout or rave like she did at the sheriff. Her voice was low and throbbing and angry and sad. Rather magnificent. "For me to lose . . . what I valued most . . . was unimaginable. But it happened. And I'm still here." Revonda said each word like a separate bead on a string. That's the only way she showed her Scotch whiskey.

Of course, every single person in that room had stopped talking at once. Sam stood over by Revonda's family pictures, silent. Cousin Edna tensed with her tray of sandwiches half-passed.

In that silence, before Revonda could finish, Knowing Agnes in her swearing reds rose up from a corner and strode over and stood in front of Revonda. Her eyes were black and empty, and yet Knowing Agnes was staring, as if something from the great beyond were staring through her. Her skin was leathery from walking outdoors in all kinds of weather, her hair windblown. She still clutched her bouquet of wilted Queen Anne's lace.

Revonda froze with surprise.

Agnes turned to look at each one of us with those empty eyes, as if she were aping Revonda. Then she fixed those eyes on Revonda. "Revonda's son died as a punishment from God," she said in an echoing monotone. "She don't go to church right. She's not saved. Her son used heathen magic. God smote him down. God smites the damned."

Dear God, who said that? Whose words was she repeating? How many people in this room think that? I shivered. Because a part of me thought that. The part that was afraid of jinxes, afraid of curses. Anne, who was coming out of the kitchen with a tray of glasses, dropped it. The crash seemed appropriate somehow. Like a clash of cymbals.

But who would actually say that God struck Paul down because he was damned?

Revonda took the floor. And the amazing thing was—she stopped looking old. Her face was still taut, but with determination. Her head high like the Statue of Liberty in a rage. And this time she swept the room quickly with proud thousand-volt eyes. "You came to stare. All right, stare hard. Because I'm rich. Because my son read books about Medieval magic. Because some of you think that's Satanism, don't you? Because a crazy woman said what you all think. Don't look shocked. Feel sorry for yourselves. You're in danger. A person or persons killed my son. Not the hand of God. I intend to find out who it was. And if you're smart, you'll help. No matter who the killer is related to. Because if a killer is out there—or even in here—and that killer believes he can kill any damned one of us who deserves it . . ." She paused and looked from face to face. "Then who is safe? Which damned one of you is perfect? My son wasn't perfect. And neither am I. And neither are you. Now get out of my house and go home."

The guests didn't quite stampede out the door. But they sure didn't linger, either.

CHAPTER
15

Boy, was I glad I'd kept Pop separate from Revonda. A lady that jet-propelled—even when bereaved, even right after her son's memorial service—would be a horrible combination with a man that anxious to stir things up.

On the day after the service I went over to see Pop in the morning to be sure he wasn't in any kind of trouble. He welcomed me with a tremendous smile, wheeling his chair forward across the living room to meet me, blue eyes positively turned to jewels with sheer determination. Bad sign.

"I've got the answer to all your worries about Cousin Clothilde's little Anne," he said. "And Mary dropped off a joke for your book before she left for the beach. Not that you deserve it. You haven't been by in days, has she, Ella Marie?" His most excitable young sitter was on duty again, sitting with him at the table.

I'd kept up by phone, but he didn't think that counted.

"Anne was upset because a woman went berserk after the service for Paul yesterday," I told him. "Everyone was."

"Yes, I know," he said. "And so many people think Paul was murdered." For a man who never goes anywhere he sure keeps up.

"So what should we do to help Anne and Sam?" I asked him.

"First," he said with a mischievous twinkle, "the joke." If he has two things to tell me and he's annoyed at me, he always leaves the one I want to hear most till last. He smiled grandly.

"This man and woman were sitting watching television, and the woman said, 'I'm going in the kitchen to get a snack. Can I bring you anything?' "

At least it was a joke I hadn't heard.

"The man said, 'Yes, I want some ice cream, but be sure to write it down.' And the woman said, 'Don't be silly, I can remember that.' "

Be patient, I told myself. It's probably just a line or two more.

"The man said, 'But I want chocolate syrup on it, so be sure to write it down.' And the woman said, 'Oh, come on, I can remember ice cream with chocolate syrup. How dumb do you think I am?'

"Now, let's see," Pop said, "what else was there, Ella Marie?"

"Nuts," she said. "The man said, 'But I want nuts, too, so write it down.' "

"Of course," Pop said. *"And the woman said, 'No. I'll remember. Ice cream with chocolate syrup and nuts.' "*

"Now listen, Peaches," he said. "This is the best part. *In a little while she came back from the kitchen with a plate of scrambled eggs. The man groaned and said, 'I told you you had to write it down. You forgot the toast.' "* Pop happily led the laughter.

"Thank you. Now about Bloodroot Creek," I said.

But Pop said, "Not one word till you write that down for your chapter on writing things down."

And after I'd written down the joke, he said, "I have the answer. This case needs a personal touch. I need your help." I smelled trouble. Pop continued: "I'm going to invite my old friend Revonda over here to dinner, and our cousins, Anne and Sam—and, of course, you and Ted—and we'll discuss magic." He all but clapped his hands with glee. "The radio and the television and the paper all say that some kind of black magic was the reason for Paul Roland's death." What he said was a gross exaggeration, but I could see it made his day.

"Pop, you can't just yank people around at a time like this," I told him, coldly. "Revonda is distraught."

"Nonsense," Pop said. "When Revonda is upset, she takes action. Everybody knows that. Once, when she was a kid, she stood perfectly still for four hours, waiting till she could shoot the fox that killed her favorite hen. She got that fox square between the eyes. Zingo! Revonda is determined! Now she needs her old friends to rally round her and help her out." He wheeled his chair back around to his favorite table and patted the chair next to him. "Sit down. We need to plan this."

I sat, and I argued. All I could finally manage was to get Pop to agree to put the dinner party off a few days, at least till after the Fourth. The further off the better, I figured. "I'm putting my birthday celebration off," I said. "Ted and I agreed. So you can put off *your* dinner to a time when it'll do the most good."

"Why do that?" Pop glared like I was the whole problem.

"Revonda says the killer will certainly come to the big Fourth of July celebration in Bloodroot Creek. So I need to snoop around. After that, I'll get together with Bessie and arrange a good dinner—but only if Revonda agrees to come." I counted on Revonda not to be so foolish.

I told myself I was lucky—at least Pop wasn't having hallucinations. He had been for a while. Mix that in with some of the stranger parts of reality, and wow! The doctor had adjusted Pop's medications, and at least he hadn't imagined men on the roof with knives or such for quite a while.

Pop picked up the newspaper from the table. He was so blind he couldn't read anything but the biggest headlines, but he probably had had Ella Marie read the story to him so often that he knew it by heart. Of course he watched TV. Perhaps he could see a little of it. And he could hear.

"I like that part about how if just anyone can be killed in a way that fits his sins, we're all in danger," Pop said. "Revonda said that, right? Boy, I can think of some people I'd like to kill to fit their sins!"

Oh, brother! "You'd get killed," I said, "with your nose caught in a mousetrap, from being so nosy."

Pop rubbed his nose and beamed. "I can't think of a better way to go!"

CHAPTER
16

Somehow, I got myself talked into helping Revonda and Anne sort Paul's things. At the time it sounded like a good chance to find some surprising clue. I was intrigued by the big black red-lined cape in the back of his closet, for instance. My imagination could do things with that. For the first time I noticed a paper knife that looked like a dagger, or was it the other way around? Revonda said it belonged to Paul's great-grandfather. Nothing we found seemed to have the killer's signature. We put clothes in boxes for the Christian Ministry's used-clothing department or the Asheville Community Theater costume collection.

I suggested to Anne that she and Sam come have dinner with Ted and me. A little healing food and conversation. Revonda intended to spend the rest of the afternoon and evening making phone calls. She'd have a sandwich on a tray next to the phone. "I will be too busy to notice whether you're here or not," she told Anne, "and as for answering the phone, I want to do it myself. I want to be positive not to miss anything or fail to speak to every person in this valley. At least one cousin will be here to answer the door. I can't get rid of cousins. They're too curious to go away."

Ted came home about five o'clock, to find me in the kitchen patting rosemary on a chicken. A member of the English Department at the University in Asheville gave me the recipe: Shakespearean Chicken. You know, *Rosemary for Remembrance*. The folks back in Shakespeare's day believed rosemary was an herb that improved the memory. Besides, the chicken is easy and good. Just pat with a little rosemary and maybe a pinch of sage and bake as usual. Serve with a wine and chicken-stock sauce, made with pan drippings, after most of the fat is skimmed off. And if Shakespeare was right—well, we could all use as much memory as we could get.

Sam and Anne ate my chicken as if they hadn't had a bite in a week. We didn't talk a lot about Paul's death. I guess we needed a respite. Sam told us how as a kid he lived on a farm in Pennsylvania. Which is maybe why he likes farm country.

Over ice cream and coffee we did recap the case, and Sam and Anne stayed late. I don't guess they were in a hurry to get back to the scene of the horror. Then their van wouldn't start. Sabotage? When things are going wrong, everything gets suspicious. But it was an old van with lots of aches and pains, Sam said. Could be just something inside it died of old age. Too bad it picked midnight in our driveway to conk out. So we gave them a ride home through the moonlit night. Sam said he'd see about the van in the morning.

As we turned into Revonda's driveway, the moon through the branches of the big trees made moving patterns. I almost missed seeing the odd light in Revonda's house. "That's a light in Paul's room!" Sam cried, just as the light went out. I don't know how he could tell where at a glance. It had been a small light, wavering. Maybe a flashlight. Otherwise the house was dark.

Ted glided us to the house and parked quietly. We heard

the dogs barking, and we jumped pell-mell out of the car. Ted called he'd cover the back door, even as he ran toward it. The rest of us spread out in front of the house. I asked Anne to run to the studio to call the sheriff.

The moon had picked this time to go under clouds. We hardly had time to feel our way in the dark when the doors to Paul's room burst open, and someone swept past us so fast that we were unable to grab him. Sam did get hold of a shirt collar, but the man—at least, it later turned out to be a man's shirt—ran right out of it. Must have been unbuttoned. Sam threw down the shirt and ran after him. I rushed into Paul's room, through the wide-swinging glass doors, and turned on the light switch.

No one was there. Revonda kept those outside glass double doors locked just as Paul had. Who had a key? The mirrors on the walls and ceiling winked. I felt like the last flash reflection of a person running had just escaped my eyes. A fallen straight-back chair lay on its side on the floor not far from the small table near the wall. As if the intruder had knocked the chair over when he ran, whoever he was. The rocking chair with the moon face in the center of the room rocked slightly, too, as if the person had brushed against it as he passed.

The door on the house side of the room burst open, and Revonda strode in in her pajamas. "My God, what's happening?" The dogs ran in past her, still barking, and took off after Sam and the burglar or whatever. Revonda was by my side, asking, "What was it?" She'd grabbed my arm and her voice slurred. She had evidently taken a sleeping pill and was having trouble shaking the drug off.

I said, "I don't know. Sam's looking." I wished he and Ted weren't both out in the dark with whatever. But it wouldn't help if I left Revonda.

I heard a car start in the distance. I prayed that didn't mean the intruder was getting away. I hoped . . . prayed . . . Sam was safe. I heard a second car start. Would that be Sam, in Revonda's car?

I told Revonda I wanted to let Ted in the back door so he could search the house. She said she'd let him in herself and be sure the door was locked. But when she did, Ted came straight through the house without searching. He said we'd better wait for the sheriff to be sure we didn't destroy evidence.

Revonda snorted, "Don't count on that fool."

I figured the best thing we could do was calm Revonda and search Paul's room, since our fingerprints and whatever were already in there. Besides, I wasn't sure I should trust the sheriff any more than Revonda did. She knew the man.

Revonda still looked groggy, standing there in her leopard-spot pajamas. I got her to sit down in the moon chair.

At first glance, nothing seemed out of place in Paul's room except the small chair knocked over. Almost everything had been put back the way it was before he died. His narrow cot was unrumpled. The face jug glared down at us from the shelf. But then my eyes were drawn to a mirror on the black floor. It was a small mirror, the kind a woman might carry in her pocketbook, glimmering between the table and the chair. So small you could hardly spot the reflection in all the other mirrors. And it was broken in three pieces.

Revonda said, "Don't pick it up. I'll call Ron. He'll get here before the sheriff since he lives just up the hill." Her voice was still slurred, but her mind was working. She walked unsteadily toward the phone, and when I moved to help, she said, "No, I want to do it myself."

Then Sam was back. "That man got a head start," he said. "I don't know which cove or driveway he turned into."

I showed the others the mirror, a woman's kind of mirror. And I wondered if it was a woman who came in that room, a woman who had a key. Perhaps she'd dropped the mirror and was going to have seven years' bad luck.

"Jinx would have a key to Paul's room." Revonda's voice was still a little slow, but she'd come awake.

I didn't believe the intruder was Paul's sad-sack-but-beautiful girlfriend Jinx. I'd only seen that intruder flash by, but I had the impression it was a man and bigger than Jinx. Still, who can be sure in the dark?

"I should have thought to ask Jinx for that key back," Revonda went on. "That girl is so vague and so promiscuous that anyone could steal her key. I wouldn't be surprised if she belonged to a cult, either. I hear there's sex in those rituals. Those people believe they have sex with the devil." That had her wide awake. She turned and stared at me. Almost as if she thought I had sex with the devil. "You are the one to go talk to Jinx, Peaches." She looked me over like I was a cat she might want to adopt. As if she was of two minds. And then she said, "People tell you things. You look sympathetic." She said that with her mouth slightly pursed and her eyebrows up almost as if it was an accusation.

I didn't like her attitude. I'm a good listener, and proud of it. I used to wonder why people like to bend my ear—me who forgets details. But then I realized people want you to hear the essence of what they say, want you to hear how they *feel*, which is just what interests me. And if they tell you their troubles or hopes, they don't care if you recall it all. In fact, sometimes they're glad you *don't*.

For detection, on the other hand, I jot down notes. For detection, I made up my mind to talk to Jinx at the Fourth of July celebration the next morning. Was Jinx involved in Paul's death? I felt pretty wait-and-see on that. But one thing seemed surer and surer: Paul didn't kill himself.

CHAPTER
17

THURSDAY, JULY 4

As I drove out to Bloodroot Creek about nine in the morning on the Fourth of July, I kept thinking about that broken mirror. The sheriff hadn't shared any thoughts, though he came in person and summoned a photographer to record the scene.

Who would come into Paul's mirror room to steal a small mirror and drop it on the way out? And where had it come from? The deputies had been over that room with a fine-tooth comb, hadn't they? Or had someone brought it in and left it there as a symbol of God-knows-what?

Jinx had a key. And who else? Marvelle was Paul's godmother, and Mert said they were close. How odd that a man suspected of traffic with the devil should have a godmother. Marvelle might have a key to the room. I'd try to talk to Marvelle, as well as Jinx.

I dropped by Revonda's to see if there were any new developments. Not yet, she said, and asked where Ted was. I said he'd be along.

"The Fourth of July could be our A-number-one chance to trap the killer," she said. "I'll bet my soul the killer is someone who could not fail to go to the celebration without causing raised eyebrows and embarrassing questions. In this valley we celebrate the Fourth of July as a favorite holiday. Even flatlanders have been asked to take part." Revonda smiled at Anne. "I'm glad you are following my advice to go on with the puppet show for the children." She turned to me. "After Paul died, they called and said they'd understand if Anne wanted to drop out, but I told Anne to go and keep a sharp eye out for anything suspicious.

"And don't forget to pick up Marvelle," Revonda commanded Anne. "Marvelle loves to be onstage so much, she'd go right on acting if the theater burned down. She's even thrilled to be leading the Pledge of Allegiance." Revonda traced a tropical flower on the arm of her chair with one red fingernail. "Marvelle needs to be looked at." A little friendly bitchiness perked Revonda up. "You'd think Marvelle had a huge career on the stage, the ways she acts. She inherited money and retired here, copying me. You know where we met? We were doing a toilet paper commercial for television, the low point in my career and the high point in hers. But she'll do the pledge well."

Anne suggested that she and I go to the Bloodroot Valley Community Center together. I figured perhaps she wanted to tell me something in private. "Revonda's in really bad shape," Anne said as we drove off in her van—Sam had found the van's problem was simple to fix in the light of day. "She's afraid to be alone. That's why her cousin Edna is still there." Then Anne explained she had to stop by and get her puppet theater at the church, where she'd done a show for the Summer Bible School kids at Mert's behest.

At the church, the Boy Scouts were putting the finishing touches on their float with the flag at one end and everybody saluting. Several boys helped Anne get the parts of her stage into the van. The stage was black with lots of rods and curtains.

Finally we got to Marvelle's house. We knocked on the door. No answer. If she was so eager to lead the salute to the flag, where was she? Maybe putting the last touches on her makeup? Switching to longer false eyelashes? I liked Marvelle, but her frantic effort to look glamorous was a little comic. Her house was small and painted white and fixed up to the nines, with gladiola and roses and a birdbath with a fountain. But cheerful.

Anne kept knocking, but still no Marvelle. The door was unlocked, so she opened it and stuck her head in and called. Silence. We stepped inside. It was all very decorated with huge cushions on the couch, a shawl on the baby grand piano shimmering with big embroidered red roses. The room was cluttered. Not like Revonda's house, where *House Beautiful* could have come in to take pictures at any moment. The morning paper was out on Marvelle's coffee table, and her sunglasses and some gardening gloves and a bandanna were on a small table by a side door. Anne stood at the bottom of the stairs and called up. Still nothing.

"Maybe she forgot you were coming," I said, "like I might have done."

"Or was I supposed to meet her somewhere else?" Anne asked. "Actually, it's not so far that she couldn't have walked."

We drove to the white clapboard community center, expecting Marvelle would already be there. No sign of her. Not many people there yet. Just children and their pets and the judges for the pet parade. A judge was pinning a ribbon on a little boy who held a chicken in a little straw hat.

We met Sam under a tree and told him we couldn't find Marvelle. "Never mind," he said. "Marvelle's a grown-up. She'll take care of herself." He began to help Anne set up her theater. I'm no good at put-togethers. I admired the crepe-paper Uncle Sam costume on the Wizard and the bonnet that made Me Too into Betsy Ross.

A small girl wiggling a loose tooth watched Anne and asked: "When does it start?" Not until after the parade and the "speaking," Anne explained. I was glad there'd be plenty of time for me to look around.

Two of Revonda's cousins commandeered Sam to help put up tents for concessions. Anne was still fussing with her scenery. At last I was on my own. The sun shone, the flag whipped gaily at the top of the flagpole in front of the community center. I was supposed to keep my mind on looking for something suspicious. What? There were lots of bouncing kids in shorts and grown-ups with cameras round their necks, beginning to line Valley Road for the parade.

I found a good place to watch in front of a log house with a hedge of shaggy evergreens on one side. I love parades. At least, while I looked for some clue, I could take in this one. And here it came! First, a pickup truck with a huge hand-lettered sign on the side that said: YOUR COMMUNITY CLUB. Must be the club's officers on folding chairs in the back, including Mert. Not one of them looked like a killer. Then came the Boy Scout float. I waved to the boys who had helped Anne move her theater. Then the regional high-school band with three drum majorettes in red, white, and blue, throwing batons in the air. A very enthusiastic short, fat boy played a tuba bigger than he was. I loved the band. The volunteer firemen rode by on their spit-and-polished red truck. A little girl with a snub nose and braids rode by on a black and white horse and waved at every single person, including me. Next came a decorated tractor. Nothing at all seemed suspicious.

After a flatbed truck with a church choir singing "Nearer My God to Thee," there was Ron-the-Deputy in full uniform, riding a big chestnut horse. He waved at three kids sitting on the top of a pickup cab to see better. He waved at two older women on a porch near the road. Then he waved even harder at someone up the road in front of him. It was Anne. He grinned, and winked. Long and slow. Anne blushed.

Then everybody began to press toward the community

center. No sign of Marvelle yet. What had happened to her? And I didn't see Jinx.

As I hurried on with the crowd to the patriotic program—the "speaking"—I passed the red-haired guy with the ASK WILL T-shirt, Paul's dinner-theater buddy. Same shirt he wore to the funeral. Otherwise he wasn't out of the ordinary. I told myself some clue would turn up in the community center. Ted had saved me a seat, on a front row next to a family of small girls with red, white, and blue bows in their hair. I looked around. Anne and Sam were standing in the back between a young man and woman each holding a child. There weren't any empty seats. Sam waved.

The M.C. was saying, "Before we get to the speakin', I want to point out that this is Mary Sawyer's birthday." We all clapped, and a young girl called out: "Tomorrow is Sally Martin's."

The M.C. had a whispered conference with the three other people in chairs on the stage, and then he said: "Does anybody know where Marvelle Starr is?"

Marvelle wouldn't miss a chance to appear onstage. Any stage. That's what Revonda had said. I wished I hadn't thought of that.

The M.C. led the pledge, and we sang "The Star-Spangled Banner." I looked around at Ted when we sat down again, and he was frowning. But Ron, who sat near the door, was smooth-browed and unruffled. He lounged back in his chair with his feet crossed in front of him.

Up on the platform Sally Martin's father told how the Fourth of July was celebrated seventy-five years ago. How they had no fireworks so every family saved scraps of wool and sewed them into balls and soaked them in kerosene the night before the Fourth. They mowed the field close and lit the balls and threw the fireballs from one man to another in the dark. "You didn't get burned," he said, "if you threw them quick enough." I could imagine Sam trying fireballs. He wouldn't be afraid.

The patriotic program ended with the "Battle Hymn of

the Republic." Ted and I wormed our way toward the door and so did Anne and Sam. "You haven't seen Marvelle?" I asked them. They shook their heads, no. "I think something is wrong," I said. We all headed toward Ron, but the crowd was thick with old friends and relatives shaking hands.

Ron stopped to talk with two pretty teenaged girls. Anne had pushed ahead of us and managed to get to him and I heard her say "Marvelle Starr" and look worried and point in the direction of Marvelle's house. I pushed closer and heard him tell Anne he'd check around. Ted said he'd keep close to Ron and see what happened.

Then the loudspeaker announced Anne's puppet show, and she ran off to get it ready. I followed along. Somehow, I felt I needed to keep an eye on her. Something was out of whack on this fine sunshiny day.

Anne's set-up stage seemed great, with the kids sitting in the shade of the tree and one branch bending over the stage like part of the scenery. The kids clapped for the Wizard, dressed up like Uncle Sam, and Me Too in her Betsy Ross bonnet.

When he saw Betsy Ross's flag, the Wizard jumped so high with enthusiasm that a bit of sharp branch hidden by leaves ripped off his Uncle Sam hat and left him bald. Some of the children giggled, and a small boy on the front row screwed his face as if he was about to burst into tears.

Anne flushed. Oh, dear, she was hating herself for being accident-prone. That wouldn't help. But the Wizard seemed to think for himself. "I did that on purpose," he said, extra stern to make up for being bald. "I did that to show you who Uncle Sam really is." He stuck out his red, white, and blue chest and leaned toward the children. "Uncle Sam stands for our country, which is all of us. Me, the Wizard, who knows everything, and also you." He pointed toward a small redheaded boy, still giggling. "And even you. Every one of us is Uncle Sam ready to celebrate the Fourth of July." He sounded downright impressive. He pointed straight to a little girl with braids and a teddy-bear T-shirt. "If you were being Uncle Sam, what would you do to celebrate your country's birthday party?"

Another girl whispered in her ear. Nobody was snickering anymore. They were all waiting to hear. Anne had pulled it off. Now, *that* wasn't being disaster prone!

The girl shouted: "I'd buy cake and ice cream for every person in the whole country!"

Me Too in her Betsy Ross costume jumped right up while the kids clapped. "Me, too!" she shouted. "That won't help the national debt, but make mine chocolate chip."

I wanted to run up and congratulate Anne, but right at that moment I began to hear a buzz and then a hum and then several screams over by the community center. A wave of agitation passed through the crowd as some kind of bad news spread. Sam came hurrying over toward us, and so did the parents of the kids. The show was over.

Sam ran, pale and upset, straight to Anne. He put his arm around her. "Anne," he said. "Marvelle is dead. Ron found her dead. He sent word for us to get back to Revonda quick. First her son, now her best friend. She'll go berserk."

I broke in—I couldn't help it. "Where did he find her?"

Sam's eyes went round with horror, and this was the man who painted bodies frozen under ice! "She was upstairs in her room, sitting in front of her mirror." Sam shook his head like a dog trying to shake off water, as if he wanted to make the picture of that go away. Then he spoke very slowly. "She was in a clear plastic bag. With a spiral over the rouge on each cheek."

When we turned off the light to go to sleep that night, that picture was still in my mind: the vain woman killed in front of her mirror with a magic mark on each painted cheek. "Ted, are you awake?" I asked.

"Umm," he said sleepily.

"I need to tell you something," I said, "or I'll have nightmares all night." He turned on the light and reached over and squeezed my hand.

"The most abominable thing about the killer," I said, "is the way he designed those murders so they stick like cement in my mind. He killed those two in such a damn dramatic way that all anyone who thinks of Paul or Marvelle will ever be able to see in his mind is how they died. He's hijacked all our memories of Paul and of Marvelle, and twisted them to suit himself."

Ted came over to my side of the bed and hugged me. How else could he answer?

CHAPTER
18

Pop had arranged his party for July fifth. I couldn't stop him. To get around any this-is-short-notice objections from me, or from Bessie, his housekeeper, he had Laurey's Catering provide a cold salmon with dill mayonnaise and other goodies. (We were spared Laurey's reaction to the short notice.) He had Bessie polish the silver and get out the pretty linen-lace placemats that my mother had saved for best. "Revonda will appreciate luxury," Pop said. "It will soften her up. She always means to have the best of everything." He sent me out to pick daisies for the table and do other errands. "No matter how many airs she put on, Revonda always liked daisies," he said. Boy, he seemed to have total recall! How hot had their relationship been?

Much to my amazement, Revonda accepted the invitation. Anne told me Revonda said it might cheer her up to get out of her house and see a friend from her youth. And she remembered Pop as pretty damned smart. Ted and I came to

Pop's dinner on the theory that he might behave worse if we weren't there.

He had invited us for eight-thirty—or about dusk. He said women all looked better in candlelight, which pleased them and him, too. He made Bessie set candlesticks around the living room and turn off the overhead lights.

Revonda and Anne and Sam all arrived together, Sam with an arm around each. Revonda was elegant in a black cotton dress with a wide collar, and her tiger earrings. She still looked drawn, but with makeup so beautifully applied that the circles under her eyes vanished. In the candlelight she looked ten years younger. Even on Ted's face, I could see appreciation.

"You're still a damn good-looking woman." Pop grabbed her hands, and pulled her down for a kiss. They got off to such a good start I caught myself thinking: You don't suppose the old coot would get into his head to marry her at this late date? I went cold and repressed the thought.

Sam was out of his mad-scientist suit, back to T-shirt and blue jeans. Anne wore a white dress with a collar as wide as Revonda's, and a tight belt. She'd pinned a rosebud at the V of the neck. They were cheering themselves up with clothes. Or was Anne trying to make sure Tiger-Woman didn't upstage her? Anne kept darting adoring looks at Sam. He winked back. What with Pop's glowing glances at Revonda we sure did prove that life goes on, even after horror.

First, we all sat around Pop's favorite table and had drinks and some wonderful hors d'oeuvres made with caviar and whipped cream cheese.

"Even at such a terrible time, it's good to see an old friend," Pop said, raising his glass of Scotch in a toast to Revonda, who was sitting on his right. "There's one kind of black magic I always approve," he said, "and that's the glamour of beautiful women." He nodded at Anne, who sat on his other side, and again at Revonda.

Gallantry did not extend to his own daughter. And each of the other two stiffened slightly. If Pop mainly wanted to talk about magic, as in doing in Paul, why should they want even a hint attributed to them? But Pop didn't notice.

"It's so good to see you again, Harwood." Revonda put on her Southern Lady manners. "And your clever mind will be an addition to our efforts to find the truth." Ha. We'd see. "The horror of my Paul's death has now been compounded by a second tragic death." She stopped, swallowed, squared her shoulders, and went on. "I'm sure Peaches has told you that the woman we call Knowing Agnes mentioned evil magic when she made that scene after the memorial service. She repeats what people in the valley say. The killer could be some religious fanatic who believes that magic is a sin that has to be punished. My poor friend Marvelle seems to have been killed in a way that highlights her sin—her vanity."

"The same magical symbols that were on Paul's hands and forehead—if that's what those whorls were—were painted on Marvelle's cheeks," Ted pointed out. Nobody commented on that.

"I have called you all here together," Pop said, leaning back grandly in his wheelchair, "to discuss the suspects in these two tragic murders, and the way each suspect may have been involved with magic in an evil way." He stretched out the word "evil" with great relish. "I have asked Ted, who is very good at that sort of thing, to draw us up a list of suspects, their opportunity, and their attitude toward magic. I believe that is the key element here." He leaned back happily in his wheelchair, overjoyed to preside. He paused and looked each of us in the eye. "I am counting on you," he said, "to come up with new information about these people."

"I have made it my business," Ted said, "in the spare time I could save from teaching and correcting all those papers, to talk to the people who might be suspects and find out where they were when."

Sam leaned back and crossed his legs, seeming ready to enjoy a game. Revonda sat straight, ready to pounce. I tried not to look skeptical. Pop loves this suspect-brainstorming business. He's done it before but never discovered a killer that way. Anne glanced around nervously. "Do we have to accuse each other?"

"If any of you knows things about yourselves that the rest of us haven't guessed, I expect you to confess right away," Pop announced pompously. "We all have guilty secrets." Nobody volunteered to confess first, including Pop.

"I've put the names alphabetically," Ted said, "which means that if you go by Peaches' writing name and call her Peaches Dann, instead of Peaches Holleran, she comes first. I come next. For motive, I guess we could be protecting Anne and Sam if we thought they were guilty. Actually, I've been too busy with summer school to murder anybody."

"You're wrong about that list," Revonda said. "Henderson comes before Holleran. Harley Henderson should come first in more ways than one. I think he's mixed up in drugs, and Paul and Marvelle somehow caught on and showed it. I bet you won't be able to pin down where he was at the time of either murder."

"He managed to be vague," Ted admitted. "We're near Asheville, which is a resort. Resorts tend to attract drug traffic. Several people told me Marvelle was a member of Narcotics Anonymous. So suppose she backslid? This could somehow be drug-related."

"Harley believes in money and in power," Revonda said. "And if you don't think that can be just as destructive as believing in devils, you're a damn fool," she said to Pop. "Put our sheriff on the list, Ted. Right at the top."

Ted pointed to the list. "The Justices are next."

"Ruth would lie for Jeeter in a heartbeat," Revonda said. "And I bet his brother Buck would, too. So who cares if they said they were together when Paul was killed. And Jeeter only has his wife to alibi him on the Fourth of July. And he gets violent if he doesn't take his pills."

Everybody nodded. Our jury wanted Jeeter to be guilty.

"And hell hath no fury like a woman scorned," Revonda

quoted. "Paul treated Jinx with scorn. He told me he also let that girl look at his magic books."

"She has no alibi for either death," Ted said. He put her near the top of his list.

"Reverend Phillipson is crazy," Revonda said. "Balmy since his wife died. Maybe he's so bound to see nothing but good that his dark side breaks loose and kills. He could have copied the marks from that thing Paul wore for good luck." She sipped her Scotch complacently. "And another good suspect is Mert's grandson Billy. He was one of those kids mixed up with that cult in the high school." Vaguely I remembered news stories of something of the sort. The kids actually stole and slaughtered a goat in some kind of ritual.

"Mert's grandson was involved?" Anne made a rejecting mouth as if she couldn't bear that.

"Of course, you two know that your closeness to the crime puts you under suspicion," Ted said to Anne and Sam. "Anne has alibis, Sam doesn't. He was seen on the Fourth, but not all morning, at least not so anyone can pinpoint exactly when and where."

"I was wandering around," Sam said. "I should have stuck with a witness."

"And just to be thorough, we have to talk about you, Revonda," Ted said. "You were with Peaches and Anne and then Marvelle when Paul died, and Cousin Edna was with you when someone killed Marvelle. Right?"

She agreed.

"It's time for us to eat dinner," I said. They nodded. Ted rolled Pop into the dining room, and we all sat down around the oval mahogany table. On one side of the room my mother's silver service on the sideboard shone, reflecting the candle flames and bits of us. On the other side of the room the windows with the light fading fast behind them turned into dark mirrors, flickering with candlelight. And I remembered something from Paul's magic stuff that I'd rather forget. That's the trouble with a bad memory. You can't count on it. Sometimes it works, even when you wish it wouldn't.

Somewhere in those copies of pages from Paul's books I'd seen one that said that of four men who set out to become magi, one would become an adept and three would go mad. That was the sort of quote that Pop would have loved. I was not about to tell him. Did Paul think he was an adept? Did he think he could use herbs and symbols, for example, to make magic work? And if he did, how did that cause his death? Did he go mad? And how on earth did Marvelle fit in? I suddenly felt nostalgic for plain old uncomplicated murder.

CHAPTER

19

SATURDAY MORNING, JULY 6

In the morning Anne called at six-thirty. She knew I was an early riser. "I got up to pick raspberries," she said in a surprised voice. "For breakfast." Pause. "I didn't sleep well. And when I went out, there was a snake." Amazed voice: "I saw a dark something on Revonda's porch steps and it was a dead snake." She was breathing hard. "Sam says it's a copperhead, coiled up—just like . . ." She sounded on the edge of hysteria. I might have been, too. I don't care for snakes.

"Ron is here," Anne said, calmer now. I heard Sam make some remark in the background, but I couldn't catch it, as she continued, "Ron says whoever it was probably walked on the gravel drive and didn't even leave footprints. He's still looking and another deputy is here, too."

"I'll come right over," I said. Ted was swamped with summer-school preparations for second session, and he'd been up working late after Pop's party. He's a night person. I left him a note and set forth.

When I got to Revonda's house, I found her and Sam and Anne peering from the end of the porch while a photographer recorded the snake, artfully coiled to look like one of the spirals that someone marked on Paul and Marvelle. Ugly.

The picture-taking ended. We talked about how strange it was that neither Sam nor Anne nor Revonda heard a thing, and that the dogs hadn't barked. Just as they hadn't barked when Paul met his end.

"We'll go pick some raspberries now," Sam told Revonda. "After this we need a super-breakfast to give us strength." He had some small red buckets in his hand. I almost laughed. Sam had such a way of finding some sunshine even in the midst of horror. Anne held his hand tight. Subdued.

He led us to the raspberries in back of Revonda's house, near the mountainside. They grew in a row at one end of the garden. On one side light green lettuce, dark green New Zealand spinach with pointy leaves, and young beets. On the other a mowed place back to a patch of weeds and wildflowers and a barbed-wire fence and, beyond that, somebody's cow. The cow gazed at us peacefully, as if everything was right with the world. Ha! But the garden was a balm to our snake jitters. It smelled of turned earth still wet with dew.

"A raspberry is about my favorite thing," Anne said. I could see she was trying to convince Sam that she felt better. Her hand hardly shook as she plunked a berry in her mouth. Behind her the sun was shining up over the blue-green mountain, but we were still in shadow. Flatlanders find that strange, that west-side-of-the-mountain people have a sunless morning time.

"My grandmother had raspberries when I was a kid," Anne said. "She'd let me eat nothing but raspberries and vanilla ice cream for a whole lunch!" She managed to smile up at Sam, who beamed back.

In the distance birds tweeted, probably wanting us to go

away so they could eat the berries. I watched around me like a hawk. I happen to know that snakes love berries, too.

"Raspberries are like skyrockets," Sam was saying. "I love that flavor-burst."

A young voice said, "They weren't pruned right!"

I turned around quick, amazed somebody got so close and we didn't hear him come. A boy about fifteen or sixteen with wild black hair and a mocking smile stood by the berry row holding a white plastic bucket and wearing dark glasses. And this was 7:30 in the morning with no sun. "Mrs. Roland told my grandmother we could pick," he said. "I'm Billy Holt. You know my grandma."

I had a feeling I'd seen him somewhere, but the glasses threw me off.

"Mert Williams," Sam guessed. "Our favorite person. She has a lot of grandsons."

Silly Billy, I thought. He was all earnestness and elbows and feet and foolish sunshades.

Sam was looking the kid over. "I wasn't here to prune these raspberry bushes. Somebody did that last fall. How do you know they weren't pruned right?"

Silly Billy adjusted his dark glasses, threw a berry in the air, and caught it in his mouth before he answered: "I read a lot. I watch a lot. I see a lot. Do you know I found these dark glasses right by the road in the grass? Glasses make people look smart. My grandmother says you paint pictures." He was what *my* grandmother called "fresh as paint."

"And you don't stake your tomatoes right," the kid said. "You have to prune them if you want them to be big."

Sam kept plopping berries in his pail. "I pruned some tomato plants and I didn't prune some. I don't believe in doing things 'right.' I don't believe in doing them all the same way. That's boring."

The kid stopped picking and just stared at Sam. "Say," he said, "that's kind of interesting. Do people think you're crazy?"

Sam said, "I can't worry about that or I'd be a lousy artist."

"I draw sometimes." Billy wiped his mouth with the back of his hand. He seemed to be a free spirit, yet he seemed nervous. When his hands weren't busy, he clenched them and unclenched them by his sides. Like a scared grown-up instead of a happy kid.

Something was familiar about him. Something about his general shape. "Turn around," I said. "Let me see all sides of you."

He made a surprised mouth, but he turned obligingly. A willowy kid. Where did that supple form fit? In some recent scene. At the Fourth of July? No. Before that. It'll come to me, I thought hopefully. If I don't force it.

And then I knew. He was the kid I'd seen from Revonda's bathroom window. The one with the black hair that I saw walking across the yard the day we found Paul dead. I'd forgotten all about it. I mean, it was before we found the body, and therefore so ordinary to see a kid pass by, it went right out of my head. So, of course, I hadn't told a soul.

"I like you, Billy," I said. "But I have to tell you that I saw you in this yard the day Paul Roland died. Does the sheriff know?"

"Oh, that wasn't me." I bet that his eyes were wide with fear if I could have seen them behind the dark glasses. He took a deep breath. "Listen," he said, "please don't tell the sheriff what you told me. It's not true. But I can't prove it. I got in some trouble last year. He won't believe me." He took his dark glasses off and looked me straight in the eye. He knew the value of eye contact.

"What kind of trouble?" I asked.

He squirmed. "They thought I was one of a group of kids in some kind of cult thing, some crazy kids that stole a goat. I wasn't. Somebody must be a ringer for me." His whole body leaned toward me, pleading to be believed.

Oh, boy, he was *that* grandson.

"Listen," he said. "You're trying to help Mrs. Roland find

out what happened, aren't you? Because she thinks the sheriff is dumb. Well, the sheriff *is* dumb. I hear things. I can tell you things that will maybe help."

"Like what?" Sam asked. Big smile, sparkling eyes. His eyes said he expected the best of Billy. He expected wonders.

"I'll find things." The kid turned to Sam. "I will. I'll be your spy." He grinned, to show he enjoyed that idea.

"O.K.," Sam said right off, "we'll take you up on that."

Anne looked surprised but didn't say a word.

Why was it up to Sam to speak for us all? Except that it took nerve. Sam had nerve, all right. Why did I accept his agreement with the kid and not object? Partly, I think, because I liked the boy. And partly because I'm so bad with forms and faces. I thought he was the kid I'd seen. But I couldn't for the life of me be absolutely sure.

Finally we left Billy picking. We nodded at a deputy still looking around outside, then went in to have breakfast with Revonda in her country kitchen, where the canisters with the herbs painted on them were in an exact line and the copper molds over the fireplace hung exactly straight. We had waffles and raspberries and whipped cream and sourwood honey. Sam fixed the waffles. Because we needed them, he said.

Revonda agreed there was no point in telling the sheriff about the kid, at least until we were sure he was the one. "And maybe we could spy on him while he is off guard pretending to spy for us." She arched an eyebrow. "Mert didn't tell any of you about Billy's trouble, did she? She could never believe one bad thing about that child. She protects him. His father drinks. You can't trust Billy for a minute," she said. "If your father drinks, you learn how to keep secrets, which means telling lies. Billy's father could drink God under the table. Only worse father I know is Jinx's father, that crazy Jeeter."

"I never saw Jinx at the Fourth of July," I said, startled. In fact so much had happened that Jinx had gone right out of my head. Poof! Not a good omission. Obviously my next step should be to go and talk to Paul's girl Jinx. I looked at my watch. Nine o'clock. "And this is as good a time as any to go talk to her. I'll call to be sure she's there."

Revonda laughed. "That girl doesn't have a phone." She drew me a map of how to get to Jinx's cabin. She said Paul's white four-wheel-drive pickup truck would be better on the back roads than my car, so please use it.

I didn't like the idea of riding to Jinx's in the very truck Paul drove just before he died. Jinx must have sat in the seat of that truck beside him. But Revonda insisted, and some of our back roads are a hazard, with sharp grades and deep ruts. Sam offered to go with me, but I was sure that Jinx would be more open with me alone.

"Take a dog," Anne said. "Baskerville is friendly. You'll feel safer."

I did not look forward to asking Jinx the question Revonda had demanded I ask: Was Jinx involved in a cult where they had sex with the devil? Now, how on earth can you ask that politely? Revonda always seemed to suspect the worst and the most dramatic thing.

I certainly wanted to know why Paul's sad-eyed girl had seemed so determined at Paul's funeral to find a chance to talk to me in private. I wished I hadn't waited so long to track her down. Because now, since Marvelle's murder, everything seemed out of control. Anne or Sam or Revonda could be next.

CHAPTER

20

LATER SATURDAY

As I drove along, the big black rottweiler named Basker-ville sat right beside me on the front seat of Paul's truck. A cheerful dog, she seemed to grin. I followed Revonda's map with only one wrong turn, and that was fortunately into a short dead end, so I didn't stay lost.

Jinx, in a neon-orange shirt, was out in her garden next to a little tin-roofed cabin, picking lettuce. Nice garden: in neat hoed rows like a picture in a book I had as a kid. When Jinx saw Paul's pickup in her driveway, she froze. She'd prob-ably never seen it there before except when it brought Paul. Sorry.

I parked under a huge old weeping willow with a gnarled trunk, and Jinx came and met me at the truck, quiet as snow. Baskerville didn't even bark to announce her.

"I'm glad to see you," she said, "though I've got a modeling job in a little bit, so I can't talk long." She had a classic oval Madonna's face and a strange air of seeming dirty when she was plainly clean. Even her hands were clean when she'd just picked lettuce. And why on earth, I wondered, did she choose to wear a bright orange T-shirt with PIKE'S PEAK OR BUST stretched across her breasts, and sexy tight jeans? She led me into the cabin, pointed to a neat cot with a faded flowered spread, and said: "Please sit a while." No place for that but on her bed, where a large black cat was already curled up. A round low table scattered with a few magazines stood in front of the bed.

Jinx put her heads of lettuce in an old white-enamel sink in one corner of that shadowy room. She sat down on the bed to one side of the table. I lowered myself down on the other side, and the bedsprings pinged with our weight so loud the cat jumped off. Those bedsprings must have pinged for Paul, only louder and in more intimate moments. Do bedsprings remember?

"Thanks for coming," she said. "You're trying to figure who killed Paul, aren't you?" She reached smooth childlike hands across the table, between the piles of *True Love* magazines, and picked up a pack of cigarettes and a box of kitchen matches. She kept her eyes on her hands, as she lit up. "Sam told me that you and he and Anne think the spirals on the bodies"—she paused and squeezed her eyes tight—"must be important."

I did not tell her about the real snake arranged in a spiral at Revonda's. I wanted her story first. "When did you talk to Sam?"

"In the grocery store. He said he was looking for a model." Her voice was hollow, as if she wanted to swallow her words. She looked up straight into my eyes. "I model naked. My father thinks I'll go to hell for that." She threw her head back defiantly. "And if I'm going to hell anyway, it doesn't matter what else I do, does it?"

"Whatever happens to you matters," I said.

"I don't guess Paul thought much of me."

I was annoyed. She had such an I'd-like-to-give-up tone in her voice, a part of me wanted to shake her. But this gal had reason to feel rotten. "Perhaps you know," I said, "that people say Paul was cruel to you." She flinched. Then she flushed. "Men treat me like that." Suddenly her soft voice rose and grated with anger, and I realized I had felt that anger all along. Right under that I-won't-hit-back-if-you-hit-me big green-eyed look. She dragged hard on her cigarette, drank in the smoke, and blew it out toward me. "I've cared for three men. It's always like that. They treat me bad. My father says it's a punishment from God. O.K., sometimes Paul hit me, but that was because he'd been drinking whiskey. He said I chased him. He said I was a slut."

Of course she was angry. Angry enough to kill? Would she have been physically strong enough to do it?

"I don't think you're a slut." Even in the orange T-shirt. Even with the pout. That wasn't what bothered me.

"But when I stayed away, Paul came and looked for me. He did. And I loved him. Sometimes I think the more he was mean to me, the more I loved him. Does that make sense? Sometimes he'd come and talk to me because I'd listen even to crazy stuff about how people could make things happen by drawing pictures and saying words. I felt like he needed me whether he knew it or not. Do you understand?"

"Not exactly," I said, "but I'm trying. I know you're a person who likes to help. You wanted to tell me something that could help us find out what happened to Paul, Jinx. Isn't that right?"

She pulled a tissue out of her pocket and blew her nose. She reached for something on the table. "The day of Paul's memorial service, I found this." She sighed. "He left it. I guess I put some magazines on top. Later I found it." She held out a floppy green paperback book the shape of a magazine. "It's about spirals."

My eyes had become used to the dim light. Even the cover of that book got to me. Pictures of the wind whirling in spirals around an Asian man. Some of the wind spirals had the heads of animals attached to them, a horse, a fish, an alligator, a giraffe. The man held his hands up together as if he was praying to the sky. The title was *The Mystic Spiral: Journey of the Soul*. How did that relate to murder?

I opened the book to see words underlined in red ink. About how a spiral tendency within each person is the longing for and a growth toward wholeness. *Wholeness?* I turned the pages. Was it Paul who'd underlined a lot of high-sounding stuff? How everything whole goes through cycles. How it starts from a point, expands, and differentiates. Was a spiral supposed to be a picture of that? Each thing contracts and disappears into the point again. That was the pattern of our lives, the underlined part said, and maybe the pattern of the universe.

"Did Paul tell you why he wanted you to look at this book?" I asked Jinx, totally puzzled.

"He said he'd not been nice to me. He actually said that. And this book might teach us how to talk. I thought he was making fun of me. But maybe not. He'd been drinking. But I was so hopeful. And then, the next day . . ." She began to cry.

I patted her hand, but I went on turning the pages. There was stuff underlined about the cycles of the moon and about whirlpools in water and much more. There were pictures of an Egyptian Pharaoh with snakes on his war helmet. *Snakes.* There was a painting by Botticelli that looked like a funnel made of stone walls and was called a spiral cross-section of the pit of hell. Good grief. A Navaho sand-painting of coiled snakes was called a mandala for healing. *Healing!* And what did all this have to do with Paul's death? With spirals painted on him? And with spirals on Marvelle? How about the coiled dead snake today? My head felt like there was a whirlpool inside.

"Paul was more complicated than I thought," I said, and Jinx smiled as if I'd given her a compliment. "May I borrow this book?" I asked. She nodded yes, and I put it in my trusty pocketbook that always hangs over my shoulder.

"There's still danger," she blurted out.

"How do you know?"

She stayed Madonna-calm. "I get feelings. I knew Paul was in danger. I tried to tell him." Such a minor tone of voice, like a sad song. She held the cigarette tight between her fingers as if it were a lifeline.

A shiver waved through me. I knew she meant something more by "feelings" than just sad or happy. "You had no reason but a *feeling* to believe Paul was in danger?"

Jinx had shut her eyes. "Marvelle, too." She blew out smoke, then took a deep breath and the PIKE'S PEAK OR BUST on her orange T-shirt rose an inch. "We're still in danger. Anne and I and Revonda."

Oh, brother!

Paul's dead image came back to me, shimmering in plastic. Then Marvelle's. I could imagine Jinx's orange T-shirt glimmering through a plastic bag. Not a pretty thought.

"Why?" I asked.

Jinx opened her eyes wide. "Paul and Marvelle were like Anne and Revonda and me. We have trouble."

"You mean you *attract* trouble?" I could see Jinx would do that with her T-shirt and no bra, and that don't-hit-me-again-unless-you-really-want-to manner and that give-up voice.

"Like I said, my father thinks I'll go to hell for posing without clothes on. That's got something to do with the danger. I don't know what. He thinks a lot of people will go to hell."

Guilt, I thought. Is that what those people "in danger" have in common? Does trouble smart-bomb its way to the people who feel like they deserve it? Jinx's father was obviously in favor of that idea.

She got up. "I have to go."

"Before you go, I need to ask you some hard questions," I said. "Were you or Paul ever part of a group that . . ." I groped for a tactful way to go on.

"Oh, you've heard that," she said sadly. "That I belong to

a cult and we sleep with the devil! It's not true, but I've had letters accusing me of that!"

"Where? Exactly what did they say?"

"I burned them," she whispered. "What would you do?"

Not destroy evidence, I hoped. "And Paul . . . ?"

"Hated to join things," she said defiantly. "He never even belonged to a Boy Scout troop when he was a kid."

"Do you believe Paul was mixed up with a Satanic cult?"

Her eyes widened. I thought: She's scared.

"No." She raised her voice. "I don't care what people say, he wasn't. He tried to talk the kids out of it."

"He . . . What kids?"

"Some of the high school kids. I don't know which. They came and asked to look at his books. They said the devil was the one with power and they wanted power. He told them they thought they were playing a game, but it wasn't a game. They could hurt themselves." Now she was eager. Willing to be late to model. Wanting me to approve of Paul, who had sneered at her.

"Was one of the kids Mert's grandson?"

She shook her head. "Paul wouldn't tell who."

"Do you think Satanism has anything to do with why people are in danger?"

"I don't know."

I was annoyed at her again, which made no sense. Her tone of voice was not going to hurt me. But I didn't like it.

She got the lettuce from the sink and put it in a plastic bag. Semitranslucent. Not thin and clingy like dry-cleaning bags. But I wished it wasn't here.

"I have to go," she said. She picked up a second bag. "I need this job. So I can eat."

I jumped up and followed.

She stood still in the doorway. "I haven't got an alibi. When Paul died, I was here alone. When Marvelle died, I was here alone with the flu." Jinx stood as still as a scared cat. Just three feet away.

I walked toward her, and she backed up. Backed right out the door into her garden. I followed.

"When was the last time you saw Paul?"

"Right here the night before—whatever."

I looked beyond her toward the growing things. There was a row of dill. Still young and short but plainly dill. I went over and picked a piece and felt the feathery leaves in my fingers. I crushed it and smelled the sour.

"There was dill with Paul when he died," I said.

Jinx swallowed and said, "There was dill and another herb Ron said was called verbena." Her voice shook. "Ron went to see my mother. My mother knows a lot about herbs. About the old-timey way with herbs. But I stay away from home. I upset my folks."

"Could I go see your mother?"

"Well, sure," Jinx said. "Go when my father isn't there. You can never tell what he'll do. Sometimes he pretends to take his pills and doesn't. He can get rough." She frowned as if the sun was in her eyes. But the sun was behind her.

"On Monday mornings at about eleven-thirty a friend comes and takes Pa to Bible study and lunch in town. He'll not get back till one or one-thirty. So go see Ma on Monday."

She stopped near an orange lily, reached into the second plastic bag, and pulled out a pair of dark glasses. "Just my things to model in. I'm doing a beach scene. I have a bikini in here." She put the dark glasses on.

They changed her face completely. I almost gasped. With the don't-hit-me eyes covered, she became sophisticated. Her shining red hair was a glory. Her Pike's Peak shirt was witty. Her faded jeans "in."

"I'm late." She ran off to her old pickup. There was room on the grass for her to drive around my car. She waved and was gone.

CHAPTER
21

IMMEDIATELY AFTERWARD

I backed out of Jinx's driveway pondering, first about spirals. And they made me think about Jinx and how she probably *did* tell me more because I'm a good listener. Revonda was right about that. Of course Revonda didn't know I'd written a whole chapter on *What to Do If You Can't Remember What to Say* in my *How to Survive Without a Memory*. You've guessed the answer. I wrote about all the useful flavors of listening including *I understand* (as with Jinx). That answer only works if you've had troubles, but, by my age, who hasn't? And then there's *You're fascinating,* which is not hypocritical like it sounds if you get the person on his best subject. The trick is to discover that subject. Works even on difficult types like *The Detail Addict* who interrupts anything you say to demand names and dates, which then go right out of my mind. Or *The Tunnel Vision* who acts like you are an idiot unless you know everything about his special field. Get those folks to declaiming their own subject quick, and they won't put you down. Except for hard-nut cases like Sheriff Harley Henderson.

Now, I know better than to drive and ponder at the same time, especially on an unfamiliar back road. I have a strong warning about that in my *How to Survive Without a Memory*. But sometimes my pondering just creeps up on me, and by the time I catch on, I'm already lost. I realized that had happened. Very annoying.

I was lost, but not alone. I reached over and patted Baskerville. She was breathing through her mouth, pink tongue lolling out. I noticed how big and powerful her teeth were. But what I evidently needed was a cross between a seeing-eye dog and a homing pigeon, and even that might not help unless the dog was driving the car.

The road had been gravel, but now it was dirt, and always curvy. At the side of the road, young trees were close together. When the dirt track branched, I took what I thought was the best fork and jounced on worse ruts. "Some of the back roads are just logging roads," Revonda had told me. And the narrow track was edged by chunky gray rocks. Not turn-around country. Finally I found a wide, weedy space at the edge of the ruts. The grass and weeds weren't deep enough to bog the track down. That's what I figured. So I backed around. Slowly. But not slowly enough. Baskerville began to bark at a brown-and-white spotted hound on the side of the road. That distracted me.

Suddenly, *bam!* The back wheels went into a gulch. The weeds had hidden it, but, boy, I felt it. The front end of the truck rose, and the back banged, and the back wheels spun in the air. My heart began to bang, too. I was lost, and the truck was stuck in a hole.

I tried to go forward. I tried rocking the truck, going forward and quickly backward and forward again. No luck. I got out and tried to push. The spotted hound sat back in the grass and watched with interest. Baskerville kept barking to get out. The truck wouldn't move.

I let Baskerville out on her leash. The spotted hound came

over and wagged his tail. A dog must mean a house nearby. The hound trotted off down a path. Baskerville tugged to follow. I locked the truck, and we ran after the dog.

He stopped once and looked back and wagged his tail, but after that he was not about to slow down. I had to scramble to keep him in sight, even if tree branches caught at me. The path was worn underfoot, but wet branches and briers leaned across it. Plainly we were following an animal trail, faintly marking the shortest way. We kept climbing up one bank and down another. With Baskerville tugging, I almost fell. I let her off her leash, rolled it up and put it in my pocket. We ran up banks of green ferns that smelled spicy when I stepped on them, then down into flat patches of wildflowers. I tried to keep my mind on flowers. That's what Sam would have done. Looked at the beauty. A branch tore my skirt. Another slapped my face. A root almost tripped me. Now how on earth did I get myself into this?

I was following the dog, but I didn't know where I was, did I? We ran over dead leaves, so deep under the trees that no wildflowers poked through. I couldn't see the faint trail at all anymore. I couldn't see a path in any direction. If Baskerville and I didn't keep up with the other dog, we were just plain nowhere.

My grandma warned me about that when I was small. About how if you didn't know how to find your way in the woods, you could wander in a circle for days and starve to death. I tried to remember what she told me. She survived the Great Depression by gathering black cohosh and ginseng in the woods. Grandma said old-timers took a dog to smell out snakes. I wished I hadn't thought of snakes. Well, I had two dogs. Herb gatherers took a gun in case they met a bear. Suppose I met a bear? I stumbled over a fallen branch, but caught myself.

I was out of breath. When I was small, Grandma impressed those lessons on me over and over. Old-timers knew not to wear perfume, not even scent from soap, or the bugs would think you smelled like flowers and bite you. Bugs were biting me.

The dog who was leading us began to trot faster. I hurried down one side of a gully and back up the other side with my feet slipping and the loose rocks rocketing behind me. And just over a small rise, I found a brook, curling dark around smooth stones and foaming over small waterfalls. "Follow a brook downhill and after a while you'll probably come to a road." Grandma had said that. God bless her.

The dogs came running back and stood with their feet in the brook and drank. Then they raced ahead and vanished. I hadn't followed the brook far when the trees began to thin, and I saw a clearing.

There, in the distance, a good-sized cabin sat in the middle of young corn. This was a fairly prosperous farm, with a big barn and a small shed. Long light-green swords of leaves in the sun. Rows and rows. I felt like crying again. For joy. And I told myself: So I get lost. But I make discoveries being lost. I meet nice people. Think positive.

But this was not a well-kept farm. As I got closer, I saw the corn was full of weeds. The rows were all full of the same weed. Then I recognized the thin leaves. Marijuana.

A man in a red plaid shirt stepped out the door of the house, holding a rifle. At least he didn't point it at me. Think positive.

A dog barked fiercely by his side, a powerful dog with the broad face and shoulders of a pit bull. Pit bulls can kill, quicker than snakes. Baskerville came running to my side again and began to growl. The man let his rifle dangle in one hand, but with the other he raised a set of black binoculars. The lenses glittered in the sun. Pointed at me.

Baskerville and the pit bull both began to bark furiously. I wanted protection, but I sure didn't want a dog fight. I ran back into the woods, calling Baskerville. She followed and we ran so fast the trees, the briers, everything melted before us. I don't know how far I ran. But finally I was so out of breath I stopped. I sat down on a rock, panting. Had I circled around to the same place? Suppose I was lost until after dark?

But no. This was not the same. Near my feet I saw a clearly marked path. A human path? And, amazingly, I was still near the brook. Or another brook. Water was what I needed. I itched and stung. I splashed water on my face and my arms and my legs.

The spotted dog had vanished, I wasn't sure when. But now the path was clear and well worn.

Just as well, since my guiding brook turned an almost right angle and then went into such a thicket of rhododendron I could never have followed it. But my luck seemed to have changed. I came out onto a hillside that overlooked a distant curve of asphalt road. A road! I thought: I'm going to be safe! Finally I came to another clearing, just below me. And there sat a small cabin, not any bigger than Jinx's, with a rusty tin roof. Nothing grew around it except in flower beds near the house. Oh, there was a small square garden on one side that looked like it might have a few tomato plants and some greens. But certainly no place for commercial marijuana.

Two cars were parked in the yard, one old and battered, the other fairly new. I approached the cabin quietly, looking around. Once stung is twice cautious. Nothing bloomed in the flower beds, but plants in different shades of green had interesting shapes to the leaves. Herbs? I picked a small saw-tooth fuzzy leaf and squeezed it. A pungent lemony smell was so sharp I was startled. There were bits of herb with Paul's body. Not this kind, though.

The cabin was made of logs and weathered wood siding and settled into the earth whopperjawed. Mint grew by the sagging wooden steps to a small porch. The grass was clipped neatly. I felt there was someone in that cabin I'd like, but I might not have had the nerve to knock if Baskerville hadn't run over to the porch steps. I hurried after her to snap on her leash. I was just leaning over, patting Baskerville and smelling the mint and deciding whether to go up on the porch when I heard the cabin door squeak open.

I looked up quickly and there was a rifle pointed at me. I looked into the glittery eyes of an old man in a battered black felt hat. He said, "I know who you are, girl. You're one of the devil's own."

CHAPTER

22

SATURDAY AFTERNOON

The gray man stood at the top of the gray porch steps, pointing a long gun right at my head. He had a face like a stone cliff—gray like stone, rugged like a cliff, impassive like a cliff—with a small wary mouth and glittering blue eyes. "You mean to help that snake-temptress," he said. "I've heard about you." A small fuzzy dog yapped beside him.

Baskerville growled. The gun wobbled. The dog kept yapping. I pulled Baskerville close to my heels.

"Revonda Roland tempts young people to the ways of the world as bad as the snake in the garden tempted Adam." His voice boomed out over the barking like a radio preacher's.

The porch door squeaked behind him. A faded older woman came out. "Be quiet," she said to the fuzzy dog, and the dog obeyed. "Jeeter," she said in a tired voice, "here's your pill."

Jeeter! Jinx's father was called Jeeter. He did violent things when he didn't take his pill. I had blundered into him!

And suddenly I found myself half-believing that bad-luck stuff—that I was drawn here somehow. Oh, come on!

The faded woman held out a glass of water in one hand and a pill in the other. "You promised," she said. "I know you're a man of your word."

He kept those glittering eyes on me. His radio voice boomed on. "She came creeping, spying. She is from that house of iniquity. Where the devil painted snakes on Paul Roland's hands and feet and forehead, and then stole away his soul."

Did this man paint "snakes" on bodies? He had alibis for the times when Paul and Marvelle died, but just from relatives.

If Jeeter's finger slipped on the trigger, I'd be dead.

"I'm lost." I said it to the woman. She apparently wasn't crazy.

"Jeeter," said the woman, "your brother Buck came to encourage you to take your pills so you can stay with us. We need you."

He kept those glittering eyes on me, but he did lower the gun and reach over and hold his free hand out for the pill. He popped it in his mouth, and then he took the glass of water from the woman, drank the whole thing, and handed the empty glass back. The pill did not stop his words. "We do not know in what form the devil came to Paul Roland, but we do know he will come again to snatch the ungodly."

"Won't you come in? Won't you have a cup of coffee?" The woman said that like I was a neighbor just dropping by for a visit. "I'm Ruth. We're having a bad day today." *Ruth* told the *truth, forsooth*. I certainly knew about bad days, being related to Pop!

Jeeter said, "You come with me. I want to ask you questions." He lifted the rifle again. If the pill was to make him calm, it hadn't worked yet. "Tie the dog to the porch rail," he commanded.

I don't argue with a gun. I tied Baskerville and said, "Sit and stay." She whimpered, but she did it.

Ruth (for *soothe*) politely held the squeaky screen door open for me. I went inside, with Jeeter still pointing the gun at my head.

The light inside was dim, and I almost tripped over a slat basket full of vegetables. "Keep walking!" Jeeter shouted. The basket was at the feet of a man in a rocking chair. He just sat there and looked surprised when I grabbed the arm of his rocker to keep from falling. But not as surprised as I'd be if I saw my brother pointing a gun at a woman.

"Sit there." Jeeter pointed to a chair right across a low table. He sat down on the other side of the table. Jeeter and the other man and me around the table, with one seat left for Ruth, who must be Jeeter's wife (and, presumably, Jinx's mother). Jeeter put his gun down on the table between us. It was in quick-grabbing reach if he took the notion, but at least he couldn't slip and shoot me by mistake.

My eyes began to get used to the dim light. I might learn something useful, right? I tried to keep my mind on that.

The man, who I figured must have been Jeeter's brother Buck, had on a red-checked shirt. Exactly like the red-checked shirt on the man with the binoculars in the marijuana field. He had the same brown hair. I hadn't seen the face well. My heart was pounding as if it knew. But I told myself it couldn't be the same man. That would be too much of a coincidence. There are lots of red-checked shirts.

Jeeter stared at me, but he didn't *do* anything. My eyes took in the room. Spartan. The lightbulb in the ceiling was bare. Almost the only decoration in the room was a bland picture of Jesus, in a white robe, that hung in back of Jeeter as if looking over his shoulder. An old leather-bound family Bible sat on the table by the gun, the same color as the gun handle. Like they were a set. I prayed Jeeter would remember what was in that Bible, about love thy neighbor and especially the thou-shalt-not-kill part.

Red-Checked-Shirt sat at right angles to Jeeter. Behind him was an unpainted wood bookshelf with all sorts of small china animals on the top shelf. Cutesy, not realistic.

Mrs. Jeeter's only frivolity? On the next shelf down were books. *Culpeper's Herbal, Goldenseal, Etc., Wild Herbs of the South,* and such. Well-worn.

And, I thought, Ruth-for-Soothe was the one I needed to talk to about herbs. But Jinx had said her mother wouldn't say much in front of her father.

Buck had narrow eyes, like he was used to looking into the sun, and a broad mouth. "Jeeter," he said, "that's a new gun, isn't it? Nice looking, like it'll shoot sweet." He leaned over very slowly and picked it up. He stared through the sight out the window. "I just shot a copperhead," he said. "You and I always was good shots, Jeeter. I hit that snake right in the head."

Was he deliberately getting that gun farther from Jeeter? Was he my friend? Or was he the man who stood in the marijuana field and watched me through binoculars? Did he know my face?

"We have a lot of snakes in these mountains." Buck turned to me. "You get lost, you'll find you a snake by mistake. It's not a good thing to get lost." Was that a threat?

Mrs. Jeeter was handing me a cup of coffee. "I'm out of milk," she said. "Have some sugar." She held out a pretty flowered sugar bowl that glowed white in that unpainted room.

"You're only safe in these mountains if you know what to do about snakes," Buck told me. There was something about his narrow eyes that made everything he said seem like he meant it two ways. If I could snitch on marijuana, was I a snake?

I sipped my sweet coffee. I don't usually take sugar, but after my run through the woods and the shock of Jeeter, I needed fuel.

"We have all kinds of snakes around here," Jeeter said. He seemed to be relaxing some. Buck was putting the gun back down on the table but almost out of Jeeter's reach. Jeeter hardly seemed to notice. "I've seen, the most, copperheads and rattlesnakes," he said. "A rattlesnake can jump eight feet to attack if it's coiled."

Eight feet! I learned back in summer camp that poison snakes have broad jaws and a pointy tail. That's all. Nothing about them jumping!

One side of Jeeter's mouth smiled, though one side was still turned down. He leaned toward me, eyes cold as a snake's. "My uncle Ezra says a rattlesnake can *spit* venom. I never did see it myself, but a big one spit at him, and the venom that hit him made him feel so woozy he couldn't kill the snake."

Buck in his checked shirt laughed. At me or at Jeeter? "Why, you all will scare that girl to death. I've lived here all my life, and no snake has ever bit me." Was Buck going to be my friend? "Nearest I came to snakebite, I was mowing, and something tugged at my pants, and I looked down, and it was a copperhead with his fangs caught in my baggy pants. I just held my snaky leg out and jumped and kicked him away with the other foot. If you're smart, you don't get bit."

And he meant if *I* wasn't smart, *I* would get bit. It was as if they—even Mrs. Jeeter—were conspiring to scare me into staying on the main roads or in the house from now on.

"You need to study on snakes," Mrs. Jeeter told me. "A rattlesnake will give you warning. A copperhead won't."

Jeeter reached for the gun again and put it over his knees. He kept gimlet eyes on me.

I tried to figure how I could get out of that place. I could say I had to go to the bathroom. Maybe I could climb out the bathroom window and run. But they probably had an outhouse. And what would I do about Baskerville?

"A copperhead is an ill snake," Jeeter said, "but a peaceable snake. They wait quiet. Then if you come close, they bite."

He emphasized *bite,* and plainly he didn't mean peaceable the usual way. He meant still. Deadly still.

If I weren't scared of Jeeter's gun and the maybe-owner

of the marijuana crop and the snakes between me and home, I might even like to sit and listen to him talk. Some older folks still used words the way the first settlers did, because for so long the valleys had been hard to get to at the end of windy dirt roads. That was why we stuck together so, especially kin. Because once all we had to fall back on was kin.

I was sure that Mrs. Jeeter, and also Buck, would stick by Jeeter no matter what. Would even help him hide my body if he shot me.

Even so, I half liked the way those older words like *peaceable* sounded in Jeeter's rolling voice. Kind of hypnotic, except that the doom in his voice made me want to get out of there. I felt like his tone could raise up copperheads in the corners. No wonder Jinx needed to run out and find people to love her. No wonder she didn't know how to find the right ones.

"Snakes have special places where they like to be," Buck said. "There's a shortcut between here and Revonda Roland's place that the rattlesnakes like. Full of sunny rocks. I'd never go that way."

"We're near Revonda's?" I'd blundered my way near someplace I knew! I could make it back to civilization. With luck.

At Revonda's name Jeeter grabbed the gun again. Mrs. Jeeter just patted his shoulder.

"Snakes know when you're afraid." Mrs. Jeeter nodded to herself. "It's like a dog or a horse. They can smell fear. They bite the scared ones. They know when you are safe in the Lord. A snake has never bit *you*." She smiled proudly at her husband. "Even that time when one ran acrost your foot."

Jeeter's gray face creased into a pleased-with-himself smile. "Why, yes. I looked down and there was a copperhead crawling right over my foot." He beamed. "I just stood perfectly still in the arms of the Lord, and it crawled right on where it was going. The ungodly are afraid," he said. "And so they die."

And I thought: Jeeter could be the killer. He feels he has a right to kill anyone who has a reason to feel guilty. So Jinx feels in danger if she's guilty.

I sat up straight, making sure to look as un-guilty as possible. "Thank you, for all you've told me," I said, trying to sound in control. "I have to go now, or they'll worry and start searching for me." I figured Jeeter wouldn't like that.

He pointed the gun at my head. "I haven't finished telling you about snakes. Snakes is like sin. You can't get away if you try to hold on too tight. I made a sermon once about the story of the boots."

What did he mean? Would he really shoot me if I ran?

"Because don't think killing snakes is enough," he sang. "You step on the fangs of a dead snake, you get the poison in your blood just the same." That's how Jeeter looked. As if there was poison in his blood. And yet his voice sang. "They's a story about a man who was way out in the woods, hunting ginseng in a pair of fine leather boots, when a great big rattler bit him right through the boots." I could see he had to finish before he let me go. If he did then.

"So when the man who was bit managed to get home, they took off the boots, and they did the things they used to do to get rid of the poison. They cut a live chicken in half and put a half against the bite to draw out that venom. And when he kept sinking, they put hot turpentine in a wide-mouthed jar and pressed that against the bite. Still he died, and they buried him proper, and his son inherited the boots."

I nodded to show I was listening and shouldn't be shot.

"Well, the son had always wanted those boots. Greed is a grievous sin. So right after the funeral, he put on those boots, and the fangs stuck in the boots bit him, and he died, too." Jeeter smiled at that. "So they hauled those boots out to the county dump to bury them with some junk. And one of the men who ran the dump saw those fine boots and pulled them out of the trash and put them on—and *he* died. Sin is like that."

I couldn't see exactly how sin was like that, but I didn't

care. I had to leave. I stood up. To my surprise, Buck stood up, too. "I'll get her out of here for you, Jeeter," he said. "I'll get her back where she belongs."

Alone in a car with Buck might or might not be worse than being with two others in a house with Jeeter. Anyway, it would be a change. I decided to take the chance.

Jeeter nodded his head. He said, "I'm tired."

At least I had a chance to untie Baskerville from the porch and take her with us. I told myself Baskerville was protection. I took her inside the truck with me. She sat on my feet with her head in my lap.

Buck started the engine and his big brown Ford truck jounced as we rolled down the rutted red clay driveway. He was silent with his eyes front.

"Suppose I did meet a bad snake, what would I do?" I asked.

We crossed a two-board bridge across the creek, one board for each wheel. "You kill it," he said. "No point in keeping danger around." Two meanings again? We swung out onto the asphalt road.

"For a copperhead, the best way is with a hoe," he said. "Stand back and chop off the head with a hoe blade."

I'd want a hoe ten feet long!

Did he hoe marijuana? "And if I don't have a hoe . . . ?" I asked. I didn't exactly keep one in my back pocket.

"Break the back," he said. "A snake can't move if you break the back." We were coming around the bend toward Revonda's. I was so glad I could have yelled hoorah. Maybe Buck was just a good neighbor who never hoed anything more than corn and beans. He turned into the driveway. The old Victorian house looked beautiful to me. Even though it still wasn't all painted.

"Throw a rock or use a long stick to break a snake's back. And keep that dog away from snakes," he added, glancing at Baskerville. "A cat is faster than a snake, but a dog will get bit. And if I were you, I'd stay away from Jeeter. He has spells."

But I stopped thinking about Jeeter, and even about snakes. On Revonda's porch I saw Sam with his arm around Jinx. Anne came out of the kitchen door. That must be a dutch-uncle arm he put around Jinx, I tried to tell myself. But how did Anne feel? Her eyes said scared. Sam was her lover and her good-luck charm. She needed him in back of her now. Did Jinx need him, too? That would be an ugly problem.

I got out of the truck with Baskerville and thanked Buck.

Sam unhanded Jinx and came and threw an arm about me. "You worried us," he said, "when Jinx came and said she hadn't seen you for hours."

"I got Paul's truck stuck in a ditch," I said. "Where's Revonda?"

Sam began to laugh. "She went off on a date. What do you think of that?" He acted like that was a big joke on me. I felt confused.

"Revonda has gone," he said, "to have a drink with your father, wearing her best black dress and real pearls."

CHAPTER

23

LATE SATURDAY AFTERNOON

It was one of those moments when I needed to be in three places at once. I needed to protect my father from dangerous entanglement with a sexy actress. (So, O.K., Revonda was suffering sorrow and loss, but that probably made her sexier to Pop.) I needed to get home and talk all this over with Ted, and then collapse. But I needed to tell Anne and Sam about marijuana and Jeeter, and show them the book about spirals. I still had that book with me in my trusty shoulder bag that—through thick and thin, lost and found, and even with a gun aimed at my head—never left my shoulder. A durable bag!

Jinx had taken off from Revonda's as soon as Buck had dropped me off. Sam offered to follow in his car to be sure she got home safe, but she said no. If she was going to live in a lonely place, she had to be independent and take care of herself. What a combination: She felt like a target and still refused help.

Sam watched her go with a frown and said, "Inviting

fate." He said it like it was the title of a painting. Anne's worried eyes darted from Jinx in her car back to Sam. I said, "Now, about marijuana and snakes . . ."

I told them about the marijuana field and then about Jeeter and Ruth and Buck and their snake talk and how I thought they were trying to scare me. "You know," I said, "in the Middle Ages they had memory systems based on the fact that you can remember something frightening and shocking better than something that's not. And it's true. I could repeat every word they said."

Sam said he thought Jeeter was a good suspect, and that in the future he'd sure steer clear of boots with fangs inside. We all agreed that I shouldn't tell the sheriff about seeing the marijuana farm, since we didn't trust him not to be mixed up with dealing drugs himself. Also, I'd been so lost and turned around in the woods that I didn't know where the place was anyway. I wasn't even sure where I'd left the truck, except that it was on a road not too far from Jinx's.

"Don't worry. I'll find it tomorrow first thing," Sam reassured me. Then he said he had to go check that all Revonda's doors and windows were locked, since she might not be back before dark.

"And then," I told him, "I need to show you the strange book about spirals."

From the studio I called Ted and told him I'd be late but, boy, would I bring news. And God bless Ted, he just said he'd be looking forward to it.

Anne put some soup to heat up and sat down at the table with me. She pulled at a strand of her hair, curled it round her finger, and shifted uneasily in her chair. "I'm sure it's true about snakes." Jeeter's snake stories were still on her mind.

"How do you mean?" I asked.

"Snakes are more likely to bite the people who're afraid. They know. When I think about that, I'm even more afraid and they are even more likely to bite me." She was dead white, almost blue-white in the pale light.

And there wasn't a single snake around. I wanted to say, "Come on, snap out of it." But I knew I should listen.

"You make it sound like Jeeter has my number," Anne said, "like he knows how to make a person afraid of their own fear. And it makes me think about Paracelsus," she said.

"You've lost me."

"I mean," she said, "in that book on magic, Paracelsus said magic came by focusing your mind and will and imagination. What kind of magic do I make when I see pictures in my mind of what I'm scared of? I can't help it. Snakes. Or losing Sam. Or a killer who will spot me as the most scared one. And the most scared one would be the one to kill." Her teeth were actually chattering.

"You stop that!" I said. I couldn't help myself, either. I have a thing about people who give up. I can stand almost anything else and be sympathetic, but gloom gets me.

"Listen," I said, "you see what could go wrong in your mind so you can figure out how to change it. That's the reason. You've got to concentrate on seeing what to do."

I wasn't getting through. "Everything went wrong for me," Anne sobbed, "until I met Sam. Sam is my good luck and my love. He says I'm O.K. And if I lose him, what will I do?" Lucky for her, I thought, that fear almost became her. She was fey like a wood nymph, not like a droopy wet blanket.

"You'd manage," I told her. "But you won't lose Sam."

"Maybe he loved me," she sobbed, "because he likes to help people who have trouble." She sobbed even louder. "And Jinx is worse off than me."

"You have a point there," I said, trying shock treatment. Anne gulped. I handed her a tissue from my trusty pocketbook, and she blew her nose.

"Jinx is the closest I ever saw to giving up," I said. "The worst. She scares me. I bet she scares Sam."

Anne blew her nose even harder. "I ought to be nice to her." Anne was struggling to be rational. I could see that.

"What kinds of things have always gone wrong for you?" I asked. Facts help.

"Oh, everything." She sighed. "They even had a fire in the hospital the day I was born."

"I'm sure that was your fault," I said sarcastically.

"And I almost flunked the first grade. I never did well in school, except on the out-loud stuff. I was fired once for filing things in the wrong place. I forget things like you do. I learn to spell things and then I forget—which sounds dumb, but I do it. And one time I somehow got turned around and found myself driving the wrong way on a divided road. I even did that."

"Would you be shocked," I asked, "if I said none of that sounds so bad to me as long as you survived it? And you're a great puppeteer."

"Oh, that," she said with a shrug. "That's easy. That's fun."

"Who keeps reminding you about those things you did wrong?" I asked. Anne plainly couldn't remind herself about the fire in the hospital.

"Well, they bothered my family," she said. "They said I better watch out or I'd be like Uncle Fred. Uncle Fred breeds schnauzers and lives with my grandma and is always broke. But Sam thought I was great. And after I married him, I felt great! And now, suppose—?"

"Be sure you don't imagine bad things that aren't true about Sam," I said. I went over and gave her a big hug. This gal needed all the hugs she could get. Because I was afraid she had a point. A bully zeroes in on someone who sends out give-up vibrations, right? Wouldn't a killer be like that?

But then, I told myself, Paul had seemed to be angry, not depressed. And Marvelle was downright perky. But the give-up thing bothered me all the same.

Sam came breezing in. Talk about never giving in to gloom. "Now," he said, radiating good cheer and anticipation, "show us the book about spirals."

CHAPTER

24

SATURDAY EVENING AND SUNDAY MORNING, JULY 7

Ted was as baffled by the spiral book as Anne and Sam had been. How could it be related to murder? We drank iced tea and conferred at the kitchen table, and were uninspired. Ted was horrified to hear of my blundering near the marijuana farm and visiting Jeeter.

"I wish I could have been along," he said. By which I figured he meant he never gets lost. On the other hand, perhaps knowing about Jeeter and the farm would turn out to be useful. You never know.

"I also wish I felt better about the sheriff," he said. "I talked about him to a source I have, and he said the down-east folks don't trust him, but it may be because of his good-old-boy mountain style." We agreed I wouldn't tell the sheriff about the marijuana, at least for the time being.

Then we took our tea over to the counter and got to work fixing supper.

"The wrong things upset me," I said as I trimmed the broccoli. "Anne and Jinx are both smart, good-looking girls.

And they both can act as limp as wet spaghetti. They make me want to scream! That doesn't help."

Ted gave me his wise-professor glance as he dotted the flounder with butter. "So who did you once know— someone who acted that way and it bothered you?" he asked. "Maybe you're reminded."

I drew a blank. "Nobody limp as they are!"

"Did you ever want to give up, yourself?" Ted asked. I thought about that while he made hollandaise sauce to go on the broccoli. A reward, because we'd both had busy days. I squeezed the lemon for him, reaming out the juice with an old-fashioned squeezer I keep for sentimental reasons. It was my mother's. My mother made lemonade after school.

"The lemon squeezer is related to something I need to remember," I said.

"Related to when you wanted to give up?" he asked hopefully.

"Yes!" It came back to me. Ma squeezing lemons and listening to my troubles, and helping me to figure how to cope. Then the time when Ma wasn't there.

"In the second half of first grade," I said, "my mother was gone for a month after an automobile accident. I had trouble learning to read. A bunch of kids ganged up and called me dumb. And some older kids got into the act and I was scared to walk to school, but I had to go. Pop was so upset, because Ma was away, that he was no help. I wanted to give up and stay in bed all day."

"So what happened?"

"Ma came back. She taught me ways to laugh at the mean kids. Do you know the one about, *'I'm rubber, you're glue, everything bad you say about me bounces off me and sticks on you'?*"

Ted said, "No," and cracked two eggs.

"Very effective," I said. "Also, with Ma back I felt better. When you're spunkier, bullies don't pick on you. But it still bugs me to deal with that give-up feeling. I need to help those gals feel spunkier, that's what! I also need to go see Pop." I sighed. "He has a date with Revonda tonight."

"Those two deserve each other," Ted hooted. "But do you think she'd take on an invalid? Never."

That cheered me up. The phone rang, and I answered. A gravelly low voice said, "You keep your nose out of other people's business, or you'll be dead." Buck-Marijuana-Field, I figured. Still, I was scared silly. I also knew that if I told Ted, he might persuade me to *give up* trying to help Anne and Sam. Or he'd worry about me all day. So I did one of the dumbest things I ever did in my life. I told Ted it was a wrong number.

Next morning Ted was bogged down in grading summer-school papers. I went out to Revonda's to show her the spiral book. *Carefully.* I watched the rearview mirror.

I found Revonda sitting in her jungle chair, flanked by dogs, and fuming. Hound growled as I came in, but Revonda said, "It's all right." Then, "What's *not* all right is a big revival on the ballfield next week. To pray for those who are under the power of Satan. I know what that means. They'll pray about Paul, without knowing Paul. He was not a bad person!"

I didn't know what to say. Fortunately, Anne came in at that point and said, "I found out something strange about Marvelle. Reverend Phillipson told me."

Revonda pounced. "That Pollyanna! He told you something useful?"

"He came by to see if we were O.K. and he was talking about how we are all under stress because the murders scare us," Anne said. "So we get fearful and clumsy. Like the way I broke that glass this morning."

Revonda's hands twitched. She hated clumsiness.

"He said people were already fearful before Marvelle was found dead. Even when the sheriff was still sure Paul had killed himself."

Revonda listened one hundred percent.

"He said Marvelle was afraid a man was peeking in her windows at night. She told the minister and the sheriff. No one else. She thought her fear made her look silly. And then, Reverend Phillipson said he supposed it didn't matter now if he told. Marvelle obviously hadn't been silly at all."

"And then?"

"Well, Reverend Phillipson said the sheriff went himself to investigate."

"Stage-struck," Revonda snorted. "He was an extra once in a movie about blockaders shot in this valley. He was impressed with any actress."

"The sheriff couldn't find a thing. Not even a footprint."

"He couldn't find a mad dog if it bit him!" Revonda shrugged. "But Marvelle imagined things. She probably liked to think men would still peek at her." Revonda leaned forward and lowered her voice dramatically. "On the other hand, if there's a deranged killer, he may have watched her from a distance, but she could feel his eyes."

Jeeter?

Revonda turned to me with a charming smile. "Peaches, you can find out about Marvelle by chatting with her psychologist. She'll tell you more than she'd tell me."

So Marvelle was getting help!

"Pretend you're taking a walk," Revonda said. "That woman works in her garden Sundays. Shocks some of the church crowd. Actually Paul went to see the woman once or twice. A while back. Her name is Octavia Morris. Paul said it was a waste of time."

I had my own reason to see the psychologist. I wanted to know if Marvelle had give-up tendencies like Anne and Jinx and hid them. I might find out about Paul, too!

I found the psychologist where Revonda's directions said she'd be—right down the road, pulling weeds in front of a white clapboard house with glorious roses. She was a slender woman in jeans, with short dark hair, yanking grass and stuff out of a circular flower bed around a tree. She was younger than I expected. Maybe thirty-five. Not a woman who minded getting her hands dirty.

I said, "Hello," and started up the gravel driveway.

She stood up. "I'm Octavia Morris." She had remarkable brown eyes that seemed to take in everything about me all at once.

I explained I was Anne's cousin and Anne worked for Revonda, and since I'd had some luck finding out who killed my aunt and such, Revonda had enlisted my help to try to discover who killed Paul, and now Marvelle. This all sounded pretty lame to me, but Octavia Morris smiled and said, "We all want to know that, even young Billy Holt who mows my lawn. That's all he talks about." So Marvelle's psychologist was friends with Mert's grandson. Everybody knew everybody in Bloodroot Creek.

She stepped forward. "I'm just going in for a cold drink. Why don't you join me?"

The house inside was cool and comfortably dark, all natural wood and bookshelves with interesting objects all around. The bronze head of a young woman stood on one side of the mantelpiece. At the other side was a painted wood carving of an American Indian dancing. He wore rows of eagle feathers attached to his outstretched arms like wings, and a blue mask. Arresting.

She asked me to sit in a chair on one side of the fireplace, then went to get us iced tea. I scanned book titles: *The Witch and the Clown, Shadow and Evil in Fairy Tales, An Archetypical Approach to Death, Dreams, and Ghosts.* Spooky.

On the edges of the shelves were small brass and ceramic animals: a white china unicorn, a brass dog with a Chinese symbol on the forehead, a ceramic winged horse, and a handmade-looking green pottery dragon. The dragon, with its horselike head and small batlike wings and pot belly, almost made me laugh. Then I noticed that on each of the handlike claws, on each of the feet, and in the middle of the forehead, were small ceramic spirals. In one claw, the dragon held what was plainly a magic wand. A stick with a triangle at the top and in the middle of the triangle a white spiral. Like the marks on Paul and Marvelle! I sucked in my breath. Imagine keeping that dragon in plain sight after a killer painted spirals on your neighbors! My heart pounded.

"Confront your fears!" She startled me. "Dragon helps my patients to do that about these murders." She had come back from the kitchen and must have seen me staring. She handed me my tea in a sweaty cold glass. Walking casually over to the chair across from me, she sat down and leaned back, so completely self-assured. "This summer is my first time to be questioned about murders. But you've had experience I take it?"

I told her as briefly as I could about the murder of Aunt Nancy and the threats against Pop, and I thought: This is not what I came for.

"They questioned you about Marvelle Starr and Paul Roland?" I asked.

"Yes. I was able to tell them part of Marvelle's schedule before she was killed. She was here at three o'clock the day before."

I felt this Octavia Morris was behind a glass wall I couldn't penetrate. Controlling the way our conversation went. Yet she seemed friendly.

"Was Marvelle Starr depressed?" I asked. "Did Marvelle talk to you about her fears of being watched?"

"I can't talk about the substance of conversations with patients," she said. Still pleasant but on guard. Both sandaled feet were straight in front of her, flat on the ground. Her hands were clasped in her lap.

"Revonda told me Paul came to see you." There was not going to be a way to ask what I wanted except to jump in.

"I really can't tell you about patients." She said it a little louder. "That would be unethical."

"But you hear what people say now about Paul. Some of them say Paul belonged to a Satanic cult. And that maybe Marvelle did, too. I hear there's going to be a revival meeting to pray for those who have been under Satan's influence. Revonda believes they'll say that Paul was one."

She looked up sharply, and I could see by a slight twitching that an inner struggle was going on.

"I *will* say that I don't believe Paul belonged to a cult," she said finally. "I think he would want me to say that much. I told that to the sheriff."

Behind her was a strange picture of a young man turning into a tree—or perhaps the other way around. A symbol for something? It reminded me of my scare in the woods. Yet I liked the picture. The young man even seemed exalted, like Reverend Phillipson when he hoped for the best. But the young man's feet were roots, going down into the ground. His fingers were twigs, with a scattering of green leaves, his bare body like a tree trunk. The picture was a dream.

"There seem to be symbols that have had meaning for our subconscious minds from the dawn of history. They appear in folktales and in dreams," she said. "Paul was interested in those symbols. I don't believe he was a joiner."

I looked back at her bookshelf. In front of a book called *Individuation* was a small sword, probably a letter opener. Not unlike the one in Paul's room.

"Symbols," I said. "Like a sword. Paul's books say a sword was necessary for some kinds of magic. And I suppose a spiral is a symbol like you're talking about?" I asked.

"A symbol can have more than one meaning." Her voice said I was jumping to conclusions. "A sword can be phallic or a symbol of a wand, of power. A spiral can be a symbol of growth or of the way we solve a problem and then come to it again on a higher level to solve again." She kept those brown eyes focused on me. Demanding that I understand. "The important thing is what the symbol means to you. In your dreams, for example."

"And spirals on a dead body?"

"What do you think they mean?" she asked, still guarded.

"I don't know."

"Do you think Paul and Marvelle were members of a Satanic cult?" she challenged. And I thought, wait a minute. Why do I get the third degree?

"I don't know." I felt kind of stupid, but that's how it was.

"Not to know, when you have no way to know, is a very healthy attitude." Octavia Morris seemed pleased. "There are people who can't admit to themselves that they are only human, who can't admit that there's bound to be some evil in every person, including themselves. Those people have to see the evil in somebody else. We call that projection." She was holding me with those brown eyes. "When you see a person who is sure without proof that another person is in league with the devil, ask yourself what the accuser is hiding. Even from himself. Ask yourself if he's unbalanced."

We were straying from the things I came to ask about.

"Revonda thinks Paul might have been killed by a member of a cult who misunderstood Paul's interest in magic," I said. "But I can't see why, unless the killer was a member of a rival cult. Do cults have turf fights?"

"I don't know any members of cults." She raised her voice, the way the television commercials are always louder than the show itself. She dropped her voice again. "I believe people who join cults are looking for someone to tell them who they are. Like all those poor people in Jonestown years back who drank cyanide because their leader said to. I don't believe Paul was like that."

"Was Paul depressed," I asked, "even though he acted angry?"

"I haven't been able to tell you much about my clients," she said firmly.

I started to get up. I was annoyed. "Thank you," I said. I probably sounded sarcastic.

"I'd really like to be helpful. I could tell you something I saw. I haven't told anyone but the sheriff, because I don't like to start rumors. But this might help you." I sat back down quick.

"I drove past Marvelle Starr's house on the morning of the Fourth of July. You remember the Fourth was warm?"

"Yes." My mouth was dry with hope. I took a sip of tea.

"Not far from Marvelle's house I saw a strange-looking woman walking," she said, "a large woman in a big flowing smock, a bandanna, and dark glasses. And I thought: one of those crazy tourists. She must be hot in all those clothes."

"Did it look at all like anyone you ever saw before?" I stood up again. I almost rose in the air with excitement. A great disguise for a killer.

"Anyone could have hidden under all those clothes," she said. "Even a man."

CHAPTER
25

I thought I was going back to Revonda's to discuss the Spiral-on-the-Dragon Lady's news, but I found Anne coming back across the street from Mert's. Jinx's battered pickup was parked by the studio, next to Paul's truck. Good for Sam. He must have found Paul's truck where I left it and brought it back. "I hope you'll come in," Anne said to me, eyeing Jinx's truck like it might explode.

Of course, I intended to come in. I could feel trouble about to come to a head, and it worried me. I was right at Anne's heels when she opened the door at the top of the stairs.

Sam was at his easel, and Jinx was stark naked. Now, I know artists paint people that way. But Jinx had looked naked even with her clothes on. And now she stood balanced on one foot on top of a rickety stool. Without her tacky clothes, even in that odd position, she was more beautiful than she was with clothes on. She was beautiful even in spite of her wide-eyed, half-frowning, off-balance expression. She was gently curved and smooth as the petals of those roses at Paul's funeral.

I turned and glanced at Anne, and what I saw was terror.

I turned back and saw fear spread to Jinx's face. She wavered like she might fall at any moment. Would Sam run to catch her if she fell?

Anne must be asking herself that. She flushed red.

Sam said, "Hi. Jinx has offered to do some modeling for me." Very casual, feet apart, brush in hand, painting full-speed ahead. He hummed to himself, concentrating so hard on his picture he didn't seem to see danger signals.

Jinx said "Hello" in that don't-hit-me-again voice and held her pose. Did she know she was so damn sexy?

Death and danger stimulate the need for sex. I heard that on television. During the Black Death, people copulated in the streets. Was Sam having a little on the side? I could see why Anne wondered.

I tried to defuse the tension by telling them all about the woman Octavia the psychologist saw in bandanna and dark glasses.

Sam said, "So it was someone who would have expected to be recognized." I suspect Anne and Jinx were both so tense they didn't hear.

"Take a break," Sam said to Jinx. "That's a hard position to hold. You look bushed. That's enough for today."

Jinx got down from the stool and wriggled to loosen her naked muscles. "Posing is hard work," she said. I knew she aimed that at Anne and me. "Even if my father does think it means I'll go to hell." She put on her clothes quickly. No underwear, just shirt and jeans.

I went over and looked at Sam's picture. Anne came, too. He was still putting dabs of paint here and there, humming to himself "The Green, Green Grass of Home."

The picture showed the rock face of a mountainside with Jinx on a narrow ledge. Naked, of course. Facing us. She wasn't balanced on one foot in the picture, but she had that same unsteadily-balanced-on-one-foot expression with the eyes wide. The picture was just roughed in. But, like all Sam's pictures, it went straight to the pit of my stomach.

I thought: For God's sake, girl, turn and hug the cliff! And however you got there, get down quick. And put on some clothes. Because in the picture her nakedness was like her not holding on. Frightening. Sexy, but frightening.

"I told Jinx," Sam said, "that this isn't a portrait of her. This is a picture of some force that has to do with the murders, a force I'm trying to explore." He smiled at me like we were co-detectives. He stopped painting and stood back and studied the picture. "When I fully understand the force, I'll be closer to knowing who killed Paul and Marvelle."

I put my arm around Anne, who was standing next to me.

Jinx had come over to look at herself on the cliff. She had on her PIKE'S PEAK OR BUST shirt again. She hugged herself. "I feel that way sometimes. I hate that picture."

Sam stood and admired it. So pleased that joy was spouting out of every pore, out of every tangled reddish-blond hair in his head or beard. "Thank you. I want this picture to make you feel. I'm getting it right." He put his arm around Jinx's shoulders and gave a squeeze. I felt Anne wince like she'd been burned.

Jinx caught Sam's joy, and she smiled up at him, softened and warmed like a red-haired angel. Then she glanced at Anne, shriveled, and left. I wanted to yell, "All of you stop and talk this out!" But would that help?

Sam was humming and adding bits of paint here and there to make his naked Jinx even more lifelike. Painting is memory on canvas. So Jinx was still with us.

"When we met, you said you wanted to paint *me*," Anne shrilled. "You've painted Revonda. You've painted Jinx. Why not me?"

Sam put his brush down. The joy shrunk out of him. I wanted to say, "Anne, this is not the way to talk." But she already knew it. Her expression jerked this way and that, like she was trying to control it, but she was too angry and scared. I felt as if little needles of anger were sticking out of her all over.

Sam stood by his easel, beyond the needles. "I'm not ready to paint you." He threw his head back and squinted the way artists do when they want to get the scale of some picture right. "I know you too well, Anne, and not well enough." He said that sadly. Then he turned back to his picture. "You and Jinx are alike in some way. I have to understand that. It's important." He reached out and took Anne's hand. Good! The right move. "I see you, but I don't see you well enough."

Behind Sam, the green leaves on the tree out the window moved gently. Maybe rain would come.

"And what do you see?" Anne challenged.

He winked at me, like he was glad I was there for a witness. "I see gentle hair that does nice things in a small wind," he said, "and hands that act out your words and make them richer, and a tentative mouth that tastes your words to be sure they're just right, and listening eyes with five kinds of light inside."

Some of the stiffness went out of Anne.

"And those wonderful eyebrows that lift and lilt at the edges like the wings of a seagull in flight."

He shut his mouth and let go of Anne's hand. His eyes had that faraway look, like he'd retreated so far inside his own head he forgot we were there. "So why do I want to paint you wrestling with a ghost? Wrestling with a white smothering thing? Wrestling with a white glob of wind?"

"So that's how you feel! You don't want to paint me in any way at all, or else you'd do it." The screech in Ann's voice was back. Oh, dear.

He started and looked at Anne as if he really saw her again. "You know," he said, "I think part of what is wrong is that you're not sure of yourself. You get lost. Why Anne, you won't even write home unless I fix your spelling, and then you feel dumb."

Anne flushed. She bent her head as if she didn't want to

see him. Why on earth was Sam bringing up spelling—of all things—at a time like this? Sometimes I thought he was a little crazy. But he wasn't about to stop.

"I saw this article in the paper about dyslexia—"

"So you think something is wrong with me, too! Just like my family! There's nothing wrong with me! I manage fine!" Anne was shouting.

And then Sam laughed, and I was afraid Anne was going to haul off and hit him. Maybe I should have left. But I wanted to know what would happen next.

"Of course something is wrong with you," he said. "Something is wrong with everybody." He threw his arms wide as if he was ready to hug everybody. "Ask Peaches!"

He went over and ruffled through the scraps of this and that. "I clipped this today." He grabbed something he'd torn out of the paper and held it up. "This is about a Dr. Zimmerman who specializes in dyslexia."

"I don't have to have it just because it's in the paper!"

Sam wouldn't give up. "Here. Read this. It tells how some people keep feeling like they fall in black holes. This Zimmerman just moved here from California."

"I am not some kind of a nut who doesn't know where I am!" Anne shouted. "You're just changing the subject so I'll forget to be mad with you about Jinx. I don't need to go to this Zimmerman from California."

Sam stayed reasonable. "You could be color-blind," he said. "You could be mean. You could have no sense of humor. Why, you could be stupid or self-righteous. You could be dull. But you're not. You've got to have something wrong, or how can you be human?"

"So what are you, Sam? How are you human?"

"They tell me I'm not practical." I almost laughed. "But it doesn't bother me." He shrugged. "And whatever is wrong *does* bother you. Go see Dr. Zimmerman. Why not?"

"What does all this have to do with why you don't want to paint my picture?" I felt the porcupine quills zoom back out. Sam actually stepped back as if he felt them, too. Stepped closer to the canvases stored against the wall.

"I tried," he said. "I tried to paint you holding a bunch of zinnias. With all those bright colors for the way you get enthusiastic. But they turned to black and white and began to whirl." He laughed a sheepish laugh as if she'd caught him at some silly naughtiness.

"Where is the picture? I want to see it."

"No, you don't. It's just a study. It turned out wrong." He moved even closer to the canvases by the window, as if he wanted to protect them.

She pushed past him and began to look.

"Please." He followed her over. "I can't hold you down and prevent you from seeing that picture. But in the stage it's in, it will hurt you to see it. I don't want to hurt you, Anne." He threw a look of appeal to me. "Ask Peaches. You shouldn't look at something that will give you wrong ideas."

Anne kept looking. Mostly Sam painted what was wrong with the world. I thought, Good Lord, what has he painted?

The picture was the next-to-the-last in the row. Anne pulled it out, and a wild sound came out of her, half gasp, half moan.

"Anne, for God's sake, I told you that picture isn't right. I'm searching for what's right." Sam was yelling as if a shout could make her hear. But he didn't grab the picture. He let her study it.

I angled around to see. The draft was rough, but there was no way to mistake that the girl looking out from the canvas was Anne.

She stood staring straight in front of her, almost trance-like. Eyes huge, like when she was scared. Bull's-eyes were painted on her in bold black and white. One target was in the middle of her forehead. And a smaller one on each hand and foot. I sucked in my breath.

Sam had painted a picture of Anne, jinxed. That's how it was: There was a girl named Jinx, a girl he was painting. She had the name, but Anne had the real thing. Anne, who was double-scared because Jeeter said that snakes bit the ones who were afraid of them. Who remembered that Paul's magic books said visualizing a thing with strong emotion could make it happen. Who visualized all the things she feared, even losing Sam.

Sam took the picture out of her hands. He didn't try to hug her or apologize or anything like that. He was dignified, like someone at a funeral, even in his jeans and SAVE THE WOLVES T-shirt. I remembered him wearing Paul's suit in the pine church banked with roses. That seemed so long ago.

"I am going to destroy this picture." He tucked it under his arm with the ugly part toward his body. He went into the kitchen and took the box of matches next to the two gas burners. He grabbed a few old newspapers and stuck those under his arm, too. He came back and took Anne's hand in his free hand and asked us both to come with him. Anne looked so in shock that I'm not sure she could have followed without his guiding grip. I followed down the steps out into the yard. He led us across the gravel driveway, around Revonda's big white house, and to the stone barbecue grill in the backyard. He removed the iron grill and balled up newspapers in the fireplace.

I thought: What on earth would some cousin think if she came to pay a visit on Revonda now and what she saw was us, burning this ghastly picture.

Sam said, "I don't quite believe in magic." I knew that had to do with the picture. The picture of Anne jinxed. He took some kindling from the pile by the grill and arranged it over the crumpled paper, tepee style.

Then he turned to Anne and said, "But there's a power in images, for good or evil. I'm sure Paul's magic books are right about that, or I wouldn't paint. We'll get rid of this image." Then he lit the fire and put the canvas on top. I wished he'd put it upside down, but he put it right side up.

We watched Anne burn, the orange flames curling through the canvas at the feet first, then the rest fast with a loud crackle and an ugly oily smell. We stayed until nothing was left but ashes and the empty charred wood frame.

Sam stood triumphant, holding Anne's hand. "There. That's the end of that!"

But Anne's eyes were still wide and scared.

I found myself thinking of a foolish expression my friend Lottie the messy poet used to say: *If a messy desk is the sign of a messy mind, what is an empty desk a sign of?* That's the kind of dumb stuff I remember.

What was an empty picture frame a symbol of? Anne's eyes were asking that.

CHAPTER

26

I went back up to the studio with Sam and Anne. Sam kept glancing at me to be sure I was coming. Anne kept holding on to my arm. Maybe they were so upset that they didn't want to face each other alone. We had tuna-fish sandwiches and coffee, sitting at the round table. (Revonda was off eating with a cousin.) My efforts at conversation sounded phony, so we ate in silence.

Then Billy showed up, complete with ever-present dark glasses. He handed Anne a platter with a big golden-crusted pie. "My grandmother sent you this. It's peach." Mert was cheering us up, with a pie fit for Sunday dinner.

Billy waited as if he was hoping for more than Anne's "thank you." He had a paperback book in his back jeans pocket.

Sam finally said, "Won't you come in and have some pie with us?" The kid beamed his "yes." Anne cut us each a piece of the juicy pie, which was totally delicious. Billy ate his slowly and toyed with the last bite, like he was putting off something.

At last he turned to Sam and said, "I'm scared." He swallowed, and his Adam's apple bobbed like he might choke. "I have to talk to somebody who thinks it's O.K. to try things. And maybe"—he turned to me—"a detective person is O.K., too." He took the book out of his pocket, hesitated, then thrust it at Sam. It was a small black paperback with a picture on the back of a hypnotic-eyed man and strange symbols.

Anne's eyes went round. Get that out of here, we have enough trouble, they seemed to say. But I was sure we needed to find out what Billy had to tell us, however frightening.

"My friend got this book when he was out in California," Billy said. "And I read it because I like to find out about things." He turned to Sam and took off his dark glasses as if he wanted to see Sam better. "Do you understand?"

Sam nodded.

Billy's eyes were extra wide, and there were circles under them. He reached out and took the book back and opened it to a page that was all underlined. Then he gave it back to Sam: "Read that."

While Sam read, Billy helped himself to another piece of pie—gulped it down like he needed the strength. He kept swallowing even between bites, and his feet kept wiggling, very uptight.

Sam took a long time reading. Anne made a pot of coffee and poured us each a cup. She dropped a cup, broke it, and cleaned up. Finally Sam turned to me, not to Billy. "The man who wrote this book was upset when terrible things happened—like murders and gory accidents, and people said, 'It was God's will.' " Sam stopped and considered the book, and then added, "He saw this as deception and hypocrisy. Hypocrisy is the hook."

"Yes." Billy's eyes burned angry. "I don't like it when people act like that. Like, if some kid's father goes to church and acts so holy and comes home and gets drunk and beats up the kids. Or even acts so great in church and outside just acts mean. I hate that."

Sam nodded strongly. "I hate that, too." Sam turned to me. "This book says that members of other religions say one thing and do another, but that Satanists do exactly what they say." He turned to Billy. "And you liked that?"

"Yes. And I wanted to know if spells and stuff could work. I wanted power." Billy grinned and squirmed so much when he said those last words that his slat-bottomed chair creaked. "It would be fun to say a spell and have money or girls or even revenge. That's what I figured. I like to try things to see if they work." His dark eyes, naked without the sunglasses, shot a hopeful glance at Sam for sympathy on that one, then at me. Anne's eyes were cast downward onto her hands, like she didn't want to hear.

"So we started a group," he said, "me and some friends and this older kid who said he knew about this stuff, and an older man he knew. But they didn't do it right!" He raised his voice, and his eyes were surprised and mad. He took the book back and turned the pages and pointed: "Right here it says that a Satanist uses the power of spells, so he doesn't need the things you get addicted to, like drugs. But those kids had a big drug party every time we met. I don't want to be smashed like my father. I hate that. That older kid kept saying how Satanism meant we should indulge in natural desires. Then we'd have no frustrations that could hurt us or hurt our friends and folks. But it wasn't like that."

Billy kept swallowing. He laced his fingers together palms up and stared at his hands. The skin was fine, mottled pink and white and damp with sweat. A sensitive kid, stressed-out. But they were strong-looking hands all the same.

"Those guys said I couldn't quit or I might tell and if I quit they'd put a spell on me." He hardly moved his lips, like the words scared him. "I kind of believed that stuff." He twisted and pulled a lock of hair near his ear. "Mr. Harder,

the principal, found out about us, and they put a spell on
him, and he wrecked his car."

"He might have wrecked his car anyway," Sam said.

"The older kid—well, he was really a man, about
twenty-one—said they'd been nice to Mr. Harder—they
didn't put the worst kind of spell on him, the kind that
would kill him. They all said they'd put the bad kind on me
if I left." Billy was breathing hard.

I wondered what I'd do if I knew somebody deliberately
put a spell on me. I guessed I'd be scared to death. I'd try
to be logical, but that would be hard.

I could see just listening scared Anne silly.

"Well, what I'm getting to," Billy said, "is that to do the
spell on the principal, so as to have enough power, they
caught a funny little dog and killed it. I like dogs." Billy had
turned light green. I was scared he might be sick.

He turned the pages of his little black book again and
thrust it at Sam: "Read that. It's about making a spell for
somebody to die."

Sam read it out loud, slow and surprised: It said a proper
human sacrifice was anyone who had deliberately and
unjustly wronged the sacrificer. It said that such a person
would have asked by their actions to be cursed. Sam ran his
finger down the page. Therefore, the book said, you had the
right to symbolically destroy that person. And if the curse
resulted in his death, you could be glad. Sam looked up. "It
says 'symbolically' destroy. That means not actually kill,
doesn't it?"

Billy was shivering hard. "It wasn't symbolic when those
kids killed the dog. I didn't read that book right. I didn't
finish it before I joined those kids. I don't want to decide
who ought to die! And suppose those kids thought that
Paul . . ." He choked.

Sam put the book down on the table. "Are you saying that
this group of kids could have killed Paul and Marvelle as
part of a spell?" His voice rose with wonder. "This group of
kids?"

Billy put his head down on his arms and began to sob in great gasps. Sam put his hand on the kid's shoulder. When the sobs let up a little, Sam asked, "What are you going to do?"

Billy pressed his hands into fists, wiped his eyes, and said: "I'm going to make them stop." I almost laughed. He sounded like single-handed he was going to be Superman.

He sat up straight, and his eyes flashed. "I wrote all their names on a piece of paper, and I put it in an envelope. I told those kids I had a way for that envelope to be found if anything happened to me. I didn't tell them how, or they'd just steal it. I told them if they let me leave, I wouldn't tell who they were. But if something happened to me, people would find out." He sat up straight and squared his shoulders and smiled. "I outsmarted those kids."

And then a sob took hold of him again. "But if they kill people and I don't tell, I'm part of it, aren't I? An accessory or something? I'm scared. But if I do tell, what will I tell? I don't know what they did."

"We are all going to try to find out who did the killing," Sam said. "It's not all up to you. You're part of a team."

"We want you to be safe," I said.

Billy nodded, as if he'd been about to get to that. "I need somebody besides me to have this list of names," he said to Sam. "I need those kids to know somebody else has a copy of the list. So if they find my list I have hidden, they still won't dare hurt me."

He handed an envelope to Sam and said, "Please promise not to open it unless something zaps me."

Anne looked up with terrified eyes. "Can't we give the list to the sheriff?" she asked. "I know Revonda doesn't trust him and thinks he's mixed up with drugs, but . . ." Her voice trailed off.

Billy shrugged. "The sheriff knows who the kids are. Same ones as before. He just doesn't have proof."

"There's no real danger unless the cult kids are killers," Sam said, "and if they are, they aren't going to like us anyway." He held up the plain white envelope. "I won't even tell you where I'm going to hide these names," he said. "I won't tell anybody. I trust you not to tell anybody I have them." Billy and Sam shook hands, dead serious. Billy grinned and relaxed a little and ate the last piece of pie. Sam put the names in his back pocket, waiting to find a hiding place, I figured, until we weren't looking.

"Did the kids use herbs in spells?" I asked. "We've never solved the riddle of the herbs in the plastic bag with Paul's body."

"The older kid used herbs," Billy said. "He said they made strong spells and were easy to get. But I never learned about how to do that because I left." He reached over and put his dark glasses back on, and immediately he looked like a trickster.

He stood up and went over past Sam's easel to peer out the window. "I have to see if anybody is watching this place," he said, grabbing the empty pie plate and sneaking off dramatically down the stairs.

"I'll go see Jinx's mother, who knows about herbs," Anne volunteered. She said it angrily, like a challenge to Sam. Maybe she wanted him to worry about her. He nodded unhappily.

"I'll come, too," I said, "tomorrow when Jeeter goes to his prayer meeting in town. I wouldn't go near that place again when that crazy man is there. But when he's gone, I bet his wife could tell us about all sorts of things, even aside from herbs."

I stood up. I thanked Anne and Sam for sharing their meal with me, and I said, "We're all stressed out, but we all need each other. Believe me, that's true!" I meant: "Listen, you two. Make up!"

CHAPTER
27

"I deserve some time to smell the roses," I told Ted. He'd finished preparing his stuff for class. We sat out on the terrace, and one rosebush by the corner of the house was in bloom, fragrant in the late afternoon.

"Someone keeps calling us up and then hanging up when I answer the phone," Ted said. "Very odd. Like a threat. I hope you're being extra careful."

I promised I was, but I was tired and I changed the subject. "I forget how distinguished you look," I said, ignoring the way his hair stands up like antennae, especially after he's been working and running his fingers through it. So he's a distinguished Martian. Just my type. Next to him on the glass-topped table was a book called *Good Magic* and another called *A History of Magic and Folk Cures*. "Are you taking over from Paul?" I asked.

"No," he said. "One of Revonda's cousins dropped these books off, with a note from Revonda that says they show that magic can be used for good purposes. She said Paul had these two in his collection, so she asked her cousin to get us copies." He laughed. "Revonda will go to any length to prove Paul never ever did anything wrong."

"I don't intend to think about Paul now," I said. I swirled my iced tea so the ice clinked, my favorite summer noise. "Thank goodness our house is our fortress," I said. "I feel safe here."

"Actually," he said, "we have a weapon on hand. I thought we'd gotten rid of every plastic bag in the house, just to be safe. But when I took the glasses out of the cupboard, I happened to look up on the very top shelf, and there's a plastic bag around the gold-rimmed china that your mother got from her grandmother. Up out of reach."

"Oh, well." I sighed. I didn't want to get up and go remove it. Who would know but Ted? We ignored it through a wonderful leisurely dinner and coffee, and then for some reason that bag on the high kitchen shelf began to prey on my mind. Our kitchen stepladder wouldn't reach, and the outdoors ladder was broken. I admit, I ran over it backing out of the driveway. I'd been meaning to buy a new one. Never mind, a chair on a table would give me a handy perch. I climbed up while Ted was watching CNN. He doesn't approve of improvised ladders, but heck, they work. Maybe just to spite me for improvising behind Ted's back, I slipped. Not with dishes in hand, thank goodness. I had them unwrapped and back in place and the plastic bag dropped to the floor. As soon as I felt unsteady, I jumped, so I wasn't hurt, but I knocked the chair over with me and made a *thump, crash.* Ted came running. I tried to look as calm and pulled-together as possible. I stared at the chair as if I were surprised to see it there, lying on its side on the red tile floor. It reminded me of something.

"It's not safe for you to climb up like that," Ted said unhappily. "You'll break something." He meant some part of me, of course. But a picture came to my mind. A broken mirror on the floor and a chair lying on its side by a table.

With a start, I remembered the chair in Paul's room, lying

knocked on the floor next to the small table. Yeah, reenactment is a good way to bring something back to mind. I'd thought the burglar knocked Paul's chair over when he ran away. But now I remembered there'd been a thump. And if we could hear it at all outdoors, it must have been a loud thump like I made when I hit the floor. In a flash I saw that the burglar who broke into Paul's room had been climbing on that chair to reach something near the ceiling. What on earth?

We could have called Revonda, but Ted said we ought to be with the first searchers for whatever it was. I agreed. I won't say I'd stopped trusting anybody else, but I'd stopped being sure who had what to hide. I stuffed the plastic bag in the garbage, and we put that in back of the house in the outdoor can as we set forth.

"Something is hidden high up in Paul's room," I said as soon as Revonda came to her door. That got her attention. We told her about the chair and table reenactment.

She gave us her Oh-come-on smile. "What could we still find? After the way the police searched?" But she called Ron.

He came right down from up the hill, off duty in an old plaid shirt and jeans. We all trooped into the mirror room, plunged into Paul's flashing world when Revonda turned on the electric light. I scrutinized the wall near the place where the chair had fallen. My heart began to beat hard. I was pretty sure I saw the high-up hiding place. Most of the mirrors on Paul's walls were odd shapes pieced together, but one was square and about the size of the door of a bathroom medicine cabinet. I bet it was just that, sunken flush with the other mirrors. "Look!" I pointed.

Ron seemed to spot the mirror door at the same time I did. He climbed up on the seat of the ladder-back chair and pried at the square mirror, which came open so suddenly that he started to fall and jumped. Just like me. Just like the burglar?

Inside, there was nothing—or that was my impression.

Just a white-painted shallow cabinet with two shelves and nothing more. But Ron climbed back up, examined the inside, and flashed us a grin, excited. "Here's a razorblade down in the bottom," he said, "and a plastic straw." He took his index finger and wiped it on the bottom of the medicine cabinet and held it up with white powder on it. "We have us a find. I think this is cocaine."

"That's ridiculous," Revonda said.

"Folks who use cocaine put the powder on the mirror, take a razor to line it up right, and sniff it with a straw, Revonda. So it seems like Paul did that," Ron said. "That could be why he didn't always think straight."

Revonda had sat down in the chair with the face. For once she was without words. All the lines in her own face drooped.

"So the burglar knew Paul used cocaine," I said, "and knew where he kept it, and broke in to get it?"

Ron whistled. "That burglar may know who killed Paul."

"Paul was killed over drugs?" I didn't believe it. Everything about Paul was too fantastic to be that simple. "And Marvelle was killed over drugs, too?" I didn't believe that, either.

Ron laughed a shallow bitter laugh. His teeth were bright white. He bit at his words: "Drugs are everyplace."

Behind him was the closed door to the living room, and I was glad Revonda had taken down that magical figure on the door, of a naked man spread-eagled in a star. The face jugs with candles in them were gone from the bookshelf. Paul's room was like a largely empty cave of ice. But that mirrored room still felt dangerous.

"Listen," I said to Ron, "something may have happened to me—or not. Related to drugs. But I'd better tell you about it." Somehow, I trusted Ron more than the sheriff. I told him about the man with the binoculars in the marijuana field. How he could be Buck, who was at Jeeter's house and gave me a ride home. But that I couldn't be sure. I said I hadn't told about coming across that marijuana between the corn because I wasn't positive that's what it was. Furthermore, I didn't know where the field was. But, I said, "the worse part is I'm getting threatening calls." Ted chipped in about the calls where someone hung up as soon as we answered.

Ron listened carefully. He took notes.

"We'd have heard if there really was a marijuana farm nearby," Revonda told him scornfully. She glared around her. "You're certainly going to find that any drugs in Paul's room were a plant."

We didn't wait to hear what Ron said. We said good night and made a quick exit.

"I wish Sam didn't have Billy's secret list of the cult members," I told Ted on the way home. "Of thrill-seeking kids. Or drug dealers. Or whatever. And something about Sam scares Anne," I said unhappily. "And why isn't Sam himself more afraid?"

"Let's go home and forget our worries in a little light reading," Ted said. "We can case the books Revonda sent and find out what kind of magic she wants us to think Paul believed in."

CHAPTER
28

MONDAY, JULY 8

When I arrived at Sam and Anne's studio on Monday, I heard laughter upstairs. Silly laughter with squeaks. The upstairs door was open, and Anne stood by the kitchen counter with a lighted candle in her hand, which was rather strange at eleven o'clock in the morning. On the counter was the book titled *Good Magic* and also *A History of Magic and Folk Cures*. So Revonda had sent them the books, too! Anne was giggling. Thank God. Sam and Anne must have made up.

"I like the one," Sam was saying, "where you can be safe from sorcery by spitting in your right shoe. Those old spells have tradition." He saw me, grinned, and winked. "I also like the one," he said, "where you light a banquet with candles made from the semen of an ass. By the light of those candles, all the guests have the heads of asses. Say, that might be kind of fun," he whooped. "Half the deputies who come around here already look like jackasses to me."

Anne blushed. Because he meant Ron? "I bet you like the

one," she said, "where a naked virgin touches you with her right thumb to cure epilepsy."

He winked again. "Too much is made of virgins. A naked wife would suit me fine."

She shrugged at me like: What can you do? and put down the candle. She grabbed a grapefruit off the counter, threw it at Sam, and missed.

He grabbed it up and threw it back. Obviously they had the sillies. Best thing in the world when you're too tense. Anne caught the grapefruit against her hip.

"Unfair magic!" he shouted. "Catching my grapefruit with your right hand at eleven A.M., near a clove of garlic, at the time of the waning moon."

"And with the wind from the west—the wind should be included." Anne threw the grapefruit back hard and missed again. "Damn," she said.

Sam stopped laughing. "Actually," he said, "those spells that make you think about exactly where you are in the world and in the universe make sense to me. Like when you're supposed to pick a certain herb with your left hand while facing north under the dog star or the full moon or whatever. The knowing-where-you-are part feels right. I do that to paint."

Anne grinned. "You mean I'd have to stop mixing up left and right and going east for west, or all the spells would work backward?"

Sam was back to whooping. "Jackasses would look like deputies!"

I looked at the lighted candle, still on the counter. "Were you going to try a spell?" I asked Anne. "Was that candle part of it?"

She shrugged. "I thought it would help me not to feel so much like a target. But Sam's been razzing me. Now I don't have time, anyway." She blew out the candle.

"The strange thing about these spells," I said, "at least the ones in the modern books Revonda sent us, is that some are listed just as historical curiosities, but the ones that are advertised as workable are a lot like the tricks I use to remember things."

They both turned, surprised, and waited for more. It was an odd connection. "One way to remember," I said, "is to turn something that makes no sense to you—like a name, say, Bill Cunningham—into a visual image. And the more that image is funny or punny, or shocking, the easier it is to remember. Like, you could picture an irate bill-collector, handing a bill to a clever and cunning ham. The more thoughts you hang on that image, the better you remember. And from Albertus Magnus in the Middle Ages to modern memory books, they all agree on that."

"How is that like a spell?" Anne asked, pulling out a chair for me and then sitting down at the table herself.

"From what I've read," I said, "in magic you make a strong image and even act that image out. Maybe you want it shocking so it's more memorable and that's part of the reason for the naked virgin and the ass's semen and touching a dead man to get rid of a mole. In one of those books I just read, it tells how to act out the image of what you want in a lot of ways at once—even by the stage of the moon and the direction of the wind. You send your mind a strong picture—well, more than a picture. You use all your senses."

"And so," Anne said, "if you kept sending negative messages, you might lose your mind."

"I never said that!" I was at a loss. I wished Sam would say something funny, or that Anne would throw the grapefruit at me.

Sam walked over to the counter and picked up a book called *Exorcism.* "And that fits with what this book says." I hadn't looked at that one. Revonda hadn't sent it to us.

"It says that strong emotion plus visualizing a thing can make it happen. Can even put on a curse or remove a curse."

I looked down at the prickle on my arms and realized I had goose bumps.

Anne swallowed. "Then you could even put on a curse by mistake!"

That seemed like half psychology, half black magic. It felt ugly. There was a weight in the pit of my stomach. I wished Ted was there to say something sensible.

At least I could bring us back to why we'd been looking at the magic books to begin with. "I wish we knew enough about Paul to know if all this strange stuff helped cause his death. But we *can* find out what the herbs with his body meant."

"Give me your right shoe, Anne," Sam called out. "I want to spit in it for protection. It's much pleasanter to spit in someone else's shoe than in your own. Right?" Back to the sillies to break the gloom.

"Anne and I need to go," I said. "To be sure we are at Jeeter's house while he's out."

Sam turned serious. "Before you go, Revonda told us about the traces of cocaine in Paul's room. She said someone planted it there. Is that true?"

"Ask Ron or the sheriff for details," I said hurriedly. "I only saw Ron find it. We have to go."

Sam picked up his brush and went back to his painting. Anne glanced at his watch, which was lying on the counter. I wondered where hers was. Mine, alas, was home by the bathtub. But, by feel, I knew it was getting late. Even Baskerville, who Anne brought along on a leash, seemed in a hurry.

"What time was it?" I asked as we came out into the driveway.

"Twenty of twelve," she said. "Time to go, quick. Jeeter is due home at one."

I saw Revonda picking yellow lilies in the circular wildflower garden. Nobody else around. "Good morning," she called, and then, "My mother loved these."

Good, at least Revonda was recovering. I waved to her and called back, "We've got to hurry over while Jeeter is out. It's already twenty of twelve."

We walked up the hill, toward Jeeter's long rutted drive.

Mrs. Justice was out on the narrow wood front porch, hanging dishtowels on a line just under the roof. They waved like worn-out flags.

She was as pale and wispy as I remembered. "Good morning," she said to me. "No snake stories today." Was she laughing at me?

"This is my cousin Anne," I said. "Your daughter tells me that you know a great deal about herbs, and how they're used in these mountains. She said she believed that if we came on a Monday you would tell us what you could."

She hesitated with arms up to the clothesline. Her voice was wooden: "I haven't seen my daughter in a while."

Keep talking, I told myself: "Of course you know there were herbs found with Paul Roland's body. The sheriff doesn't seem to be doing much to find out why. Not that we can discover. We thought it might help us know what happened if we found out what those herbs meant, maybe help prevent more killing."

"Deputy Ron talked to me." She lowered her arms but didn't invite us in.

"Did he ask you about the herbs?" I asked.

She sighed. "You can come in, but please tie the dog on the porch, and you have to be gone before my husband comes back."

She opened the door slowly as if she was tired and led us over to the bookshelf. The books were almost the only color in the whole dimly lit room. What a place to grow up. I tried to picture Jinx as a child in this gray room. Jinx, who inspired Sam to hug her. I hoped Anne wasn't thinking about that.

The only furniture in that room other than the bookshelf was the low table Jeeter had laid his gun on when he tried to scare me, and a few assorted chairs. His gun hung on the wall now.

"When I talked to Ron, my husband was here," she said. She fingered an old leather-bound book on the shelf. "Jeeter doesn't like me herb doctoring. He says only faith can heal. But I figure God made the herbs, too. I didn't tell Ron much. Just that those herbs do grow around here. Most anybody with a sharp eye could find some. I told him Paul came to see me to ask me where wild herbs grew. Some only grow on south slopes. Some want sun, some want shade." But dill was one of the herbs found with Paul—and dill isn't wild.

She pulled an old book out of the bookcase and stared down at flowers and leaves embossed on the leather cover. She stroked the book like it was a pet. Her hands were worn shiny with work. Large hands for such a small woman. "My husband was glad to see Paul come, at first. My Jeeter thought he might save Paul. But Paul wouldn't be saved, and Jeeter decided all herb doctoring was the devil's work."

She opened the book and leafed through the pages. "After they found Paul, I was curious myself," she said, "and I looked in this book that tells some of the old lore about herbs. I found this." She pointed to a picture labeled "Verbena officinalis." I pulled my sketch of the herb that had been on Paul out of my pocketbook. That was it. She handed me the book, and I began to read the quaint old type. Boy, did verbena have a lot of names: verbenacaea, enchanter's plant, herb of the cross, holy herb, Juno's tears, pigeon's grass, pigeonweed, simpler's joy and vervain, blue vervain and hyssop. And lots of uses. Good for eczema or skin conditions, had been used for whooping cough, dropsy, jaundice, liver and kidney problems, and to heal wounds. Once thought to be a cure for the plague. But Paul didn't have those problems. Certainly not the plague.

Mrs. Jeeter ran her finger over the picture of the spiky flower. "Some people call verbena 'herb of Grace,'" she said. "They say it grew on the mount of Calvary, and stanched the wounds of the Saviour. They say it has the power to protect."

I looked down the page: Albertus Magnus said verbena was a love charm. Why would Paul need a love charm when his girl ran after him? Nicholas Culpeper in the seventeenth century said you could mix verbena with lard to help pain in secret parts. A sexy herb.

"Maybe this is what you want," Mrs. Jeeter said and pointed to a couplet down at the bottom of the page:

> *Vervain and dill*
> *Vervain and dill*
> *Hinder witches from their will.*

Vervain and dill! Exactly the herbs found with the body. To protect Paul from *witches*?

"There are witches in the high school," she said. "Jeeter says it's one sign the end of the world is coming."

Was Paul afraid of the cult of kids? Were they afraid of Paul? That was a weird thought. Did the person who killed Paul, or more than one person, put the herbs with his body for protection from him? From maybe a curse as he died? I shuddered.

"I couldn't tell Ron about this with my husband here," Mrs. Jeeter said. She glanced around the room nervously, as if she expected Jeeter to be hiding in a corner. "You understand, don't you?" she asked. "You saw how he can get. And yet he's a fine man with a great faith until the sickness makes him misbehave."

She found a flyer for some carpet-cleaning service. "Lord knows I don't have a carpet," she said. She wrote the lines about vervain and dill on the back.

I put the verse in my pocket and promised to get it to Ron. I turned the shiny old pages of her herbal to dill. Nothing about magic there. Just said that infused with water or white wine, dill was good for the stomach.

"Paul saw this book?" Anne asked.

"Yes, he surely did." She bent her head as if she felt she'd helped to cause his death by letting him look at the book.

I was trying to think of something helpful to say when I heard Baskerville begin to bark. Mrs. Jeeter turned white. But it couldn't be time for Jeeter. I glanced at my wrist—

and remembered. I'd left my watch by the tub. I took no chances. I ran out on the porch and undid Baskerville from the porch rail, fumbling at the knot in the leash. By the time I got it loose a car was coming into sight around the bend.

I pulled open the screen door, ran through the house with Baskerville, and out through the back door, which Mrs. Jeeter was holding open. Anne ran with me, both of us breathing too hard to speak. I heard the front screen door slam, high pitched and flimsy compared to a real door, but it must mean Jeeter was in reach of his gun. Maybe this isn't one of his bad days, I told myself, but I didn't believe it. I ran for the nearest opening in the weeds around the mowed part of the backyard, praying I'd find the shortcut there, and thank God I stumbled onto a path formed mainly from chunks of flat rock—uneven, but I could run on it. Anne being younger ran past me like a frightened wood nymph in her long paisley skirt and white blouse. "Hurry," she called. Briers caught at her skirt. She stumbled, but quickly righted herself. Baskerville ran just after her. A gun boomed behind us, and I almost tripped on a rough part of the rock. The path had grown narrow with weeds at both sides: The briers leaned across and grabbed at us.

Suddenly Baskerville stopped ahead of me. I tried to slip around her and see the trouble. Right across the path there'd been a rockslide. On one side of us was a cliff, too high and straight up to climb. On the other side were high weeds. Covering the path, and jutting out into the weeds, was a huge boulder and a bunch of small rocks that had evidently broken loose from the face of the cliff. Thank God they hadn't fallen just as we were passing. Anne was struggling through the weeds. Was Jeeter just behind? The boulder leaned toward us. We couldn't possibly climb over it. I plunged after Anne.

I let out my breath with relief when we came to the path again on the other side of the rock slide. My foot slipped on a rock, and into a crevice between two rocks. Ouch, my ankle turned. My whole leg cried alarm. I listened. No more gunshots yet. I limped onward, after Anne and Baskerville.

A stone floor stretched five to six feet wide, even wider in some places. The midday sun shone down into this corridor of rock from high above. A pine tree grew out of a crevice on the cliff side of the rock path, as if to say, "You see, I can grow anywhere."

Baskerville began first to growl and then bark. Anne tried to shush her. We didn't want to remind Jeeter where we were. The hair on the dog's back got dull black as it stood on end. Anne stood stock still. Stopped by a snake.

Right in the middle of the path, about ten feet ahead of us, a snake was stretched out in the sun. At least six feet long, with the wide ugly jaws that meant poison. Poison. Before I could even be sure that was a diamond pattern on its back, the snake coiled back, raised the tip of its tail, and began vibrating.

"Rattlesnake!" I called to Anne. "Stay back." She had already frozen.

Baskerville barked louder and crouched as if she was about to lunge. I threw my weight against Baskerville's leash, wrapped the leash around the pine tree, and tied it in three knots. Dern, I turned my ankle worse. I held the dog's mouth shut. I said, "Be quiet," then remembered what Revonda said, and added, "It's all right." Baskerville was a well-trained dog. She barked no more except for an occasional whimper.

Meanwhile, beyond Anne, the snake had moved to coil itself into a shallow mini-cave in the rock wall on the mountaintop side of the path. That cold metallic rattling was too even and shrill to seem like it came from a live thing. I felt the hair on my spine stand up like Baskerville's. I sat down. My ankle throbbed. "We can't go back," I said. We couldn't go forward past the rattler, either. In front of us, the path narrowed. "And I've sprained my ankle," I told Anne. "I'll do what I can, but I can't move fast. Above all, stay clear. I hear they can jump eight feet."

"How can we kill it?" Anne asked. She gave the snake a

wide berth, but she didn't run. I was surprised how calm she was in a real crunch.

That coiled rattler was thick as my arm, thick in a way that said "power." Those bulges at the back of his triangular head made him look cruel, as if he enjoyed being poison. He watched us with alert eyes set under bony ridges, and the tip of his tail vibrated so it blurred and the ugly sound of the rattle went on and on. One brier grew out of a crevice on one side of his ugly coil.

"You can throw a rock to break a snake's back," I said. I noticed a flat rock near the bluff. Anne began to pry it up.

She picked up the rock, stood very straight, and took a deep breath. "I want to be the one to kill the snake," she said. "You can tell me how."

I was amazed. "You're not afraid?"

"I am terrified of snakes," she said, lifting her chin. "And that's why I'm going to kill this one. I'm going to send my mind a strong image, of me being brave. I'm not a target. That will be my magic."

Good Lord, I thought, that's what I get for spouting forth my silly theories about magic. I started to say, "Just get a good-luck charm." No, that wouldn't do.

"You have to break his back," I said.

"Yes," she said. "I'll throw this rock with all my strength."

There weren't but a few loose rocks I could see. Anne had to hit him just right. I thought: The gal who can't even *thunk* a two-hundred-pound husband with a grapefruit in the kitchen wants to try to hit the snake.

I wanted to say, Look: I know how to do this. Even if I'm scared sick. Even if I have to hobble on a bum foot. Why, you can't hit the broadside of a barn.

But I knew I would sound just exactly like Cousin Clothilde. Like poison. Just what Anne had heard all her life: You can't. Anne certainly didn't need to hear that now.

The rattler watched us with those small round eyes with yellow slits in the middle. Pitiless eyes.

"I know you can do it, Anne," said the part of me that feeds stray cats and hugs kids.

The rest of me went cold and thought: What does a rattlesnake do if you attack it and miss?

CHAPTER

29

MOMENTS LATER

"Stay at least ten feet back." My voice quavered. I think watching Anne was worse than trying to kill that snake myself. She had to throw that rock from a distance and at an odd angle, throw a curve to hit the snake square and hard.

She raised the rock and threw with all her strength. There was a loud *thunk*. She'd nicked the side of the snake's little cave and that took the force from her rock. The snake curled back tighter and rattled louder. Coiled in a spiral. Like the marks on Paul.

"Almost!" I said.

She looked around for another rock, but the stone floor of the path was solid, the top of a buried ledge. All I saw was a dead piece of tree limb which must have fallen down from high above. The dead limb might not be strong enough to kill the snake.

On the other side of the rock slide, there'd been a lot of stones. On this side on the stone floor of the path, nothing loose.

"There's a ledge above us," I said. The side of the rock wall up the mountain was at a steep slant, but there were cracks and crevices in it here and there. About halfway up was what looked to be a fairly wide ledge. "Rocks could be up there."

In fact, when Anne started to climb, I noticed the crevices arranged themselves nicely for easy toe- and hand-holds, almost to the ledge but not all the way. She reached up into the unknown. Her hand came down with a good-sized rock. Thank goodness. She dropped it down to the path below for ammunition. Baskerville let out a low growl. I held my arm around her. "It's all right."

Anne put her hand back and pulled down another rock and something clear. It was a folded-up plastic dry-cleaning bag!

I sucked in my breath. Somebody was hiding his murder weapons here. Or some group was doing it. In this snaky place where nobody wanted to come. Anne reached again, but I called, "Leave what's there. The sheriff will need to see." I hoped no one could hear me.

"More plastic bags," she called. "They were under the rock." So they wouldn't blow away, of course. She put the first bag in the pocket of her India-print skirt.

We had to get past the snake before the killer or Jeeter joined us. And the killer might be Jeeter. Anne climbed down. Pale but determined. I wanted to say "O.K., now let me try to hit the snake." I didn't really want us to be found dead with a plastic bag in Anne's pocket. But I knew how important it was to her to kill that snake. And I'm not the best shot in the world myself.

I said: "You'll get him now."

But with the snake farther under the overhang and as much in back of the brier as he could get, the aiming would be even harder. Anne got down on her knees and tried to skim a rock in. It hit the brier, which must have been tougher than it looked, and the rock shunted to one side. The snake went on rattling. The next stone had the same fate. I felt sick.

Now what? Anne came back and picked up the dead branch. It was about the length of a hoe, but twisted rather than straight. She would have to get close enough to hit the snake directly. The stick might break in her hands if she put force on it. But she'd have to put force to break the snake's back.

She walked toward the rattler, leaning forward so that her arm plus the stick put as much distance between the snake and her body as possible. With the tip of the stick, she pushed the brier-cane aside. I could see the snake coiled under the overhang watching us. He moved his head from side to side above the coil of his body, as if positioning himself to strike. She shoved the stick at him quickly. I prayed she'd break his back against the stone with the thrust. The stick broke. She jumped back. The snake was still moving. But the noise of the rattle had stopped. After my heart stopped thunking, I managed to pull myself up with the help of the tree and hobble over to look. Anne just stood there, a little stunned, I think. The stick still lay where Anne dropped it, holding the brier down so I could see Mr. Snake, coils pushed lopsided, head no longer held above them. I picked up the broken stick-half nearest me and threw it at him. His coils moved feebly. He did not rattle or try to strike.

I put my arms around Anne. "You did it." I laughed. "We're safe!" Well, more or less.

I undid Baskerville, and Anne helped me hobble down the path, past the snake, now definitely harmless, through a long patch of woods, through the edge of someone's pasture, and out into a pasture with three cows. I knew where I was when I hit the road. Just up from Revonda's. Hoorah!

But as I got my bearings, I saw flashing blue lights ahead in Revonda's driveway, through the trees. "Something's wrong," I told Anne. "What now?" My stomach turned over.

With Anne's help, I hobbled as fast as I could, down the road toward the lights, and turned in the driveway. I told her to go on ahead, but she wouldn't do it.

We pushed our way through a knot of neighbors, not even stopping to ask what was wrong, and hurried toward Sam, who was standing on the porch talking to Ron and another deputy. Sam looked half sick, leaning on the porch rail. I also saw several men in uniform by the springhouse.

"I need to talk to you alone right now," Ron said to Anne. He took her arm, even before she could hug Sam, and pulled her through the kitchen door.

One of the deputies told me. "It's that girl named Jinx. She's dead. "

I saw the sheriff and hurried over. "Where have you been?" he asked accusingly.

"Is Jinx dead?" I asked. He said yes, but that he was the one asking the questions. So I told him as briefly as possible where we'd been. When I finished, he looked at my swollen ankle and said, "There's bound to be trouble when amateurs get mixed up in these things." I bit my tongue. He softened slightly. "I guess we're lucky to find those plastic bags. These were pretty handy to the perpetrator, weren't they? Why, you could be at that shortcut from Revonda's place and back in five minutes if you ran, and most of the way you'd be out of sight. I'll send somebody to look at the scene right now.

"I reckon you want to see the body," he said. *Want* was not the right word. "Well, you can't," he said.

"I bet I can tell you how you found her," I said sadly. "In the springhouse, since your photographer just went in. And it must be in a plastic bag, and I'm sure poor Jinx is naked." He gasped. I could see I was right.

"She felt guilty about her body," I said. "This killer goes for guilt. What kind of marks were on her?"

He blushed. The marks, I was sure, would be related to her sex. Because that was the seat of her guilt.

CHAPTER

30

The sheriff gave me permission to wait for Anne in the studio. "I am her nearest relative now here in the continental United States," I told him. He did believe in kin. I watched through the window as his men searched the place. Finally Anne came out of Revonda's house, almost staggering. Ron held her arm and walked her over to the studio. As soon as he left, she threw her arms around me and held tight.

She sat down at the table, eyes not quite focused, stunned. "They think it's Sam. It's my fault. What if it was Sam?" Her voice was flat.

I sat next to her and took hold of her icy hand. "You've got to tell me about this," I said. "I can't help if you don't."

"It's about the time." She almost choked on the words. "You remember I looked at Sam's watch. It said twenty of twelve."

I did remember because we had to be sure to get to Jeeter's house while he was gone. Much good it did us, but we tried.

"When Ron asked me about what time we left, I told him because I had no reason to lie. That I knew of."

"Of course not," I said.

"Ron asked me was I absolutely sure of that time, and I said we knew we had to go see Mrs. Jeeter and get back while her husband was still gone to prayer meeting. So I'm sure I remember right. And Revonda saw us go."

"You told me what time it was, and you told her," I said. "Two witnesses."

"Ron asked me when I'd seen Sam after that, like it was some big deal. But I had to tell him, the first time I saw Sam was after we killed the snake and came home just now. And Ron said 'Jinx is dead,' like that's connected." Anne took a great breath, as if to pull in strength. "He said Billy found Jinx in the springhouse. Dead. In a plastic bag. There were those spiral marks. On each nipple." Anne put her hands over her own breasts and shuddered. "And like a target with an arrow—down there." She was so devastated just telling me that it took her a while to go on.

Markings of Jinx's guilt, as she and her killer saw it.

Finally Anne was able to speak in a weak and wondering voice. "Ron said that at quarter of twelve Jinx had stopped at Revonda's and left a picture of Paul she'd found on the last roll of film in her camera. Revonda and her cousin Edna were there, too, and saw her." She breathed deeply several times, as if that gave her strength to go on. "At about quarter to one Billy came to get springwater and found the body." Her voice became angry. "Revonda and her cousin and Billy all swear to that. So he knows Jinx was killed between those times." She twisted her hand and squeezed mine tight as if she needed something to hold on to. "He says Sam swears we were with him at noon. Sam says we were actually with him till twenty after twelve. He says he looked at his watch right after we left and was worried that we were so late."

"Have you talked to Sam?" I asked. "A madman killed Jinx. Sam isn't a madman."

"No, but I don't think Ron would have lied. Why would

Sam lie?" Her eyes grew dark with terror. "I know what Ron thinks. He thinks Sam killed Jinx—and that means . . ." She put her hands over her face. She massaged her face as if she could rub those words away. She took her hands down and clamped them together.

"I'm not good at most things," she said, "but I've always been good at picking people. But maybe I only thought so. Because why would Sam lie? Why?"

"There must be an explanation for all this," I said firmly. "You *are* good at picking people. So am I. And I don't believe for a minute that Sam did that."

I said that to buck her up. But the truth is, my biggest fault as a sleuth is that I tend to like people, at least at first, and see their good sides. If I'd met Jack the Ripper, I would probably have been impressed by how nice he was to his dog.

But in Sam's case I felt rock-solid sure. He was much too charming to be a crazy killer. "What motive could he possibly have to kill Jinx?" I asked Anne.

"I don't know, but Jinx is dead and Sam lied about what he was doing at the time she was killed. Sam has no alibi, and Ron knows it. All because of me. How could I be such a fool," she demanded, "as to think that if I killed a snake I'd know I was O.K.? Jeeter kills snakes, and look at him. He's a nut."

"Yes, but a nut with an alibi," I said sadly.

CHAPTER

31

Revonda had asked us all to come over and brainstorm because none of us believed that Sam had killed Jinx. Yet Sam stuck to his story, saying that we were with him at noon whether we knew it or not. How could he be so stubborn?

I sat on the couch next to Ted. Revonda sat next to her vase of yellow lilies. Sam was at his easel, working on her portrait even while we talked.

I got up and hobbled over and looked over Sam's shoulder at the portrait. Under his brush, Revonda was both beautiful and elegant, because her bone structure was good, her chin was firm, her brows were high and arched. Her black silk dress was a subtle backdrop for her diamond necklace. Perhaps that's why she liked the picture. But I studied the anger in that face, so subtle I could hardly see how Sam put it across except in the tenseness at the corners of the mouth, the brilliance of the eyes. There was fear in that face, not too obvious, but it came across, maybe in the same tension that held the head high like a queen's. To me, it was a disturbing picture. Almost a hypnotizing picture. The eyes grabbed, the way Revonda's eyes did in real life. It was a face with charm in the small smile, but, underneath the charm, no hope. I'm not sure how the paint strokes showed a quality that wasn't there, but they did. If I had been Revonda, I would have wanted Sam to burn that picture, like he did Anne's. Revonda probably didn't know about Anne's.

But I figured Revonda must have some hope left. She kept talking about how we were going to find the killer. She had hope of being avenged.

Sam said, "O.K. That's it. I'm finished." Revonda got up and went over to admire her picture and talk about how talented Sam was and how she'd help him gain the recognition he deserved as soon as we found the killer.

Revonda turned to me and raised an eyebrow. "How do you like it?"

I said I thought Sam had an amazing talent for catching the essence of the subject of a picture.

"Then don't look so sour," she commented. "It doesn't become you."

At least Sam hadn't been formally charged yet. That was something. We sat in a rough circle and tried to add up what we knew. Now, at least, we knew where the killer had kept the master supply of plastic bags even after the sheriff had made sure there were none left in the valley.

We added to Ted's list of people and time and alibis. For Jinx's death, Anne and I alibied each other. Cousin Edna had been in the house with Revonda. Billy had told us he'd been at his grandmother's. Not that she'd ever admit if he wasn't. We didn't know about the kids in the cult yet.

Revonda talked about all the artists Jinx worked for and how artists were not very stable people, except, of course, for Sam. And how Jinx had almost asked to be killed. By living off by herself, by wearing those provocative clothes, by associating with the wrong people.

Those words brought out the cruelty in the lines around

Revonda's mouth. I kept seeing her as she was in Sam's portrait. I wanted to believe her when she said one of Jinx's artists must have killed Paul out of jealousy, Marvelle because she saw something, and Jinx in a rage. Artists, she said, have the imagination to find power in spreading terror. The killer, she said, "is the most powerful person in this valley right now. He has us all afraid. We expect horror. When Billy came running to my door, so scared he didn't even scream, I expected the worst." I saw the fear in her eyes glitter, just like in the picture, only more so.

Before we could say a word more, the doorbell rang. Revonda jumped up out of her chair and said, "You go, and if it's someone I want to see, I'll come out. I'm going to my room." She strode off through the hall to her bedroom while I went through the living-room to the front door. I opened it to Reverend Phillipson. I greeted him loudly. Revonda certainly wouldn't want to hear him talk about how good would come from evil. Or see him try to break bunches of twigs to show that we have strength when we stand together.

Sam said he had jobs to do. Ted said please to excuse him, he had to help Sam. Anne and I stayed.

Personally, I felt comforted by the Reverend, even as he stood there in the doorway. He really did have the face of a happy baby, round, innocent, with fine skin, blue eyes beaming kindness. His white hair was as fine as dandelion fuzz and circled his bald dome like a monk's. He reached out and touched Anne's hand lightly. "I have been thinking of you and hoping for the best." He turned to me. "And I'm so glad you're here with Anne. How can I help?"

It was a pleasure to be with someone who didn't seem a bit afraid. He smiled gently, like he believed in Santa Claus all year round—not for him, but for us. His ears were baby pink. His small pink hands were peacefully folded in front of him.

We sat down in three carved rosewood chairs near the front door. "Can I tell you things you won't tell anybody else, not even the sheriff?" Anne asked.

"I might advise you to tell the sheriff," he said. "But rest assured, I won't tell him myself."

She had lowered her voice, and he lowered his, too. I realized he'd inadvertently picked the chairs farthest from Revonda's closed door. She wouldn't be able to hear.

Anne gave him a pleading look: "I'm afraid."

He nodded. "That seems natural. We're all afraid right now."

"But I'm afraid of everybody. I'm even afraid of my husband. I'm even afraid of myself. I'm afraid of being afraid."

Too bad, because she had seemed so bold facing the awful reality of that snake.

She told the whole story of her relationship with Sam, beginning with Boston, including the fact that she didn't really have any way to know anything about Sam except what he told her and her gut hunch, which had been that he was the very best thing in her life. "But now . . ." She swallowed and took one of those I-absolutely-won't-cry deep breaths. Then she told the Reverend with his pink hopeful ears how Sam seemed to tell a lie. How there were witnesses that what he said wasn't true. "I know in my gut he wouldn't lie. But I'm not sure I can trust my gut."

He put his hand over hers. "Trust is a great gift," he said. "Why don't you trust yourself?"

"Things go wrong for me," she said. And she told him about the time she took a turn and thought she was going the right way down the road, and suddenly she was going the wrong way, against the traffic. "Things like that are always happening to me."

"Traffic is different from a gut hunch," he said. "I would trust you with a gut hunch. I bet Peaches here does, too."

I nodded.

"I wish," Anne said, "that I hadn't read Paul's magic books. Because one kind of magic in Paul's books makes sense to me. And that's if you concentrate one hundred percent on visualizing a thing, with strong emotion, that's the way to make it come true."

The Reverend frowned like he didn't agree.

She explained faster, "I mean maybe you could change things in your own life."

He sat perfectly still, hands clasped. And nodded. "That sounds a little like prayer, if there could be prayer without God."

"The trouble is," Anne sobbed, "that I can't help visualizing what can go wrong, visualizing the things I fear, like me dead in a plastic bag. So maybe I'm making bad magic against myself. And the more that scares me, the more I can't stop."

He stopped patting her hand and got up from his chair. He wandered over to the whatnot shelf where Revonda kept the little sewing basket I'd never seen her use and the pearl-handled revolver, which must have belonged to her grandfather. He picked up the gun and weighed it in his hand. How odd. And I thought, suppose Revonda is right? Suppose he's crazy?

He took a small brown paper sack out of Revonda's sewing basket with the red satin lining. He shook something out of the sack into the pink palm of his hand: a bullet. "Most people don't know Revonda keeps bullets hidden in her sewing kit," he said. Calm as ever. "I found out one day when I was waiting for Revonda and a button came off my jacket. I'm going to load this gun," he said, in the kind of warm melodic voice he might have used to say, "What a lovely baby."

"My father taught me how to do that," he said sweetly. "He collected guns. You never forget those things." He turned around and I heard clicking noises of bullet going into gun. I was so surprised that I froze, staring at the back of his humbly bent head. Suppose we'd escaped Jeeter and the rattlesnake and the marijuana farmer only to be shot by a preacher who looked like a cross between a monk and a Kewpie doll. He'd been so one-sided good he'd gone crazy—that was it. Yet we'd trusted him. So much for *my* gut hunch. I heard Anne laughing. She sounded hysterical.

He turned and aimed the gun at her head. I wondered what to do. You don't want to startle a madman. "This gun is magic." He nodded to himself, as if approving his own wisdom. His small mouth curved in a gentle smile. He kept the gun aimed. "Paul talked to me about magic. Most people wouldn't talk to him about that. He used to come by when I was working in my garden. Don't move away," he ordered me. Anne sat perfectly still in her chair. Stunned?

"My father taught me to hit the target." The Reverend turned to Anne. "I'm a good shot. I could hit you right between the eyes. Are you visualizing that?"

I was. Even seeing the headlines: INSANE MINISTER MURDERS PUPPETEER. How could I think about headlines when I needed to be defending us? Somehow the whole situation seemed unreal.

"This gun is Paul's kind of magic," the Reverend repeated. "Aimed at your head because that magic means thinking it's all up to you to do things exactly right, to visualize exactly right. You are alone."

I remembered a charm in the stuff Sam copied from Paul's books that said the devil would drag you down to hell if you got it wrong. I could see what hell it was for Anne, being scared of her own fear.

"If I killed you and put you in a plastic bag in a way that showed what I thought you ought to be punished for, that might be black magic," he said. I figured he was even crazier than Jeeter. He needed pills, and no one knew it. So was he saying the murders were some kind of magical human sacrifice? He still looked as kind and gentle as a baby. The gun was now pointed at Anne's heart. What on earth could I do?

"Don't you see, each of these murders can be a kind of cruel magic to make the people of this valley focus their minds on a wrong idea: that each of us is alone with his sin, alone with his guilt." He was beginning to use his singsong sermon voice. I wondered if he'd shoot too quickly if I tried to hit the gun out of his hand, and decided he might.

"There is no good magic but love," he sang. "Love is God's magic."

Then all of a sudden he lowered the gun and beamed and raised his voice to a friendly triumphant bellow: "We are not alone with our sins. We are never alone when we can pray."

He turned to Anne. "You were certain I would shoot you. You saw it. But you saw wrong. It was your fear you saw, not your future."

He went over and put the gun back on the whatnot, just as casual as if he hadn't almost given me a heart attack. I still felt weak. He strode back, eyes flashing joy. "I believe these terrible murders can teach us that lesson. They're dramatic enough so the whole community, and maybe eventually the whole nation, will finally learn that lesson. That would be a blessing." He was radiant, arms raised.

I was glad Revonda wasn't there, or she would have choked him in a rage.

Anne's mouth was open in amazement. I thought: He's so wrapped up in his lovely ideas he doesn't even see us. He doesn't know what he just put us through, making his point. He came back and took Anne's hand. She stared at her hand in his as if it might explode.

"You believe that, if you visualize your death in fear, that will help to make it happen."

"Or losing Sam," she said tentatively. "Or anything I'm afraid of."

"But you see," he said, beaming, "God has the last word. So visualize God helping you. Have faith." He hugged Anne. "You're going to be all right. I'll see you soon. Give Revonda my love." He came over and hugged me, too. And with that he left.

I sat. I felt like I'd been picked up by a tornado and put back down again. Anne looked dazed. "He does have faith," she said, "gun and all. I'd like to have that kind of faith. But I'm still scared."

His words were still whirling round in my brain, but I did have the gumption to say, "He's right about your intuition, Anne. You've got to trust it."

CHAPTER
32

I walked Anne back to the studio, through the early evening cool, just at the time when the light begins to get blue. I was still favoring my ankle. We found Sam at his easel, painting furiously, seeming isolated in an island of bright electric light. He was humming cheerfully to himself.

"Reverend Phillipson pointed a loaded gun at me, Revonda's pearl-handled pistol," Anne told him in a flat voice.

"Umm," he said. He was entirely focused on his picture. He didn't even say "Hi" to me.

Anne repeated the gun bit, somewhat louder. He glanced up. He laughed. "He was illustrating some noble truth, right? He is a character." Sam hummed louder, wiggling his bare toes and dabbing paint. He could have acted a little bit concerned. This was the evening of the day a young woman he knew had died. And he was the prime suspect. So who was the real Sam?

"The Reverend scared me a lot." Anne hugged herself,

and I thought: She wishes he'd hug her in one of his great bear hugs.

"He likes a good image," Sam said, hardly looking at Anne. "He got your attention. Religious shock treatment." He kept right on painting sixty miles an hour.

"You don't intend to let anything upset you, even a pearl-handled dueling pistol. Loaded and aimed at your own wife. If you think you've got a picture right, nothing else matters to you, does it, Sam?" Anne's voice rose harshly. "Not even me."

He looked up, eyes wide with surprise.

I walked around behind him to see what kind of picture had grabbed his whole attention like that.

The picture under his brush was glimmery, reflective, but warmed by touches of red and green. Pretty. But I'd learned never to trust my first glance at one of Sam's pictures. Beneath the pretty colors I always suspected booby traps. I kept studying the canvas, and suddenly it sorted itself into a crucifix . . . under ice? Very odd.

Then, like a hit over the head, I understood what I was looking at. I saw Christ on the cross in a plastic bag tied shut with Christmas ribbons. Sam was just dabbing more red on a ribbon. Anne let out a gasp so loud I was afraid the sheriff's men would come running. She'd seen it, too.

"Sam! You can't paint that!"

He turned and looked at her, feet apart, head back, and those bushy eyebrows up. "I *am* painting this." He actually smiled.

"You've got to get rid of it. Someone from the sheriff's department might come in here and see it."

"I'll tell them I'm painting it for them." He grinned so broadly his beard wiggled. He winked at me.

"Oh, Sam, don't joke," Anne begged. "Three people are dead from plastic bags."

"You've got to understand." He had turned around and was giving us a lecture. "I explore things in paintings. This painting probes the killings. Otherwise, the very thought of them would drive me mad. I think I know the essence of what's wrong. I have it here even if I don't have the details yet." He was actually bouncing on his toes with satisfaction.

"You mean you don't know the details of who did it and why?" Anne sounded scornful.

He completely missed her sarcasm. "No," he said. "I don't have those details quite yet."

"You don't have an alibi for any of the killings, and we're flatlanders, and you're a suspect. You're a fool." I had never heard Anne so bitter. She was rigid with anger.

"I have to finish this picture." So he was going to be a mule. Too bad.

"My God, Sam," she exploded, "you're in the Bible Belt. Jinx's father would lynch you if he found this picture. Even Revonda, who loves you so, will think you're crazy. Unless you get rid of this quick, I'll think you're crazy. If the sheriff wants any further excuse to arrest you, he'll think this is it." Her voice came out sharp and raspy.

"I can't get rid of this picture." He crossed his arms. He sounded hurt. "I have to explore further. Also, I think this is one of the best things I've ever done. Someday this picture will make me famous."

"Famous in the electric chair!" Anne yelled. "You're pigheaded. You'll never change."

Should I leave? I asked myself. Should I try to mediate? Curiosity got the best of me. I listened. But I said, "Better keep your voices down."

"Don't you even care about the people who are dead?" Anne whispered.

"I care." He didn't even lower his voice. "Just like I care about you."

Anne opened her mouth and shut it. She hugged herself harder. "All right," she choked. "What does this picture mean? What does it prove?"

"It's about having to hide what's ugly," he said. "About having to cover agony and pretend it's something else: a Christmas present. About how something in us always sees through and knows the agony is there but can't face it. That's what's wrong with the world. It's worse wrong with somebody here in the valley." He was waving his arms, full of himself. Anne wasn't going to be impressed.

"If we can't find the killer, that's all bullshit!" she yelled.

Sam drew himself up, dignified. "I believe that if I keep working on this picture, I'll know who the killer is," he said. "I intend to keep working." He raised his voice angrily: "If you want to change somebody, then change yourself."

Oh, dear. He needed to hug her, not say that. But something had hold of him. I hoped to God it was his muse and not some hidden inner demon.

"My mother and father were right about you!" Anne yelled. She turned to me and said, "I need air."

And I thought: Good. A cooling-off period. That might help.

We walked up and down the driveway in the half light. Revonda had turned on the outdoor lights, and the last daylight and the electric mixed, making the leaves on the trees vibrant green.

"I hate Sam," Anne seethed. "And I love Sam. He must be crazy. But he's what I count on." Her voice rose with surprise at that. "I know he told a lie about the time. But I want to trust him. I'm so confused. I feel like there's no central me to tell all the other parts how to behave or what to think."

"There is a central you, and you have to be very still and listen for it," I said. "That's what works for me. Sleep on this."

We walked round and round and finally went back inside. We found Sam still painting like there was no tomorrow. "I think I'll work all night. I feel as if I have a deadline." He sounded frightened.

"I'll be back in the morning," I said. Something was out of kilter between these two, about to run amok. I wished I could stop it. But I couldn't spend the night. I hadn't been invited, and I needed to get back to Ted.

Love needs to be nourished and cared for. I couldn't bear to see Anne and Sam ignoring that, so I went home to nourish and care for my own.

CHAPTER
33

Tuesday was a day when nothing fit together. It began with a dream. I saw a spiral just like the spirals painted on the bodies, except this spiral stood alone in the air. It began to revolve and a voice said, *"Clockwise."* Then the spiral turned the other way into a vortex, a whirlpool. I fell into it headfirst and was sucked down, struggling while the voice said, *"DAB is BAD."* I opened my eyes, and it was morning, and I was tangled in the sheet.

I struggled loose and sat up. Ted was awake, too. "Nightmare?" he asked. I told him about it. I said, "Dab is what Sam does with paint." I threw myself over next to Ted and said, "I want people to love each other. I can't help it. When they do love each other a lot, and then it looks like they may stop, I almost can't stand it."

We loved each other a lot, and that helped. "Thank God I trust you," I said. "To care this much for someone you didn't trust would be awful."

"Likewise," he said.

"I wish I could find somebody *besides* Sam to confess to three plastic-bag murders quick," I told Ted at breakfast as I stared out the kitchen window at the rain. He pointed out that it was always possible Sam was guilty. That made me feel so sad I could have cried. At least we hadn't had any of those strange hang-up calls this morning.

After Ted left for the college, my car just naturally found its way to Bloodroot Creek. The rain was lifting. Clouds came and went. Mist clung to the mountaintops. I met Knowing Agnes in her mismatched reds, walking along the road picking wet wildflowers, and on a hunch I stopped the car in a wide grassy spot by the road and offered her a ride. After all, if she repeated word for word what she heard, here was a whole source of information we hadn't made the most of yet. After Paul's funeral something had triggered Agnes to repeat what she heard about Paul. She didn't just say gibberish. We couldn't ask her questions, but maybe I could find some way to guide her talk.

She stood near the door I'd opened on the passenger side and peered at my face as if I was a sign she couldn't quite read. "You can't come in," she said. "We don't let anybody in our house now except our kin."

I smiled in what I hoped was an encouraging way and held out my hand. "We never used to lock our door," she quavered, "but now we don't know who to trust." A tear rolled down her weather-beaten cheek.

So the murders had made her less welcome. I supposed even Agnes could kill, at least in theory. She could have a plastic bag in that big battered red pocketbook, hanging over her shoulder just like mine. She felt rejected. I reached in my pocketbook and took out a chocolate bar, insurance that if I'm lost I won't be hungry, too. I patted the seat in welcome and held out the candy. She took the bar and handed me her bunch of wildflowers. "All our sympathy," she said. She climbed into the car, gave me a glowing smile, unwrapped the chocolate, and took a bite.

I noticed how her nails were cared for, how neatly her

skirt was mended where it must have been torn by briers and such. Somebody loved Agnes enough to take good care of her and leave her free. She sat back in the car seat and made herself comfortable.

"Revonda Roland," I said to her. "Anne Newman. Sam Newman." She took another bite and licked her lips. "Marvelle Starr," I said. "Paul Roland." I paused a while between names, also between first and last names in case she only knew the first. "Sheriff Henderson," I said. "Ron Brank, Mert, Octavia . . ." I couldn't remember Mert's or the psychologist's last names because I hadn't given them my *How to Survive Without a Memory* treatment. Never mind. "Jinx Justice, Jeeter Justice, Buck Justice," I said.

I guess I hoped it would be a little like seeding clouds to get rain. I'd drop a subject, and it might pull out more. But Agnes quietly finished the chocolate bar, and then she seemed restless. How could I jog her mind before she left me?

Words wouldn't work. I'd try reenactment. The couch cover I meant to take to the dry cleaners was in the backseat of the car. I reached back and got the middle seat cushion cover that is shaped a little like a short plastic dry-cleaning bag. Shirt model. I put it over my head. Any sane person who'd come along would have been sure I'd lost my mind. But I'll try anything.

Agnes cried out, "No! No! No!"

I pulled the cover off quick. She was reaching for the door handle and wrenching it open. She jumped from the car. I figured I'd blown it. But then she turned and made a pronouncement. "Nobody will ever suspect me."

The killer had said that. I was sure! Who'd care what Agnes heard?

She left me in a hurry and took off in a flash of red down the first driveway. I hoped she found a welcome.

I sat there in the car and pondered. Whoever felt above suspicion had someone to confide in. Or it could be someone who talked to themselves out loud. So it could be almost anybody. Except Sam! So he wouldn't have said "nobody will ever suspect me."

Wow! I could tell Anne why it couldn't have been Sam! I'd felt so bad about that girl. I wanted to bring her hope.

I set right out for the studio, singing to myself. Things are going to be better, I told myself. They are. Outside the sky opened up again and cried in a steady light rain.

CHAPTER
34

IMMEDIATELY AFTERWARD

The sheriff's car drove into Revonda's driveway just ahead of me. I followed him in to see what was up, crossing my fingers. He parked in front of the house, got out of his car, and when he saw me get out of mine, too, he waited for me on Revonda's front steps. "I was hoping you'd be here." Nicest thing he ever said to me. It wasn't mutual. "I want to talk to the lot of you." He seemed pleased with himself. If you could cross a steam shovel and a grinning Halloween pumpkin, that was him. Still wearing those fancy cowboy boots.

Anne met us at the door, and the sheriff strode over to Revonda's chair. He was really in luck if he wanted all of us toge:her. Anne and Sam were sitting in the living room, drinking coffee with Revonda. One on each side of her, pointedly not looking at each other.

"Revonda, honey," the sheriff thundered, "you need to be sure that anybody who works with you lets me know right away about anything like a threatening phone call or a marijuana field." He said that straight to Revonda, implying the rest of us were deaf and blind and under Revonda's thumb.

Hey, he meant me! "I told your deputy," I said. "I didn't tell him right away, because the calls were so vague, and I wasn't sure where the farm was, or if that really was marijuana." That sounded pretty lame, and his shrug said he didn't believe me, but it wasn't really me he stayed mad at. It was Revonda. He glared at her like it was her fault that I fell short.

"Since we heard, we've been tracing calls to your number," he said directly to me. "Some came from a farm in the area where you say you got lost and then saw marijuana between the corn rows."

"So what are you coming to tell us?" Revonda demanded. "Why are you beating around the bush, Harley? Making my friend stand here like a schoolkid." (I wasn't sitting because I didn't want Man-Mountain looking down at me.)

The sheriff kept grinning. "I went with my men to that farm yesterday morning, Buck Justice's place. Jeeter's brother."

So. It was Buck.

The sheriff turned to me and raised his voice. "But we didn't get there soon enough. No marijuana growing there."

I kept my mouth shut and waited. What was he about to spring?

"We did find traces of leaf they left when they pulled it up." His grin turned into a grin of rage. His voice went higher. "Somebody warned Buck. Now, which of these folks did you tell before you told the law?" he asked me. "Somebody saw to it that Buck knew before we got there." He swept us with a triumphant glance.

"Evidently," said Revonda, "Buck had the elemental intelligence to know that if you had a hint of where the farm might be, you'd have a plane in there searching before breakfast. Even you would be smart enough to do that, Harley."

"I was smart enough to find a lot more than marijuana when Peaches Dann here finally gave us the facts." He pointed a finger so close it almost jabbed me. "We went to that farm and we found cocaine in the house—two pounds, hidden good. In a shed out back, we found black candles and feathers and bones and a knife." He said that like it was what he'd always wanted to find, and like it proved me guilty.

"We also found a list of high-school students. Kids who got in trouble a while back. We've brought them in for questioning, and some of those kids admit they were members of a cult that met on that farm and helped distribute drugs. What do you think of that?" I thought it was amazing we hadn't heard about it. He must have scared the families into silence, or Mert would have picked it up on the grapevine.

I wondered where Sam had hidden the list of cult members that Billy gave him. Sam, sitting there next to Revonda, kept his mouth shut tight.

"Now, what I came here in person to say is that, this time I'll give you the benefit of the doubt about deliberately withholding information. But if it happens again, I will arrest every one of you for obstructing my investigation."

With that he stomped out, still grinning like he had the best of us and meant to keep it that way.

I felt sorry for Mrs. Jeeter and almost sorry for Jeeter. I bet they hadn't known they were related to the man behind such ugly goings-on. I also felt like another shoe was going to drop. Certainly the sheriff would send someone over to question me further. And maybe the others. I still worried he might arrest Sam. Suppose they found the list of cult members Sam had hidden goodness knew where?

"That Harley is full of himself," Revonda said. "I could have told him Buck Justice was no good."

"I have some good news," I said and told them about Knowing Agnes. But Anne wouldn't give up being mad with Sam. And as I say, Revonda didn't look well. We were not a lively group.

"What did you discover by painting your picture last night?" I asked Sam. "Did you sort out your intuition while you painted? Did you find any answers?"

He perked up. "Partly." He put his coffee cup down on the little table that held Paul's picture. "The killer is getting desperate because he can't control things. Because he can't commit the perfect crime." Sam began to expand, almost glow. Anne watched him coldly, Revonda with interest. "Whoever is killing isn't doing it for normal reasons—not for greed or lust or revenge," Sam said. "So any one of us could be the killer and not show a sign of those passions." He glanced at us eagerly, like we might enjoy a chance to confess.

"Is that all that came to you from painting that picture?" Anne asked. Her scornful eyes said "crazy picture." That wouldn't help.

"Yes," he said. "If the world ends it will not be for greed or lust or revenge, either." He said that like an added inspiration. "It will be from self-deception."

Poor Anne wanted to throw something at him, I could tell. Theorizing about the end of the world while we had to deal with a real pickle. So I shouldn't have asked him—but I was intrigued.

"Why self-deception? I think that's a pretty tame sin. I indulge in it myself, sometimes."

"Think about it!" he cried. "The greatest realistic greed still wants the world to exist to enjoy possessions in. Same with lust, same with revenge. But if you pretend the world can't end, then here comes the end of the world."

"This is a hell of a time to worry about some end of the world," Anne snapped. "We might be killed today, before we find who's dangerous here."

"A killer who deceives himself is the most dangerous." That rolled off his tongue like one of the Reverend's sermons. "So I'd like to suggest we stick together in twos or threes. I may get arrested at any moment," he said, "because nobody will believe that you-all got the time mixed up yesterday, and I did have an alibi." He said that rather casually, as if it didn't matter in the long run.

Anne looked at her feet.

"Even you can be wrong, Sam," Revonda said, "but that doesn't mean you're guilty. Maybe your watch was wrong and you forgot you reset it."

"My watch keeps excellent time!" he announced. "I never reset it. But let's talk about the future, not the past." He sure didn't help the people who wanted to believe he had a future.

"And since we're sticking together," he said, "Peaches and I can both go with Anne to her puppet show. I hope you didn't forget it, Anne. Because it's nearly time now." He glanced at his controversial watch.

Puppet show! I was amazed. In the middle of all this?

Anne said, "Oh, dear. That. I'd like to forget it. But they called and reminded me. I signed a contract for a family reunion. The descendants of James Norwood. Now I think they want me especially because I'm notorious. I'm on the news. When they called up yesterday, they offered to pay a bonus if I'd still do it."

Revonda put her hand over Anne's. "Those Norwoods are related to Jeeter's wife. You certainly ought to look them over. This may be an opportunity."

"Come on," Sam said to Anne. "We need to get the puppet stuff in the truck." She didn't answer him, but she got up to go.

Good, I thought, this'll get us out of this house before somebody shows up to give the third degree. Why hadn't the sheriff told us to stick around? Did he think we'd lead him somewhere?

I sat down next to Revonda, patted the dog, and tried to sort out my thoughts. "Is this Hound or Baskerville?" I asked. They were so alike.

"Hound," Revonda said. "Sam took Baskerville to the vet yesterday. She was throwing up."

One less protection for Anne, I thought. Baskerville had

attached herself to her since Paul died. I didn't trust Hound. "Even Hound is acting oddly," Revonda said.

Sam came back and said the puppet stuff was ready, and we set out, three of us together in the van. Anne still glowering at Sam.

We hadn't gone far when we saw flashing lights from the sheriff's department car in our rearview mirror. The car zoomed up behind us and blinked us over to the side of the road. When two deputies took Sam, that shook Anne out of her anger. She hugged him goodbye like he was more valuable than gold. He seemed to take this all in his stride. "I expect you to find the real killer," he commanded us grandly.

I offered to drive, since the tears streaming down Anne's face would have made it difficult for her to see the road. We agreed that returning to the studio would be more depressing. We had directions to get to the Norwood family reunion, but we got lost. Unfortunately, I'm good at that. So is Anne. And I'm sure we were more prone to it because we were upset.

This wasn't a good day to get lost. Someone was following us. I noticed that almost as soon as we were on a totally unfamiliar stretch of road. The houses were few and far between: a small clapboard cabin, glimpsed down a drive with a big bushy dog barking as I passed; a pink trailer with no car in sight. If I turned into a driveway to ask for help and nobody was home, we might be trapped. I mustn't panic. But that blue car reflected in the rearview mirror followed every turn we made. Suppose . . . ? Stop it, I told myself, trying to keep my mind on the road. But the car kept following. Way far back. When I slowed down, it slowed down. When I speeded up, it speeded up.

And as we drove along, I found myself wondering: If the cult killed, why hadn't they killed me when I found the farm where they met? If they knew the sheriff found their list of members there because of me, what might they do to get even now? Or was the cult a diversion, and the killer was out there, totally unknown?

Anne turned and looked behind us.

"Pretend you don't see that car," I said.

If I kept turning uphill, maybe I'd get to the Blue Ridge Parkway, which tended to be a high road. If I got there, I could get my bearings.

CHAPTER

35

EARLY TUESDAY AFTERNOON

The car behind us vanished around the curves as the road wound up and up. Then we began to descend. I guess God does look after fools, drunks, the USA, and me. Thank goodness, we came to a TO-THE-PARKWAY sign. Perhaps I could get out of sight around a curve before the blue car came close enough to see whether I went left or right. I whisked past two young men on motorcycles.

I was going way over the speed limit, but I sure didn't care if I got arrested for speeding. In fact, I thought of jail as a nice safe place. How fast would I have to go to be hauled in on the spot? My tires squealed on a curve. I hoped our follower wasn't in hearing distance. A side road went downhill from the Parkway. I turned down. The more turns, I thought, the more I can hope to lose the blue car.

Suddenly houses were closer together. The road straightened and ran along the side of the mountain. That ominous car came back into view, then curves hid him again. I began to look for a driveway I could zoom into and hide behind a house. But on the steep hillside, most of the driveways were in front of the houses. The road straightened again. No hiding place once he got to the straight part. He could see my every move.

I saw a sign in front of a house on the down side of the road. "There's a great drive!" I said. "It goes around in back of the house. And that building has offices in it. Someone is sure to be there. We won't be trapped by ourselves."

I zoomed into the driveway, trying to slow down bit by bit, but the wheels squealed again. I parked in back and was pleased to see there was a back door. We jumped out of the car and hurried over. The sign on the door there was smaller: RONALD ZIMMERMAN, PH.D. SPECIALIST IN DYSLEXIA AND OTHER LEARNING CHALLENGES.

"Zimmerman," Anne said. "That's the man Sam told me to go see! The one he said helped people who did dumb-seeming things and had trouble in school."

"Don't just stand here," I warned. "Let's get inside."

We went into a dim hallway, but I could see that the brass doorknob inside had a little turnable piece in the center. A knob lock. I latched it behind us. The narrow hall ran from back to front. We followed it to a brightly lit room with a reception desk, and a woman behind it, who looked like the universal grandma. White hair, glasses halfway down her nose, pink cheeks. She smiled and said, "Oh, one of you must be Marcia Albert. We were afraid you'd forgotten your appointment for an evaluation. You're late."

I pointed to Anne. "This is the gal you want," I said.

Anne blinked, but then she followed the receptionist. Well, after all, if Marcia Albert wasn't coming, why waste the doctor's time? What better place to hide? Wasn't it fate that we ended up where Sam said to go? I bet that's what Anne thought. The receptionist said the basic evaluation took two hours. I asked to use the phone. I called Revonda and told her where we were and that I needed the name and number of the people with the family reunion. She didn't know it. I called Ted. No answer. Anne might know, but I wasn't about to disturb her appointment with Dr. Zimmerman. The family reunion would have to amuse itself with speculation about why we vanished.

I almost tripped over a lamp cord that snaked out into the room. Some hyper kid with an earlier appointment must have pulled it out. Part of me noticed, but most of me began thinking about loose ends. Good old one-track-mind.

I made a list of all the odd pieces we were trying to fit into the puzzle. Someone that no one would suspect, in a bandanna, a loose smock, and dark glasses. Someone near Marvelle's house, near the time she was killed. A large enough person so it could be a man. Jinx had favored dark glasses, but she was dead. Billy wore dark glasses even in dim light. He said he found them by the road near Revonda's house. Which could unfortunately point to Sam, since he lived in the studio.

Revonda had an alibi from Cousin Edna for the time of Marvelle's death. Cousin Edna was pretty vague. But Revonda would *never* have killed Paul, and besides she was with us at the time he died. The psychologist wore snake earrings and flaunted a dragon with spirals in the same spots they'd been painted on Paul. Very odd. The sheriff definitely had it in for Revonda. How could I find out more about him?

Jeeter was certified to have a mental illness, controlled by medication, except sometimes he didn't take it. If the Reverend Phillipson had flipped out after his wife died, as Revonda thought, he was not certified and not on medication. None of that particularly fit with what the sheriff said about a cult.

Ron was definitely taken with Anne, but I didn't think he'd go far enough to try to frame Sam, and besides, there was no need. Sam spent every free moment framing himself!

No matter how I tried to fit the pieces together, I couldn't get a picture. I got up and wandered back down the narrow hall and looked out the back window. A blue car was parked next to Sam and Anne's van. No person in sight. Now what?

Finally Anne came out. I never saw anyone glow with happiness so in my whole life. "Hey, there's a reason," she cried, "a real reason why I do things wrong. Like when I get lost or perceive things backward."

"So that's good?" I asked, surprised.

"Not bad luck, and not that I don't try. It's not that I'm lazy or mean. It's something real I can even do something about. I feel so relieved. It's great!"

Dr. Zimmerman had come out, too. He shook my hand. Maybe he thought I was Anne's mother. "And you have a talent," he said, turning to Anne. "So often, we find a special creative talent. That's why you have those puppets you told me about."

"That goes with the problem?" I asked. "What *is* all this?" Wasn't one of them going to tell me?

"Anne has a perceptual problem," the doctor said. "The term most people know is *dyslexia*. But each case is different."

"That's where you read words backward, right?" I asked.

"What you see," the doctor said, "is a smart girl who has trouble in school. Who has to work to read. She needs a special way to learn. And yes, sometimes she does read a word backward."

All of a sudden I remembered my dream. "I must have known it in my gut. I dreamed about that," I said, amazed. But why? My whole mind is on trying to solve three murders. Why would I . . . ? And then it hit me with a jolt. "In my dream someone said, '*Dab is bad*.'" I heard my voice screech with excitement. Anne, the doctor, and the receptionist all stared at me.

"If you could flip a word," I said to Anne, "you could flip a clock, couldn't you? See it backward, so to speak?" I was so excited I could hardly get the words out.

"Yes," the doctor said, eyeing me like I might have flipped. "I had a patient who did that."

Light dawned on Anne's face. "Twenty *of* could be twenty *after!* I saw Sam's watch wrong! Sam didn't lie!"

The doctor blinked and turned to one of us and then the other, totally confused—especially when Anne rushed over to throw her arms around him, tripped over the stray light cord, and she and the lamp fell to the floor with a loud crash.

The front door burst open, and Ron rushed in. Ron?

He had a gun in his hand, and it took him a minute to figure out there was no one to point it at. I introduced Dr. Zimmerman. I explained that nothing was wrong except someone had been following us.

Ron acted embarrassed. "I followed you," he said. "Heck, it's my day off, and I can do what I please, and I was scared maybe Sam was not the perpetrator." He flushed. "I didn't mean that like it sounds," he said quickly. "Mrs. Holleran here gets herself in jams," he said. And remembering the rattlesnake, I couldn't argue. "I was worried about Anne. Heck, I don't like to see any more pretty girls get killed. We never have enough of those."

"Would you write a letter that says I might see a clock backward?" Anne asked Dr. Zimmerman. Of course she had to explain to him what this was all about. He said he'd be delighted. In fact he said this was the most unusual case in his entire career.

"Would you take me right to the sheriff?" she asked Ron. "I want to tell the sheriff what happened. And I have to tell Sam I'll always trust him from now on, no matter what."

That was going to be exciting, I bet. But then, Anne was a playwright. Whatever happened would be grist for the mill.

CHAPTER
36

TUESDAY AFTERNOON

After Anne left with Ron, I asked to use Dr. Zimmerman's phone again and called home. Ted was off teaching. But I had a hunch that, with events moving so fast, I should try my answering machine. I have a special code for picking up messages.

The first message was from Pop. "Peaches," he said, "I want you to be sure to take Revonda's advice. She says she's going to be the first one to figure these murders out. I told her I thought you were close to figuring who did it, but she said she thought that she'd be first." That was all. No explanation.

The second message was from Octavia-the-Psychologist. "I have something you may need to see at the first possible moment," she said. "I'll be here all day." I called her back. No answer. Strange.

The last message was from Revonda. "I've made an important discovery about the murders," she said. "Get back to me." So I called her immediately, and she said to be at her house at three o'clock. "The time is important." Dr. Zimmerman's round clock on the wall said 2:30. When I asked Revonda what was up, she said, "I have a friend with me," in that I-can't-talk-now tone of voice. "The front door is unlocked," she said. "Come right on in."

I called my answering machine again and left word of what Octavia and Revonda said for Ted. "Revonda seems nervous about something," I said. "That's not like her." I asked him to meet me at Revonda's as soon as possible after his class that ended at three o'clock. Of course, he might have conferences with students. He might not even check the machine till quite late. I also left a message at the English Department Office, but he might not check that, either.

I figured I had time to get to Revonda's comfortably. But I was held up ten minutes in back of a fender bender while a tow truck hauled a smashed Honda out of the way, then I had to honk at two teens who were leaning out of their car windows, talking in the middle of the road. By the time I came to Octavia-the-Psychologist's house, I was running late. She was out weeding, saw me coming, and waved. When did that woman see patients? At midnight?

"Wait just a second," she called. "Billy gave me a picture he said he wanted you to see. He said not to give it to anybody else. He'd have asked his grandmother to give it to you, but she's off somewhere. He wouldn't tell me why it was so important."

Why didn't Billy leave whatever at Revonda's? Or get it to my house? But perhaps he didn't know where my house was. Anyway, this was ridiculous. But I waited a minute and she went inside and came back out bearing a white envelope, which she handed to me. Billy the envelope boy. I took a quick peek, even late and annoyed as I was. Some sort of group photograph at a picnic. And most of the people were squinting in the bright sun, but Revonda and Mert were both smart enough to have dark glasses on. No note. This didn't make sense. I'd ask Revonda about it.

A car I didn't recognize stood in Revonda's driveway, an old red Volkswagen convertible. Dashing but battered. Why had Revonda asked me over? I had just stepped up onto the porch when I heard barking and screaming. The front door was unlocked as advertised. I opened it and heard Revonda's voice, outraged and frightened: "You'll never get away with this!"

The Persian rug hid the sound of my feet as I slipped in to find out what was wrong. I passed the shelves with all the mementos on them. A brass bowl of pennies teetered on the edge. Old coins, no doubt. No time to worry about that. My eye fell on the small pearl-handled gun. Loaded! That fact had gone right out of my mind from the moment Reverend Phillipson had put the gun down. How could I forget a loaded gun? Thank goodness no kid had come along and shot himself by mistake. But the gun might be useful now! I'd never shot one. I hoped I wouldn't have to. I took the gun and slipped it in my skirt pocket. The door to Revonda's bedroom was half open, so I could hear but not be seen.

"Where's the money? Paul owed me money. You admit that, and I mean to have it. I'll use this knife. I'd enjoy using this knife on a bitch like you." The man's voice was hysterical.

I peeked through the crack near the door hinges. The man's back in a black T-shirt was toward the door. He had red tousled hair. Revonda sat at her desk, turned sideways toward him, in a red pants suit and lots of gold. The dog by her side was growling but not advancing on the man. Why not? Revonda needed help.

I backed up from the crack. *Thud!* I'd knocked against that derned bowl full of pennies. They fell on the floor and rolled in all directions.

The man sprang to the door and opened it wide. I recognized him. Paul's dinner-theater buddy. Who wore his TO BE IS BETTER THAN NOT TO BE T-shirt, of all things, to the memorial service. He had it on now. While his back was turned to Revonda and before I could even think, she reached in the drawer of her desk, took out a black pistol, and with both hands aimed the thing at his head. "Drop that knife."

He turned back around and dropped an ugly hunting knife with a clunk. Revonda nodded toward a roll of package tape on her desk, the brown shiny kind that's so hard to get off when you're opening a package. "Put this around his wrists," she said to me. She kept her gun on the young man.

"March him over to the closet," Revonda ordered. "He'll be safer in there till we get help. Now tape his ankles together."

The looks he shot me were as poisonous as tarantula bites. While I taped, he went on yelling at Revonda.

"Why did you call me and tell me to come for the money? You never meant to give me that money, did you? Why in hell did you call me here?"

The dog kept growling but sat quite still.

What he said didn't make sense. "You must be the one who broke in last week," I said.

"Paul gave me a key, and I want what's mine!" he yelled. "The cocaine or the money. I didn't find cocaine, and this bitch used the money to lure me here." I put the roll of tape down. Something was definitely wrong.

"Did you ask him to come here, Revonda?"

"That's not enough tape," she said. "Put some more." She shook the gun at me. "Go on, or I'll shoot."

I caught my breath. Billy had tried to warn me. That dawned on my thick brain with a thunderclap. Revonda was the one who dropped the dark glasses. He found the picture and recognized them! But I didn't. And me with my bleeding heart—I had to help Revonda in trouble. I'd thought I was helping the mother of a murdered son. But she was using me. I mustn't let the hot anger that surged through me trip me up.

"Put tape over his mouth," she ordered. "Put more. Now push him in the closet and shut the door. Now, put your hands up." Revonda stood so she could watch my every move. "He's going to die, but let him die ignorant of what becomes of you." After I shut the door, I could hear him making moaning noises through the tape.

With eyes and gun still on me, Revonda went to her desk. Holding the gun in one hand, she pressed or moved something on the side, and a small compartment came open. Two markers clattered to the floor and a piece of paper fluttered down. She pulled out a plastic dry cleaning bag and put the other things back. The thin plastic glimmered in folds of liquid ice.

"You're the killer!" My voice squeaked. I began to back up slowly. With her hawk's eyes fastened on me, I couldn't reach down into my pocket for the gun. She followed me. The dog followed us both, as if we were a small parade. Revonda shut the door to her bedroom, blocking out the young man's moaning noises. I backed through the dark of the small hallway into the light of the living room, past Revonda's childhood pictures framed on the wall. Past her father holding up a snake. How appropriate. If I turned and ran, she'd certainly shoot. We were like a silent movie, without a piano player.

Just as I stood near the front door, someone knocked. Ted! I thought in hope and terror. "I'll shoot if you scream," Revonda hissed. "And I can shoot through the door, too." Then, more loudly, she called, "Come in."

The door opened and Anne backed in calling, "Thanks for the ride, Ron. Thanks for trying to help." My heart sank as I heard a car drive off. If I called out to Anne, one or both of us would be dead. She came all the way in, before she looked up and saw Revonda and the gun. "Both of you keep your hands up and stand together," Revonda commanded. She wanted an easy target. She walked over to the door and locked it. "We don't want to be disturbed. Keep moving. I don't care for all these windows. We'll go in Paul's room."

She stood sideways, keeping the gun on us, and opened the door to the mirror room. "Go ahead of me," she said.

"And don't bother to run for the French doors. They're locked."

We went into an ice cave, stripped of Paul's magic things now. The face chair was still there, and Paul's cot with a white throw. But the face jugs, the candles, the books were all put away somewhere by efficient Revonda. The room which had felt like it hid demons was now just icy cold as death.

Anne seemed speechless. And what could either one of us say? But Anne rose to occasions. At least she'd risen to the occasion of the snake. And she moved with more assurance now than she had then. If we kept our wits, we might survive.

"You'll never get away," Revonda said. "Why fight?" She laughed, and red Revonda with her red lips laughing was reflected in the ice around us. "As for you, Anne, you told me yourself you have bad luck. You might as well get this over with." Her eyes were hypnotic, the white large around the blue, the blue darkened like a storm, the pupils growing large.

Anne stood tall and straight, still silent. Stunned silent? Or quietly gathering force?

Revonda held the plastic bag in front of her, glimmering, gun in one hand, bag spread between the two hands, bag moving in the mirrors, almost mirror colored. Ice colored.

Anne and I had to divert Revonda. God willing, help would come. Yet if Ted or Sam came and didn't suspect Revonda, they could be trapped with us. If Anne was here, did that mean Sam was out of jail? Billy must suspect Revonda, or why the picture? Would anyone listen to Billy? Who would he go to for help? If we could divert Revonda, I might get the pistol out of my pocket and shoot quick.

Suddenly there rose into my mind a picture of that day when Revonda said to me, "People tell you things." She'd looked at me in that strange way, half admiring, half something else. I couldn't figure out what that something else was. It was fear. My heart began to beat faster. I *was* good at listening, and all at once I knew why that scared Revonda. Because she needed so desperately for someone to listen. She needed to justify herself.

Around her, the mirrors glittered cold, even with me and Anne and Revonda, all reflected in them. Her life was like that. Self-justification was the nearest thing she had to warmth. And, therefore, precious to her.

"You've fooled everyone," I said as we backed farther into the cave of mirrors. "You killed Marvelle and then Jinx, and nobody even suspected you. Did you kill Paul?"

Her eyes widened. She clenched her hands tight around the gun and the bag. "I was a good mother!" That was a cry of pain. I was almost sorry for her. Her face of pain reflected all around us.

"Listen," she said, "everything I did was for my son. I got away from this place where everyone treated me like the daughter of a man who drank himself to death in a privy. That was the first step. I became the sort of woman who could someday bear a happy child."

Anne backed against the face chair, and the grinning face went up, down, up, down reflected and rereflected the mirrors. And the bouncing reflections still made me a little dizzy. But this time I thought that strange carved face was laughing at Revonda. Laughing at the good mother of the happy child. I almost laughed. I steeled myself. Don't get hysterical.

Revonda still held herself like a queen. "I married a rich man and he helped my career. I was a star." Her voice thrilled at the word *star*. "I came back here, and nobody treated Paul like they'd treated me. Nobody. He had a chance to be whatever he wanted to be, and he threw that away. All he could do was this." She waved the gun at the mirror room, which gave her back a hundred waving guns. "I've fought so hard to be what I am. The fools in this valley are not going to put me down. I would not let them say that my son killed himself. He was all I had. All I cared about. And then I found him dead like that. With a terrible note."

She shut her eyes, but opened them so fast that I couldn't take advantage of the moment. " '*Better my own self dead than your puppet alive. You are a witch.*' He wrote that to me. His mother." Revonda tossed her head back like an angry horse, and all the reflections tossed. I felt woozy. "He was never my puppet. I tried so hard to help him be what he could be, but he would never listen."

I saw Anne start to speak and then restrain herself. Her eyes were angry.

A witch. In my head that strange jingle from Mrs. Jeeter's herb book read itself out loud: *Vervain and dill, vervain and dill, hinder witches from their will.* I saw Paul's body with those herbs showing through the plastic, and the strange whorls painted on it. He was crazy. But he was crazy in a logical way.

"I did what I had to do!" Revonda glared at us. "I hid that note in my desk. Fortunately, the sheriff is too naive to look for anything as simple as a secret compartment. And with the note I hid the markers Paul used to paint those crazy marks on himself. I should have thrown the note away. But somehow, I couldn't. Not his last words. Although I hated them." Her voice wavered. Then she stiffened her spine and began to move toward us.

The dog, by her side, let out a low growl. The dog's eyes followed us, and I felt like now she was just waiting in case Revonda needed help. I was the one who needed help. I wished to God the dog in the room was Baskerville, who loved Anne, instead of Hound, who always obeyed Revonda.

"I knew what I had to do." Revonda moved closer. We backed a few steps, but there wasn't far to go. I knew my listening face turned toward her was keeping us alive. That and her need to be heard. "I had to prove Paul was murdered." Her voice rang with drama. "I had to prove to the people in this valley that they were wrong about me." She spit the words. "They said my grandfather killed himself, my father drank himself to death, my husband drank and killed himself in his car. They weren't going to say my son was a suicide, too! That I was a black widow. No." She raised the plastic bag.

"So why did you kill Marvelle?" Keep her justifying. She was an ice witch, not a tiger.

"That cruel Marvelle told me Paul had told her he wanted to die. He opened up to that show-off, not to me, his mother. I needed someone else to be killed just in the way he was. To prove we had a serial killer, not a suicide."

"So you disguised yourself," I said, "in dark glasses and a bandanna and a big floppy dress, not your style. And took the nye way, mostly cross-country, to get to Marvelle's and back as quick as you could."

She laughed, and that tinkly-ice-cube laugh in this ice room was wildly eerie. "I knew I had to do it during Edna's favorite TV program. Nothing pulls that old fool away from that. I even told her to feel free to take the phone off the hook, that a half an hour wouldn't matter." That splintered laugh again.

Anne clenched her fists. Oh, dear, I thought, Anne's going to let fly and lose her temper, and perhaps our lives. But she stayed frozen.

"Then Jinx came to me," Revonda said solemnly, "with some crazy idea about how the marks on Paul's body meant personal growth. Which was like that terrible note from Paul which said death was the only way he could be his own self. That fool girl talked about how Paul had been depressed, had threatened to kill himself. She couldn't keep her mouth shut. She'd make my son look like a coward who couldn't face life. So I killed her." Revonda became clearer. "Besides, serial killers keep killing, don't they? That's why a serial killer will put you both in plastic bags, marked with the fingerprints of that stupid young man in the closet. And he'll be dead because he attacked me." She raised her eyebrows and smiled in a knowing way.

"Our serial killer will put Anne here in a bag with a

broken mirror, a well-known symbol of the bad luck she's so proud of."

Anne erupted. "You're telling me I'm such a fool I'll almost help you kill me. Is that right?" Anne's voice was strong and angry. She held her head high.

"Yes," Revonda said. "Now."

"That's like a curse."

"Yes," Revonda said, "you can call it that. You know you're cursed. Something is wrong with you."

"I know something is wrong," Anne said proudly. "And therefore I can figure out how to get around it. That's more than I can say for you!"

I kept expecting Revonda to pounce, but she didn't. She seemed unsure. Surprised to be challenged.

"You also told me what Paul said about curses," Anne went on. "That if the intended victim refuses a curse, it goes back on the sender. You believe that, don't you?" Anne raised her voice and threw the words at Revonda: "I refuse your curse!"

I caught my breath. Of course. Anne knew first-hand. If you let yourself believe you're jinxed, then you are. Could she turn what she knew into a weapon to save our lives? It might work. Combined with every other way, we could fight back.

The dog growled again. Her eyes were still on us, ears pricked.

Revonda stopped dead still, as diverted as she'd ever be. I reached down for the gun in my pocket. The time had come when I had to do the best with it I could. But before I could do more than get my hand in position around the cold metal, Revonda turned to the dog and yelled, "Sic 'em!" Anne screamed in terror. I raised the gun aimed as best I could, and pulled the trigger. There was no bang, only a sick click as the dog bounded forward and arched into the air. The Reverend Phillipson had only loaded words. Even in terror, a part of me almost laughed. I should have known!

A scream and a crash!

The dog had lunged at Revonda, not at me or Anne. Revonda lay on the floor near the table, quite still, with the dog holding her down. As I tried to sort that out, there came a pounding on the French doors. Anne ran to open them.

And there were Ted and Sam and the sheriff, and also Billy—a mob. And I'll tell you, a mob of moral support was just what I felt we needed. Now that the threat was over, I was shaking. I hugged Ted. Anne hugged Sam. We were like the last scene in an operetta. Except for the sheriff and Billy, who were staring at Revonda on the floor.

"I told you I suspected her," Sam said to the sheriff, over Anne's shoulder, "but it took Billy and Ted both to convince you to come see. You were sure pigheaded at first," Sam scoffed, "not even letting Anne see me." He hugged her extra tight.

It was the first time I ever saw the sheriff look humble. "I never thought Revonda . . ." He stared at her hard. "You know what, she's breathing. She's still alive!"

I knew she would hate that anticlimax. She would prefer to be dead.

"Is this dog dangerous?" the sheriff asked no one in particular.

"Of course not," Sam said, with a huge self-satisfied grin. "Anne, call off Baskerville. It was Hound I took to the vet. I don't trust Hound. I figured that was one way I could stack the odds for Anne in case I was arrested."

Baskerville bounced over and began to lick Anne as soon as she called. Baskerville, who jumped to protect Anne when Revonda threatened and Anne screamed.

The sheriff leaned over Revonda. "She's hit her head," he said. "On the table, I think. She's knocked out. But she's breathing." In fact, Revonda stirred and moaned. The sheriff pulled out a pair of handcuffs. He sighed. "I guess she's a dangerous woman," he said. I was surprised to see tears in the sheriff's eyes. "But she was a lovely young girl."

I was glad he remembered that. Because even for Revonda I felt some pity. A woman that proud would find worse than hell in prison. Execution, if it came, would be a reprieve.

Poor Pop. He'd feel bad. But not so bad that he wouldn't be thrilled to have been in the middle of the action. The boyfriend of the killer. Pleased as pie that with a little help from his friends he'd trapped the Bloodroot Creek killer, before she killed me in some appropriate way.

And do you know? I was just a little bit disappointed. I would never know how Revonda would have done it: what she would have thought was my most dramatic sin.

CHAPTER
37

A Year Later

Ted was standing by the table near the front door, looking through the mail. He picked up the *Citizen-Times*. A headline said: MAGIC MURDER TRIAL BEGINS TODAY.

"But it wasn't magic that killed Paul and the others and destroyed Revonda," I said.

Ted raised both eyebrows, which I knew meant: *What wild conclusion have you drawn now?* I'd been trying to digest the whole Revonda-and-Paul thing, mostly out loud.

"Magic," I said, "was the symptom. Paul was looking for a way to believe he had some kind of power, some way not to feel overwhelmed by Revonda. He picked a way that made things worse, that cut him off from most of the people around him." I thought of his ice-palace room and shivered.

Ted put the paper down on the table and began to go through the envelopes. "But it did seem that the curse Revonda wanted to put on those around her came back and zapped her." Logical Ted said that! He picked up a heavy ivory envelope and began to rip it open.

"Revonda has a desperate need to be in power," I said. "So when Anne refused to be controlled, Revonda lost her cool. But we weren't really dealing with magic as such," I said, "unless imagination is magic. We were certainly dealing with sick imagination."

"Hey, look at this!" Ted handed me an ivory card.

The True Spiral Gallery
invites your presence
at the opening of an exhibit of
the paintings of Sam Newman

Including a collage incorporating news stories
of the murders in Bloodroot Creek
and excerpts from a speech on the U.S. Senate Floor
denouncing the artist as well as praise for the artist from a
sermon by the Reverend G. O. Phillipson of Bloodroot Creek

Friday evening, August 15, at 7 P.M.

The True Spiral Gallery will be representing Sam Newman
jointly with The Grombrach Gallery, New York

"Well," I said. "That should help Sam to become famous. Just like Anne always said he would be. Talk about imagination—Sam's got it in spades! And maybe the right kind of imagination *is* magic," I said, "in art and music, and writing, too."

"And you even use imagination in order to remember." Ted shook his head and grinned. "Some of the ways you use to remember are beyond anything I could possibly dream up. Would you please tell me why you have an upside-down soup pot in the middle of the dining room table, and a stack of books on top of that, and a ceramic tiger on the very top?"

"Certainly," I said. "The tiger stands for Revonda. When I go to set the table at six-thirty, that's exactly the time I need to call Pop and remind him to see how they cover the opening of Revonda's trial on television. Pop begged me not to let him miss it. He wants to write Revonda a note and tell her she looked lovely on television. Which, knowing her, I'm sure she will. He says they'll both be condemned to die. Revonda by the state, and Pop by Father Time. So they need to cheer each other up."

I wandered over to admire my wild tiger assemblage. "You've heard of Found Art," I said, "made of whatever comes to hand. Well, I call this Temporary Found Art, and it's a great memory-jogger. Because you can't miss it— right? And the surest reminders are the ones you can't miss, even if you try."